R.O. Saunders

September 1972.

Rochdale.

HANS

AN OUTLINE O
THE NEW

C. F.

FLOYD

new
test
ament
lib
rary

HANS CONZELMANN

AN
OUTLINE OF THE
THEOLOGY OF THE
NEW TESTAMENT

SCM PRESS LTD
BLOOMSBURY STREET LONDON

Translated by John Bowden from the German
Grundriss der Theologie des Neuen Testaments
second edition, published 1968 by
Christian Kaiser Verlag, Munich

334 01195 7
FIRST ENGLISH EDITION 1969
© SCM PRESS LTD 1969
PRINTED IN GREAT BRITAIN BY
W & J MACKAY & CO LTD, CHATHAM

CONTENTS

PART TWO
THE SYNOPTIC KERYGMA

PART THREE

THE THEOLOGY OF PAUL

A. Theological Method and Basic Concepts

PART FOUR

THE DEVELOPMENT AFTER PAUL

PART FIVE

JOHN

ABBREVIATIONS

AThANT	Abhandlungen zur Theologie des Alten und Neuen Testaments
Bauer (– Arndt-Gingrich)	W. Bauer, *Griechisch-deutsches Wörterbuch zu den Schriften des Neuen Testaments* (1958⁶); English translation by W. F. Arndt and F. W. Gingrich, *A Greek-English Lexicon of the New Testament* (1957)
BFChTh	Beiträge zur Förderung christlicher Theologie
BEvTh	Beiträge zur evangelischen Theologie
BHTh	Beiträge zur historischen Theologie
Bill.	H. L. Strack and P. Billerbeck, *Kommentar zum Neuen Testament aus Talmud und Midrasch* (1922ff.)
BWANT	Beiträge zur Wissenschaft vom Alten und Neuen Testament
BZ	*Biblische Zeitschrift*
BZNW	Beiträge zur Zeitschrift für die neutestamentliche Wissenschaft
CN	*Coniectanea Neotestamentica*
EvTh	*Evangelische Theologie*
FRLANT	Forschungen zur Religion und Literatur des Alten und Neuen Testaments
HAW	Handbuch der Altertumswissenschaft
HNT	Handbuch zum Neuen Testament
HThR	*Harvard Theological Review*
JBL	*Journal of Biblical Literature*
KuD	*Kerygma und Dogma*
LThK	*Lexikon für Theologie und Kirche*
LUÅ	Lunds Universitets Årsskrift
LXX	Septuagint
MThS	Münchener Theologische Studien
MThZ	*Münchener Theologische Zeitschrift*
NF	Neue Folge (New Series)
NGG	Nachrichten von der Gesellschaft der Wissenschaft zu Göttingen
NovTest	*Novum Testamentum*
NTA	Neutestamentliche Abhandlungen

NTS	*New Testament Studies*
PL	*Patrologia Latina*. ed. J. P. Migne
RGG³	*Die Religion in Geschichte und Gegenwart*, Third edition
RHPR	*Revue d'Histoire et de Philosophie religieuses*
SAB	Sitzungsberichte der Berliner Akademie der Wissenschaften
SAH	Sitzungsberichte der Heidelberger Akademie der Wissenschaften
SBT	Studies in Biblical Theology
SGV	Sammlung gemeinverständlicher Vorträge
SHT	Studies in Historical Theology
StANT	Studien zum Alten und Neuen Testament
St Th	Studia Theologica
SupplNovTest	Supplements to *Novum Testamentum*
SyBU	Symbolae Biblicae Upsalienses
ThB	Theologische Bücherei
ThBl	*Theologische Blätter*
ThExH	Theologische Existenz Heute
ThF	Theologische Forschung
ThLZ	*Theologische Literaturzeitung*
ThQ	*Theologische Quartalschrift*
ThR	*Theologische Rundschau*
ThViat	*Theologia Viatorum*
TThS	Trierer Theologische Studien
TThZ	*Trierer Theologische Zeitschrift*
TU	Texte und Untersuchungen
TWNT	Kittel, *Theologisches Wörterbuch zum Neuen Testament* (1933ff.; English version, 1964ff.)
UNT	Untersuchungen zum Neuen Testament
WA	Weimarer Ausgabe (Works of Luther)
WMANT	Wissenschaftliche Monographien zum Alten und Neuen Testament
WuD	*Wissenschaft und Dogma*
WUNT	Wissenschaftliche Untersuchungen zum Neuen Testament
ZNW	*Zeitschrift für die neutestamentliche Wissenschaft*
ZSavRG	*Zeitschrift der Savigny-Stiftung für Rechtsgeschichte*
ZSTh	*Zeitschrift für systematische Theologie*
ZThK	*Zeitschrift für Theologie und Kirche*

PREFACE AND FOREWORD

I

Themes treated in different places and in different ways in discussions over the whole field of New Testament exegesis come together in the study of the 'Theology of the New Testament'. At any given time, 'New Testament theology' provides as it were a model, presenting a whole theological period in perspective; this may happen in the synthesis of an F. C. Baur, in the historicism of the liberals, in the programme to replace the theology of the New Testament with a history of the religion of primitive Christianity, or most recently in the monumental summary which has been made by Bultmann of the productions of the age which has taken its stamp from dialectical theology. Once again – and certainly not by accident – Bultmann has succeeded in making a comprehensive synthesis: by means of his concept of theology he has been able to embrace both the unity in the New Testament and the multiplicity of approaches, types, outlines, beginnings of systems, which it contains, even if he does put the emphasis on the side of historical multiplicity.[1] The work of the last two decades has brought out the historical differences even more strongly. Among other things, the theology of the individual authors of the synoptic gospels has become a much-ploughed field. This has given rise to the impression – which is widespread among students today – that the New Testament tends to break up into a more or less fortuitous accumulation of 'conceptions', types or 'theologies'. This impression has become even stronger by being associated with a new tendency towards historical positivism and relativism. The upward trend in which biblical scholarship delighted for decades itself proved to be a piece of escapism – into the historical.

There is a danger that, as a result of the new positivism, the criteria for exegesis worked out by dialectical theology will be lost, especially as this positivism has an immediate influence on exegetical theses and hypotheses. Thus, for example, the assertion that the real moving force in primitive Christian theology is to be found in the interaction between enthusiasm and apocalyptic has not been demonstrated

[1] R. Bultmann, *Theology of the New Testament* II (1955), p. 251.

exegetically; it is an evaluative interpretation, developed on the basis of certain premises from systematic theology: it arises from a diastasis of *fides quae creditur* and *fides qua creditur*. This division is then projected into the history of primitive Christianity. As a result, primitive Christianity appears as the outline of an objective, apocalyptic world-picture on the one hand and as a psychological experience on the other.

The question whether stress is to be laid on historical reconstruction, i.e. the presentation of the thought-world of the New Testament as conditioned by its time, or on 'interpretation', points in the same direction. Bultmann carried through the latter approach and thus provided a corrective for the element of *historical construction* in his account. After a period of the positivistic collection of material, causal and genetic explanations (the history of motives), and psychological interpretation of the texts, it was indeed important to make a thematic interpretation of the *meaning* of what was said and the *message* presented by the texts. In other words, there was a need, for example, for an investigation not only of the *concept* of faith in Paul and John but also of the understanding of faith itself.

Here, too, perspectives have shifted. The retreat into historical investigation is paralleled by a remarkable tendency to take over statements of the New Testament directly, as teaching for today. It is, of course, realized here that the New Testament is conditioned by the period in which it arose, and so people feel it necessary to select what can 'still' be of use 'today'. The unconscious assurance with which this criterion is used seems to me to be one of the most dangerous symptoms of the frame of mind which prevails today among the younger theologians. If experience and the spirit of the age are to be the controlling factors in theology, then theological work is on the way out.

II

The impression made by Bultmann's account seems to have been so strong that no comprehensive treatment has since appeared in German (with the exception of the Catholic presentation of the subject by Meinertz). That does not, of course, mean that Bultmann has dominated this discipline. There are rather different, characteristic positions (to mention only that of Oscar Cullmann). But there is no other new textbook, nor even another guide.

Bultmann's work will remain basic for a long time yet, and the outline presented here betrays its indebtedness to him in a number of places. Nevertheless, I feel that an attempt at a new account is justified. Some reasons for this have already been hinted at. The progress of theological work, the historical character of theology, the shift in the questions asked, the emergence of new ones, are all obvious motives. For example, Bultmann does not include the content of the synoptic gospels in the concept of 'theology'; as a result, he does not discuss them in a way which does justice to the recent work done in this sphere.

A further reason for a new attempt is that – at least as far as I know – students are on the whole no longer aware of the presuppositions, the main interests, the criteria which shape Bultmann's work. Even terminology has changed significantly. For Bultmann and his day, the concept of 'decision' served to exclude psychologizing and to provide a positive account of the self-understanding posed by faith. Today the word is used in the sense of a superficial understanding of the freedom of the will, in other words, in exactly the opposite sense.

Bultmann's account of the theology of Paul (man prior to the revelation of faith – man under faith) was developed in the light of an understanding of faith in which faith was completely determined by its object, and not by subjective experience. Once this is no longer clear (and it is no longer clear to students today), the construction can look like a pietistic scheme and give the impression that the theme is not so much faith as *man* outside faith and *man* under faith. Indeed, even the catchword 'anthropology' is understood in this sense today, not least among the theological descendants of Bultmann.

Bultmann's existentialist interpretation (not of the cross, as an ineradicable popular misunderstanding assumes, but of the *text*) can give the impression (particularly in the sections on Paul and John) of sipping the result of interpretation as a pure distillation. I therefore feel it appropriate to give prominence once again to the historical components, thus for example in the case of Paul to begin with the form of his thought as it was conditioned by the period in which he lived. The present outline seeks to avoid the danger of historicism by regarding theology not only in general terms, as the interpretation of the faith made at a particular time, but in a more special sense as an exegesis of the original *texts* of the faith, the oldest formulations of the creed. An attempt is made here to set out the theology of the New Testament in accordance with the present state of the history of the tradition and thus to provide the reader with a unitary perspective for exploiting this discipline. Such an arrangement may perhaps help to show a way beyond the alternatives 'unity or multiplicity', which are still so dominant today (see above), so that the multiplicity can be seen to be a mark of the content, while the unity is a historical one.

The unitary starting point and focus also determines the arrangement of the post-Pauline epistles. Bultmann discusses them in the final section of his work under the heading 'The development towards the early church'. This is sensible, and historically correct. But the classification can also suggest a value judgment, as though the movement towards the 'early church' was a retrogression. The slogan 'early catholicism', which has done considerable mischief (both historically and in systematic theology) in recent years, can only serve to reinforce such a value judgment. In the present outline, this literature is therefore dealt with in connection with Paul. Three reasons influenced this course:

1. That named above, the need to avoid the intrusion of an unhistorical judgment.

2. The post-Pauline literature not only occupies a place in the larger context of the church, but also has special associations with Paul and his letters in the tradition. The existence of a school of Paul, as a prominent contributor towards the formation of theological ideas in this period, must be given its due.

3. The account must do justice to the fact that the 'apostolic' and 'post-apostolic' ages are not realities in the history of the church, but a historical idea; they are not so much a presupposition as an ingredient of New Testament theology.

III

This book has primarily been written as a textbook for students. It is hoped that the student will use it as an introduction to the present state of study and find in it as much material, and information about the interpretation of the material, as he needs for working in this field. I also hope that the book will serve the parish clergy, teachers of religion and interested laity as a useful means of orientation. It is set out in such a way as to be comprehensible even to the reader who has no Greek. Most of the Greek words and quotations come from the Bible and can be interpreted by reference to the passages indicated.

My concern is not so much to describe my own position (though that cannot always be avoided) as to give a general report. Of course, selections must be made from the mass of material (especially with the present over-production of secondary literature), so that a subjective element of judgment cannot be excluded. But that affects the periphery rather than the core of the material. And theological understanding is something very different from knowing the titles of a large number of books. At any rate, I have attempted to indicate characteristic contributions to particular themes while at the same time keeping the bibliography short enough to enable the reader to see the wood among the trees. At present in academic work there is something like a perfection-psychosis which confuses students: they find themselves being conditioned to the feeling that academic theology is something for initiates, of whom the normal user must be somewhat in awe and to whom he has to defer. But they should be helped to pluck up the courage to think for themselves and to understand that the greater part of literary productivity is superfluous. The brevity of the sketch offered here is not only a necessary expedient, but is also intentional: it is meant to provide a quite possible and appropriate simplification, a picture which can be taken in.

An invitation to study the text is far more important than an accumulation of references to literature. So the themes and problems are demonstrated as far as possible from 'classical' texts: this method should also help to stamp them on the memory. In short, this is meant to be a work-book which will help students to form their own judgments through exegesis and to gain a general view of the New Testament.

IV

One point in particular may incur criticism. There is no section in this book on the 'problem of the historical Jesus'. I am quite aware that it is not sufficient excuse for the omission to say that I find this problem a baffling one. It might be objected that the reader, at any rate, needs to be informed about the course and state of a discussion which has been recently carried on so extensively. But I feel – not for arbitrary reasons, but out of methodological consistency and as a result of the exegetical basis to my approach – that I must nevertheless insist that the 'historical Jesus' is not a theme of New Testament theology. It is nowhere doubted that the work of Jesus determines church, faith and theology. The question is, how? This book attempts to provide an answer by discussing the teaching of Jesus (including the problem of his understanding of himself) within the framework of the section on the synoptic gospels. But I feel that we owe it to the text not to introduce into it any alien problems. The basic problem of New Testament theology is not, how did the proclaimer, Jesus of Nazareth, become the proclaimed Messiah, Son of God, Lord? It is rather, why did faith maintain the identity of the Exalted One with Jesus of Nazareth after the resurrection appearances? This continuity is maintained in very different ways. Paul reduces it to the work of salvation in the strict sense; the gospels consider it in the perspective of the transmitted words and deeds of Jesus. But the identity itself remains. Where it is surrendered, we have the separation into orthodoxy and heresy, and the conflict between them.

The author gratefully remembers Rudolf Bultmann on his eighty-third birthday. Two assistants, Heinz-Dieter Knigge and Wolfgang Hinze, have been tireless in helping to prepare the manuscript. Their independent suggestions have played a real part in giving it its final form.

Göttingen,
20 August 1967

INTRODUCTION

1 · THE PROBLEM OF A THEOLOGY OF THE NEW TESTAMENT

R. Bultmann, *Theology of the New Testament* II (1955), pp. 237ff.; H. Braun, 'Die Problematik einer Theologie des Neuen Testaments', Beiheft 2 to *ZThK* (1961), pp. 3–18 (= *Gesammelte Studien zum NT und seiner Umwelt* (1962), pp. 325–341); R. Schnackenburg, *New Testament Theology Today* (1963), pp. 16ff.; H. Schlier, 'Über Sinn und Aufgabe einer Theologie des Neuen Testaments', *BZ* NF 1 (1957), pp. 6–23.

I   The Subject Matter

There are several problems. Which approach is to be stressed more in New Testament theology, the systematic or the historical? In the former case, the chief question is that of the validity of the canon; in the latter that of the wealth of the thought-world of primitive Christianity. In the former case the account will be limited to the New Testament corpus; in the latter it will also go beyond it. Representatives of a historical approach are H. Weinel, who defines his subject as, 'The religion of Jesus and of primitive Christianity', and R. Bultmann, who in the fourth part of his book describes the development towards the early church and thus goes beyond the New Testament canon.

II   History of the Discipline

H. J. Holtzmann, *Lehrbuch der neutestamentlichen Theologie*, 2 vols (1897, 1911²); H. Weinel, *Biblische Theologie des Neuen Testaments* (1928⁴; the introductory paragraphs in each case); R. Bultmann, *Theology of the New Testament* II, pp. 237–251.

The *Reformation*, and Protestant orthodoxy, do not know biblical theology as a special discipline. For them, all theology is biblical, and agreement with scripture is the criterion of truth: by reference to scripture it is possible to exclude human additions, and therefore the traditions of Catholic dogma. This presupposes that scripture is clear in itself.

Luther openly notices the differences in the Bible, e.g. between Paul and James. But they do not worry him. For he is quite certain of the material centre of scripture: justification by faith alone. His relationship to scripture is determined by the predominance of the *viva vox evangelii*.

Protestant orthodoxy systematizes what the Reformation has begun. The content of scripture is now regarded as a *summa* of pure doctrine. This leads to the discipline of 'topics', in which proofs for individual dogmatic *loci* are assembled from scripture. It is taken for granted that there is a material agreement between the Bible and dogmatics.

This presupposition became questionable, on the one hand in *pietism*, and on the other hand in the *Enlightenment*. The expression 'biblical theology' occurs for the first time in pietism. It indicates the new consciousness that the content of scripture and that of dogmatics are not identical. Over against pietism stands the Enlightenment. Here criticism clearly breaks through. The moving force is reason, which – in the controversy with orthodoxy – becomes conscious of its power.

The Enlightenment recognizes the difference between the Bible and the orthodox system of doctrine, measures the latter against its own standard, reason, and sketches out a 'natural' religion, in conformity to reason. Its verdict on the Bible is that the Bible does in fact contain the religion of reason; but this has been interpreted unreasonably by theology. The Enlightenment is confident that it can make good the damage. It sees that not everything, of course, in the Bible is reasonable, e.g. the miracle stories. This, however, is not the fault of the Bible, but of the limited powers of comprehension in the men of that time. When the Bible came into being, men were not yet enlightened; therefore some truths had to be communicated in a way that they could understand. Thus the Enlightenment distinguishes between what is timeless and rational and what is temporally determined. Naturally, it is principally interested in the former. But this distinction is a preparation for historical understanding in its recognition of the uniqueness of the historical.

The turning point is to be found in *Romanticism*, the philosophical conclusions of which are drawn by Hegel. He works out the understanding of reason as a historical factor. Truth is not simply given, but unfolds in a historical process. Hegel's philosophical insights were employed in the study of the New Testament by Ferdinand Christian Baur ('Tübingen School'). The New Testament writings are not simply documents of human religion, but of a historical process. This can only be understood if their historical context is recognized. The history of primitive Christianity, according to Baur, runs in the dialectic of thesis, antithesis, synthesis. The thesis is the legalism of Jewish Christianity, the antithesis is Paul's freedom from the law; the synthesis follows in post-Pauline Christianity. The writings of the New

Testament are witnesses to this controversy, or rather, they themselves form the historical process leading to the synthesis. The investigation of the history of primitive Christianity is the method of understanding the nature of faith, which for Baur is identical with the truth of the spirit. New Testament theology is the account of the self-understanding of the spirit, which comes to itself in the historical process.

Baur sets out the task of historical understanding. The period after him seeks to do it justice by describing the various 'doctrinal concepts' in the New Testament. The classic figure of this period, H. J. Holtzmann, differentiates between the 'transitory' and the 'permanent'. The content of the proclamation is not a doctrinal concept, e.g. that of Paul, but is something that lies behind it. What is that? There is a conviction of the validity of certain moral and religious norms; these are found in the teaching of Jesus, and it is these that are permanently valid.

In his book, *Über Aufgabe und Methode der sogenannten neutestamentlichen Theologie* (On the task and method of 'New Testament theology'), published in 1897, William Wrede challenges this approach. In his view, the method of doctrinal concepts is intellectualistic. Faith is not a system of ideas, but – religion. Hence the task of scholarship is to depict primitive Christian religion. Wrede puts it this way: we do not want to know what was *written* at that time about faith, love, hope, but what was actually believed, thought, taught, hoped, demanded.

Wrede's work is the programme of the 'History of Religions School'. The history of primitive Christian religion takes the place of New Testament theology.[1] The historical presuppositions of Christian ideas are found in Judaism and Hellenism, and attempts are made to understand them by investigating their historical origin.

This produces a completely new understanding of the *spirit*, which since Baur had been understood in idealistic terms. It is now recognized that the New Testament *pneuma* is not a matter of intellect; on the contrary, its effect is anti-intellectual, as it produces ecstasy. There is a realization that primitive Christianity did not seek salvation in pure thought but in 'mystery'. Thus Paul is brought close to the religious mysticism of late antiquity. The Christian sacraments are

---

[1] For this programme, see the article 'Biblical Theology', by H. Gunkel (OT) and M. Dibelius (NT) in J. Pelikam (ed.), *Twentieth Century Theology in the Making*, Vol. 1 (1969), pp. 23–31. It is carried out in the accounts by W. Bousset, *Kyrios Christos* (1913), and H. Weinel.

approximated to the Hellenistic mysteries. It is clear how alien the thought of the New Testament is to that of the modern world.

The second area investigated by the history of religions school was that of *eschatology*. Previously, the kingdom of God had been understood as a spiritual and moral entity, as a condition which was unfolding in the world, towards which the world was developing. Now, however, it became clear that the kingdom of God, as Jesus proclaimed it, is a supernatural condition. It cannot be created by moral, religious conduct. The world is not developing towards it. Rather than being a condition of the world, it represents the end of the world, that breaks in, like the flood, from outside.

Does this historical investigation not make Christianity a relative historical structure? What about its truth? The problem could be formulated either in historical terms: 'Primitive Christianity and the history of religion' (Karl Holl; Rudolf Otto), or systematically: 'The absoluteness of Christianity' (Ernst Troeltsch).

The history of religions school produced results which are still valid today: Christianity does, in fact, have certain historical presuppositions. Above all, this approach represented a liberation from the attempt to read modern ideas back into the Bible. It led to an understanding of the Bible in all its peculiarity. But the problem remained: what about the truth of the statements of the Bible? Weinel gives a typical answer: 'Thus biblical theology does not pass judgment on the value and truth of Christianity, but on its nature in comparison with other religions.'

Attempts were made to demonstrate that Christianity represents the highest type of religion (Weinel: as the monotheistic, moral religion of redemption). This, of course, produced a circular argument: what is to be proved is already presuppoesd, namely the particular concept of religion which provides the standard for demonstrating Christianity to be the highest of religions. The history of religions school did not clarify its own presuppositions. It did not ask whether Christian faith is aptly described if it is defined either as a religion or as Christianity.

Historical thought brought about a crisis in theology. The crisis is documented in two processes: the collapse of the 'Quest of the historical Jesus' as a result of 'form criticism'; and the emergence of 'dialectical theology'.

Form criticism asserts that an essential part of the tradition about Jesus is not faithful to history, but represents a theological construction made by the community. A mass of questions accompanies this recognition. Does it not destroy the foundation of Christian faith?

What is the relationship between faith and history? Are particular historical facts the presupposition of faith? Dialectical theology is certain that the answer is 'no!'. *Dialectical theology* does not attack historical critical scholarship itself, but the way in which its results are made absolute and developed systematically. Historical research prompted the conclusion that all theological ideas are relative. The result was the slogan: not theology, but religion. By way of a counter-attack, dialectical theology pronounced the slogan to be a symptom of collapse. The programme was not 'Less theology', but simply 'Theology'.[1] Of course, dialectical theology works out a new understanding of theology altogether. It regards theology as the understanding of the message in the texts – not as a system of propositions, not as the ultimately superfluous theory of religious experience, but as 'theological existence today' (Karl Barth).

III Literature

The textbook of the history of religions school was Heinrich Weinel's *Biblische Theologie des Neuen Testaments* (1928[4]). Its conservative counterpart was Paul Feine's *Theologie des Neuen Testaments* (1951[8]). Adolf Schlatter, *Die Theologie des Neuen Testaments* (2 vols, 1909/10; 1922[2]), is much more sharply concerned than the two previous books to penetrate the understanding of faith in the New Testament. It is, however, unsuitable as a textbook, as only the author's own view is given. Historical criticism is ignored. Schlatter does not help one to form an independent judgment. Ethelbert Stauffer, *New Testament Theology* (1955), is a reconstruction of the apocalyptic view of the world. The following Roman Catholic accounts are available: Max Meinertz, *Theologie des Neuen Testaments* (1950); Rudolf Schackenburg, *New Testament Theology Today* (1963), who provides an introduction to the literature and questions raised by its content; K. H. Schelkle, *Theologie des Neuen Testaments* (4 vols, 1968ff.), who is in process of providing a systematic account.

At present, the standard work is Rudolf Bultmann's *Theology of the New Testament* (2 vols., 1952; 1955). Bultmann's book provides an essentially historical treatment. In this way, the particular characteristics of individual types of theology emerge. But in contrast to earlier

[1] For the history of religions school, 'theology' as the content of the NT writings was unsatisfactory; they wanted to find 'more' in them. On the other hand, Bultmann makes the programmatic statement, 'that the historical significance of Paul lies precisely in the fact that he was a theologian' (*ThR* NF 1 (1929), p. 59).

accounts, Bultmann does not set out to describe the primitive Christian religion, but New Testament theology. Theology is defined as interpretation of the 'kerygma'. The kerygma, in turn, is not understood as a communication of statements about belief but as a communication of faith itself. The object of faith is not a sum of propositions; it is not even the content of New Testament theology, but the Lord himself, to whom the kerygma bears witness. The kerygma must be expounded on each occasion, because its formulations are historical. The same is true of exegesis. It, too, is historical. There can be no final, complete interpretation. For the kerygma is address and must always be heard anew as such on each occasion. This understanding of theology makes it possible for Bultmann to recognize all the influences of the history of religion on primitive Christianity without apologetic. He can equally readily recognize the different types of theology in the New Testament. Because his questions constantly refer back to the kerygma, a material unity becomes evident in the multiplicity of theological outlines. But what can be said about the truth of this faith? It cannot and may not be demonstrated; that follows from the self-evident quality of the message, which shows itself to be absolute in so far as it makes the one Lord known.

Bultmann's understanding of New Testament theology can be read off from the construction of his book. First he describes the 'presuppositions' of New Testament theology. The primary feature here is the historical teaching of Jesus. According to Bultmann, this teaching is not an element of New Testament theology, but material with which it works. There follow: 'The kerygma of the earliest church'; 'The kerygma of the Hellenistic church before and alongside Paul'. The two sections dealing with these questions are also headed 'Presuppositions and motifs of New Testament theology'. The strictly defined concept of theology is thus maintained: we are only to begin to talk about 'theology' when we come to Paul and John. The second part deals with this. The third part depicts the 'Development towards the early church'. Bultmann includes the Apostolic Fathers in this account. His approach illuminates the connection between the New Testament and church history.

Bultmann may be criticized for taking too little notice of one element, the synoptic tradition. The only part of it to appear is what criticism has shown to be the authentic teaching of Jesus. In addition, the third part contains a sketch of the characteristics of the individual evangelists.

IV Consequences for Method and Construction

The following account does not begin with the reconstructed teaching of Jesus. It starts where the themes of New Testament theology first become perceptible: in the kerygma of the primitive community. It must then show how the traditional material about Jesus is worked out in this context, first at the pre-literary stage of the synoptic tradition, and later at the literary stage, with the evangelists. By beginning with the kerygma, the account gains a unitary perspective on the two parts of the New Testament, the gospels and epistles: they show themselves to be two different kinds of theological development of the kerygma.

If we begin with the kerygma, we avoid the problem of the alternatives, whether greater stress is to be laid on the unity within the New Testament or on its multiplicity. The historical variety is made plain, and at the same time the unity is demonstrated by the way in which theology is related to its object, the Lord to whom witness is being borne in the kerygma. This produces the following scheme:

Survey of the historical setting

I The kerygma of the primitive community and of the Hellenistic community

II The interpretation of the teaching of Jesus through the report of his ministry and teaching: the theology of the synoptic tradition

III The conceptual development of the kerygma: Paul

IV Developments after Paul

V The conceptual development of the tradition of Jesus: John.

2 · THE ENVIRONMENT: HELLENISM

H. Preisker, *Neutestamentliche Zeitgeschichte* (1937); B. Reicke, *Neutestamentliche Zeitgeschichte* (1965); J. Leipoldt–W. Grundmann, *Umwelt des Urchristentums* I: *Darstellung des neutestamentlichen Zeitalters* (1965); III: *Bilder zum neutestamentlichen Zeitalter* (1966): *RGG*³ III 209ff., s.v. 'Hellenismus' (and the literature cited there); P. Wendland, *Die hellenistisch-römische Kultur*, HNT I/2 (1907); F. Cumont, *Die*

orientalischen Religionen im römischen Heidentum (1959[4]); H. Gressmann, *Die orient-*
alischen Religionen im hellenistisch-römischen Zeitalter (1930); G. Kittel, *Die Religions-*
geschichte und das Urchristentum (1931); R. Bultmann, *Primitive Christianity in its*
Contemporary Setting (1955), pp. 159ff.; W. W. Tarn, *Hellenistic Civilization* (1952[3]);
K. Prümm, *Religionsgeschichtliches Handbuch für den Raum der altchristlichen Umwelt*
(1954); C. K. Barrett, *The New Testament Background: Selected Documents* (1956);
M. P. Nilsson, *Geschichte der griechischen Religion II: Die hellenistische und römische*
Zeit, HAW V/2 (1961[2]). For gnosticism, see: *RGG*[3] II 1648ff., s.v. 'Gnosis' (and
the literature cited there); W. Bousset, *Hauptprobleme der Gnosis*, FRLANT 10
(1907): H. Jonas, *Gnosis und spätantiker Geist* I, FRLANT NF 33 (1964[3] with
supplement); II/1, FRLANT NF 45 (1966[2]); id, *The Gnostic Religion* (1963[2]).

Hellenism is a term used to describe the epoch of the Greek dominance
of world culture after the time of Alexander the Great. The attitude
of classical Greece towards the world was primarily determined by the
city-state and its law. Religion was a city cult, a demonstration of the
respect due to the gods of the city. Hellenism brings about the transformation of the city state into the territorial state, the extension of
city culture into a world culture. As a free citizen, the individual is no
longer directly involved in the state. This makes possible the development of the private sphere. Philosophy directs itself to questions of
personal conduct. The horizon is now the cosmos and its law. True,
the ancient religion lives on, but for educated people it has largely
been replaced by philosophical enlightenment. This latter, however,
penetrates only to limited circles. Into the gaps between national
religion, which does not solve the problems of the individual, and
philosophy, stream new religions from the East. Originally they, too,
were national religions. But they transform themselves into cults
which are related to individuals. The individual obtains a share in
salvation by participating in their mysteries. As in philosophy, a
tendency towards monotheism prevails. Gods are identified with one
another: the Baal of Dolicheum with Zeus; Isis with Ishtar and with
Aphrodite. The many gods are regarded as manifestations of the one
supreme God under many names. The character of these manifestations is no longer Greek. The new gods appear as 'lords'; their worshippers are 'servants'.

    Examples: *The Syrian star-gods*. The stars determine fate. The cult
brings about the ascent of the soul into the upper world of light. The
world is no longer the harmonious cosmos. It is divided into two
spheres. The laws of the world are no longer investigated by philosophical thought and natural science, but by interpretation of the paths of

the stars. Freedom is no longer gained by knowledge, but by redemption and ascent.

A second type is made up of *the gods who die and rise again*. Originally they represent the course of nature. Now they become 'saviour gods': 'Rejoice, initiates, that the god has been delivered; so deliverance comes to us, too, out of suffering'.[1]

A new form of *religious community* appears. The cult is no longer celebrated by the nation, but by a community of people who meet together voluntarily (e.g. that of Isis in Corinth, Rome, etc.), in which national and social distinctions are transcended (cf. Gal. 3.26ff.).

A further religious feature is the Hellenistic *ruler-cult*.[2] The king is the 'saviour'. His enthronement is the dawn of the time of salvation.[3]

The most luxuriant growth of syncretism, which is at the same time an independent phenomenon, is gnosticism. It is already a pre-Christian manifestation.[4] Gnosticism is a tremendous pot-pourri of Iranian, Babylonian and Egyptian ideas. They are already permeated with Greek elements under the influence of syncretism. Nevertheless, the result is a formation with characteristics all of its own, a comprehensive outline of an understanding of being (H. Jonas).

Gnosticism sets out to penetrate the depths of the world and of being – not, however, through investigation so much as on the basis of supernatural transformation. The goal is divinization (*Corpus Hermeticum* I 26). Gnosticism takes up the ideas of Hellenistic dualism and goes beyond them: this world is not only the dark place from which men long to be removed into light; it is an active, demonic power. The soul is shut in the cosmos and wanders about in it without being able to break out. For the Greeks, the courses of the stars represent the harmonious regularity of the world. For the gnostics, the stars are demonic watchers which frighten the self, if it sets out to ascend into the light, back into the cosmos, into an alien realm. Pre-gnostic dualism saw man as a dichotomy, consisting of soul and body, with the soul banished to the body. Gnosticism goes one step further: even the soul is still a cosmic entity. The true 'I', which comes from

---

[1] Julius Firmicus Maternus, *De erroribus profanarum religionum*, XXII 1.

[2] L. Cerfaux and J. Tondriau, *Le culte des souverains* (1957).

[3] Virgil, *Eclogue* 4; inscription from Priene (text in Preisker, *op. cit.*, p. 301; cf. Nilsson, *op. cit.*, pp. 370f.).

[4] E. Haenchen, 'Gab es eine vorchristliche Gnosis?', *ZThK* 49 (1952), pp. 316–49; A. Adam, *Die Psalmen des Thomas und das Perlenlied als Zeugnisse vorchristlicher Gnosis*, BZNW 24 (1959); C. Colpe and E. Haenchen, *RGG*³ II 1648ff.

the beyond, must be freed from both body *and* soul. But what is this 'I', apart from body and soul? It can no longer be visualized, and is only to be experienced by the gnostic in spiritual illumination. In the inward ascent, he experiences the spark of light in himself which is an ingredient of the divine, primal light. The light from beyond sends an emissary into this dark world, to call together the scattered particles of light, collect them to himself and ascend again to his home of light. The process of redemption is represented in cosmological myths. Salvation is experienced in the myth of the fall and forgetfulness, the sending and call of the emissary, his raising and illumination. The gnostic understanding of salvation is summed up in a text of the Valentinians: gnosticism is about:

τίνες ἦμεν, τί γεγόναμεν·	who we were, what we have become;
ποῦ ἦμεν, ποῦ ἐνεβλήθημεν·	where we were, whither we have been thrown;
ποῦ σπεύδομεν, πόθεν λυτρούμεθα·	whither we are hastening, whence we have been redeemed;
τί γέννησις, τί ἀναγέννησις.[1]	what birth is, what rebirth is.

3 · THE ENVIRONMENT: JUDAISM

E. Schürer, *The Jewish People in the Time of Jesus Christ* (1885); W. Bousset-H. Gressmann, *Die Religion des Judentums im späthellenistischen Zeitalter* (1966⁴); P. Volz, *Die Eschatologie der jüdischen Gemeinde im neutestamentlichen Zeitalter* (1934²); G. F. Moore, *Judaism in the First Centuries of the Christian Era* I–III (1954⁷); K. Schubert, *Die Religion des nachbiblischen Judentums* (1955); H. Braun, *Qumran und das NT* (2 vols., 1966); H. H. Rowley, *The Relevance of Apocalyptic* (1963³); F. V. Filson, *A New Testament History* (1965).

Sources: (a) LXX. (b) *The Apocrypha and Pseudepigrapha of the Old Testament*, ed. R. H. Charles (1963²). (c) Rabbinic writings: H. L. Strack provides an *Introduction to the Talmud and Midrash* (1931). *The Mishnah*, ed. H. Danby (1933). *The Babylonian Talmud*, ed. I. Epstein (London 1935). P. Billerbeck, *Kommentar zum NT aus Talmud und Midrasch* (1922ff.). (d) The Qumran texts: *The Dead Sea Scrolls in English*, ed. G. Vermes (1963).

---

[1] The text is quoted in Clement of Alexandria, *Excerpta ex Theodoto* 78.2. For exegesis, see H. Jonas, *op. cit.*, I, p. 206; cf. pp. 108, 261.

Judaism not only provides the setting for Jesus and the primitive community, but is also their religion. So in this section we are already concerned with the material of New Testament theology.

The Judaism of this period is not, of course, a unity. It was only made so after the Jewish War (AD 70). The groups of the Pharisees and Sadducees are known from the New Testament. The Qumran texts offer a view of a special group with a rigorous observance of the law and a syncretistic twist to their view of the world. We have further reports of baptist groups in the Jordan valley. We know of the Samaritans, with their own sanctuary on Mount Gerizim, and also the oriental and Hellenistic diaspora, which was partly drawn into a whirlpool of syncretism. Apart from this peripheral phenomenon, monotheism and the law are common to all groups. A connection with the Jerusalem temple is usual; the Samaritans and the people of Qumran are an exception to the rule. The authority of the one God is respected in obedience towards the law and in the regulation of life and the cult. This very much limits the religious productivity of Judaism; the law stands firm. But it is still possible to compose prayers and hymns. The apocalyptic view of the future also offers scope for free elaboration.

I   The Idea of God

Judaism has no epistemological reflections about God and the make-up of the world. It has no concept of nature except for what it takes over from the Greeks (Philo). The world is God's creation; but this truth is not worked out theoretically. It is an insight of faith, which leads to obedience and praise. This fact still holds, even where doubts emerge about the make-up of the world (IV Ezra). The author of this apocalypse no longer understands the world. But in puzzling over the riddles of the world he is asking about God.

The factors in the idea of God are: the creation and guidance of the world, the election of Israel, the giving of the law. Israel has experienced God's guidance (leading, punishment, re-acceptance) in its history and can draw the appropriate conclusions for the present. God is not nameless, nor is he invisible; but it is not in accordance with his majesty for him to be seen. One can note a tendency to accentuate increasingly the transcendence of God. His name, originally his revelation and the possibility of calling upon him, now itself becomes so holy that people avoid mentioning it.

Intermediate beings have their abode in the realm between God and the world, and maintain the connection between the two:

(a) Hypostases: God's 'wisdom', 'dwelling', etc. In effect, this means that revelation becomes a mediating factor between God and man.

(b) The angels: these are arranged in a hierarchical order.

(c) On the opposing side: Satan and his host.

Influences from oriental demonology can be recognized. This is especially true of Qumran, with its doctrine of the two spirits. The Persian influence is clear. Some features of Persian religion may serve for comparison: two realms at war with one another; a conjunction of cosmology and ethics; a dualism of decision; man is at war and must decide actively. In this struggle he is determined by the two spirits. The eschatological orientation is part of dualism. Consideration extends beyond this world to the outcome of the world-wide struggle, the kingdom of God. Before the kingdom, however, comes the judgment. Persian religion knows of a double judgment, an individual one immediately after death and a general one at the end of the world, at the general resurrection of the dead. This twofold judgment has found its way into Jewish and Christian eschatology. The idea of an individual judgment means that the individual bears the whole weight of responsibility. He does not achieve blessedness as the member of a people or a church, but exclusively through his own actions. The idea of the general resurrection, however, makes it clear that the final victory falls to the good. This guarantees the certainty of salvation.

The view that man is justified only by his works is carried through consistently. There is no room for grace. The judge is bound by his own law.

Parseeism develops into a radically worked-out system the idea that blessedness is achieved by works and by decision understood as works. It knows only absolute contrasts: good or evil. There are no degrees, even psychological ones: man is wholly on one side or the other.

II Elements of the Picture of the World

The New Testament has no special doctrine of cosmology. There is no particular 'Christian' view of the world. It is significant that a view of the world is simply taken over from the environment, whether Jewish or Hellenistic. There is no concern in primitive Christianity that cosmological views should agree together. Clearly there is some idea of the fabric of the world, but it is not taught in the creeds. Christians and Jews do not argue over the make-up of the world, but whether Jesus is the Messiah.

1 The World

The Old Testament has no concept to correspond to the Greek 'cosmos'. The whole of the world is called 'heaven and earth'; both are God's creation (Gen. 1.1). God rules over both (Matt. 6.10; 11.25; Acts 17.24). As creation, heaven and earth are transitory, and they will pass away (Mark 13.31; Matt. 5.18; II Peter 3.7), whereas the words of Jesus will remain. There are hopes for a new heaven and a new earth (Rev. 21.1; II Peter 3.13). In Judaism and Christianity, the original, Old Testament faith in creation has been changed into an eschatological hope.[1] Alongside the idea of the transitoriness of this world and the new creation of another we have the notion of the transformation of this world, but the difference is not particularly significant. For even in the second approach there is no expectation that anything of the present world will remain; the coming world of salvation will be completely different, 'new'.

In addition to heaven and earth, a third constituent part of the world should be mentioned – the sea (Ps. 146.6; Acts 4.24; 14.15; Rev. 14.7; cf. Ex. 20.11). The sea acquires a special significance in apocalyptic speculation. There it represents mythical chaos. So in the new creation there can be no more sea (Rev. 21.1).

Heaven and earth can be considered together, for example as the realm of God's rule (and in Christianity as the realm of Christ's rule): 'All authority in heaven and on earth has been given to me' (Matt. 28.18). Alongside the aspect of heaven as a constituent part of the universe, however, we find another: heaven is the *abode of God*, and as such is, of course, changeless. Both aspects can remain side by side without difficulty. Even as God's dwelling place, heaven is conceived in spatial terms: God is enthroned on high. Heaven is his throne and earth his footstool (Isa. 66.1=Acts 7.49). God is called ὁ ἐν τοῖς οὐρανοῖς. In Judaism, 'heaven' is used as a periphrasis for the divine name (Bill. I 862ff.). The divine pronouncements, e.g. at the baptism and transfiguration of Jesus, come from heaven.

To the God of heaven belongs the host that surrounds his throne, the angels (Mark 12.25; 13.32; Matt. 18.10; Gal. 1.8, etc.). On the

[1] G. Lindeskog, *Studien zum neutestamentlichen Schöpfungsgedanken* (1952), pp. 46ff. A model is offered by Isa. 65.17 and 66.22; beginnings like this are developed in apocalyptic.

other hand, heaven – as a constituent part of the world – can also be the realm of evil powers (I Cor. 8.5; cf. Eph. 2.2).

As the abode of God, heaven is at the same time the place of *paradise* and the blessedness of the faithful. It is there that our hope is preserved (Col. 1.5; cf. I Peter 1.4; Phil. 3.20).[1] Even more exact knowledge is possible: e.g. that paradise lies in the third heaven (II Cor. 12.2–4; Slavonic Enoch 8). Singular and plural forms of 'heaven' are to be found side by side. In the latter, two groups of passages are to be distinguished: οὐρανοί can simply be an echo of the semitic שָׁמַיִם or שְׁמַיָּא; in that case it may be translated as singular. But the idea of a number of heavens can also be present (there are three in II Cor. 12.2).

A quite different conceptuality and therefore a quite different picture of the world is to be found in the epistle to the Ephesians. The earth is the lowest part of the cosmos. The ἐπουράνια stretch above it to the highest point, the throne of God. In the lowest level of the ἐπουράνια, the air, Satan has his throne with his satellites. Thus according to Ephesians, hell is up above.

2 Heaven and the Saving Event of Christ

We can distinguish *two basic christological patterns*. One is developed in the light of apocalyptic ideas: resurrection or exaltation – parousia of Christ; the other in the light of mythical cosmological ideas: descent – ascent of the revealer.

For the second pattern see I Cor. 2.6ff.; Eph. 4.9f.; heaven and earth form the realm in which the saving event is played out; redemption is an ascent. There is no place in this picture of the world, taken by itself, for a future parousia, but only for a passage by Christ through the spheres (cf. Heb. 4.14; 7.26; 9.24). Here, therefore, a spatial aspect is added to the apocalyptic temporal aspect of the pattern of the parousia. In one context the kingdom of God is future, in the other it is timeless and transcendent.

The Jewish picture of the world includes the *underworld* as well as heaven and earth (and sea) (Rev. 5.3). There, too, there are powers (Phil. 2.10). Two originally different ideas, of Hades and of hell, have been combined here.[2] Hades (שְׁאוֹל) is first simply the world of the dead below. In addition, there is γέεννα, the place of punishment. It is not expressly said in the New Testament where that is. But it is clear that it is thought of as being below.

---

[1] J. Jeremias, παράδεισος, *TWNT* V 763–71.
[2] P. Volz, *Die Eschatologie der jüdischen Gemeinde*, pp. 327ff.

Cf. Matt. 11.23: one goes below. Occasionally another picture can be detected in the terminology: the place of punishment is the uttermost darkness at the edge of the world. In Jewish writings we also find the idea of hell as a place in the world above, over against paradise (Sl. Enoch 10; cf. Bill. IV 1084).

According to the original idea, darkness predominates in Hades and a consuming fire in hell. But an exact distinction is no longer made between the two, so that hell can also be imagined as being hot and cold and dark at the same time: there is fire at the same time as gnashing of teeth. It is the abode of the beast (Rev. 11.7; 17.8), the devil's dungeon (Rev. 20.2). All spheres of the world are inhabited by beings. There are heavenly beings and demonic beings and others which are to some extent neutral, or have a twofold potentiality:

3 The Angels

In the Old Testament we find the 'messenger of Yahweh' as a manifestation of God. Where the New Testament mentions the ἄγγελος κυρίου (Acts, Lucan birth narrative, Matthew), we have a creaturely being rather than the Old Testament figure. The Old Testament knows of further heavenly figures: cherubim, seraphim, a whole 'host'. But this does not explain the dominant role of angels in the late-Jewish view of the world. The Persian belief in demons evidently influenced Judaism outside the Old Testament. It is, however, more important to see the function of this speculation in the picture of the world than to determine its historical derivation. The angels are called the 'holy ones' (Dan. 4.14; Mark 8.38). It is their primary task to stand before God and to form his court.

Judaism has a whole hierarchy of angels. The best-known are the archangels. If one compares the New Testament picture of the world with that of Judaism, an astonishing restraint in angelology becomes plain. The New Testament is simply not interested in hierarchies of angels and the formation of groups of angels. Individual names of angels appear only occasionally (Gabriel: Luke 1.19, 26; cf. Dan. 8.16; Michael: Jude 9; Rev. 12.7; cf. Dan. 10.13, 21; 12.1). Michael is the heavenly vizier. In the War Rule of Qumran he seems to be identical with the Prince of Light (1 QM 9.15f.; 17.6f.). In the New Testament, the angels only play a marginal role: they are messengers (Christmas stories, Acts). They guide the departed faithful (Luke 16.22). There is acquaintance with the figure of the personal guardian angel (Matt. 18.10; cf. Tobit 5.6). The role of the angels is, of course, most strongly marked in the Revelation of John. One special idea is that they mediated the law to men (Acts 7.53; Gal. 3.19; Heb. 2.2).

Further names of 'powers' are: ἀρχαί Rom. 8.38 (cf. ἄρχοντες τοῦ αἰῶνος τούτου I Cor. 2.8) and δυνάμεις; ἐξουσίαι Eph., Col.; πνεύματα Heb. 1.7, 14; Revelation.

More important than the way in which these powers are conceived is the attitude of men towards them. The angels are subordinate to Christ (Matt. 4.11; 13.41). They will accompany him at the parousia.[1] For the believer, the hostile powers have already been brought to nothing (I Cor. 2.6). The same is true of *Satan*.

He is called διάβολος, Belial or Beliar, Bee(l)zebub. He is ἄρχων τῶν δαιμονίων Mark 3.22; ἄρχων τοῦ κόσμου τούτου John 12.31; θεὸς τοῦ αἰῶνος τούτου II Cor. 4.4. His abode is in the depths or in the air (Eph. 2.2). He, too, has his angels (Matt. 25.41; II Cor. 12.7; Rev. 12.7, 9). The myth of the fall of the angels appears peripherally (Jude 6; II Peter 2.4). The figure of Satan rarely appears in the Old Testament. There he is not the evil one, but the heavenly prosecutor. His role as prince of evil was developed in Judaism, though his figure was accommodated to Jewish monotheism. Satan is not anti-God. At the end he will be cast out (Rev. 20.7–10).

In the New Testament, the devil is the tempter (temptation narrative; I Thess. 3.5) and the seducer (Acts 5.3). He seeks to hinder the mission (I Thess. 2.18) and unleashes persecution (I Peter 5.8f.). He has the power of death (Heb. 2.14); he has the kingdoms of the world in his gift (Luke 4.6) and can change himself into an angel of light (II Cor. 11.14).

There is no question of reconstructing a 'New Testament doctrine of Satan' from these hints. They are simply fragments. For example, the devil acts in the passion, but his work there has no significance for theological understanding. No account is taken of him in the description of God's rule. Paul outlines man's position before God, the nature of sin, judgment and salvation, without using the idea of Satan (Rom. 5; cf. on the other hand the account in the Wisdom of Solomon). In the New Testament, Satan is not a being with whom one can explain e.g. sin and death. He is the evil one against whom precautions must be taken, and who is driven away by the confession of faith.

4 The Temporal Aspect of the World

It is significant that some originally spatial concepts are transformed into temporal concepts. The most important are:

κόσμος: the meaning of this word overlaps with that of αἰών. The cosmos is creation and therefore limited; it is 'this' world. In comparison with Judaism and gnosticism, one can see an extreme reduction of cosmological speculation in the New Testament: 'cosmos' primarily describes the world of men. There is no account of chaos, none of apocalyptic astronomy and astrology. Christian groups who reverence the cosmos in a religious way by making its 'elements' the object of their worship are sharply rebuked: Gal. 4.3; Col. 2.8, 20.

[1] The Lucan doctrine of angels forms an exception: here the angels stand immediately below God, and not Christ. Cf. Luke 9.26 with Mark 8.38.

αἰών: this word is equivalent to the Hebrew עוֹלָם, 'long time', 'eternity'. The word designates on the one hand the eternity of God: εἰς τοὺς αἰῶνας (doxologies); βασιλεὺς τῶν αἰώνων (I Tim. 1.17), and on the other the period of this world, which is bounded by creation and the end of the world. Men look forward to the συντέλεια τοῦ αἰῶνος (Matt. 13.39f.).

5   The Relationship of Time and Eternity

In the Old Testament, eternity is primarily imagined as unlimited time. God always has been and always will be (Ps. 90.2). This is the support for the theory that this idea of eternity as time lengthened to infinity is a constitutive part of the biblical revelation. But it must be pointed out that there are also timeless ideas about the world and eternity in the New Testament (John; Ephesians). Above all, we must ask whether this idea is determinative in itself. Is it an appropriate description of the eschatology of the New Testament to say that the New Testament represents the beyond as an extension of time? Or does this idea arise simply because the world beyond is presented in the form of a picture which is to be interpreted and not taken literally? If we put the question in this way, we quickly discover that time is merely the formal determination of the picture and not its content.[1] The essence of eternity is not that it is extended in time, but that death and sin are no longer. Even the imagery is appropriate for timelessness: eternal worship, eternal feasting. The intention of the expressions is not directed towards a continuity between this world and the beyond, but towards the infinite difference: things will be very different there from here; a new world is coming, and it will be of a miraculous kind. That is the significance of the apocalyptic schema of the 'two ages', 'this' one and the one 'to come': הָעוֹלָם הַזֶּה and הַבָּא הָעוֹלָם. This pattern of two ages is presupposed in the New Testament, but it is not developed. The pattern plays no part in the eschatology of Jesus. It is only hinted at in Paul, who never uses the expression 'the age to come' (it first occurs in Eph. 1.21). It is already the case in Jewish apocalyptic that the idea of time is not constitutive of the eschatological hope:

'When all creation . . . shall end, . . . all time shall perish, and the years, and thenceforward there will be neither months nor days nor hours. There will be one aeon, and all the righteous . . . shall be collected in the great aeon, and they

[1] Cf. H. Sasse, αἰών TWNT I 205.

will live eternally, and then too there will be amongst them neither labour, nor sickness, nor humiliation, nor anxiety, nor need, nor violence, nor night, nor darkness, but great light . . .' (Sl. Enoch 65; cf. the prospect of the 'rest' in Heb. 4.9).

III Man and Salvation

God is the creator who has made the *world* good. But is it really good? It is an expression of faith for Judaism that it is good, but this expression is true in the sight of God rather than in empirical reality. The world does not simply correspond with its nature as creation; it has been corrupted through sin. It must therefore be restored to its rightful condition. The harmony between God and the world is not an obvious datum, but requires a new act of creation in the future.

This insight, that salvation lies in the future, can be established in respect of the *world*: a picture of the new world is then outlined. Alternatively, the *individual* becomes the focal point; in that case, the factors of existence come into the foreground: law and sin; the need to be concerned for righteousness: the future judgment. Anthropology is added to cosmology.

What is true of the world is true of *man*: he is a creature, i.e. he is created good by God. No part of him is evil *per se*. Judaism has no dualistic rejection of the body and matter, and no dualism of body and soul.

נֶפֶשׁ does not mean 'soul' as an immortal part of man, but the power of natural life.

Man can be lost as a whole or win salvation as a whole. If he wills the latter, he must exert himself. The way to salvation is the fulfilment of the law. God has taught what is to be done and demands unconditional obedience. Man has not to ask why this and that are commanded; he is to carry out what he has been told. The meaning of the commandment is not therefore felt to be a problem and is not discussed. A command is not valid, for example, because it may help a man. That may indeed be the case. But formal authority comes first.

There are apparent exceptions. The best known can be found in the tradition about Hillel: the Golden Rule is the sum of the whole Torah (Akiba: the commandment to love). But this explanation does not limit individual casuistic precepts in a critical way, as is the case with Jesus; it even strengthens them. Johanan ben Zakkai: 'A dead body does not make a man unclean, nor does water make him clean. But the Holy One has said: I have established a law, I have made a decision. You are not at liberty to transgress my decision, which is written.'[1]

As the precept applies formally, and is therefore not comprehensible in itself, it needs exposition if it is to be applied rightly to individual cases. So the exegete, the scribe, is a part of the law. Exposition aims at complete fulfilment by comprehensive regulations. But is formal fulfilment really obedience? Is fulfilment to be achieved by quantitative accumulation, and complete obedience by a comprehensive regulation of individual instances? Can the law be fulfilled at all? And if not, what then?

This group of questions must, of course, be put in historical perspective.

We cannot make the Reformation's dogmatic judgment on the law as a means to salvation into a historical verdict on the Jewish understanding of the law. Nor may we be guided by modern sensibilities. If we read the Talmudic debates, we have the impression of a tremendous disorder. But it is important to understand this is a Jewish perspective.

For Judaism, the law is not primarily a sum of precepts, but the sign of the election of Israel, the ratification of the covenant. It is not a burden, but a delight (Paul: Phil. 3.4-6).

It should be noted that the Talmud does not consist of instructions for daily life, but is a comprehensive collection of possible instances with extensive discussion. It can be compared with a modern law book together with commentary and specialist literature. For example, none of the legislation about the temple cult affects daily life at all, particularly after the destruction of the temple. What regulations for daily life remain (the commandments and prohibitions, see Bill. I 900f.) are largely a matter of customs with which the Jew is familiar from childhood on. The sense behind each individual regulation is felt to be that the law is the condition for Israel's existence. It can only be had in its entirety or not at all. However, it remains to be seen whether this intention can really be maintained.

The question is: can obedience be achieved by legalistic casuistry at all? What is sought after is not just formal fulfilment, but the correspondence of my will with the will of God, the overcoming of the conflict against him, in which I find myself involved. On the basis of the law, man's relationship with God is necessarily a legalistic one, even if he recognizes the priority of the covenant. There is also the limitation of all law; what is not prohibited is permissible. The law

---

[1] Passages quoted are: *Shabbat* 31a (cf. Bill. I 460); *Siphra Lev.* 19.18 (cf. Bill. I 357f.); *Pesiqta* 40b (cf. Bill. I 719).

leaves certain areas free by providing no regulations for them. Here man can move freely.

The decisive issue is not whether the orthodox Jew really makes use of this free area. The decisive thing is the phenomenon as such, that the law *qua* law leads to this possibility; not only can I ask what I should do, but I can also ask what I need not do. So the law seduces a man into a broken obedience. A symptom of the situation is the attempt to slip round the commandments. An instructive example is offered by the tractate *Shabbat*. Radical obedience would not begin to be interested in such expedients.

There is a further issue: if I have fulfilled the demand, I am free to do what is over and above the demand; for the moment, I have settled accounts with God. The law opens up the possibility of acquiring merit. But this is to pervert its significance, as it demands the whole man for God. As it is, it becomes a means by which a man can stand before God through his own efforts. This makes certainty of salvation impossible. An indication of the problem is the Jewish *consciousness of sin*: men know that they keep failing to fulfil the commandments and that altogether there is an excess of transgression. Exceptions (the awareness of individual devout men, cf. Phil. 3.2f.) prove the rule. But the consciousness of sin is also broken, as sin is primarily understood to be the individual transgression which can be compensated for by good works. Nevertheless, the Jewish consciousness can come to the point at which people no longer get by with good works. What help is there then? Objectively, there is the cult, which has atoning power. Of course, Jerusalem is a long way away, and the cult is primarily directed towards the nation, and not towards the individual. So as a last resort there remains humble submission, the appeal to God's mercy.

One might also add, 'righteousness'. 'There is none of the earth-born who has not dealt wickedly, who has not sinned . . . For in this, O Lord, shall thy righteousness and goodness be declared, if thou wilt compassionate them that have no wealth of good works' (IV Ezra 8.35f.). 'If I stagger because of the sin of flesh, my justification shall be by the righteousness of God which endures for ever' (1 QS XI 12).

The idea of the *law* consistently leads on to the idea of *judgment*. In the Old Testament, judgment is a historical event. In Judaism, it becomes a transcendent act, after the death of the individual or at the end of 'this world'.

Jewish eschatology is not a unitary system. But some of its main outlines may be stressed. On the one hand, we have the influence of the Old Testament, national eschatology. In addition, there is a cosmological picture of the future ('apocalyptic'). Neither type ever appears in a pure form; even the cosmological hope remains bound up with the Jewish people.

The most important problem from the point of view of the history of religion is that of the origin of apocalyptic. Persian influence is determinative. It is confirmed by the Qumran texts (see below). The main characteristics are: (a) the association of the end of the world and the resurrection of the dead; (b) the juxtaposition of the cosmological act of the general resurrection of the dead and the individual judgment immediately after death. In the first case, the hope is for the new age, in the second for paradise. Both forms of expectation have, however, become involved in each other and are sometimes deliberately brought together by attempts at compensation: there is an expectation of an intermediate state for the individual until the dawn of the new age. This juxtaposition has also found its way into Christian eschatology. Cf. I Cor. 15 (the general resurrection of the dead) with Luke 16.19–31 (the story of the beggar Lazarus). Sometimes there is an expectation of the resurrection of the righteous only: the sinners remain in death (Test. Sim. 6; Test. Levi 18). Sometimes a general resurrection is expected, with vindication or condemnation (IV Ezra 7.32f.; Eth. Enoch 51.1–3).

A particular figure to accomplish the last things (for the righteous, a saviour) is not necessarily part of the eschatological expectation. Such a figure is to be found comparatively seldom, in two types, the national and the apocalyptic: the national Messiah appears in Ps. Sol. 17, the apocalyptic Messiah in Ethiopian Enoch and IV Ezra; cf. Dan. 7.

The eschatological picture is motivated by the consciousness that salvation has indeed still to come, but that it is certain to come and demands decision and obedience. The new world may be depicted in bizarre imagery, but there can be no mistake about what is really meant: the world of salvation is a wonder, an object of hope, the realization of which transcends all imagination. It is salvation *par excellence*. The purport of eschatology is radical concentration on God. But this significance is largely concealed by exotic pictures. They are indeed outlines of hopes, but they are drawn in fear. Where they are really transcended, one need no longer be concerned about heaven and earth. But this very concern is the theme of apocalyptic. Of course, we must note when apocalyptic took its rise historically: in a time of persecution.

That the connection of law and eschatology is constitutive for the shaping of life and understanding of salvation is particularly clear

from the *community of the new covenant* at Qumran. The world-view of
this group has been influenced by syncretism (apocalyptic, Parseeism)
and its practice is rigoristic. It represents itself as the group of the
elect, and in so doing passes a verdict on all Israel. The people of God
is not the empirical Israel, but this circle which must detach itself
from Israel. Thus a decision is required of each individual: entry into
the covenant is the condition of salvation. In the covenant, radical
obedience to the law is dominant. This is fulfilled when a man subjects himself to the rule of the sect. Like the Christians, the members
of the sect call themselves 'saints', 'elect (of God)'.

The primitive Christian community also sees itself as an eschatological community of the elect of Israel, separated from the world. But its organization does
not have saving significance in itself: the Christian community has no common
order which must be followed to achieve salvation. Community of goods may
serve as an example. Even if the Acts of the Apostles does present an ideal, rather
than an accurate picture, it shows that the sharing of goods was at least an ideal
among Christians. It is understood as a free community of love. Each gives of his
own as is necessary. In the sect, on the other hand, community of goods is the law.
On entering, a man gives up his possessions; otherwise he endangers his salvation.

This latter view is also that of Jesus and the primitive church. The difference
is that in the church each is responsible for himself and is therefore free. The sect,
on the other hand, removes the risk from the individual. It receives his offering
and in exchange guarantees him material security. Jesus demands decision with
utter risk. In one case the saving power is the regular observance of the law of the
group, in the other the important thing is the acceptance of the kingdom of God
like a child. The attitude to the world is basically different in the two instances.
This is expressed in the respective views of the world.

The community of Qumran forms the group of the 'children of
light'. They have to love one another, but hate those outside, the
children of darkness. Their thought is dominated by a dualistic idea
of predestination, of Iranian origin: the decision of the individual is
predetermined by the two spirits of truth and falsehood. True, the
monotheism of the Old Testament is maintained: God is the creator
of the two spirits, and their Lord. But in fact man's being in the world
is determined by his link with one of the two realms.

Of course, these ideas are not developed consistently and logically. In one
stratum of the community rule there is only the pure either-or: one moves in
either one or the other sphere. Doctrine here is enlightenment about being and
the requirement to maintain it fully. In the same context, we can also find expressions in which the dualism is weakened psychologically: the individual has a
larger or smaller share in one or the other kingdom. Here doctrine means ethical
instruction, education.

Texts

1.   1 QS III 15ff.:
'From the God of Knowledge comes all that is and shall be. Before ever they existed He established their whole design . . . (These are) the spirits of truth and falsehood. Those born of truth spring from a fountain of light, but those born of falsehood spring from a source of darkness. All the children of righteousness are ruled by the Prince of Light and walk in the ways of light, but all the children of falsehood are ruled by the Angel of Darkness and walk in the ways of darkness . . . It is He who created the spirits of Light and Darkness and founded every action upon them and established every deed (upon) their (ways).'

2.   1 QS IV 15f.:
'The nature of all the children of men is ruled by these (two spirits). They walk in (both) their ways. And the whole reward for their deeds shall be . . . according to whether each man's portion in their two divisions is great or small.'

3.   The most important Persian parallel is Yasna 30.3–4:
'These are the primeval spirits who as a pair (combining their opposite strivings), and (yet each) independent in his action, have been formed (of old). (They are) a better thing, they two, and a worse, as to thought, as to word, and as to deed. And between these two let the wisely acting choose aright. (Choose ye) not (as) the evil-doers!

(Yea) when the two spirits come together at the first to make life, and life's absence, and to determine how the world at the last shall be (ordered), for the wicked (hell) the worst life, for the holy (heaven) the best mental state.'[1]

---

[1] English translation by L. H. Mills in: F. Max Müller (ed.), *Sacred Books of the East* XXXI (1887), Zend Avesta, Part III, pp. 29f. Cf. K. F. Geldner, *Die zoroastrische Religion, Religionsgeschichtliches Lesebuch* I (1926), p. 2.

PART ONE

THE KERYGMA
OF THE PRIMITIVE COMMUNITY AND THE
HELLENISTIC COMMUNITY

PREFACE

We still would not have a really historical account if we were to attempt to reconstruct the doctrine of the early church from the texts available. First, there is the question how far an account of this doctrine is possible at all. For the doctrine of God matches that of Judaism. The same is true of the picture of the world. Jewish ideas are even taken up in christology and ecclesiology (Messiah, people of God). It must also be noted that the doctrine of the church is meant not only to communicate knowledge, but to bring man into a particular situation before God, to salvation. The proclamation is itself a factor in the communication of salvation, but so, too, is the proclaiming church. The church's understanding of itself must therefore be included in the account.

4 · HISTORICAL PROBLEMS

R. Bultmann, *Theology of the New Testament* I, pp. 33ff.; 63ff. (and the literature cited there); C. Weizsäcker, *Das apostolische Zeitalter der christlichen Kirche* (1901[3]); A. Seeberg, *Der Katechismus der Urchristenheit* (1903); E. von Dobschütz, *Probleme der apostolischen Zeitalters* (1904); J. Weiss, *Earliest Christianity* (1959[2]); A. Oepke, *Die Missionspredigt des Apostels Paulus* (1920); R. Asting, *Die Verkündigung des Wortes in Urchristentum* (1939); W. G. Kümmel, *Kirchenbegriff und Geschichtsbewusstsein in der Urgemeinde und bei Jesus*, SyBU 1 (1943): O. Cullmann, *The Earliest Christian Confessions* (1949); id., *The Christology of the New Testament* (1963[2]); J. N. D. Kelly, *Early Christian Creeds* (1950); C. H. Dodd, *The Apostolic Preaching and its Developments* (1956[8]); E. Schweizer, *Lordship and Discipleship*, SBT 28 (1960); F. Hahn, *Christologische Hoheitstitel*, FRLANT 83 (1963); W. Kramer, *Christ, Lord, Son of God*, SBT 50 (1966); V. H. Neufeld, *The Earliest Christian Confessions* (1963): L. Goppelt, *Die apostolische und nachapostolische Zeit*, in: *Die Kirche in ihrer Geschichte*, Vol. I (A). Further literature in RGG[3] VI 1192f. (s.v. 'Urchristentum'); III 972f. (s.v. 'Judenchristentum'): III 141 (s.v. 'Heidenchristentum').

I   The Sources for the Reconstruction of the Early Kerygma

We have no writings from the earliest church before Paul.

One partial exception here is the source Q, which can be reconstructed from Matthew and Luke. But it gives no historical information about the primitive community. It is meant to transmit the teaching of Jesus. Nevertheless, it reflects ideas of the community, which not only handed down this teaching but at the same time put it into practice. So the outlines of a type of early theological thinking can be regained by critical analysis.

We have the account in the Acts of the Apostles. It makes use of ancient reports. But even Luke's material has legendary colouring. And he himself uses it in order to shape his picture of history. For example, the picture of the 'twelve apostles' at the head of the church is unhistorical. There never were 'twelve apostles'. There were the 'twelve', but their position is no longer clear; and there were apostles (see below). But the Lucan picture of the apostolic period is the picture of a later era. Nevertheless, there are positive starting points for reconstruction, e.g. in the disputes over questions of the law, in the sketches of a community order which have been preserved for us in the synoptic gospels. The letters of Paul have also preserved pre-Pauline material, e.g. credal formulas and hymns, as have the post-Pauline letters.

II The Primitive Community and the Hellenistic Community

It is confusing for the beginner to find differing uses of the term 'Hellenists' in the literature. It describes members both of Hellenistic Judaism (Acts 9.29) and of Hellenistic Christianity, and here again there are two shades of meaning. Acts 6 gives an account of a group of Christians in Jerusalem who are described as Hellenists (the group round Stephen). Since the time of the history of religions school (Heitmüller, Bousset), a further usage has emerged: the word describes the missionary church outside the narrower realm of Jerusalem, because within it ideas and patterns of life from Hellenistic (Jewish and non-Jewish) religion were at work. We can see them first in Paul. But it is still clear in his case that he became acquainted with these Hellenistic themes in a church which had already been shaped by them.

THE HELLENISTS IN JERUSALEM

N. A. Dahl, *Das Volk Gottes* (1941), pp. 193ff.; A. Oepke, *Das neue Gottesvolk* (1950), pp. 188ff.; M. Simon, *St Stephen and the Hellenists* (1958); see, too, the commentaries on Acts 6.

The primitive community did not see itself as a new religious society, but as part of the society of the Jewish religion, indeed as the true Judaism, which believed in the fulfilment of the promise for Israel in Christ. It also kept to the regulations of the law.

The isolation of the primitive community from Judaism is – externally speaking – less marked than that of the baptist sects in the Jordan valley (Qumran), which maintained an outward detachment from the temple cult. Nevertheless, there is a much sharper material differentiation. By refraining from isolating itself, the church demonstrated the public nature of its message and existence. It did not go into the wilderness, to look after its own life there, but confronted Israel with its message in Jerusalem.

The decisive point at debate between the church and the rest of Judaism is the message that the crucified Jesus is the Messiah of Israel. Judaism could have contented itself with the mere observance of the teaching of Jesus. But now an attitude towards his person is required, as a condition of salvation. This already means that salvation is brought about, not by the fulfilment of the law, but by faith. First, however, the scope of the message of Christ must be made clear in the context of particular controversies. Then the relationship of faith and law, church and Israel, and even of faith and the world will become the central theological theme.

The problem raised by the preaching of faith as such breaks out for the first time in the Jerusalem community and leads to the conflict with the group of the 'Hellenists'. Unfortunately the account in the Acts of the Apostles is highly coloured. The event, and above all the theological position of the Hellenists, can only be reconstructed conjecturally. With caution, it can be affirmed that even these Hellenists regard themselves as Jews and know themselves to be involved in the continuity of the saving history and bound to the Old Testament. They base their picture of history upon it: the history of Israel is the history of disobedience (this is the basis of Stephen's speech, to be reconstructed from Acts 7). Jesus taught true obedience. A further feature is his criticism of the casuistic fulfilment of the law, of the sabbath and of the temple. Here the Hellenists do not dissociate themselves from the law, but from the Jewish way of fulfilling the law, in the non-Hellenistic primitive community.

This conjecture about the teaching of the Hellenists is supported by the fact that their persecution came about in Jerusalem. Stephen is stoned, the rest of the primitive community remains unmolested. There is further confirmation in the fact that the Hellenists' criticism of the law does not coincide with that of Paul. Paul does not criticize the temple cult, but questions the law as a way to salvation and its validity for the Gentiles. He does not criticize the law as such, but only the cultic law. Evidently he sets monotheistic faith and the moral law over against it.

The expulsion of the Hellenists from Jerusalem leaves the problem of the law latent in the primitive community for the moment. But their expulsion leads them to a mission to the Gentiles (Acts 11.19ff.). Here they can join forces with the mission of Hellenistic Judaism. As a result, the Hellenistic church in the wider sense comes into being, with new forms of thought and life. Of course, we cannot make a sharp distinction in detail between the primitive community and the Hellenistic community. Common factors appear here and there. Nevertheless, the two can be distinguished clearly enough. It is not a question of assigning each particular idea schematically to this group or that, but of recognizing the existence of the two types. The difference is perceptible in christology ('Kyrios'), in the shaping of the liturgy, in the significance attached to the spirit, in the understanding of the sacrament, in the idea of the church, in organization and in attitudes to the law. Of course, we cannot postulate any uniformity of modes of thought and life.

The Hellenistic church displays tendencies which could lead to a detachment from its historical presuppositions, to a transformation of Christianity into an unhistorical mystery religion. But the presence of the Old Testament, and with it the link with Israel and salvation history, always exercises pressure in the other direction.

It is essential to differentiate between the two types (the primitive community and the Hellenistic community) if we are to understand the theology of Paul.

A recurrent picture of Paul seems to be that of the individual genius, the man who detached Christianity from the historical Jesus and orientated it towards a mythological picture. But Paul already found this orientation towards the exalted Lord in the Hellenistic church when he became a member of it. His contribution is to work out the faith in the Kyrios in theological terms. The same is true of his doctrine of the law.

The existence of a law-free Gentile Christian church raises basic questions about the nature of the law. The answer is obtained in the hard struggles carried on by Paul. It is not enough just to find a practical *modus vivendi* between Jewish Christians and Gentile Christians. Their life together must be *theologically* possible.

5 · THE ORIGIN OF THE COMMUNITY AND ITS UNDERSTANDING OF ITSELF

R. Bultmann, *Theology of the New Testament* I, pp. 33ff.; E. Schweizer, *Church Order in the New Testament*, SBT 32 (1961).

I   The Origin

Of course, the career and teaching of Jesus is the presupposition for the origin of the church. But Jesus did not found a church. It was assembled as a community through the appearances of the Risen One and the preaching of the witnesses to these appearances. From the beginning, the church has been associated with the resurrection. The church looks back to the completed earthly work of Jesus.

This assertion does, of course, contradict a famous passage, Matt. 16.18–19: 'You are Peter, and on this rock I will build my church, and the powers of death shall not prevail against it. I will give you the keys of the kingdom of heaven . . .' But is this a genuine saying of Jesus[1] ?

[1] F. Obrist, *Echtheitsfragen und Deutung der Primatstelle Matt. 16.18f. in der deutschen protestantischen Theologie der letzten dreissig Jahre*, NTA 21 (3/4) (1960); R. Bultmann,

The hypothesis that this is a later interpolation into the text of Matthew has now been generally abandoned. It represents a misguided interpretation of an apt observation: this passage does not appear in Mark and it disrupts the context in Matthew. The doublet Matt. 18.18 indicates that the passage was inserted by Matthew himself into his source (Mark). Matthew found the saying in his special tradition. It is a section of considerable antiquity. This is clear from its content and language: the Aramaic background can still be seen clearly. That is not, of course, a proof of its authenticity; in fact, the following arguments tell against it:

The word *ecclesia* occurs in the synoptic gospels only in this one passage and in the doublet, Matt. 18.17. The use of the word in the singular is not in itself a sufficient argument against authenticity. It is more serious that the eschatology of Jesus, the announcement of the imminence of the kingdom of God, does not fit in with the idea of an organized church. The usual counter, that the two nevertheless fit together, runs as follows: the people of God belongs to the Messiah and therefore the church belongs in the eschatology of Jesus. If Jesus regarded himself as Messiah, he not only could have, but must have founded a church. But in the first place, it is questionable whether Jesus regarded himself as the Messiah; and secondly, the founding of an organization is not part of the work of the Messiah. Therefore, if Jesus regarded himself as Messiah, the saying must be taken as inauthentic; and if he did not regard himself as Messiah, the same thing still applies.

The historical Jesus did not detach a group from the Jewish people as the host of the elect; he called the whole people. He assembled the elect only by means of his preaching. Men were not shown to belong to Jesus through membership of an organization; their status is to be made clear by the decision for acceptance or rejection at the coming of the kingdom of God. The fact that Jesus does not make membership of the people of God empirically visible distinguishes him from the Jewish sects. True, he demanded discipleship, and there were people who were his disciples in a special sense in that they travelled with him. Jesus could require such discipleship in particular instances, but he did not generally make it a condition of salvation.

The group of disciples was not organized. It had no constitution, no fixed ordering of life. Even if the 'twelve' were in fact already constituted during the lifetime of Jesus, the very choosing of 'twelve' contains a claim on all Israel and a reference to the coming rule of God. It does not point to the founding of a church. Jesus' eschatological awareness of himself excludes the idea of a present church.

The recognition that here is no authentic saying of Jesus does not of course 'settle' the matter theologically. Liberal theology drew from its inauthenticity the conclusion that Loisy put so perversely: Jesus expected the kingdom of God – and

---

The History of the Synoptic Tradition (1968²), pp. 138ff.; id., *ThBl* 20 (1941), cols. 265–79: W. G. Kümmel, *Kirchenbegriff und Geschichtsbewusstsein in der Urgemeinde und bei Jesus*, SyBU 1 (1943), pp. 37ff.; id., 'Jesus und die Anfänge der Kirche', *StTh* 7 (1954), pp. 1–27; K. L. Schmidt, 'Die Kirche des Urchristentums', *Festschrift für A. Deissmann* (1927), pp. 258ff., esp. pp. 281–302; id., ἐκκλησία, *TWNT* III 522ff.; A. Oepke, *Das neue Gottesvolk* (1950), pp. 166ff.; O. Cullmann, *Peter. Disciple, Apostle, Martyr* (1962²), pp. 162ff.; A. Vögtle, 'Messiasbekenntnis und Petrusverheissung', *BZ*NF 1 (1957), pp. 252–72; 2 (1958), pp. 85–103.

the church came. This statement is historically correct. But what does it mean? The pertinent theological question is whether and to what extent Jesus and his work were rightly understood and carried on after his death, through the formation of the church. If God's salvation is validly communicated in Jesus, and is thus offered on occasions even after his death as a present possibility; if the revelation is understood not only as a communication of doctrinal propositions but also as an actual event, then its constant actualization in preaching is also part of the revelation. At the same time, however, this is also true of the place in which the preaching takes place, the visible church assembled for the hearing. The church is therefore not the direct continuation of the disciples' life together with Jesus. It arose when the one who was dead appeared to them alive. The most important evidence for this is I Cor. 15.3–5.

II   The Church's Awareness of Itself

The Christians remained Jews first and foremost. In forming a special group within Judaism, they were simply following a trend of the time (Qumran, baptist groups). But how did the Christian community understand itself in positive terms? Its *self-designations* give some indication: οἱ ἅγιοι, οἱ ἐκλεκτοί, ἡ ἐκκλησία (τοῦ θεοῦ). ἅγιοι and ἐκλεκτοί are eschatological terms in Judaism. They describe the assembling of the (few) elect of the end-time out of the empirical Israel. In giving itself titles like this, a Jewish group (e.g. the group at Qumran) would express its exclusiveness; only in it does a man find access to salvation. It is taken for granted that Israel is the elect people of God, that it has forfeited its election as a whole through its conduct, and that therefore only a 'remnant' will gain salvation.

In the Qumran sect, the person who fulfils the law achieves salvation by taking upon himself the regulations of the community rule; among Christians, salvation comes to the person who acknowledges Jesus Christ as the saviour of Israel. The decisive question is: will this confession lead to a sectarian exclusiveness – as with the sect at Qumran? Will the elect be content with being themselves destined for salvation? Or will faith be understood as a positive possibility for existing in the world? What constitution will the church then assume, and how will it shape its teaching?

The Concepts in Detail

οἱ ἅγιοι

In the Old Testament, 'holy' was originally not a moral but a specifically religious concept; what is holy is marked off from the profane, as a holy area, a holy object, a holy person. What is holy appears in manifestations of power: anyone who touches the ark of Yahweh dies. Judaism describes as the holy ones: (a) Israel – in

The spirit appears more to be personal being in I Cor. 2.10ff.: τὸ . . . πνεῦμα πάντα ἐραυνᾷ; in Acts 10.19: 'the spirit' speaks to Peter. But these passages are rather personifying expressions, and do not characterize the spirit as a person. The spirit usually appears as a working of power, which is imagined in Hellenistic thought as a substantial fluid. This view is present where there is talk of 'pouring out of the spirit'. Closely related to spirit is *dynamis*.

Luke 1.17: the Baptist will work ἐν πνεύματι καὶ δυνάμει. I Cor. 2.4: the proclamation does not offer rational proof of its truth (σοφία), but the 'proof of the spirit and power' (cf. I Thess. 1.5). Acts 10.38: God anointed Jesus πνεύματι ἁγίῳ καὶ δυνάμει. δόξα (glory) is also related; cf. the variants in I Peter 4.14: ὅτι τὸ τῆς δόξης (+ καὶ δυνάμεως manuscripts except B;pᵐ) καὶ τὸ τοῦ θεοῦ πνεῦμα ἐφ᾽ ὑμᾶς ἀναπαύεται. χάρις (grace) also appears as pneumatic δύναμις. Stephen is πλήρης χάριτος καὶ δυνάμεως (Acts 6.8); thus in 6.5 we have: πλήρης πίστεως καὶ πνεύματος ἁγίου. So the concrete manifestations of the spirit are called both πνευματικά (gifts of the spirit) and χαρίσματα (gifts of grace; I Cor. 12ff.).

The harmless way in which animistic and dynamistic modes of expression are juxtaposed is an indication that the ideas are taken over as they are and that the new, specifically Christian, element does not lie *in the ideas* as such. The recognition that the spirit is thought of as a kind of substance can offer a safeguard against idealistic interpretation. This is the progress which the history of religions school achieved. But the meaning of the concept is still not properly understood. The very fluctuation in the concepts raises the question, what is really *meant*? Here we come up against the following problems: how is the relationship between spirit and community, the relationship of the saving event to the community – and to the individual – understood? What is the relationship between the community – and the individual – and the world? The analysis of the history of religions school must culminate in a phenomenological definition.

III   The Working of the Spirit

Again we can note a duality: (a) the spirit is regarded as a power which manifests itself from time to time in special phenomena, above all in worship. (b) But it is also regarded as the power which constantly fills the new man, the man of faith, because it has been once for all infused in baptism. So, on the one hand, particularly eminent individuals, prophets, miracle workers are regarded as pneumatics and, on the other, so are all believers, i.e. those who have been baptized.

Examples: (a) the pneumatic man is described in I Cor. 2.10ff.: his being is of a supernatural nature; the spirit knows all; the pneumatic has the power to judge all men; he himself is judged by no man. Paul contrasts him with the Corinthians: they are still σαρκικοί, or ψυχικοί.

(b) On the other hand, Paul speaks of all believers simply as those who have received the spirit or who live in the spirit (Rom. 8.9ff.). Thus at the end of the Pentecost speech, Peter promises the spirit to all who repent and let themselves be baptized (Acts 2.38). Again, also in Acts, Stephen is described as a man of the spirit to a supreme degree. The Acts of the Apostles is the book in which the spirit shows itself to be at work in particular moments.

The most important evidence about the rule of the spirit is the great catalogue of spiritual gifts (=charismata) in I Cor. 12–14[1]. Ecstatic manifestations of the spirit dominate worship at Corinth. Here a scale of valuation can be seen: the supreme working of the spirit is 'speaking with tongues', i.e. ecstatic speaking. A further charisma is the capability of understanding and translating this speaking. The next lower gift is prophecy which is delivered in a comprehensible way. It does not disclose the future, but what is hidden: what is within man (I Cor. 14.25). Paul reverses the Corinthians' assessment: prophecy is more than speaking with tongues, because it is comprehensible. The standard of the Corinthians is ecstasy as such. Paul, on the other hand, declares that ecstasy is ambiguous and therefore must itself be assessed critically: there are also pagan ecstasies (I Cor. 12.2). He puts forward two criteria: 1. the confession (I Cor. 12.3); 2. the οἰκοδομή (building up) of the community. The person who speaks with tongues only edifies himself; the prophet edifies the community. Therefore prophecy is the higher gift.

Paul goes on to describe as workings of the spirit those actions which are not connected with ecstasy, in the light of this double criterion. Every contribution towards building up the community, whether it is the provision of help (diakonia) or tasks of administration, i.e. 'profane' services, is a work of the spirit. This accords with his understanding of the place of the church in the world: its form is profane because its nature is eschatological. It does not live alongside the world, but in the world, though not from the world. Paul here applies his insight into the 'secularity' of Christian existence to the

---

[1] H. Greeven, 'Die Geistesgaben bei Paulus', WuD NF 6 (1959), pp. 111–20. See the excursuses in J. Weiss (Meyer Kommentar) and H. Lietzmann (HNT) on I Cor. 14.

idea of the church. The same thing will appear again in Pauline ethics.

7 · COMMUNITY, WORSHIP, SACRAMENTS

The dispute over the original character of the primitive church has been governed down to the present time by the controversy between Rudolf Sohm and Adolf Harnack[1]. The question is: what is the relationship between the nature of the church, its outward form, the concept of the church, church law and the ministry of the church? The theme can only be discussed in detail at a later stage. For it leads far beyond the early period to the early catholic development of the concept, constitution and ministry of the church. Here we can only discuss the first beginnings of church order.

I Organization and Ministry in the Primitive Community

K. Holl, 'Der Kirchenbegriff des Paulus im Verhältnis zu dem der Urgemeinde' (SAB 1921), Gesammelte Aufsätze II, pp. 44–67; H. von Campenhausen, Kirchliches Amt und geistliche Vollmacht in den ersten drei Jahrhunderten, BHTh 14 (1953); E. Schweizer, Church Order in the New Testament, SBT 31 (1961); R. Schnackenburg, The Church in the New Testament (1965).

Sohm argues that the church and church law, the church and the ecclesiastically appointed ministry are in fundamental opposition to each other. The nature of the church is determined by the rule of the spirit. Thus the only order possible in it is one which is directly brought about by the spirit. Only the man who is directly called by God, i.e. only the charismatic, can exercise a leading role by being endowed with the spirit. He makes his decisions in the light of the spirit. He is not bound by legal precepts. There can therefore be no 'ministry' in the church. Against this, Harnack argues that ministry and legal ordinances were present from the beginning; they do not

---

[1] R. Sohm, Kirchenrecht I (1892); A. Harnack, Enstehung und Entwicklung der Kirchenverfassung und des Kirchenrechtes (1910); cf. O. Linton, Das Problem der Urkirche in der neueren Forschung (1932); R. Bultmann, Theology of the New Testament II, pp. 95ff.

contradict the nature of the church. Karl Holl sets out to take the argument further by distinguishing two concepts of the church. That of Paul is in fact determined charismatically, that of the primitive community (of James) legally. Are Sohm and Harnack, then, both right? That, however, is hardly possible; for we must ask which concept of the church is the legitimate one.

Holl has rightly pointed out that in the faith itself there is a principle of tradition and therefore a legal factor: there is reference to the testimony of eyewitnesses which must be accurately handed down (I Cor. 15.3ff.).[1] Bultmann, following Holl, points out that the spirit can itself be a principle of church order: the word of the charismatic is legally valid and creates church law.[2]

THE EVIDENCE IN THE PRIMITIVE COMMUNITY

Our source material is scanty. Above all, the idea of the eschatological people of God, which expresses itself in the community's designations of itself, ἡ ἐκκλησία, οἱ ἅγιοι, οἱ ἐκλεκτοί, is still recognizable (see above, p. 34). The most important problems concern the significance of the city of Jerusalem for the idea of the church, the role of the twelve, the nature of the apostolate, the beginnings of a constitution and ministry, the understanding of worship.

If Christians are the *people of God*, the consequence for an understanding of the church is that what makes the church the church is not the decision of individuals to gather together to cherish their religious conviction. The church is there before the individual and even before the individual community. It is constituted by God's act of election. An individual community is possible because the church exists beforehand.

The idea of the people of God contains a critical definition of the understanding of the church. It can become effective against the development of the church into a

---

[1] Holl is challenged by W. G. Kümmel, *Kirchenbegriff und Geschichtsbewusstsein in der Urgemeinde und bei Jesus*, SyBU 1 (1943), pp. 1ff.

[2] H. von Campenhausen, *op. cit.*, pp. 324f.; E. Käsemann, 'Sentences of Holy Law in the New Testament', *New Testament Questions of Today* (1969), pp. 66–81: the spirit is the power that proclaims God's law on earth. This is expressed in legal sentences couched in a special style, e.g. I Cor. 3.17: εἴ τις τὸν ναὸν τοῦ θεοῦ φθείρει, φθερεῖ τοῦτον ὁ θεός. H. von Campenhausen, 'Tradition und Geist im Urchristentum', in: *Tradition und Leben* (1960), pp. 1–16. J. B. Leuba, 'Der Zusammenhang zwischen Geist und Tradition nach dem NT', *KuD* 4 (1958), pp. 234–50.

religious society, a gnostic association or a catholic institution of salvation. Of course, the salvation-historical, eschatological idea of the church is not in itself the only possibility of expressing the priority of the church to the individual. Even it is not sufficient to describe the nature of the church. The church as the people of God can be understood in terms of a radical Judaism. In Paul, the idea of the people of God is supplemented by that of the church as the body of Christ (see below, pp. 26off.).

That the church is there before the empirical Christian community is demonstrated by the fact that the *history of Israel* is claimed as the *earlier history of the church*. The church is not, however, a direct continuation of Israel. A gulf has appeared. In designating itself the true Israel, the church declares that the empirical Israel was not adequate for its task, that it refused faith. In the church, the promise has become reality: fulfilment is realized by being proclaimed.

Luke 16.16: ὁ νόμος καὶ οἱ προφῆται μέχρι Ἰωάννου· ἀπὸ τότε ἡ βασιλεία τοῦ θεοῦ εὐαγγελίζεται . . . This raises the problems into which Paul goes in Rom. 9.11: the nature of proclamation and the relationship between the church and Israel.

The relationship between promise and fulfilment, between church and Israel, is not wholly clear. Of course, there is an external continuity in that the first Christians are Jews who take over not only individual Jewish ideas but also the Jewish faith in the one God. The Father of Jesus Christ is identical with the God of the Old Testament. But the relationship between the church and Israel is not exhausted in these empirical facts. It first appears in the accomplishment of the proclamation, and is thus a matter only of faith. The historical self-awareness of the church that it is the true Israel is evidenced in the way in which it not only 'takes over' the Old Testament as its Holy Scripture but also keeps to it. This fact alone displays the judgment on the Israel which did not follow faith. Keeping to the Old Testament is a counter against a possible narrowing of faith to an unhistorical doctrine of redemption. For the church is convinced that the God who acts in Christ and occurs in the proclamation is none other than the creator and ruler of the world. The Old Testament prevents the isolation of redemption from the world. And it keeps in mind God's commandment, i.e. the character of faith as obedience. Even the Gentile Christians believe in this God of Israel. Thus the Old Testament brings about the unity of the church of Jews and Gentiles – in faith in the God who is not reached by mythical speculations and the practice of mysteries, but perceived in his words.

The Old Testament[1] is not only read and recited, but also expounded. The exegesis can be very simple: passages like Isa. 53; Ps. 22 are read as an account of the passion of Jesus.

So, conversely, the passion narrative can also be supplemented from the Old Testament. That is where, for example, the sum which Judas received for his betrayal is established.[2]

The contemporary Jewish methods of scriptural exegesis, allegory (Gal. 4) and typology (Heb.), are used. There is at first no concern about the Old Testament cultic law. It must be considered at a later date, because it now stands in scripture.[3]

The idea of the people of God means that the primitive community is conscious of its links with *Jerusalem*.

This is strongly stressed in Luke: the Risen One appears only in Jerusalem. He commands the disciples to remain there. From there, the church must be extended into the world; even the Gentile church maintains links with Jerusalem.

Karl Holl understood the place of Jerusalem in terms of church law: Jerusalem is the legal centre of the church (as was Rome later). In reality, while Paul recognizes the predominance of the city of Jerusalem, in tradition, this is not a legal superiority. There is no authority which exercises a legal supervision over the whole church. Neither the twelve nor the apostles had such a function.

If the nature of the church is determined through the ordering of the proclamation, then organization and ministry do not *per se* have power to save.

This must be made clear over against the catholic understanding of the church and ministry. It is occasionally argued that there were ministries in the church from the beginning. But this does not imply anything about the *understanding* of the ministry. The question is whether the ministry is determined by the word or the word by the ministry.

On the other hand, the church is not an *ecclesia invisibilis*, but the visible community which is gathered through the preaching. The nature of the church is not guaranteed by a special ministerial office. On the contrary, it is constantly achieved anew through preaching,

---

[1] W. Dittmar, *Vetus Testamentum in Novo* (1903); B. Lindars, *New Testament Apologetic* (1961); C. Smits, *Oud-Testamentische Citaten in het Nieuwe Testament* I–IV (1952ff.).

[2] Matt. 26.15 goes back to Zech. 11.12. See M. Dibelius, *From Tradition to Gospel* (1934), p. 188.

[3] Hebrews! Bultmann discusses other attempts to solve the problem of the Old Testament in *Theology of the New Testament* I, pp. 108ff.

which not only narrates the saving event but actually brings it about. Thus the tradition of the church is formed as the tradition of preaching. The question, therefore, is what must the ministerial office look like if it is to be commensurate with the church as the church of the word?[1]

We know little of individual ministries in the early period. The picture given by the Acts of the Apostles is unhistorical, above all in identifying the apostles with the twelve. The two must, however, be differentiated.[2]

The function of the *twelve* is not a legal one; they do not occupy the position of an authority, but represent the church as the true people of the twelve tribes (Matt. 12.28). We learn virtually nothing about their particular activity. Peter is the only exception, and we know extremely little about him – only that he carried out missionary work outside Jerusalem and Palestine. Nothing is known of any mission by the others.

The three 'pillars', Peter, John the son of Zebedee and James the brother of Jesus, are also named as an authority. Paul mentions them in Gal. 2 in his account of the apostolic council. On the other hand, he does not mention the twelve here; they were evidently no longer together as a group, even at this stage. The twelve gain their predominant significance only in retrospect, in the development of the idea of tradition. In the third generation, the title 'apostle' is transferred and at the same time limited to them. In Jerusalem, James the brother of the Lord seems to have taken their place as the authority. We do not know more.

The concept of *apostle* is hardest of all to define. Even the origin of the designation is disputed.

The title cannot be derived from the Greek meaning of ἀπόστολος ('sea-going expedition'). The usual reference is to the Jewish institution of the שָׁלִיחַ (*shaliah*:

---

[1] Bultmann, *Theology of the New Testament* II, pp. 95ff. In clarification: one possibility is the catholic one: the ministry is an authoritative teaching ministry and a ministry of the administration of the sacraments within the church, understood as an institution of salvation. The opposite possibility is pure spiritualism, in which authority is only given by subjective inspiration. In the former case, there is a church, but the word is no longer free; in the latter, the word is free, but there is no longer a church.

[2] H. von Campenhausen, *op. cit.*, pp. 13ff.; id., 'Der urchristliche Apostelbegriff', *StTh* 1 (1947), pp. 96ff.; G. Klein, *Die zwölf Apostel*, FRLANT NF 59 (1961); W. Schmithals, *Das kirchliche Apostelamt*, FRLANT NF 61 (1961).

one who is sent). The *shaliaḥ* is a plenopotentiary with a particular task.[1] But his position is a temporary one, while that of the apostles is permanent. The task of the *shaliaḥ* can be anything, but that of the apostle is definite.

The commission is constitutive of the concept of the apostle, and it is given by the exalted Lord himself. There is no other appointment to this ministry. So, too, there is no other limitation of its authority than that contained in the commission itself. The position of the apostles, whose number is open, extends over the whole church. The way in which they are bound by their commission links their authority with the kerygma. As its proclaimers, they become the first bearers of the tradition. Therefore later, when the idea of tradition is understood more and more in terms of church law, the title of apostle can be applied to the first known guarantors of doctrine, the twelve.

II Worship

For the reconstruction of the early kerygma see: H. Lietzmann, 'Symbolstudien', *ZNW* 21 (1922), pp. 1ff.; 22 (1923), pp. 257ff.; 24 (1925), pp. 193ff.; 26 (1927), pp. 75ff.; W. Bauer, *Der Wortgottesdienst der ältesten Christen*, SGV 148 (1930); G. Delling, *Der Gottesdienst im NT* (1952): O. Cullmann, *Early Christian Worship*, SBT 10 (1953); H. Conzelmann, 'Christus im Gottesdienst der neutestamentlicher Zeit', *Pastoraltheologie* 55 (1966), pp. 355–365.

If cult is defined in general terms as a means of influencing the deity, then it is doubtful whether the primitive community knows of a cult at all.[2] There is no sacrifice; there are no holy places and times, no priests. The ingredients of worship are reading of the scripture, preaching and address to God in prayers and hymns (I Cor. 14; I Tim. 4.13). Influence on God thus takes place in the verbal forms of praise, thanksgiving and intercession. In addition, there is acclamation of the Kyrios. So the whole of the 'cult' is verbal. Is this renunciation of cult simply a negative attitude, or is there behind it a positive understanding of the new intercourse with God?

If we discount human actions of blessing, there is clearly a strong feeling that the only power of blessing is the grace of God shown forth in Christ. There is therefore no longer any material holiness. λογικὴ λατρεία takes the place of the cult (Rom. 12.1; cf. I Peter 2.5). The perspective from which to assess further development is to ask whether this worship will in time again become a cultic action of blessing, a

[1] Cf. especially K. H. Rengstorf, ἀπόστολος, *TWNT* I 414ff.
[2] Bultmann, *Theology of the New Testament* I, pp. 121f.

new Christian mystery with Christian holy actions and persons. This question arises particularly in respect of the two procedures which are often called 'cultic': baptism and the eucharist, the two 'sacraments'.

III Baptism

R. Bultmann, *Theology of the New Testament* I, pp. 133ff. (and the literature there); W. G. Kümmel, 'Das Urchristentum', *ThR* NF 18 (1962), pp. 32ff. (survey of scholarship); W. Heitmüller, *Taufe und Abendmahl im Urchristentum* (1911); J. Leipoldt, *Die urchristliche Taufe im Lichte der Religionsgeschichte* (1928); O. Cullmann, *Baptism in the New Testament*, SBT 1 (1950); N. Adler, *Taufe und Handauflegung*, NTA 19 (3) (1951); J. Schneider, *Die Taufe im NT* (1952); G. Delling, *Die Zueignung des Heils in der Taufe* (1961); G. R. Beasley-Murray, *Baptism in the NT* (1962); G. Braumann, *Vorpaulinische christliche Taufverkündigung bei Paulus*, BWANT V 2 (1962); W. F. Flemington, *The New Testament Doctrine of Baptism* (1948); J. Ysebaert, *Greek Baptismal Terminology* (1962). For further literature see *RGG*[3] VI 637.

Recent discussion has been vigorously stimulated by Karl Barth,[1] who questions the church's practice of infant baptism. It cannot strictly be denied that infants were baptized in the early church, but still less can it be proved. A survey of church history shows that infant baptism appeared about the year 200 (with Aland against Jeremias).[2]

From the beginning, baptism has been the universal rite of acceptance into the community.

Paul presupposes that all Christians have been baptized (Rom. 6.3; I Cor. 12.13). The church took this practice over from John the Baptist. The further historical question of how baptism arose at all in the first place will not be discussed here. There are the following hypotheses:

(*a*) Baptism was derived from Jewish proselyte baptism.

(*b*) It was taken over from Jewish baptist groups in the Jordan valley.[3]

---

[1] K. Barth, *The Teaching of the Church regarding Baptism* (1948).

[2] J. Jeremias, *Infant Baptism in the First Four Centuries* (1960); against this: K. Aland, *Did the Early Church Baptize Infants?* (1963); in reply, Jeremias, *The Origins of Infant Baptism*, SHT 1 (1963); and again Aland, *Die Säuglingstaufe im NT und in der Alten Kirche*, ThExH NF 86 (1963[2]); and id., *Die Stellung der Kinder in den frühen christlichen Gemeinden – und ihre Taufe*, ThExH NF 138 (1967). Cf. also A. Strobel, 'Säuglings- und Kindertaufe in der ältesten Kirche', in: *Begründung und Gebrauch der heiligen Taufe* (1963); id., 'Der Begriff des "Hauses" im griechischen und römischen Privatrecht', *ZNW* 59 (1965), pp. 91–100. W. Grundmann, 'Die νήπιοι in der urchristlichen Paränese', *NTS* 5 (1958/9), pp. 188ff.

[3] J. Thomas, *Le Mouvement Baptiste en Palestine et Syrie* (1935), discusses these groups (even before the discovery of the Qumran writings).

The significance of the baptism of John is also hard to reconstruct. Christians describe it in two ways:

(a) Negatively: it does not confer the spirit, which is given only by Christian baptism. It may be relevant that the spirit plays no part in the preaching of John the Baptist. The question is, however, whether the bestowing of the spirit was associated with Christian baptism from the beginning.

(b) Positively: the baptism of John is described as a βάπτισμα μετανοίας εἰς ἄφεσιν ἁμαρτιῶν (baptism of repentance for the forgiveness of sins; Mark 1.4). Is this historical, or a Christian interpretation? H. Thyen argues that this was already the Baptist's understanding.[1]

It is clear that Christian baptism is associated with repentance from the beginning (Mark 1.4 presupposes that this is the case even with John). It confers forgiveness for sins committed before baptism. But it is not only a cleansing of the past but also the opening of a new life: the baptized are like new-born children (I Peter 2.2). What does this life look like? Is it a life under new, rigorous law (cf. Qumran)? Part of baptism is indeed baptismal paraenesis, teaching about putting off the old man and putting on the new. Everything will depend on how the new community, into which the baptized enters, understands itself and shapes its existence in the world. Will it remain in the world, or exclude itself from the world, as a sect? Will the new obedience itself be understandable as the new life, or will it be regarded as a way of ensuring salvation?

On the rite: evidently baptism is first practised as immersion (Acts 8.36; Heb. 10.22; Barn. 11.11; presupposed Didache 7.1-3, where the sprinkling of the baptized person is allowed if there is insufficient water). But the external rite is not constitutive; water as an element plays no significant part. It is not taken as the 'water of death'. There is no symbolism of entering and rising from the water. Baptism is effective because it is baptism 'in the name' or 'into the name' of the Lord.[2] Heitmüller understands the baptismal formula to mean 'by naming the name of Jesus': it represents the act of the appropriation of the baptized person by the Lord. For this interpretation one can also refer to the use of the name of Jesus in exorcism. Delling objects that the element of the name plays no independent role in the phrase 'in the name of Jesus'.[3] It corresponds

---

[1] H. Thyen, 'Βάπτισμα μετανοίας εἰς ἄφεσιν ἁμαρτιῶν', in: Zeit und Geschichte (Bultmann Festschrift, 1964), pp. 97–125.

[2] See A. Schweitzer, The Mysticism of Paul the Apostle, p. 20. The use of prepositions in the baptismal formula is: (a) εἰς I Cor. 1.13, 15; (b) ἐν Acts 10.48; (c) ἐπί with dative, Acts 2.38.

[3] G. Delling, op. cit, pp. 68ff.

to the formula 'in Christ' (Paul can omit the catchword ὄνομα). The meaning is that one is baptized on the basis of the name. Baptism is not the appropriation of the baptized person by the Lord; on the contrary, it is the appropriation of the saving event by the person baptized.

It is true that the saving event is transferred to the baptized person 'in the name of Jesus'. But, on the other hand, there is no doubt that the name of Jesus is mentioned here. That means that the baptized person belongs to him and stands under his protection. Cf. the phrase Χριστοῦ εἶναι (Gal. 3.27ff.). The oldest baptismal formula has one member. There is a triadic formula in Matt. 28.19; later in Didache 7.1–3; Justin, Apol. I 61. The confession of faith in a summary formula is a part of baptism. It is not clear whether it was spoken before or after the immersion. There is remarkably little interest in liturgical regulation in the New Testament. In Acts 19.5f., the laying on of hands (with naming of the name?) is part of the rite; in Didache 7.4 there is a preparatory fast. The idea of protection is expressed in the designation of baptism as a sealing (II Cor. 1.22).

In Acts, there are apparent exceptions to the connection between baptism and the spirit. (a) Acts 8: the spirit does not come with baptism (through Philip), but only with the laying on of hands by the apostles (Peter and John). (b) Acts 10: the spirit comes before the baptism. But it should be noted in both passages Luke presupposes that baptism and spirit are not to be separated.

The designation of baptism as a 'bath of rebirth' (Titus 3.5; cf. I Peter 1.23) is reminiscent of the mysteries. Paul himself does not use the concept of rebirth. Baptism brings 'enlightenment' (Heb. 6.4; 10.32).

In what way is baptism associated with the historical saving work, the death and resurrection of Jesus? A first indication is given by the meaning of the name (see above). The saving work is transferred to the person baptized. Another idea related to the mysteries crosses this one; baptism confers a share in the fate of Christ. It is a dying and rising again with him.

The most important text for this interpretation is Rom. 6. The connection with the ideas of the mystery religions is disputed by G. Wagner[1]; but it is probably there, as one cannot develop the idea of a community of destiny from the baptismal

---

[1] G. Wagner, *Das religionsgeschichtliche Problem von Römer 6, 1–11*, AThANT 39 (1962).

rite itself. The closeness of the ideas of the mystery religions is shown by I Corinthians, precisely in the qualifications which Paul has to make (I Cor. 10).

One qualification over against the mysteries already emerges with the idea of the church: the mystery groups are limited to the cult: the church, on the other hand, embraces the whole of life. In the light of the idea of the church, it becomes clear how baptism is objectively effective, and at the same time is not a matter of magic.

IV   The Supper Meal

M. Goguel, *L'Eucharistie des origines à Justin Martyr* (1910); W. Heitmüller (see iii above): H. Lietzmann, *Messe und Herrenmahl* (1926): O. Cullmann, *La signification de la Sainte Cène dans le Christianisme primitif* (1936); E. Lohmeyer, 'Vom urchristlichen Abendmahl', *ThR* NF 9 (1937), pp. 168–227; 273–312; 10 (1938), pp. 81–99; E. Käsemann, 'The Pauline Doctrine of the Lord's Supper', *Essays on New Testament Themes*, SBT 41 (1964), pp. 108–35; G. Bornkamm, 'Herrenmahl und Kirche bei Paulus', *ZThK* 53 (1956), pp. 312–49 (= Gesammelte Aufsätze II, pp. 138–76); J. Jeremias, *The Eucharistic Words of Jesus* (1966²); P. Neuenzeit, *Das Herrenmahl*, StANT I (1960): J. Betz, *Die Eucharistie in der Zeit der griechischen Väter* II/1 (1963²); E. Schweizer, *RGG³* I 10–21 (and further literature there).

There are four fairly independent *problems* here: what is the relationship between worship, the service of the word of God (with the reading of scripture, prayer, glossolalia, prophecy), and the celebration of the eucharist, the sacramental meal? Are both celebrated separately or are they constantly associated, so that each meeting of the community also includes a sacramental feast (thus O. Cullmann)?

2. In the early period, the eucharist seems to be associated with a true meal, the agape, which the community celebrates as a sign of its fellowship. What is the relationship between eucharist and agape?

3. The third problem concerns the eucharist itself – quite independently of whether it was celebrated along with a service of the word of God or by itself.

Lietzmann put forward the hypothesis that there were two different types of eucharist, that of the primitive community and that of Paul. In the primitive community, the eucharist was not understood as a repetition of the last meal of Jesus with his disciples, as a memorial of his death, but as a recollection of the constant table-fellowship of the disciples with Jesus; the eucharist is the continuation of this after his resurrection. This 'bread-breaking' with its ἀγαλλίασις can still be detected in the Acts of the Apostles. Paul, however, understood the meal as a memorial of Christ's death.

4. What is the meaning of the 'words of institution'?

I MINISTRY OF THE WORD AND EUCHARIST

We can hardly presuppose a uniform rite. We cannot postulate that the ministry of the word and the eucharist were always combined nor that both were always celebrated separately. Their connection can be recognized in I Corinthians, particularly in its construction.

Paul connects instructions for the meal with those for worship: (a) meal: 10.14ff.; (b) worship: 11.2ff.; (c) meal: 11.17ff.; (d) worship: 12.1ff. The connection is also presupposed in Acts 2.42.

On the other hand, the analogy of synagogue worship, which is purely concerned with the word of God, tells against their always belonging both together. It had a strong influence on the shaping of Christian worship. Mission preaching, too, tells against it.[1] In I Cor. 14.23ff., Paul presupposes that even unbelievers come to the gathering of the community. Only the baptized, however, are admitted to the eucharist. We must therefore posit at least two separate liturgical acts.[2] We may perhaps suppose that where the synagogue tradition was followed, the service of the word took place in the morning, and the meal in the evening.

In his famous letter to Trajan (Ep. X. 96), Pliny reports that the Christians assemble *stato die* (on Sunday, of course) *ante lucem* in the open, and then again in the evening *ad capiendum cibum*. Lietzmann wanted to understand the morning celebration as a baptismal celebration rather than as a liturgy of the word. But Pliny speaks of a regular juxtaposition.[3] Thus we find that about AD 100, in Asia Minor, the liturgy of the word and the eucharist were separated. The two were later combined in the time of Justin. Here, however, there is a further difference: in Pliny, the meal still appears to be a proper meal, whereas in Justin, eucharist and agape are separated.

The oldest designation for the supper is κυριακὸν δεῖπνον (Lord's supper; I Cor. 11.20). Later, εὐχαριστία makes itself prominent (Didache, Ignatius, Justin). This word first describes only the prayer of thanksgiving, but it is later extended to the whole meal. The expression 'breaking of the bread' still occurs in Acts. It is a matter for debate whether this is meant to be a technical term or whether it is

---

[1] For further non-Christian analogies see: W. Bauer, *Der Wortgottesdienst der ältesten Christen*, SGV 148 (1930).

[2] Bultmann, *Theology of the New Testament* I, p. 145; W. G. Kümmel, 'Das Urchristentum', *ThR* NF 17 (1948/9), p. 21. Cf. Justin, Apology I 66.1. Against the interpretation given above: G. Bornkamm, *Gesammelte Aufsätze* I, pp. 123ff.

[3] Kümmel (see previous note), p. 43.

simply meant to characterize the celebration as a meal (cf. Acts 27.35). An answer to the question how often a celebration was held is given in Didache 14.1: κατὰ κυριακὴν κυρίου (every Sunday).[1]

2 EUCHARIST AND MEAL

Originally the sacrament was taken within the framework of a proper meal. This is clear not only from the reports in Acts and from the fact that the cult formula (see below) puts the founding within the framework of a meal, but also from what happens in Corinth (I Cor. 10f.).

Paul gives a further indication. He transmits the founding of the sacrament in the following way: Jesus gives the bread and then – μετὰ τὸ δειπνῆσαι (after the meal) – the cup. That means that when this formula was constructed, a meal lay between the two sacramental acts of the giving of bread and the giving of wine.[2] But we can see that at the time when Paul writes I Corinthians, the development has already gone further. For, from further indications in I Cor. 11, it becomes clear that meanwhile the two acts of the sacrament have found a place at the end of the meal, as a rite which is complete in itself. Paul evidently has no interest in going back on this development. The misuses against which he fights are of another kind: the rich eat by themselves at the proper meal which precedes the sacrament, whereas the poor have to starve. This destroys the life of the community. Paul wants to counter the development by separating the meal completely from the eucharist. I Corinthians is thus the first evidence of the development which is complete with Justin.

The background to the Corinthian misunderstanding is as follows: It was generally assumed earlier that these gained ground because the Corinthians did not take the sacrament seriously as such: they made a sort of banquet out of it (Lietzmann, Karl Barth). But this does not match the attitudes of the Corinthian enthusiasts elsewhere (H. von Soden, E. Käsemann, G. Bornkamm). The perversion arose, rather, because the Corinthians were crude sacramentalists (along the lines of the mystery religions). They thought that sacramental food worked as a substance. Each ate it for himself. This pneumatic individualism destroyed fellowship. Paul does not appeal to the Corinthians to recognize the sacramental significance of the consecrated food – they do that already. They should rather

---

[1] Cf. Justin, Apology I, 67: on Sunday; *ibid.*, 65: after baptism.

[2] G. Bornkamm, *op. cit.*, p. 154; W. Schmithals, *Die Gnosis in Korinth*, FRLANT 66 (1965²), pp. 238f., differs.

understand that the sacrament takes place in the context of the church and is thus to be actualized by the realization of their community.

Two further problems are more difficult.

3 LIETZMANN'S THEORY OF THE TWO TYPES OF MEAL

Meals were already celebrated in the primitive community. But we should hardly assume that the community originally understood them, as did the Hellenistic community, in a specifically sacramental sense, as the eating of a spiritual substance. Lietzmann interpreted the evidence in the following way: the primitive community did not celebrate the memory of Jesus' death, but continued its table fellowship with Jesus.

Thus, too, Bultmann (*Theology of the New Testament* I, p. 151). The theory was modified by:

(*a*) Lohmeyer: he wanted to find both types in existence as early as the primitive community, in two different groups, the Galilean and Jerusalem communities. The only correct element in his thesis is that the sacramental interpretation was not the creation of Paul. It was already there beforehand.

(*b*) Cullmann wants to derive the bread-breaking in the primitive community, not from table-fellowship with the historical Jesus but from meals with the risen Lord. But a meal is not an essential element in the Easter appearances.

What Acts says about the meals, and the joy that prevailed at them, does not point to particular cultic feasts, but to the main daily meal which was eaten ceremonially. In being called 'the breaking of the bread' it is equated with Jewish meals, which are opened with blessing and bread-breaking (Mark 6.41; 14.22; Luke 24.30; Didache 9.3; 14.1).

Wine can, of course, be drunk, but it has no cultic significance, as the name 'bread-breaking' shows. Lietzmann refers for comparison to Jewish meals eaten in a 'company'. But see J. Jeremias, *Eucharistic Words of Jesus*, pp. 29-31.

The meals of the Qumran community are a closer parallel: there bread and wine were blessed and distributed.[1]

The connection with Jewish table customs is shown by the eucharistic prayers of the Didache. They are Jewish prayers revised in a Christian direction.[2] Their content is thanksgiving for gifts and prayers for the eschatological consummation. It is illuminating that Didache 9.1–10.5 is primarily a meal without

---

[1] K. G. Kuhn, 'Über den ursprünglichen Sinn des Abendmahls und sein Verhältnis zu den Gemeinschaftsmahlen der Sektenschrift', *EvTh* 10 (1950/51), pp. 508–27.

[2] M. Dibelius, 'Die Mahlgebete der Didache', *ZNW* 37 (1928), pp. 32ff.

reference to the death of Jesus and without sacramental communion, and that the transition to the sacramental eucharist follows in 10.6. This passage is one of the strongest supports for Lietzmann's thesis. Here the two types seem to have been combined subsequently. Of course, this interpretation of the evidence is not certain; all that can be proved is that the eucharist is associated with a meal. Didache 9f. is therefore hardly evidence for the juxtaposition of two types of meal, but rather for the combination of eucharist and agape. All that can be said is that there were different interpretations of the meal and that there were even meals of a non-sacramental character which represented the table-fellowship of the believers. It cannot be proved that these meals were regarded as a continuation of table-fellowship with the historical Jesus. It is even extremely improbable, as we nowhere find evidence of such a view. If there were this interpretation, there would have been mention of such meals during the time of Jesus. The passage which is usually referred to, the feeding of the five thousand, proves the opposite, because it does not deal with a meal of the disciples but with a public miracle. Nor can it be proved that there were only such meals, without sacramental significance, in the primitive community.

If we compare the evidence in the Acts of the Apostles, Paul and the Didache, we do not find Lietzmann's two types of supper and with this two different ways of deriving the supper from Jesus. We find, rather, on the one hand communal feasts with a commemoration of the Exalted One, and on the other hand the supper, in which the feast is associated with the death of Jesus and the act of its founding.

4   THE WORDS OF INSTITUTION

The institution of the Lord's supper has been handed down in four variant forms: Mark 14.22–25; Matt. 26.26–29; Luke 22.15–20; I Cor. 11.23–25.[1] Matthew's version is based completely on that of Mark and has no independent value as a source.

I Cor. 11.23–25

Paul expressly quotes a stereotyped tradition of the community. The quotation extends to v. 25 ('Do this in remembrance of me'). Verse 26 is an addition of Paul's by way of comment: in the meal, the death of the Lord is proclaimed 'until he comes'. Part of the understanding of the meal is thus the prospect of the parousia, the knowledge of the provisional character of the salvation in which the believers share. The meal is not an anticipation of the heavenly meal, but a substitute for it in the intermediate period.

[1] There is a convenient survey by Lietzmann in the HNT on I Cor. 11.25.

Although v. 26 is no longer part of the cult formula, Paul has added it in agreement with the tradition. One can also find an eschatological prospect in Mark and Luke; in their tradition it is taken up into the very words of institution.

The content of the cultic formula is as follows: (a) the introduction, 'the Lord Jesus on the night when he was betrayed', depicts the situation. This remark is more than a mere historical reminiscence. It establishes the foundation of the sacrament in sacral law and guarantees its validity. This prevents it from being a non-historical mystery.

The mysteries know only of a mythical 'institution'. It is celebrated, not as a 'remembrance' but as a repetition of the dying of the cult god.

Paul does not say that the original supper was a passover meal (see below, p. 59).

(b) The action and the words of interpretation form the act of institution. At the beginning stands the prayer of thanksgiving; this is a Jewish custom at meal-times, which was taken over by the church. There follow the breaking and giving of bread with the significant words: the bread is the body of the Lord, the '(body) for you'. The word ὑπέρ interprets Jesus' death as a sacrificial death, either 'for you' (expiation) or 'in your place' (representation). Finally, its repetition is enjoined. Here again, more is meant than 'remembrance', namely, effective realization. This happens with the eating of efficacious food which is given its power through the rite. That the rite is related to the death of the Lord is clear, but the way in which it is related is not shown by the text in any way that can be given precise and dogmatic definition. Only the understanding of the death could be further clarified to some extent: it is interpreted as an expiatory or representative sacrificial death (see above). In addition, there is in the word over the cup the idea of the establishment of the new covenant, that is, the founding of the new people of God. The command for repetition stands once more at the end of the saying over the cup.

ποιεῖν (do) in itself limits the cultic-technical sense that this word can have: 'perform a ritual act'.[1] The command for repetition will not belong to the earliest stratum, but will be a liturgical addition (G. Bornkamm). It is missing in Mark. In fact, however, it does not add anything new, since the tradition of the cult formula already requires repetition in itself.

The difference in form between the words over the bread and the

[1] H. Braun, TWNT VI 481f.; Bauer (–Arndt–Gingrich), Lexicon s.v. ποιέω I b.

words over the cup (rightly stressed by Käsemann and Bornkamm) is particularly striking. The parallel is not between σῶμα (body) and αἷμα (blood), but between σῶμα and διαθήκη (covenant). The understanding of the sacrament is not, therefore, orientated to the elements, but to the Lord present in the community.

The fact that we do not have 'flesh' and blood but 'body' and blood shows that these are not regarded as parts of the Lord. They were, however, understood this way at a later date; at that time, σάρξ quite consistently took the place of σῶμα (cf. John 6.51ff. and Ignatius). Finally, the sayings over bread and cup do not have to be combined to make up the whole sacrament; each is, rather, a complete communication in itself. It is clear from I Cor. 10.16f. that the offering of the bread in itself presents the Lord: here Paul describes the meaning of the sacrament, as participation in the body of Christ, exclusively in the light of the body and the bread. As the words over the bread and the cup were originally separated by the meal, each had to be independent in itself.

σῶμα should not be translated 'person' ('I am this myself'), but 'body'. This is the only way of making sense of the addition τὸ ὑπὲρ ὑμῶν. In other words, the bread offers real participation in the body of death, in the διαθήκη founded by Jesus' death.

Paul develops the paradosis of the meal theologically, by interpreting the community in terms of his idea of the church. What gives the sacramental elements their spiritual character and transforms food and drink into a spiritual substance (I Cor. 10.3f.) is the presence of the spirit, which represents the Lord. It confronts man with the choice of proclaiming the death of the Lord, with the community, or being guilty of his death, with the world.

Mark 14.22–25

The interpretation τὸ ὑπὲρ ὑμῶν does not occur in the saying about the bread. In the saying over the cup, its place is taken by a corresponding addition: τὸ ἐκχυννόμενον ὑπὲρ πολλῶν. The interpretation with ὑπέρ can thus be added to 'body' or 'blood' as desired. We can see here that the elements as such are not the significant factor.

As in Paul, the blood is interpreted as blood of the covenant, but with a characteristic variation. In Paul, σῶμα and διαθήκη stand parallel: αἷμα is a closer definition of διαθήκη. In Mark, on the other hand, διαθήκη is a definition of αἷμα: τουτό ἐστιν τὸ αἷμά μου τῆς διαθήκης (this is my blood of the covenant). Thus σῶμα and αἷμα now stand parallel. This makes possible a further development in which σῶμα is understood in the sense of σάρξ. There is no command for repetition in Mark. Of course, it is in fact presupposed. The eschatological expectation is taken up into the saying of Jesus. He declares that this is his last meal on earth. This stresses its farewell character and the hope for the future, heavenly meal.

Which version is the original one? The question cannot be put in this way. It presupposes that a uniform original form existed. But if there ever was such a thing, it can no longer be reconstructed from the present material. There is a widespread view that Paul made simplifications in comparison with the Marcan version. The reason for this is that in Mark the two attributes to αἷμα clash harshly: (a) τῆς διαθήκης (of the covenant); (b) τὸ ἐκχυννόμενον ὑπὲρ πολλῶν (poured out for many). Attempts have been made to overcome this harshness by arguing that in an abbreviated, linguistically easier version, ὑπὲρ πολλῶν referred to σῶμα. On the other hand, G. Bornkamm rightly stresses that there are earlier and later elements in both versions.

The incongruity in Paul seems more original than the parallelism of σῶμα and αἷμα in Mark. Even the harsh juxtaposition of the two interpretations of the blood (as a covenant offering and as an expiatory offering) is not the original form, from which Paul's text can be derived, but a secondary accumulation of interpretative themes. On the other hand, Mark, with his eschatological view, may be primary in comparison with Paul. That does not, however, mean to say that he offers the earliest version. By this comparison we can see stages which are present in both the Marcan and Pauline forms of the text.

If we look at the original version of the words of interpretation, three possibilities emerge:

1. The original theme of interpretation is the ὑπέρ, the idea of expiatory or representative *sacrifice*. The Marcan text would then probably be earliest, but without the addition τῆς διαθήκης: τοῦτό ἐστιν τὸ αἷμά μου ἐκχυννόμενον ὑπὲρ πολλῶν.[1]

2. The words of interpretation speak of the covenant: in that case, the original version would be: This is my body; this cup is the new covenant in my blood.[2]

3. Both the idea of expiation and that of the covenant were originally absent; in that case, the words simply ran, this is my body, this is my blood. Here the idea of sacramental communion with the cult Lord would be the constitutive element.[3]

[1] J. Jeremias, *op. cit.*, p. 193, who points out that the expression 'my blood of the covenant' (suffix) is very difficult in Aramaic.

[2] So W. G. Kümmel, in H. Lietzmann, *An die Korinther* I, II, HNT 9 (1949⁴); E. Schweizer, *op. cit.*, p. 14.

[3] Bultmann, *Theology of the New Testament* I, p. 146: of the three motifs, sacramental communion, expiation and covenant, the first must be primary, as the act is a meal. That means that these words could only have arisen in the Hellenistic

The fact that the parallelism, corresponding to liturgical style, would have to have been severely disturbed, speaks against the third interpretation. As far as the two other hypotheses are concerned, it must be pointed out that the original form can no longer be reconstructed. There are two traditions side by side which are closely related, and both contain secondary elements. We can therefore assume that there were still earlier stages. But this reaches the limits of our insight.

The third text, Luke 22.15ff., or 19f., is very strange.[1]

The 'Western' text (D it sy^sin. cur.) presents vv. 19f. in an abbreviated version. For a long time this was regarded as the original text. To account for the difference, it was supposed that the longer version had been expanded from Paul. But a reaction has now set in.[2] Today the longer form of the text is widely regarded as the original one. It can, in fact, be shown that the shorter form arose secondarily in order to remove a difficulty. It deletes the interpretation of the bread and the giving of the cup because in Luke's account the cup already appears earlier (vv. 17f.). Thus in the longer text we have a twofold giving of the cup which attempts were made to remove by abbreviation. The twofold giving of the cup can be explained on literary grounds. Luke combined two traditions, the Marcan account and a further description of the meal. This, too, had the ingredients of bread, wine and eschatological expectation. In addition, it designated the meal as a passover meal. The original form of this further (third) account of the institution can no longer be reconstructed, as Luke does not give it complete, but has abbreviated it in combining it with the Marcan text. By combination and abbreviation, the present remarkable sequence, cup — bread – cup, was arrived at. We can, however, still see that even in this third account the eating had originally been mentioned before the cup (cf. vv. 15f.). It thus contained the following elements: eating (of the Passover) with an eschatological reference; drinking with an eschatological reference. The idea of sacrifice was absent.

Leaving aside the special Lucan tradition, we can see that the question of a passover meal played no role in the account of the

---

community. Jeremias, on the other hand, lays all the stress on the fact that the basic element in the tradition goes back to Jesus himself. We reserve judgment here. In any case, Bultmann has aptly characterized the sacramental thinking of the Hellenistic community. That does not, however, mean that his literary-critical thesis holds.

[1] J. Jeremias, *op. cit.*, pp. 114f.; H. Schürmann, *Der Paschamahlbericht Lk 22, (7–14) 15–18*, NTA 19 (5) (1953); id., *Der Einsetzungsbericht Lk 22, 19–20*, NTA 20 (4) (1955); id, *Jesu Abschiedsrede Lk 22, 21–38*, NTA 20 (5) (1957).

[2] H. von Soden, 'Sakrament und Ethik bei Paulus' (1931), in: *Das Paulusbild in der neueren deutschen Forschung* (1964), p. 368, n. 37; W. G. Kümmel, HNT 9 (1949⁹), p. 185; J. Jeremias, *op. cit.*, since the second edition.

institution. In Paul, the passover does not appear at all, and it occurs only in a secondary framework in Mark.

This state of affairs is particularly remarkable, as Paul certainly knows the interpretation of the death of Jesus as a passover sacrifice – but outside the tradition of the last supper (I Cor. 5.7).

Attempts to reconstruct the course of Jesus' last supper and by this to prove that it was a passover meal are useless. They rest on a *petitio principii*, as does the whole discussion about the authenticity of the words of institution. It is clear that for Jesus they cannot have a Hellenistic, sacramental sense. So it is asked whether the words of institution could not also be understood in a non-sacramental way. Then authenticity is proved from the non-sacramental sense and the non-sacramental sense from the authenticity. But the present texts are clearly sacramental. Their meaning is bound up with the death and resurrection of Christ. But that means that the eucharist was founded by him in the same way as the church.

I Cor. 10.16 shows that the idea of sacramental communion predominates in Hellenistic Christianity. It need not be thought of in substantial terms. There is also the idea of sacral table-fellowship, in analogy with the pagan cultic meals: the eucharist is participation in the τράπεζα κυρίου (table of the Lord; I Cor. 10.18ff.). But the idea of substance can already be detected in Paul. It appears more strongly in the interpolated passage, John 6.51b–58.

One much-disputed question is whether participation in the sacrament offers a share in the fleshly body of the Crucified One or in the spiritual body of the Exalted One. Bultmann rightly remarks that this question is put wrongly: the body of the Crucified One and that of the Exalted One are identical – that is the basic idea behind the sacrament (cf. Rom. 7.4: the body that was put to death is the efficacious resurrection body).

As in the interpretation of baptism, so in that of the Lord's supper there are ideas from the mystery religions. But here, too, they are given a historical sense by the understanding of the church. This already happens in the reference to the act of its institution, and again in the association with the idea of sacrifice. In this way, the effect of the sacrament does not rest on a magical belief in substance, but on the acceptance in faith of the death of Christ as a saving act.

Paul shows particularly clearly in I Cor. 10f. that the sacrament does not change a man in a mysterious way, but brings him into the historical fellowship of the faithful in the church; it is not a magical protection, but leads to life in community. Of course, it must be granted that ideas from the mysteries appear in the Hellenistic milieu. In Ignatius, the sacramental food has become the φάρμακον ἀθανασίας (medicine of immortality). In that case, the cult no longer serves to establish 'everyday' faith in the world, but to mark out a holy realm from the world.

8 · THE CONCEPTS OF PROCLAMATION AND FAITH

R. Bultmann, *Theology of the New Testament* I, pp. 87–92 and the literature cited there; G. Friedrich, εὐαγγελίζομαι etc., *TWNT* II 705ff.; id., κηρύσσω, *TWNT* III 695ff.; R. Bultmann, πιστεύω etc., *TWNT* VI 197ff.; R. Asting, *Die Verkündigung des Wortes im Urchristentum*, 1939; H. Conzelmann, *The Theology of St Luke* (1960), pp. 221f.

A technical usage of concepts which describe the contents of the proclamation and of faith develops early. The two most important are the groups εὐαγγέλιον/εὐαγγελίζεσθαι and πίστις/πιστεύειν.

εὐαγγέλιον

The etymology and history of this concept are not very useful. In secular Greek, the word means the messenger's fee and also the message itself. It is often asserted that εὐαγγέλιον was a technical term in the emperor cult and came from there into Christianity. The true Lord of the world is contrasted with the political ruler. But its use in the emperor cult is not technical.[1] In the LXX, εὐαγγέλιον is a translation בְּשׂוֹרָה. But the word is not significant, and is not used either technically or in a specifically religious way.

Genitives can be attached to the word. (*a*) Objective genitives: Mark 1.1: ἀρχὴ τοῦ εὐαγγελίου Ἰησοῦ Χριστοῦ; Matt. 4.23: τὸ εὐαγγέλιον τῆς βασιλείας; cf. Matt. 13.19: ὁ λόγος τῆς βασιλείας. (*b*) Subjective genitives: in Mark 1.14, Jesus proclaims the εὐαγγέλιον τοῦ θεοῦ. Alongside this a technical usage develops, without the genitive. For exegesis, this means that the word must not be translated emphatically everywhere as 'the good news'. Where there is no special stress on τὸ εὐαγγέλιον/εὐαγγελίζεσθαι, it simply means 'preaching/preach'.

The word can also be used where the tidings are not 'good': Luke 3.18; Acts 14.15; Rev. 10.7; 14.6. Similarly, the LXX can say εὐαγγελίζεσθαι ἀγαθά (Isa 52.7, quoted in Rom. 10.15). εὐαγγελίζεσθαι in fact means the same as κηρύσσειν τὸν λόγον τοῦ κυρίου, κηρύσσειν τὸν λόγον, κηρύσσειν τὸν Χριστόν (Acts 8.5; cf. Acts 8.4), or even simply κηρύσσειν. διδάσκειν also has the same meaning. In Matt. 11.1 it is associated with κηρύσσειν. It is often alleged that διδαχή describes ethical teaching

---

[1] Inscription from Priene (A. Deissmann, *Light from the Ancient East* (1927²), p. 366; W. Dittenberger, *Orientes Graecae Inscriptiones Selectae* (1903), 458. 40): ἦρξεν δὲ τῷ κόσμῳ τῶν δι' αὐτὸν εὐαγγελί[ων ἡ γενέθλιος] τοῦ θεοῦ (sc. of Augustus).

in contrast to the eschatological kerygma. But in Mark 8.31; 9.31, the content of the διδαχή describes ethical teaching in contrast to the eschatological kerygma. But in Mark 8.31; 9.31, the content of the διδαχή is christology.

πίστις

On the side of the hearer, faith corresponds to preaching. The New Testament can borrow from Jewish terminology. πίστις can, on occasions, designate the faithfulness of God (Rom. 3.3), and in the miracle stories of the synoptics it can also describe trust in the miracle worker (Mark 5.36) or his miraculous power (Mark 9.23). But we cannot understand the special element in New Testament terminology in the light of the meaning 'trust'. πίστις rather means the acceptance of the message of the saving event in Christ. This meaning, too, is derived from Jewish terminology. There, faith means maintaining the creed of the one God and faithfulness to the law.[1]

Faith is not understood in psychological terms (as in Philo), but exclusively in the light of its content: 'Faith comes from what is heard' (Rom. 10.14ff.). *Fides quae creditur* and *fides qua creditur* are a unity in the act of hearing and understanding oneself in the light of the message. This sense is expressed in the terminology: there is the absolute usage: οἱ πιστεύοντες or πιστεύσαντες. These are not those who are religiously inclined, but the Christians. πίστις is the act of becoming a Christian (Acts 20.21) and the state of being a Christian (I Cor. 2.5). πιστεύειν εἰς does not mean a psychological relationship to Jesus, but is simply a shorter version of the statement: 'I believe that God raised Jesus from the dead' (Rom. 10.9).

The LXX does not use πιστεύειν εἰς to describe man's relationship to God, but the dative, or ἐπί with the dative. This terminology is again rare in the New Testament for belief in Christ: the dative occurs in Acts 5.14; 18.8; ἐπί with the dative in I Tim. 1.16; ἐπί with the accusative in Acts 9.42; ἐν with the dative in Mark 1.15; πρός in Philemon 5 (Bultmann, *Theology of the New Testament* I, p. 91).

As faith is acceptance of the message, there is no collective 'faith'. Faith primarily qualifies the individual. It summons him from his previous position in collectivity. In the moment of hearing the message, the hearer is neither Jew nor Greek, but simply the person addressed, who perceives his salvation. But the isolation of the individual through the word does not amount to religious individualism. For faith refers to the saving act which applies to all and incorporates them into the community of hearers. The decision is mine, but not as my work or

[1] Bultmann, *TWNT* VI 200f., 205f.; H. Lietzmann in HNT on Rom. 4.25; A. Meyer, *Das Rätsel des Jacobusbriefes* (1930), pp. 123–41.

my achievement, which can be credited to me. Decision is made in the hearing. In faith I cannot look at the fact that *I* have decided. I can recognize it only as a relationship to the word. In believing, I am not orientated to myself as a believer, but know that through grace I am what I am.

9 · THE CONTENT OF THE PROCLAMATION

C. H. Dodd, *The Apostolic Preaching and its Developments* (1936; 1956[8]); O. Cullmann, *The Earliest Christian Confessions* (1949); O. Michel, ὁμολογέω, *TWNT* V 199–220; J. N. D. Kelly, *Early Christian Creeds* (1950); R. Bultmann, *Theology of the New Testament* I, pp. 66ff.; H. Conzelmann, 'Was glaubte die früheste Christenheit?', *Schweizerische Theologische Umschau* 25 (1955), pp. 61–74; H. W. Boers, *The Diversity of NT Christological Concepts and the Confession of Faith*, Diss. Bonn 1962; V. H. Neufeld, *The Earliest Christian Confessions* (1963).

From the beginning, faith is expressed in formulated statements. These undergo a historical development. The Apostles' Creed, or its earlier form, the Roman Creed, already represents an end-point.

F. Kattenbusch, *Das Apostolische Symbol* I (1894), II (1900); A. Seeberg, *Der Katechismus der Urchristenheit* (1903=ThB 26, 1966); K. Holl, 'Zur Auslegung des 2. Artikels des sogenannten apostolischen Glaubensbekenntnisses' (1919), *Gesammelte Aufsätze* II, pp. 115–122; H. Lietzmann, 'Die Anfänge des Glaubensbekenntnisses', *Festgabe für Adolf von Harnack* (1921), pp. 226–42; id., 'Symbolstudien', *ZNW* 21 (1922), pp. 1ff; 22 (1923), pp. 257ff.; 24 (1925), pp. 193ff.; 26 (1927), pp. 75ff.; E. von Dobschütz, *Das Apostolicum* (1932); *Die Bekenntnisschriften der Evangelisch-Lutherischen Kirche* (1963[5]), XIff., 21ff.

I   The Reconstruction

Stereotyped traditional material is easiest to recognize where it is expressly said to be such. In I Cor. 15.3, Paul introduces a formula: παρέδωκα γὰρ ὑμῖν ἐν πρώτοις, ὃ καὶ παρέλαβον.

παραλαμβάνειν and παραδιδόναι are fixed concepts of tradition. They correspond to the Hebrew קִבֵּל מִן and מָסַר לְ (cf. I Cor. 11.23) [1].

---

[1] O. Cullmann, 'The Tradition': in *The Early Church* (1956), p. 63; this is disputed by E. Norden, *Agnostos Theos* (1913), p. 270, who finds Hellenistic terminology here.

The words πιστεύειν and ὁμολογεῖν can provide a further clue. Both acquire a technical sense early: that of reproducing the material of faith in stereotyped speech; cf. I John 4.15: ὃς ἐὰν ὁμολογήσῃ, ὅτι ᾽Ιησοῦς ἐστιν ὁ υἱὸς τοῦ θεοῦ with I John 5.5: ὁ πιστεύων, ὅτι ᾽Ιησοῦς ἐστιν ὁ υἱὸς τοῦ θεοῦ. This technical usage can be traced back to Paul. It serves to indicate formulations which were already tradition for him. The classical passage is Rom. 10.9: ὅτι ἐὰν ὁμολογήσῃς ἐν τῷ στόματί σου κύριον ᾽Ιησοῦν καὶ πιστεύσῃς ἐν τῇ καρδίᾳ σου, ὅτι ὁ θεός αὐτὸν ἤγειρεν ἐκ νεκρῶν, σωθήσῃ. Here the two key words describe two basic forms, the 'homology' and the 'creed'. The two are different in form and content. The creed describes the saving work: God has raised Jesus from the dead. The homology is a call to the person of the Exalted One. The acclamation of him is a constitutive part of the liturgy. Part of the acclamation is the proclamation before the world; the community declares publicly who is its Lord.

The confession not only demands a decision but has the power to bring one about. The person who confesses, knows that his faith is not his own achievement. Similarly, the creed also determines who refuses faith. The decision does not have a limited, inward character; it rather represents attachment to the community of those who confess. Christ's rule is confessed before the world because his sphere of rule is not only the church but the world. The church knows that, whereas it is hidden from the unbelieving world. Therefore the church must reveal the truth about itself to the world, over and over again.

A further criterion for reconstruction is offered by form analysis. Occasionally sentences recur in different writers, which are the same in form, terminology and content. In that case, we can conclude that they are traditional material, especially if such sentences stand out from their context, whether through rhythmic division (Rom. 4.25; I Tim. 3.16), through relative or participial style (ibid.), through a vocabulary which is alien to the author, or through different ideas. Thus un-Pauline concepts, in which an un-Pauline christology is expressed, are piled up, for example, in Rom. 1.3f.

Finally, one can begin from the later, developed credal formulae and follow their earlier stages back into the New Testament.

Albert Seeberg assumed that all formula-like statements in the New Testament were allusions to a comprehensive formula, a kind of catechism, which could be reconstructed by the combination of the individual passages. Against this, Lietzmann showed that each formula, however short, is not a part of the creed but the whole creed. The position can be illustrated from the case of the person who confesses before judgment. He is required to sacrifice before the image of the emperor. But he answers this with his creed: κύριος Ἰησοῦς. In so doing, he has (1) confessed the whole faith; at the moment there is nothing further to say. He has (2) confessed clearly, and the court understands him; it demonstrates that in the very act of condemnation. He has (3) made a binding confession, and (4) not only asserted, but brought about the Lordship of the Kyrios. His confession has subjected the worldly *imperium* to the Lord Jesus, in the form which is appropriate to the cross.

II   The Content of the Confession: the Person and Work of Christ

The credal formulae can be classified according to whether they contain only *one* article of faith, the confession of Christ (as do the majority of formulae) or *two*: the confession of God and Christ. The christological article can be an expression of the person or the work of Christ.

1   Statements about the Person of Christ

He is confessed (*a*) as the Messiah: Mark 8.29: σὺ εἶ ὁ Χριστός, par. Luke 9.20; τὸν χριστὸν τοῦ θεοῦ, and Matt. 16.16: σὺ εἶ ὁ χριστὸς ὁ υἱὸς τοῦ θεοῦ ζῶντος; (*b*) as the 'Son of God': I John 4.15, etc.; (*c*) as the 'Lord': Rom. 10.9; I Cor. 12.3.

2   Statements about the Work of Christ

The basic position is given by the statement that God has raised Jesus (Rom. 10.9). It is expanded by statements about his death and its saving significance (Rom. 4.25; I Cor. 15.3–5; see III below).

Both expressions are then combined in such a way that the statement about the person comes into the foreground and the statement about the work interprets the title of Jesus.

III   The Interpretation of the Resurrection

There is no uniform idea of the raising or resurrection of Jesus in the early period. Side by side, one can find the views (*a*) that Jesus went straight from the grave to heaven, i.e. that resurrection and ascension, resurrection and exaltation are identical; (*b*) that he first returned to earth from the grave and only ascended after he had spent some time with his disciples. There are no agreed details about the time of this ascension. Even in the Lucan history work, the ascension on Easter Day and the ascension after forty days stand side by side.

Similarly, the views of the nature of the appearances of the Risen One are also modified. If Jesus ascended directly from the grave into heaven, then he appears from time to time from heaven. If he only ascended after appearing on earth, the Easter appearances are fundamentally different from all later appearances of the exalted Lord (e.g. before Paul at Damascus).

This difference plays a role in the Acts of the Apostles. The conversation of the Risen One with the disciples has a different quality from later epiphanies of the risen Lord. The conversation with the disciples before the ascension is the basis of the unique status of the witnesses of the resurrection. Paul does not have this role in Acts – in contrast to his own view.

If the church confronts the world with its Easter testimony, it must vindicate its truth. This is done (1) by reference to the eyewitnesses: I Cor. 15.3ff.; Acts 1.22; 2.32; 3.15; 10.40f.; (2) by reference to the testimony of scripture: I Cor. 15.4; Luke 24.27; Acts 2.30ff.; 13.34ff. The basic text is the formula quoted by Paul in I Cor. 15.3ff:[1]

ὅτι Χριστὸς ἀπέθανεν	ὑπὲρ τῶν ἁμαρτιῶν ἡμῶν
	κατὰ τὰς γραφάς,
	καὶ ὅτι ἐτάφη,
καὶ ὅτι ἐγήγερται	τῇ ἡμέρᾳ τῇ τρίτῃ
	κατὰ τὰς γραφάς,
	καὶ ὅτι ὤφθη Κηφᾷ,
	εἶτα τοῖς δώδεκα.

The conceptuality of the formula is un-Pauline. This confirms that it was already shaped before Paul.

Un-Pauline elements are: the plural ἁμαρτίαι, ὤφθη, ἐγήγερται, κατὰ τὰς γραφάς, οἱ δώδεκα. The terminology shows semitic influence. It is usually concluded from this that the original form of the formula was Aramaic; it therefore arose in the earliest

---

[1] Literature: W. G. Kümmel, *Kirchenbegriff und Geschichtsbewusstsein in der Urgemeinde und bei Jesus*, SyBU 1 (1943), pp. 2ff.; E. Schweizer, *Erniedrigung und Erhöhung bei Jesus und seinen Nachfolgern*, AThANT 28 (1962²), pp. 89f.; K. H. Rengstorf, *Die Auferstehung Jesu* (1960⁴), *passim*; H. von Campenhausen, 'Der Ablauf der Osterereignisse und das leere Grab', SAH (1966³), pp. 8ff.; H. Conzelmann, 'Zur Analyse der Bekenntnisformel I Cor. 15.3–5', *EvTh* 25 (1965), pp. 1–11; J. Jeremias, 'Artikelloses χριστός. Zur Ursprache von I Cor. 15, 3b–5', *ZNW* 57 (1966), pp. 211–15; H. Grass, *Ostergeschehen und Osterberichte* (1962²), pp. 94–106. For further literature, see K. Lehmann, *Auferweckt am dritten Tag nach der Schrift*, Quaestiunes Disputatae 38 (1938).

period, even in Jerusalem. But an exact analysis of style shows that we do not have a translation from the Aramatic here, but a passage influenced by the language of the LXX – hence the impression of Semitic colouring. That means that the community which composed this formula used the Old Testament in the Greek translation, i.e. spoke Greek. This is not, however, to deny that a Jerusalem tradition was incorporated in it.

The subject of the sentence is 'Christ'. It is a stereotyped usage to have the designation 'Christ' where Jesus appears as the active subject of the saving work. It is significant that the resurrection is spoken of in the passive. From the four statements in the formula, ἀπέθανεν—ἐτάφη—ἐγήγερται—ὤφθη, two stand out as the real saving statements: ἀπέθανεν and ἐγήγερται. Both are doubly grounded, by reference to scripture (κατὰ τὰς γραφάς) and by a historical proof (ἐτάφη or ὤφθη) in each case. ἐτάφη and ὤφθη have no independent significance. ἐτάφη is meant rather to accentuate the preceding ἀπέθανεν: Jesus was really dead and he was raised from the dead.

Some exegetes find a reference to the empty tomb in ἐτάφη. But this interpretation is refuted by the fact that ἐτάφη is not subordinated to the resurrection, but to the dying.

The temporal detail 'on the third day' has still not been explained.[1]

It is widespread in the early Easter kerygma, in two versions: 'on the third day' and 'after three days'. There is no difference in the meaning. Attempts at explanation are: 1. The first appearances took place at this time. This explanation is possible. 2. According to H. von Campenhausen, the phrase refers to the time of the discovery of the empty tomb. On the other hand, however, the information is earlier than the legends about the tomb. 3. The information has been conjured up out of the fact that the Christians used to assemble on the first day of the week. But precisely the opposite is probable: this day became the day for assembly because it was regarded as the day of the resurrection. 4. Three is a typical number. There are parallels in the history of religions, e.g. the idea that the soul remained in the neighbourhood of the body for three days. But the analogy is vague. 5. The information is read out of scripture. But if we ask what scriptural passage is involved, confusion abounds. There is, of course, an explicit scriptural proof from Jonah 2.1 in Matt. 12.40. But this passage is late in the tradition. Nor can the formula 'on the third day' be derived from it, because it does not correspond with the details of the quotation: τρεῖς ἡμέρας καὶ τρεῖς νύκτας. Others refer to Hos. 6.2: ὑγιάσει ἡμᾶς μετὰ δύο ἡμέρας, ἐν τῇ ἡμέρᾳ τῇ τρίτῃ ἀναστησόμεθα καὶ ζησόμεθα ἐνώπιον αὐτοῦ. It has properly been argued against a derivation from this passage, however, that it is not quoted expressis verbis as a scriptural proof for the resurrection in the early period. Nevertheless, it may offer the key to the phrase. For it is characteristic of early scriptural argument that it does not give explicit quotations but contents itself with general hints.

---

[1] H. Grass (see previous note), pp. 127–38.

Resurrection and ascension are not differentiated in the formula. The appearances are thus regarded as appearances from heaven. The saving significance of the events described lies in the expiatory effect of the death and in the existence of the Risen One for his own.

Further exposition of this faith will have to include: (a) more discussion about the meaning of the death; (b) a survey of the interpretation of the historical existence of Jesus; (c) the expectation of the parousia; (d) the working out of the nature of the intermediate period between resurrection and parousia, the relationship between the Risen One and the community, as long as it continues in the world. The alternatives will be: is this intermediate period merely a time of looking back and looking forward, a time of recollection and apocalyptic hope, or has time itself become new?

The texts tell us nothing about the psychological side of the Easter appearances. We must therefore ask about their material significance. At the beginning of the Easter tradition we do not find a cycle of stories, but a series of single narratives independent of each other. Distinct types are:[1] (a) stories of appearances. Their point is the appearing of the living Jesus as such; their significance is that of describing the reality of the resurrection; (b) appearances which culminate in a command for mission (the end of the gospel of Matthew); (c) the stories of the empty tomb. The empty tomb is unknown to the early kerygma. There is a dispute whether the stories about the tomb are equally early and compete with the appearances – in that case, they would really be assumption stories, and presuppose that Jesus was already in heaven – or whether they form no independent narrative tradition but are simply late, apologetic constructions.

Originally, resurrection and exaltation are identical: I Cor. 15.3ff. The division into two acts, resurrection from the tomb and ascension into heaven, is secondary. The meaning of the resurrection is from the beginning the appointment of Jesus to his heavenly glory.[2] Now he sits at the right hand of God.

This idea derives from Ps. 110.1, the most important psalm in a christological interpretation. According to Hahn[3], the idea of the exaltation of Christ is secondary, only read out of Ps. 110 at a later date. The early community

[1] H. Grass (see p. 65, n. 1), passim; R. Bultmann, History of the Synoptic Tradition, pp. 284–91; L. Brun, Die Auferstehung Christi in der urchristlichen Überlieferung (1925).

[2] This significance is then developed consistently in John: the crucifixion is identical with the exaltation: 'ascension from the cross'.

[3] F. Hahn, Christologische Hoheitstitel, FRLANT 83 (1963), pp. 112ff.

understood Jesus' resurrection as an anticipation of the parousia and his ascension merely as a temporary absence; not positively, as an exaltation and entry into a position of honour. Only on the basis of the delay of the parousia was the ascension then interpreted as an enthronement, on the basis of scribal work on Ps. 110.

This interpretation stands things on their head.[1] The *maranatha* tells against Hahn. In addition, it is improbable that the primitive community differentiated two acts, the raising from the dead and the entry into heaven. The idea of the exaltation already occurs in some of the oldest passages in the tradition, I Cor. 15.3ff.; Rom. 1.3f., etc. Furthermore, the idea of exaltation is by no means everywhere associated with Ps. 110, e.g. Rom. 1.3f.; Phil. 2.6f.; the gospel of John. It was, rather, there from the beginning: and later it was found to be prophesied in Ps. 110.

The significance of the idea of the exaltation is that the exaltation guarantees hope. The community knows that it has an eschatological security.

Is the resurrection a 'historical event'? What the historian can infer from the texts is not the reality of the resurrection as a historical event, but the Easter faith of the disciples. The well-known objection that in that case the objective fact of the resurrection of Christ is dissolved into a subjective idea does not meet the point. If the resurrection is claimed as a historical event, it cannot be the foundation of faith. The alternative: did something objective or only something subjective happen?, is a false one. This is already clear from the fact that the resurrection of Christ is not recognizable to everyone in an objective way; it only discloses itself to faith. Thus the alternative is transcended. The element of event in the resurrection is rather to be characterized thus: faith understands the resurrection objectively as the prior element of the action of God, by understanding that it is founded precisely on this resurrection by God. Resurrection is thus visible only to faith and its truth cannot be proved historically. The only proof is that of faith itself: that in it this Lord shows himself to be Lord, that the proclamation of his Lordship itself produces a demonstration of the truth, in that today the gospel is preached to the poor and they are given forgiveness of sins, and in that the power of the world is unmasked as the world. Jesus cannot be recognized as the Risen One other than in this event of proclamation.

The texts do not describe the subjective side of the Easter appearances, the psychological element of the experience. True, they strongly stress the surprising, compelling character of the appearances, but they do not do so in order to set them off against the feeling of the disciples, but rather to show that here something new happened that aroused faith: there is no witness of the resurrection who did not become a believer.

The resurrection brings the parousia into view.

---

[1] Cf. P. Vielhauer, *EvTh* 25 (1965), pp. 42ff.

It is not introduced in formulations, since they deal with the past saving event. From this, however, hope is produced. One example is I Thess. 1.9f., a schematic summary of mission preaching. It contains: (a) conversion to the 'true' God; (b) teaching about correct worship; (c) καὶ ἀναμένειν τὸν υἱὸν αὐτοῦ ἐκ τῶν οὐρανῶν, ὃν ἤγειρεν ἐκ τῶν νεκρῶν, Ἰησοῦν τὸν ῥυόμενον ἡμᾶς ἐκ τῆς ὀργῆς τῆς ἐρχομένης. Here Jesus appears, not as the judge, but as the saviour, σωτήρ. I Thess. 4.13ff. shows how Paul imagines the happening: at the coming of the Lord, the believers will be snatched away to him in the air. Alongside this we also find the idea of Jesus as the future judge of the world. According to Jewish expectation, God is the judge (I Thess. 3.13, etc.). In that case, the Christian view is that God delegates his office to Jesus (II Cor. 5.10). The juxtaposition of God and Christ as judge does not cause Paul any headaches. Daniel 7.13 became important for the idea of the parousia; cf. Mark 13.26; 14.62. The new element of Christian expectation lies in the fact that the judge is known, as the saviour. Thus eschatology is no longer a formal expectation, but a positive hope. It is not based on apocalyptic pictures but on the saving work, on faith. We thus find little interest in painting pictures of the process of the parousia or reckoning the time when it is to come. Interest is concentrated on the proclamation of faith. Eschatology is developed in a christological manner.

The resurrection of Christ forms the basis for the hope of the resurrection of believers. The connection between the two is described as follows: (a) as Christ, so too the believers; (b) because Christ, therefore also the believers.

This 'as' or 'because' could, of course, always be understood in the sense of an apocalyptic picture of the world, and remain imaginary. The key theological question is whether hope is part of the apocalyptic world-picture or whether it can be seen as an element of faith itself.

Paul links the resurrection of Christ and the resurrection of believers in I Cor. 15. By not only basing the hope outwardly on the creed but also interpreting the creed existentially, he shows the extent to which our own fate is bound up with that of Christ. In Rom. 5–8, hope appears as a form of existence in the face of the world and the powers of the world, sin, death, temptation. The new life is already there in the spirit. The material of hope is thus not only promised but already guaranteed today as life in the spirit.

IV The Interpretation of the Death of Jesus

Cultic and juristic ideas are used to interpret the death of Jesus. They are not kept strictly apart, as the cult itself does in fact have juristic elements. The purpose of the following survey is not simply the ordering of each passage in a particular category, but the presentation of an overall impression.

1. The death of Jesus is regarded as a *ransom* (Gal. 3.13; 4.5; I Cor. 6.20; 7.23); his blood is the price (1 Peter 1.18f.). The result is

described by the word-group *(ἀπο)λύτρωσις*. Thus there is a material bridge between the idea of ransom and that of

2. *Representation*. This is expressed most clearly in the fragment of a hymn in I Peter 2.21–24. There is also no clear division between this and

3. The idea of *sacrifice*, as is shown by Mark 10.45; I Tim. 2.6; cf. Rom. 4.25; Eph. 5.2. Occasionally the sacrifice is defined more exactly, (*a*) as a passover sacrifice (I Cor. 5.7) in which the idea of the covenant is also to be found; (*b*) as a covenant sacrifice (Heb. 13.20); (*c*) by far the most important is the idea of the expiatory sacrifice. Christ is called ἱλαστήριον (Rom. 3.25; cf. Heb. 2.17; I John 2.2; 4.10).[1] It is above all the expiatory sacrifice that is borne in mind when it is simply said that he died ὑπὲρ ἡμῶν.

But ὑπέρ can also express the idea of ransom (Gal. 3.13) and of representation (II Cor. 5.21). The key word ὑπέρ is not found in Acts, James, Jude, II Peter, Didache, II Clement, Hermas.

Isaiah 53 has had some influence on the formulation (Rom. 4.25). Christ's action is described with the words παραδιδόναι, διδόναι (Rom. 4.25; Mark 10.45; Gal. 1.4).[2]

The notion of the ὑπὲρ ἡμῶν plays a dominant part in the eucharistic tradition. The idea of sacrifice is accentuated by the reference to the blood, i.e. the blood shed in sacrifice.

Cf. I Peter; Hebrews; I John; Revelation; Acts 20.28. Paul speaks of the blood of Christ only where he quotes a tradition or where one is echoed (Rom. 5.9). For the deutero-Pauline literature see Col. 1.20; Eph. 1.7. The sprinkling with sacrificial blood signifies purification, expiation (I Peter 1.2; Hebrews 9.13, etc.).

The result of the saving work is defined as deliverance: *(ἀπο)λύτρωσις*, forgiveness of sins (see below), purification, sanctification (Eph. 5.25f.), reconciliation (Paul, Colossians, Ephesians), justification (a key concept in the theology of Paul, but developed from pre-Pauline beginnings, as is shown by two passages quoted by Paul: Rom. 4.25; 3.24ff.).

---

[1] G. Fitzer, 'Der Ort der Versöhnung nach Paulus', *ThZ* 22 (1966), pp. 161–83, challenges the meaning 'expiatory sacrifice' for ἱλαστήριον; but this is also suggested by the context. It is, however, true that no isolated theory of expiation is developed.

[2] The un-Pauline language (plural of ἁμαρτία) and a comparison with other passages (Rom. 4.25, a traditional formula; Eph. 5.2, 25; Titus 2.14), show Gal. 1.4a to be traditional material.

Both style (*parallelismus membrorum*) and content show Rom. 4.25 to be traditional material. In this formula, expiation is subordinated to death as the negative condition of salvation, and the positive transmission of salvation, righteousness, to the resurrection. Paul comments on it in Rom. 5.1ff., by introducing the concept of faith and drawing the consequences: εἰρήνην ἔχομεν.

In Rom. 3.24ff. we have an accumulation of un-Pauline concepts and ideas: ἱλαστήριον, πάρεσις, ἁμάρτημα, αἷμα, elsewhere only in Rom. 5.9 and the text describing the last supper. The meaning of δικαιοσύνη is characteristically different from that in Paul[1]: God has shown his righteousness, his faithfulness to the covenant, by the institution of an atoning sacrifice. Why this complicated procedure, for God to make a reconciliation with himself? The following factors have to be explained: (a) that the old covenant cannot simply be continued, as it has been broken; (b) that the guilt cannot be dealt with by being overlooked by God. It must be blotted out. (c) On the other hand, the sacrifice shows that we are pointed towards God's grace. This cannot merely consist in a disposition of God, but must be an effective act. The train of thought is not illustrated by an abstract concept of God and an idea of sacrifice. We have an attempt to interpret faith; it is the foundation of a new relationship to the past (guilt), present and future (new covenant).

The limitation of this exposition of the saving event is, however, that expiation covers only past transgressions. What about the present and the future? The formula is not concerned with the individual, but with the collectivity of the people of God. The individual is sanctified by his acceptance here. New transgressions are no longer a possibility.

It is clear that this theory of expiation is not permanently adequate. It relates only indirectly to the individual. It cannot describe existing in the world positively. Nor is even the concept of the forgiveness of sins adequate. Paul knows that. He does not use it in any of his own formulations. The keyword ἄφεσις does not occur in his writings; πάρεσις occurs only in the formula just quoted, and in addition we have ἀφιέναι in a quotation from the Old Testament (Rom. 4.7). The idea of the forgiveness of sins is orientated to the past, and understands by 'sin' a single transgression of God's commandment. Paul develops the idea further: (a) He interprets δικαιοσύνη as the making of men righteous by God in the present. (b) He sees ἁμαρτία, not as the individual transgression, but as the power of sin. This is made clear by the terminology: he uses the word in the singular (in the plural only where he is taking up the tradition). Attention is not directed to the past, but to the future, to freedom from sin as the freedom of the new life.

---

[1] E. Käsemann, 'Zum Verständnis von Römer 3, 24–26', *ZNW* 43 (1950/1), pp. 150–54 (= *Exegetische Versuche und Besinnungen* I, pp. 96–100); W. G. Kümmel, 'Πάρεσις und ἔνδειξις', *ZThK* 49 (1952), pp. 154–67 (= *Heilsgeschehen und Geschichte*, Marburger Theologische Studien 3 (1965), pp. 260–70).

10 · THE CHRISTOLOGICAL TITLES IN THE KERYGMA

O. Cullmann, *The Christology of the New Testament* (1963[2]); H. W. Boers, *The Diversity of NT Christological Concepts and the Confession of Faith*, Diss. Bonn, 1962; W. Kramer, *Christ, Lord, Son of God*, SBT 50 (1966); F. Hahn, *Christologische Hoheitstitel*, FRLANT 83 (1963); P. Vielhauer, 'Ein Weg zur neutestamentlichen Christologie?', *EvTh* 25 (1965), pp. 24–72 (= *Aufsätze zum NT*, ThB 31 (1965), pp. 141–198) – against Hahn; R. H. Fuller, *The Foundations of NT Christology* (1965).

I Messiah

Two types of terminology are to be distinguished:

1. 'χριστός' is a title, 'the Messiah'; Mark 8.29: σὺ εἶ ὁ χριστός.
2. 'Christ' has become a mere name in the composite phrase 'Ιησοῦς Χριστός.

This is the case even where Paul puts the article, which is used only for formal reasons (Kramer, pp. 206ff.). The development of the significance of χριστός in the direction of becoming a name took place naturally in the Greek-speaking world. The Greeks do not understand the title Messiah. So the nature of the redeemer had to be explained to them by other titles.

By origin, the 'Messiah' belongs to the nationalistic type of Jewish eschatology. 'Anointed' is a designation of the king in the Old Testament.

The king is (in the oriental court style) a bringer of salvation. The best known passage is Ps. 2, which in Judaism (Ps. Sol. 17.32; 18.7) is interpreted eschatologically, though of course within a this-worldly eschatology. It is also taken up in the New Testament (Acts 4.25f.).

Thus from the beginning the Messiah is no supernatural figure, but a human saviour. Of course, over the course of time the different types of hope coalesce, and with them the ideas of the saviour. The figure of the Messiah is accentuated until it becomes transcendent. But basically Messiahship always remains alien to apocalyptic thought. It is missing from wide stretches of apocalyptic writings (Ethiopian Enoch 1–36; 91–104; Slavonic Enoch; the Assumption of Moses; Jubilees; etc.). Where it has found its way into apocalyptic (Enoch; IV Ezra; Baruch) there is a secondary stage of development.

For a saviour really only fits into the restoration of the earthly kingdom of Israel, and not into the kingdom of God which comes from above. So in Judaism, Messiah and kingdom of God are not conceptually linked;[1] the idea that the Messiah brings in the kingdom of God is missing.

Where a link is nevertheless established between the eschatological saviour figure and a new world, we no longer have a living hope but an academic construction, showing that the Messiah and his kingdom precede the future era; this is the well-known idea of the thousand year kingdom (Bill. IV 968f.).

A unique type which also seems to have been constructed artificially is represented by the Qumran texts. Two Messiahs are expected, the Messiah of Aaron and the Messiah of Israel. The former is superior. This corresponds to the organization and ideas of the sect. The hierarchical ordering of Israel is superior to the political.[2]

NEW TESTAMENT

The Messiah is the eschatological bringer of salvation; in contrast to the tradition, however, every political element has disappeared. Of course, the meaning of the concept has above all changed, in that it no longer expresses a pure expectation of the future which can be elaborated as desired, but is used to interpret a particular, historical person. The new element lies in the claim that the Messiah has already come.

A particular tendency dominates the Christian use of the word χριστός: it is used by preference when the remark is made that 'Christ' has died and risen (been raised) again. Christ here is the subject of the sentence. The style is that of the establishing of facts (Rom. 5.8; 8.4; often in I Cor. 15). Jesus is thus called 'Christ' when he is to be designated as the one who accomplishes the work of salvation. The temporal aspect of this title is principally the past, which is understood as saving event. As a consequence, the death of Jesus comes more to the forefront here than in the case of the other titles.

The negative consequence stems from the orientation of the title to the saving work (death and resurrection): in the early period there is no interest in when or how Jesus became Messiah.

[1] K. G. Kuhn, βασιλεύς, TWNT I 573.

[2] Passages are: Test. Jud. 21; cf. also the significance of Levi in Test. Levi 4, 18; 1 QS IX 11; Dam. B XIX 10f.; XX 1; 1 QSa II 11ff. (seating at the messianic banquet, which is anticipated in the sect). K. G. Kuhn, 'Die beiden Messias Aarons und Israels', NTS 1 (1954/5), pp. 168–79; H.-W. Kuhn, 'Die beiden Messias in den Qumrantexten und die Messiasvorstellung in der rabbinischen Literatur', ZAW 70 (1958), pp. 200–08.

The titles 'Son of God' and 'Kyrios' yield a different finding. They primarily designate a status. Now, it must also be said how Jesus acquired this status. 'Messiah', on the other hand, primarily points to what he did. Ferdinand Hahn (pp. 179ff.) sees the situation in different terms. The primitive community had, in his view, a one-sided outlook: forward, to the parousia, and not back to the work of Christ. All christological titles originally had a strictly eschatological meaning. Even χριστός designated Jesus' eschatological position. Examples: Mark 13.21f., 26; 14.61f.; Acts 3.20f.; Matt. 25.31–46; Rev. 11.15; 12.10.

It may be argued that these are all late passages. Therefore we must disagree with Hahn when he understands the link between 'Christ' and the passion tradition as a completely new development. The oldest instances of Jesus as Messiah in the tradition are the formulae about his death. In Paul, Christ is already a name. On the other hand, the titular sense ('the Messiah') is reactivated in some later writings, particularly those of Luke. For this title can be used to demonstrate the anchoring of the work of salvation in the history of salvation and to show the truth of the revelation of Christ with the help of scripture. The association of 'Christ', passion and scripture can already be found in the formula in I Cor. 15.3ff. Cf. also Acts 17.2f. A hermeneutical circle can be seen in Luke 24.26f., 44f.: the fate of Jesus is understood in the light of the Old Testament, where it is prophesied, but the Old Testament is in turn understood in the light of the resurrection of Christ.

The Messiah is regarded as a descendant of David (in pre-Christian literature only in Ps. Sol. 17.21).[1] Hence Jesus, too, is called 'Son of David'; not frequently, but already at an early stage, in two ancient formulas (Rom. 1.3f.; II Tim. 2.8). That is primarily a dogmatic assertion. Later, a 'historical' proof is introduced, in that a genealogy of Jesus is constructed. The remarkable reflection in Mark 12.35–37 shows that the title was first meant dogmatically, without reference to the physical descent of Jesus.

Mark 12.35–37: It is taught that the Messiah is David's son. But in the Old Testament David calls the Messiah his lord (Ps. 110.1). So how can he be his son? Some exegetes interpret the passage this way: according to Jewish teaching, the Messiah should be a son of David. Jesus was not. So if the community still wanted to champion his Messiahship it had to show that the Messiah was not the son of David on the basis of the Old Testament. A polemic of this kind is in fact to be found in John, but not in Mark, who uses the title 'Son of David' in a positive sense. He must therefore have understood the psalm passage quoted in a different way. One can, of course, argue that the pericope originally had this meaning, but that Mark no longer understood it or deliberately reinterpreted it. However, it must then be assumed that Matthew and Luke did not note the secondary interpretation by Mark. A comparison with other passages (Rom. 1.3f.; Acts 2.25f.) shows that the meaning can nevertheless be recognized. In his lifetime, Jesus is the Messiah,

---

[1] Cf. F. Hahn, pp. 242ff.; Bill. I 525; P. Volz, *Die Eschatologie der jüdischen Gemeinde im neutestamentlichen Zeitalter* (1934²), p. 174; W. Bousset, *Die Religion des Judentums*, pp. 226f.

i.e. the son of David. He was then exalted to be David's lord, i.e. to be Son of God (Rom. 1.3f.). Two periods in his work must therefore be distinguished, corresponding to the two stages of his being.

According to Mark 11.10, the coming lordship of David is greeted on Jesus' entry into Jerusalem (Matthew 21.9: the son of David; Luke 19.38: the king; John 12.13: the king of Israel). The birth narratives in Matthew and Luke construct a genealogy for Jesus which leads from Abraham (Matthew) or Adam (Luke) through David to Jesus.[1] A division of salvation history into periods underlies this.

The scheme involved is one of sevens, which is directly characterized in Matthew but is only to be recognized with variations in Luke. Originally the genealogies led up to Joseph as the father of Jesus, but this produced a contradiction with the other theme of the birth narratives: that Jesus was son of the virgin Mary. Both themes have, however, already been combined before the time of Matthew and Luke. In Ignatius they are both taken up into the creed (Eph. 18.2; Trall. 9.1). The Sinaitic Syriac undertakes a remarkable effort at reconciliation.

The title βασιλεύς for Jesus is in practice identical with 'Son of David'.

This title is given to Jesus by Luke and John in the narratives of the entry into Jerusalem. In the passion, Jesus is mocked as 'king of the Jews'; this is matched by the *titulus* on the cross (Mark 15.26 par.). The historicity of the *titulus* is disputed.

There is another striking piece of evidence. On the one hand, Jesus is called βασιλεύς; on the other, there is mention of his βασιλεία. But the two stand side by side without any connection.[2] The situation can be explained from the history of the themes. 'Jesus is king' is just another way of saying 'Jesus is Messiah'. On the other hand, the concept of Jesus' kingly reign is not derived from his status as Messiah, but is formed in analogy with the kingly rule of God.

The two are artificially combined: the kingdom of Jesus lasts from his exaltation to the dawn of the kingdom of God (I Cor. 15.25ff.; cf. Matt. 13.41).[3]

---

[1] F. Hahn, pp. 242f. (who assumes that Jesus really did descend from David): originally the genealogy in Matthew only reached as far as David. But this is no more than a hypothesis. That the genealogies are christological constructions is shown (a) by the fact that there are two different ones; (b) by a comparison with the Old Testament.

[2] Jesus' title of 'king' and his βασιλεία are only linked by John: 'Are you the King . . . ? . . . My kingship is not of this world' (18.33ff.).

[3] Matthew, however, has: βασιλεία 'of the Son of Man'.

II   Son of God

W. Bousset, *Kyrios Christos* (1913; 1965⁵), pp. 52–57; G. P. Wetter, *Der Sohn Gottes* (1916); E. Klostermann in HNT on Mark 1.11; W. Bauer in HNT on John 1.34; R. Bultmann, *Theology of the New Testament* I, pp. 50f., 128ff.; H. Riesenfeld, *Jesus transfiguré* (1947); E. Schweizer, *Erniedrigung and Erhöhung*, AThANT 28 (1962²), pp. 62ff.; O. Cullmann, *Christology*, pp. 270ff.; W. Grundmann, 'Sohn Gottes', *ZNW* 47 (1956), pp. 113–33. For material see: H. Braun, 'Der Sinn der neutestamentlichen Christologie', *ZThK* 54 (1957), pp. 353–56 (=*Gesammelte Studien zum NT*, pp. 255–59); Bauer (-Arndt-Gingrich), s.v.

The historical origin of the title Son of God, unlike that of Messiah, is obscure. Whether Jesus himself used the title or whether it was first applied to him by the community makes no difference to the question of its derivation and meaning. In the Old Testament, both Israel (Ex. 4.22) and the king are called 'Son of God' (in the latter case it is therefore synonymous with 'Messiah').

Ps. 2.2: 'anointed'; v. 7 υἱός μου εἶ σύ, ἐγὼ σήμερον γεγέννηκά σε. This is oriental court style. Of course, in talking of the son of God, Judaism cannot have in mind either physical begetting by God or an incarnation of God. It is often assumed on the basis of this verse that the Old Testament title for king was transferred to Jesus, and that the meaning of 'Son of God' is thus the same as that of 'Messiah'. Against this, however, is the fact that there is no evidence in Judaism for the use of the title 'Son of God' for the Messiah.

True, Bill. III 17 gives some examples from Ethiopian Enoch and IV Ezra. But none of these examples stands up to scrutiny. The passage from Enoch, 105.2, is a later addition; in IV Ezra the original text has 'servant' (παῖς) and not 'son'. Ps. Sol. 17 applies Ps. 2 to the Messiah, but the concept of 'Son' is not used. Were the Jews afraid of the word because it had associations with the pagan 'sons of God' in their environment? Despite the lack of evidence, some exegetes want to keep open the possibility that Judaism applied this word to the Messiah (Bultmann, Cullmann, H. Riesenfeld).

In Jewish writings, an individual man is occasionally called the Son of God (Ecclus. 4.10). Wisdom 2.10ff. is particularly illuminating: this describes the suffering undergone in the world by the righteous man. He is called in succession παῖς κυρίου (v. 13) and υἱὸς θεοῦ (v. 18). Is the title, then, meant to describe Jesus as the suffering righteous one? The fact that the terminology is confined to Wisdom tells against this. υἱὸς θεοῦ is not a title here. In addition, 'Son of God' in the New Testament has no particular reference to suffering.

Walter Grundmann has put forward a new hypothesis: in Test. Levi 4, Levi is promised that he will become God's son and helper. The Testament of Levi has connections with the Qumran texts: Levi is the tribal ancestor of the priests, and in Qumran a high-priestly Messiah was expected. Grundmann concludes that in this esoteric circle the high priest was called 'son'. In the New Testament, the title described Jesus as the eschatological high priest. But this assumption is improbable, as the word 'son' is not used as a title in the Testament of Levi. Moreover, in the New Testament the designation of Jesus as high priest belongs to later strata. It would be better to refer to Joseph and Aseneth, where Joseph is clearly described as a redeemer figure and called 'son of God'.

The New Testament evidence is not a unity. Examples are:
In Rom. 1.3f., Paul quotes a traditional formula:

περὶ τοῦ υἱοῦ αὐτοῦ,

τοῦ γενομένου ἐκ σπέρματος Δαυὶδ κατὰ σάρκα,

τοῦ ὁρισθέντος υἱοῦ θεοῦ ἐν δυνάμει κατὰ πνεῦμα ἁγιοσύνης ἐξ ἀναστάσεως νεκρῶν.

The formula is distinct in style and terminology: participial style, prepositional phrases, parallelism; concepts and imagery are un-Pauline. Whether there are Pauline additions in it is a matter of doubt. The question is particularly pressing in the case of the κατὰ σάρκα—κατὰ πνεῦμα. E. Schweizer and F. Hahn (pp. 251ff.) do not regard this as a Pauline addition. It is not a matter of the Pauline contrast of σάρξ and πνεῦμα, but of a confrontation of two spheres which also occurs in other christological confessions and hymns: I Tim. 3.16; I Peter 3.18; Ignatius, Eph. 7.2; 10.3; Smyrn. 1.1; 3.3; 12.2; Magn. 13.2; Polycarp 1.2; 2.2.

The meaning is that during his lifetime, Jesus was the Messiah (Son of David); after his death,[1] he was appointed by God to be Son of God. This sonship of God is understood in legal, and not in physical terms. The formula does not distinguish two 'natures', but two stages in the existence of Jesus. There is no knowledge of pre-existence. As Messiah, Jesus was not a supernatural being, but a man with a particular status.

Bultmann, *Theology* I, p. 26: In Rom. 1.3f., the Messiahship of Jesus is only dated from the resurrection onwards. This gives Bultmann support for his thesis that in the earliest period, the earthly life of Jesus was still not regarded in Messianic terms. This, however, is to misinterpret the evidence: it is not Jesus' 'Messiahship', but his divine sonship which begins with the resurrection. Before that, he was David's son, i.e. Messiah. That is his earthly status.

The formula shows an early stage of an 'adoptionist' christology which was also to be recognized in Mark 12.35ff.

It could also be present in II Tim. 2.8: μνημόνευε Ἰησοῦν Χριστὸν ἐγηγερμένον ἐκ νεκρῶν, ἐκ σπέρματος Δαυίδ. The exact meaning of the present text can no longer be understood. But evidently in the background there is a formula associated with Rom. 1.3f.

---

[1] ἐξ ἀναστάσεως: since, or, on the basis of, the resurrection.

This understanding of the divine sonship is also presupposed in the synoptic stories of the baptism and transfiguration of Jesus.

In both, there is heard the voice, 'You are my son'. That means that at this moment Jesus is appointed to his status. Both stories are originally independent, separate narratives. Each is meant to report the foundation of the divine sonship. When they were subsequently inserted into the framework of the gospel, the meaning was modified. The transfiguration now becomes a confirmation of the divine sonship which Jesus has had since the baptism. In Mark, the latter is still the act of appointment. In Matthew and Luke, the birth narrative is placed before it. In this way the story of the baptism already becomes the confirmation of Jesus' appointment.

The birth narratives contain another understanding of the divine sonship: Jesus is God's son by virtue of his miraculous conception. This idea is un-Jewish. It derives from polytheism. It is widespread in the ancient East and in Hellenism.

Two types may be distinguished: (a) the incarnation; (b) the epiphany.

(a) The Egyptian Pharaoh is son of God, i.e. begotten by God. The Greeks say the same thing of great men: kings (Alexander the Great), philosophers (Pythagoras and Plato) and miracle workers (Apollonius of Tyana). In Hellenism, Heracles is the son of God and saviour *par excellence*. A further theme can be associated with that of the divine conception, namely that the mother of the divine child was a virgin until she was touched by God. This idea also permeates into Hellenistic Judaism, even in Egypt (Philo). It can be sublimated, so that the conception does not follow from physical contact with the god but through his *dynamis* or *pneuma*.[1]

(b) For the epiphany-type, the stress does not really lie on the birth. It is only a secondary explanation for the miraculous acts performed by a θεῖος ἀνήρ, as ruler, thinker, etc. Here the basic idea is that a divine power is at work in him. In the first type, the nature of the God-man is described; in the second, the manifestation of the divine in his actions. This Hellenistic idea of inspiration can be associated with the Jewish one. This is shown by the synoptic (birth) narratives, where the theme of the saviour child and that of inspiration permeate each other. In Acts 2.22, the idea of Jesus as the θεῖος ἀνήρ is summed up in a formula: cf. Acts 10.38. The son-deities who come from the East and are worshipped in the mysteries represent quite another type. Here there is no account of actions, but of the dying and rising again of the god; i.e., the myth has soteriological significance. Here the fate of the god is the key element. The meaning emerges still more clearly when the soteriology is bound up with cosmology: when the descent and ascent of the revealer God portray the saving event.

In a further group of passages, 'Son of God' contains the ideas of

---

[1] Parallels to the birth narratives in Matthew and Luke in Plutarch are presented by H. Braun, *op. cit.*, p. 354 (= pp. 256f.); cf. M. Dibelius, 'Jungfrauensohn und Krippenkind', *Botschaft und Geschichte* I (1953), pp. 25–35.

the pre-existence, career and destiny of the revealer. Pre-existence is presupposed when Paul writes: 'God sent his son' (Rom. 8.3). But the idea is already firmly shaped before Paul. In order to understand it, however, we must go beyond the statistical evidence for 'Son of God'. The most important indication is Phil. 2.6ff.:[1]

. . . Jesus Christ . . .

ὃς ἐν μορφῇ θεοῦ ὑπάρχων
οὐχ ἁρπαγμὸν ἡγήσατο τὸ εἶναι ἴσα θεῷ,
ἀλλ' ἑαυτὸν ἐκένωσεν
μορφὴν δούλου λαβών,
ἐν ὁμοιώματι ἀνθρώπων γενόμενος
καὶ σχήματι εὑρεθεὶς ὡς ἄνθρωπος
ἐταπείνωσεν ἑαυτὸν
γενόμενος ὑπήκοος μέχρι θανάτου [θανάτου δὲ σταυροῦ].

διὸ καὶ ὁ θεὸς αὐτὸν ὑπερύψωσεν
καὶ ἐχαρίσατο αὐτῷ τὸ ὄνομα τὸ ὑπὲρ πᾶν ὄνομα
ἵνα ἐν τῷ ὀνόματι Ἰησοῦ πᾶν γόνυ κάμψῃ
ἐπουρανίων καὶ ἐπιγείων καὶ καταχθονίων.
καὶ πᾶσα γλῶσσα ἐξομολογήσηται
ὅτι κύριος Ἰησοῦς Χριστός,
εἰς δόξαν θεοῦ πατρός.

The form indicates a division into strophes (though there is dispute over the details). The conceptuality is pre-Pauline: μορφή, σχῆμα. The meaning is no longer that of classical Greek concepts of form, but of Hellenistic concepts of manifestation. The first part describes the descent as an act of the revealer which ends with death; the second the exaltation as God's act. At the turning point, Paul has added 'even death on a cross'. To exclude anything else as Pauline additions is neither possible nor necessary.

Granted, the title 'Son' does not occur here, but it is indicated by the content. The revealer is like God, and like him in substance; that

---

[1] Literature: E. Käsemann, 'Kritische Analyse von Phil. 2.5–11', *ZThK* 47 (1950), pp. 313–60 (= *Exegetische Versuche und Besinnungen* I, pp. 51–95); G. Bornkamm, 'Zum Verständnis des Christus-Hymnus Phil. 2, 6–11', *Studien zu Antike und Urchristentum, Gesammelte Aufsätze* II, pp. 177–87; J. Jeremias, 'Zu Phil 2, 7', *NovTest* 6 (1963), pp. 182–88; G. Strecker, 'Redaktion und Tradition im Christushymnus Phil 2, 6–11', *ZNW* 55 (1964), pp. 63–78; D. Georgi, 'Der vorpaulinische Hymnus Phil. 2, 6–11', *Zeit und Geschichte* (Bultmann Festschrift) (1964), pp. 263–93.

is, of the same nature: ἐν μορφῇ θεοῦ ὑπάρχων. The servant character of the Incarnate One is set over against this divinity. Underlying it is the pattern of incarnation, death and exaltation. But Paul has reinterpreted it along the lines of his pattern of cross and resurrection. In this hymn, it is paradoxically death that constitutes salvation. God reacts to it by exalting the dead one beyond his original rank. Originally, in his pre-existence, he had been God's son. Now he is appointed 'Lord'. The saving work is completed with the exaltation. Here there is no prospect of a future parousia.

No gospel could be written in the light of this christology, because the actions of the Incarnate One have no role in it. On the other hand, it can easily form the basis for a mythical christology, in which case one is immediately involved in the dilemma of the mythical doctrine of redemption, namely that it cannot show the relationship of the saving event to the individual. How can my salvation be demonstrated in the course taken by the redeemer? How can this event determine my present existence in the world? If the doctrine of salvation is mythical, then salvation is also mythical – other-worldly – fantastic. All that is left in the end is spiritual transmigration from the world. It makes no difference that salvation is transmitted sacramentally, through mysteries. The question therefore is whether there is a positive possibility of demonstrating the relationship between this cosmic event and my existence. Paul works out the meaning of the mythical idea for human existence in his *theologia crucis*. (One example is the transition in thought from Rom. 4.25 to 5.1ff.). There still remains, however, the question of the mythical idea itself and its meaning. Is this to be given up?

The hymn contains not only objectifying description but also an element of appropriation. It comes to a climax, ending after the account of the enthronement in a homology. The community is drawn into the cosmic event. It is shown what is real in the world, but still concealed – the Lordship of Jesus. In its own existence, it must accord with this reality. How? One possibility is for it to become a mystery community. In that case it would honour the Lord in the cult, by retreating from the world into an unreal, religious sphere. But this possibility is denied it by virtue of the very nature of the Lordship of Jesus: he is not merely a religious redeemer or Lord over the heavenly world, but rules over the earthly world, too; he demands an obedience which not only involves the observation of cultic and moral rules, but also embraces the whole of existence. The community is not only a cultic community, but a community of people living in the world. Concrete obedience consists in the proclamation – including the risk which arises through confession. The freedom of faith is represented in the proclamation. Thus the way from the content of the confession to existence is shown through the text itself.

This hymn and its 'realized eschatology' have already introduced us to the title κύριος. Before we discuss it, however, we must look at some other passages which likewise depict the saving work as already complete and demonstrate its cosmic extent.

I Tim. 3.16:

ὃς ἐφανερώθη ἐν σαρκί,
ἐδικαιώθη ἐν πνεύματι,
ὤφθη ἀγγέλοις,
ἐκηρύχθη ἐν ἔθνεσιν,
ἐπιστεύθη ἐν κόσμῳ
ἀνελήμφθη ἐν δόξῃ.

Content: epiphany, enthronement, proclamation, universal scope of the saving event. σάρξ and πνεῦμα here do not designate opposites, but spheres: the world and the upper world (see above on Rom. 1.3f.).

I Peter 3.18ff.:

⟨ὃς⟩ ἅπαξ περὶ ἁμαρτιῶν ἔπαθεν,
δίκαιος ὑπὲρ ἀδίκων,
ἵνα ⟨ἡ⟩μᾶς προσαγάγῃ τῷ θεῷ,
θανατωθεὶς μὲν σαρκί
ζωοποιηθεὶς δὲ πνεύματι.
ἐν ᾧ καὶ τοῖς ἐν φυλακῇ πνεύμασιν [. . .] ἐκήρυξεν,
ὅς ἐστιν ἐν δεξιᾷ θεοῦ,
πορευθεὶς εἰς οὐρανόν
ὑποταγέντων αὐτῷ ἀγγέλων καὶ ἐξουσιῶν καὶ δυνάμεων.

Here, too, flesh and spirit are the two spheres mentioned. The cosmic aspect becomes visible in the preaching to the spirits in prison. The text is uncertain. Evidently the original did not envisage a 'descent to hell', but an ascent – corresponding to the picture of the world in Eph. 2.2[1] (similarly Polycarp, Phil. 2.1; cf. Bultmann, *Theology* II, pp. 153, 156).

Here the cosmic doctrine of redemption is linked with the traditional doctrine of expiation; cf. I Peter 2.22ff. In this connection, we see the intention of working out the reference to 'us'.

Another related passage is Eph. 4.8–10. This passage is also often interpreted in connection with the descent to hell. But the κατώτερα μέρη are not the underworld, but the earth as the lowest part of the cosmos.

In these passages, as in Phil. 2, the saving event is depicted as the course of the redeemer. Unlike there, however, the key points are not humiliation and obedience, but appearance in the world and ascent.

The nature, rather than the career, of the redeemer can also be

[1] Cf. R. Bultmann, 'Bekenntnis- und Liedfragmente im 1. Petrusbrief', *CN* 11 (1947), pp. 1ff.; J. Jeremias, *ZNW* 42 (1949), pp. 194ff., differs.

described: he is the 'image' of God (II Cor. 4.4; Col. 1.15ff.).[1]

εἰκών is a Hellenistic term used in connection with manifestations. It does not describe the form, but the being (as in Phil. 2.6ff.: μορφή and σχῆμα). In the original version of this hymn, the *cosmos* was the body of the redeemer; redemption is the reconciliation of all things. The author of the epistle to the Colossians then interpreted the body of Christ in terms of the church. To him, redemption is expiation of guilt through the blood of Christ.

Historically the most significant of the manifestation concepts to express the idea of the divine sonship is ὁ λόγος (John 1; see 42 I below).

III   Kyrios

W. Bousset, *Kyrios Christos* (1913; 1965[5]); W. Foerster, κύριος *TWNT* III 1081ff.; H. Lietzmann in HNT on Rom. 10.9; O. Cullmann, *Christology*, pp. 195–237; I. Hermann, *Kyrios und Pneuma* (1961); F. Hahn, *Christologische Hoheitstitel*, pp. 67–125; P. Vielhauer, *Gesammelte Aufsätze*, pp. 147–67.

This title offers a particularly clear reflection of the change from the primitive community to Hellenistic Christianity. Two questions are still vigorously disputed, even today: 1. What was the origin of the title? 2. When and where did it find its way into Christianity – in the primitive community or only in the Hellenistic community?

It is possible that even the primitive community called upon Jesus as Lord. The Aramaic cry *maranatha* has been preserved.[2] More important than the question whether the primitive community already used this title, however, is the question of its significance. At this point a fundamental change is to be observed as soon as one considers the Hellenistic milieu. The cry *maranatha* is an expression of a purely apocalyptic christology. The community understands itself as those who wait in hope. In Hellenism, on the other hand, the horizon is no longer the eschatological people of God which waits for the Coming One, but the community which gathers to worship the Lord who rules in the present. The cry is now: κύριος 'Ιησοῦς. It is no longer a petition, but an acclamation and proclamation. (Bousset gives the evidence.) But one should not talk of cult-mysticism and the presence of the Lord in worship. It is not the Lord, personally, but the spirit which is present. Nor is his relationship with worshippers a mystical one; it is determined by confession and acclamation. By it,

[1] H. J. Gabathuler, *Jesus Christus, Haupt der Kirche – Haupt der Welt*, AThANT 45 (1965).
[2] It is probably to be translated as an imperative, 'Come Lord'. See K. G. Kuhn, *TWNT* IV 470ff.

the liturgy is made a legally effective institution. Thus this appeal is the real essential characteristic of Christianity. The Christians are named simply 'those who call upon the name of the Lord' (I Cor. 1.2; Rom. 10.13). The phrase comes from the Septuagint (e.g. Joel 3.5; cf. Acts 2.21). The Christians have reinterpreted it, transferring it from God to the Lord Jesus.

Paul found the title κύριος already used in a regular way, as is shown by the stereotyped acclamation and the matter-of-fact way in which he uses the title.

The use of 'Son of God' and 'Kyrios' can overlap; nevertheless, some tendencies can clearly be recognized. As a rule of thumb it can be said that υἱός is the nature, whereas κύριος designates the status accorded to the Son. Therefore one says κύριος in calling to him.

Faith uses this title to represent the present character of the relationship to the Exalted One. It is therefore closely associated with the concept of the spirit: the spirit is the effective presence of the Lord.

II Cor. 3.17; ὁ δὲ κύριος τὸ πνεῦμα ἐστίν. This is the famous *locus classicus* of the mystical interpretation of Paul. But the statement does not mean that the Kyrios is a sort of fluid in which we are mystically immersed: it means, rather, in that particular context that the Lord is freedom.

To call upon the Lord is itself an act brought about by the spirit (I Cor. 12.3).

The historical derivation of the title is an unsolved problem. Judaism did not call the Messiah 'Lord'. There are two alternative hypotheses: the Christians took over the title (a) from the Septuagint; (b) from the pagan environment in which Kyrios was used as a designation for God.

The Septuagint renders יהוה by κύριος. It is often concluded from this that the Christians identified Jesus with Yahweh. Against this, however, there are the following arguments:

1. In Paul, the title *Kyrios* in fact serves to distinguish Jesus and his position before God (I Cor. 8.6).

2. There is no explanation of the fact that this title is used primarily in acclamations.

3. Outside the Septuagint, *Kyrios* is unusual in Judaism as a designation for God.

4. It has recently been disputed that the Septuagint in fact renders יהוה by *Kyrios*.[1] *Kyrios* occurs only in Christian manuscripts of the LXX, and not in Jewish ones:

---

[1] P. Vielhauer, *Aufsätze*, pp. 148–50, against Hahn; S. Schulz, 'Maranatha und Kyrios Jesus', *ZNW* 53 (1962), pp. 125–44.

(a) Papyrus Fouad 266 (second century BC): it has יהוה in the quotation from Deut. 31f.: cf. O. Paret, *Die Bibel, Ihre Überlieferung in Druck und Schrift* (1949), p. 75 and table 2.

(b) 4Q Minor Prophets: also tetragrammaton.

(c) 4Q fragments of Lev. 2–5 LXX: *ΙΑΩ*.

(d) Aquila fragments from Cairo: tetragrammaton.

(e) Fragments from the second column of the Hexapla: tetragrammaton (cf. Origen and Jerome).

(f) Examples for ΠΙΠΙ in Hatch and Redpath, *A Concordance to the LXX, Supplement* (1906), p. 126.

(g) Symmachus: cf. *TWNT* III 1082, lines 12f.

Compare, too, the use of the Old Hebrew script in the tetragrammaton in the quotations of the Q *pesharim*: 1 QpH; 4QpPs 37; אל: 1 QH I 26. II 34. XV 25; 1 Q 35 I 5.

Thus the Christian use of κύριος cannot be derived from the LXX. The reverse is in fact the case. Once the title began to be used, it was found again in the Bible.

κύριος is, of course, a designation for God, not among the Greeks, but in Syria, Egypt and Asia Minor.

In the Hellenistic ruler-cult, the king is also called Kyrios. W. Foerster (1053f.) wants to explain this in purely political terms, in contrast to θεός. But this distinction is impossible. F. Hahn (pp. 81f.) assumes that 'Lord' was not originally a title, but an address to the historical Jesus (Monsieur, or Sir). The use as a title only developed gradually, under the influence of the LXX. For a critique see P. Vielhauer, *op. cit.*

The New Testament usage and its significance: The use in cultic acclamations and in blessings is primary. Baptism takes place in the name of the Lord (Acts 22.16). The eucharist is a participation in the table of the Lord (I Cor. 10.21).

On the one hand, Jesus exercises the functions of God as Lord: he rules over the world. On the other, however, he is clearly distinguished from God. The view is that God has delegated the rule of the world to Jesus for a particular time, from the exaltation to the parousia, and for a specific end, for the completion of the saving work, the subjection of the powers. Above all, 'Lord' designates Jesus as the permanent mediator of the relationship with God. So men call upon him.

Calling on Jesus is to be distinguished from prayer. Only God is worshipped. But that one can pray at all is a miracle, mediated through the Lord. Consequently men call upon him; they pray in the name of the Lord.

IV Further Titles

1. Occasionally, Jesus is called 'prophet'.[1] Deuteronomy 18.15 is referred to Jesus (the expectation of a prophet like Moses in the end time).

Acts 3.22; 7.38. On the Jewish expectation of an eschatological prophet, cf. John 1.21; 1 QS IX 11: 'Until there shall come the Prophet and the Messiahs of Aaron and Israel'. See also 4 Q Test. 5 (Deut. 18.18f. in a series of testimonies for the coming of the prophets and the two anointed ones).

2. παῖς θεοῦ:[2] This title is often thought to be particularly old: Jesus is said to have understood himself to be the suffering servant (according to Deutero-Isaiah, especially Isa. 53). But this hypothesis is untenable.

Prominent individual men of God are said to be 'servants of God' in the Old Testament, especially Moses, David and the prophets. 'Thy servants, the prophets' is a regular phrase in the Qumran texts. In Judaism, 'servant' stands only at the periphery as a designation for the Messiah (IV Ezra: Syrian Baruch). But there is no thought of the suffering of the Messiah here, only of his glory. Only in one place might one find a pattern for the suffering servant: Wisdom 2.13–18; there the suffering righteous man is called παῖς and υἱός in succession. On closer consideration, however, it seems that παῖς points not to the suffering but to the knowledge of God on the part of the righteous.

The New Testament evidence

παῖς occurs once in the gospels, in Matt. 12.18, a late passage, a redactional addition of Matthew to a Marcan summary (Mark 3.7–12), i.e. to a passage which was itself already secondary. Here Matthew quotes Isa. 42.1–4, not, however, to point to Jesus' suffering, but to his healings.

Jesus did not refer Isa. 53 to himself. This was only done by the community, because it found here the explanation of his death. It should be noted that where Isa. 53 is quoted, the title παῖς does not occur; where it occurs, there is no reference to suffering.

The word also occurs in the prayer in Acts 4.27–30. But even there, it does not point to the suffering, but to the acts of Jesus. True, Acts

---

[1] G. Friedrich, προφήτης, TWNT VI 829ff.; O. Cullmann, Christology, pp. 13–50; F. Hahn, Hoheitstitel, 351–404.

[2] J. Jeremias, παῖς θεοῦ, TWNT V 698ff.; O. Cullmann, Christology, pp. 51–82.

3.13 speaks of suffering, but Jesus is again called παῖς particularly in respect of his exaltation.

Some exegetes assume that the voice at the baptism originally called Jesus παῖς instead of υἱός. The formulation of the saying here does in fact derive from Isa. 42.1 (Bousset, *Kyrios Christos*, p. 57, n. 2; Jeremias, *TWNT* V 699). But the voice also recalls Ps. 2.7, where there is υἱός.

The title was used to a limited extent in liturgical language, cf. Didache 9.2f.; 10.2; I Clement 59. It does not have a peculiar christological significance.

3. Ναζωραῖος:[1] there is dispute as to whether this title can be derived from the place name Nazareth,[2] i.e. whether originally it simply described Jesus' place of origin. In any case, Mark already understands the word as a description of Jesus' origin (from Nazareth), for he regularly writes Ναζαρηνός. Matthew refers to this derivation (2.23), although he says Ναζωραῖος.[3]

4. σωτήρ:[4] this title only belongs to the Hellenistic stratum of christology. It is not a Jewish title for the Messiah. In some places it is not yet used strictly as a title, but simply describes Jesus' saving activity (Phil. 3.20). This use has its model in the Septuagint. The word is used strictly as a title only in the later writings, above all in the Pastorals. Here we find ourselves in an area of terminology which has its parallels in the Hellenistic religious attitude surrounding the idea of the epiphany of the saviour, which is expressed above all in the piety of the mysteries and in the ruler-cult.

To sum up: in the development from the earlier strata to the later, one can note a certain tendency to use the titles more and more loosely. There is a tendency to put several together, cf. Peter's confession in the Marcan and Matthaean versions. For the first time, Jesus is also now called 'God' directly: in John 20.28, the Risen One is addressed as ὁ κύριός μου καὶ ὁ θεός μου.

---

[1] H. H. Schaeder, Ναζαρηνός, Ναζωραῖος, *TWNT* IV 879–84; B. Gärtner, *Die rätselhaften Termini Nazoräer und Iskariot* (1957).

[2] Schaeder takes an affirmative view; the opposite position is adopted by M. Lidzbarski, *Mandäische Liturgien* (1920), pp. XVIff. and K. Rudolph, *Die Mandäer* I, FRLANT 74 (1960), pp. 112ff.

[3] The form Ναζωραῖος also occurs in some stereotyped formulas in Acts: 2.22; 3.6; 4.10; 6.14.

[4] W. Staerk, *Soter* I (1933); II (1938); M. Dibelius/H. Conzelmann in HNT on II Tim. 1.10.

11 · THE STRUCTURE OF THE KERYGMA

I   The Confessional Formulae

The majority of ancient formulae have only one 'article', the christo-logical one. The content of the confession is not the whole religious conviction, but only the new element, i.e. Christ as the Messiah, his death as saving event and his resurrection. The presupposition of this faith, faith in God, need not be incorporated into the confession, as it is self-evident to the Jews. In the understanding of the primitive church, Christianity introduces no new idea of God. In the Gentile mission, of course, there must be explicit teaching about God. Here a link can be made with the Jewish mission.[1] So now the confession of the one God is expressly taken up into the creed. As a result, we have formulae with two 'articles': I Cor. 8.6; I Tim. 6.13.

In both passages, stress is laid on the nature of God as the creator. This point will become effective later in countering the negative gnostic attitude to the world.

Further development takes place in two directions: (1) towards a triadic confession; (2) by the arrangement of the christological article in a framework with the addition of a detailed excursus. Ephesians 4.4 shows the framework and its construction (as does I Cor. 8.6):

ἓν σῶμα καὶ ἓν πνεῦμα . . .
εἷς κύριος, μία πίστις, ἓν βάπτισμα·
εἷς θεὸς καὶ πατὴρ πάντων.

The insertion of the christological excursus into the framework is shown in I Thess 1.9f.: the framework speaks of the true and living God and of the expectation of his Son. In this passage, an insertion is now made:

(a) ὃν ἤγειρεν ἐκ τῶν νεκρῶν
(b) τὸν ῥυόμενον ἡμᾶς.

A conclusion of a kind is reached with the second article of the Roman Creed (c. AD 150).[2]

[1] Bultmann, *Theology of the New Testament* I, pp. 65ff.
[2] K. Holl, *Aufsätze* II, pp. 115ff.; E. von Dobschütz, *Das Apostolicum* (1932).

πιστεύω

    εἰς θεὸν πατέρα παντοκράτορα

καί

    εἰς Χριστὸν Ἰησοῦν
    (a) υἱὸν αὐτοῦ τὸν μονογενῆ
    (b) τὸν κύριον ἡμῶν
        (α) τὸν γεννηθέντα ἐκ πνεύματος ἁγίου καὶ Μαρίας τῆς παρθένου,
        (β) τὸν ἐπὶ Ποντίου Πιλάτου σταυρωθέντα καὶ ταφέντα . . .

καί

    εἰς πνεῦμα ἅγιον,
    ἁγίαν ἐκκλησίαν,
    ἄφεσιν ἁμαρτιῶν,
    σαρκὸς ἀνάστασιν.

A quite different type of formula is developed in the Deutero-Paulines.[1] The regular outline is: once salvation was hidden, now it has been revealed. II Tim. 1.9f.: . . . κατὰ ἰδίαν πρόθεσιν καὶ χάριν, τὴν δοθεῖσαν ἡμῖν ἐν Χριστῷ Ἰησοῦ πρὸ χρόνων αἰωνίων, φανερωθεῖσαν δὲ νῦν διὰ τῆς ἐπιφανείας τοῦ σωτῆρος ἡμῶν Χριστῷ Ἰησοῦ . . .

This framework is already hinted at in Paul (I Cor. 2.7ff.), but it is first developed in the Deutero-Paulines: Col. 1.26f.; Eph. 3.4f., 9f.; II Tim. 1.9f.; Titus 1.2f.; the non-Pauline closing doxology Rom. 16.25–27.[2] This type of formula introduces not only the appearing of the revealer but also the salvation brought through him, and also explicitly the permanent presentation of the historical revelation through the proclamation. It is thus itself part of the saving event, a communication of grace revealed. This type of soteriology contains no apocalyptic statements about the future. It does not look forward to a parousia. It merely makes the existential statement that hope of eternal life is revealed, brought to light. The taking of the preaching into the creed is a defence against gnosticism; the world-situation is determined, not by gnostic inwardness, but by the proclamation. And in so far as salvation is revealed to the church, gnostic individualism is rejected.

II   Preaching

No primitive Christian preaching has been transmitted to us.[3] But the gist of the preaching is to be found in the epistles, from which types and patterns can still be reconstructed:

(a) Promise of salvation (creed) – paraenesis. This pattern, re-

---

[1] N. A. Dahl, *Formgeschichtliche Beobachtungen zur Christusverkündigung in der Gemeindepredigt*, BZNW 21 (1954), pp. 3–9; D. Lührmann, *Das Offenbarungsverständnis bei Paulus und in paulinischen Gemeinden*, WMANT 16 (1965), pp. 124–33.

[2] E. Kamlah, *Traditionsgeschichtliche Untersuchungen zur Schlussdoxologie des Römerbriefes*, Diss. Tübingen, 1955.

[3] The oldest is II Clement.

cognizable in Romans, Galatians, Colossians and Ephesians, depicts the primacy of the saving event (of the gospel); this is actualized in ethics.

(b) The connection with scripture appears in surveys of the history of the people of God which end with a didactic conclusion: Acts 7; 13.1ff.; Heb. 11; cf. I Clement.

(c) The newness of Christian existence in contrast to the past is depicted in the pattern 'once – now'; once Gentiles in blasphemy and darkness, now enlightened (Rom. 7.5; Gal. 4.3ff.). Paganism is not described neutrally, but is evaluated exclusively from the perspective of what is new.

When it is said, for example, that the Gentiles do not know God, it does not mean that they have no belief in God, but that they do not know the 'true' God. The ideas and expressions of Hellenistic-Jewish polemic literature are used. Cf. Wisdom: idols have no power, therefore idolatry is 'vain'. They are φύσει μὴ ὄντες θεοί (Gal. 4.8; cf. I Cor. 8.1–6). People speak of the ἄγνοια or πλάνη of paganism, and positively of the 'knowledge' of the true God. The knowledge of God includes the acknowledgement of him in practice. Cf. Wisdom 13–15: false views of God end in blasphemy.

This connection between knowing and acknowledging, indicative and imperative, is presupposed by Paul in Rom. 1.18ff.: blasphemy is the consequence of a primal sin, the confusing of creator and creature. Christians must therefore, on the basis of knowledge, no longer walk like the Gentiles (Eph. 4.17). Vices can be enumerated in the form of a catalogue (see below).

The 'sermons' in the Acts of the Apostles are neither sermons which were really given nor extracts from them, but purely literary creations from the hand of Luke. Dibelius has rightly established this. Nevertheless, he believes that here Luke used the church-preaching of his time as a model, so that it can still to some extent be reconstructed from Acts. The pattern of the Acts speeches is not, however, homiletic, but purely literary.[1]

III Paraenesis

R. Völkl, *Christ und Welt nach dem NT* (1961); R. Schnackenburg, *The Moral Teaching of the NT* (1965).

The early church was dominated by the expectation of the end of the world. What does that mean for the pattern of its life? Ascesis, seclusion from the world, indifference?

[1] Following U. Wilckens, *Die Missionsreden der Apostelgeschichte*, WMANT 5 (1961).

One could interpret the primitive Christian communism in the sharing of goods in this sense. But in reality this is an ideal picture which is meant to show Christian fellowship as a fellowship of love. It is in no way the realization of a programme in principle. That no ascetic principle has been developed is clear from three areas: (a) food: fasting is not ascesis, but is determined by ritual. True, ascetic tendencies emerge here and there, but they are rejected, for the earth is the Lord's and all that is in it (I Cor. 10.26; cf. Rom. 14.14, 20; I Tim. 4.3f.); (b) sexual ascesis: Paul approves of it in view of the fact that this is the last age of the world, and of the dangers attached to it. But he does not make any law (I Cor. 7); (c) possessions: riches are not in themselves evil, but they are dangerous. This danger cannot be escaped by legal regulations (in the style of Qumran), but only through the practice of love, which becomes possible in community.

The Motives of Ethics

Of course, ethical appeal can be grounded in eschatology: 'The Lord is at hand' (Phil. 4.5; cf. Rom. 13.11). The call to be ready, to watch, to be sober, is also eschatological (Mark 13.35–37). But primitive Christian ethics are no 'interim ethics'. They are not thought of as a regulation only for the end-time. True, there are instructions about conduct in the last evil days (I Cor. 7: it is better not to marry). But the expectation of the end is not a principle from which all or even most ethical regulations can be derived. There is rather the rule: God does not will anything that he has not always willed, in other words, that he has laid down in the commandments.

There are references to the will of God in Rom. 12.1f., and to the example of God (who makes his sun rise over good and evil alike) in Matt. 5.45.

The content of ethics is thus the same as in Judaism, as it is to be found in the Old Testament and particularly in the Wisdom literature. The appeal is strengthened by the reference to judgment (Matt. 25.31ff.) and reward (Luke 6.32ff.). Further motives are discipleship and the imitation of Jesus.

Neither means the ideal of the imitation of Jesus as the imitation of his earthly way of life, but obedience towards the commandments in faith in him. Discipleship and imitation are orientated to the saving work, and especially to the lowliness of Jesus (Mark 10.43ff.).[1]

These motives are an influence in the collecting of the words of Jesus and setting them out in the form of catechisms (Mark 9.33–50; Sermon on the Mount; Sermon on the Plain; 'Q' source).

Paraenesis is associated with baptism. Baptism communicates

[1] A. Schulz, *Nachfolgen und Nachahmen* (1962); H. D. Betz, *Nachfolge in Nachahmung Jesu Christi im NT* (1967).

strength for the new life. In paraenesis, the new life is depicted for the person being baptized. The remark about putting off the old and putting on the new man is a reference to baptism (Col. 3.5, 9f.; Eph. 4.22–24). The baptized are 'the saints'. Now they must live in a manner appropriate to their saintliness (I Thess. 4.1f.).

Forms of ethical instruction

The tradition of the words of Jesus has the utmost historical significance. In the early period, however, it reached only a limited part of the church. In Paul's circle and the Hellenistic church which is illuminated from his letters, other forms are dominant, which essentially derive from the Hellenistic synagogue. This is in turn influenced by the form of Greek ethics. Sometimes there is an obvious synthesis. Judaism has its broad and ancient tradition of wisdom sayings (Proverbs; Ecclesiasticus). Hellenism, too, knows collections of sentences (one Christianized collection is the sentences of Sextus). Thus there develops as a form of ethical instruction the loose arrangement of short sentences on different ethical problems.

One example is Rom. 12.3ff.[1] It is an important point of method to note that no logical sequence of thought can be constructed in such passages. The arrangement of sentences is to some extent arbitrary. However, we must ask whether some leading idea cannot be recognized in the background.

Two special typical forms are the catalogues of virtues and vices and the house-rules.[2] The rule pattern points to a Greek origin. There are different types of ethical rules: patterns for rulers, teaching on professional duties and general catalogues of virtues and vices, such as were developed above all by the Stoa.[3]

The antithetical account of virtues and vices is produced as a result of the subject-matter itself. The Stoa knows no psychological gradations, but only the absolute definitions of virtue or vice. There is therefore no need for a dualistic world-view as a presupposition for this antithesis. The reverse is rather true, that such tables are naturally suitable for incorporation into a dualistic world-view. Judaism takes this form of presentation from the Stoa, but the strictness of the form

---

[1] For this form, see M. Dibelius, *Jakobusbrief*, Meyer Kommentar XV (1964[11]); id., *ThR* NF 3 (1931), pp. 212ff.

[2] M. Dibelius/H. Conzelmann, in HNT, Excursus on I Tim. 3.1; A. Vögtle, *Die Tugend- und Lasterkataloge in NT*, NTA XVI (4./5), 1936; S. Wibbing, *Die Tugend- und Lasterkataloge im NT*, BZNW 25 (1959); E. Kamlah, *Die Form der katalogischen Paränese im NT*, WUNT 7 (1964).

[3] Vögtle, pp. 56ff.; Kamlah, pp. 139ff.

is relaxed. In Judaism, the enumeration follows another pattern. The justification of ethics is no longer philosophical, nor is it gained from a picture of the world and man worked out by philosophy. The presupposition is no longer autonomy, but God's commandment. As the basic philosophical system thus becomes insignificant, the form breaks up.

In exegetical terms, the recognition of the presence of a fixed stylistic form means that the catalogues are not to be evaluated historically as a realistic picture of real circumstances. Paul does not compile a table of vices like I Cor. 6.9f. because the prospect presented by the port of Corinth occasioned him to, however much he might have found illustrative material there. Rather, he uses the Jewish 'Gentile-model'. The un-Pauline phraseology ('inherit the kingdom of God') shows that this had already been used by Christians before Paul. True, Paul continues 'such were some of you'. Nevertheless, we may not draw conclusions from this about the past of individual members of the Corinthian community. Paul is rather saying: you were entangled in this world, you yourselves were part of this world.

The catalogues are not an expression of the personal views of individual writers, either. Of course, they correspond to the moral views of these writers, but they are not constructed by them, but simply taken over. There is a certain stereotyped basic material.[1]

There is no particular 'Christian' significance in the individual concepts. No new morality is developed here; the teaching is about what is moral. There is, in fact, no doubt about what morality is; according to Rom. 2, the Gentiles know this as well as the Jews, for all men have a conscience.

A characteristic example is Phil. 4.8; 'Finally, brethren, whatever is true, whatever is honourable, whatever is lovely, whatever is gracious, if there is any excellence, if there is anything worthy of praise, think about these things.' None of these terms is explained to the (Gentile-Christian) reader. It is wrong to look for a special Christian content in them. The significant thing is that these are generally current moral values.

The Christian element is found elsewhere: in the context, there is a summons to joy in the Lord and it is stressed that the Lord is near. The place in which such paraenesis is given is also to be taken into account: it is the community. There these demands become clear as rules of conduct among the brethren.

[1] Wibbing, pp. 87f. E.g.: πορνεία 8 times, μοιχεία 3, ἀκαθαρσία 5, ἀσέλγεια 6, ἔρις 5, βλασφημία 6, πλεονεξία 6.

The freedom of faith is represented as a critical mean between worldliness and withdrawal from the world. Eschatological neutrality towards the world does not mean indifference, but freedom to love. The narrow divide between happiness and ascesis, between Christian justification of the world and practised withdrawal from it, is maintained.

What is true of the catalogues is also true of the 'house-rules'.[1] Their form, too, is of Hellenistic origin. They were taken over somewhat later than the catalogues, in Colossians, Ephesians and I Peter; they are altered in the Pastorals; Didache 4.9–11; Barnabas 19.5–7; I Clement 1.3; 21.6–9. For the Pastorals, cf. Polycarp, Phil. 4.2–6.3. It is instructive to note the increasing permeation of specifically Christian ideas which is shown, for example, by a comparison of Ephesians and Colossians. This does not contradict the statement that the morality is that generally common to social life. For of course there are also specifically Christian rules, as the community exists as a special organization with a particular form of life. This does not, however, create a special Christian ethic: the concepts have no new Christian content; the precepts themselves have no saving significance. This has already been given in the presupposition of this ethic, in kerygma and faith.

[1] D. Schroeder, *Die Haustafeln im NT*, Diss. Hamburg, 1959.

PART TWO

THE SYNOPTIC KERYGMA

12 · THE PROBLEM OF TRADITION

See the works on form criticism: M. Dibelius, *From Tradition to Gospel* (1934; in later editions of the German original, *Die Formgeschichte des Evangeliums*, e.g. 1966⁵, there is a useful supplement by G. Iber); R. Bultmann, *The History of the Synoptic Tradition* (1968²). Cf. also R. H. Lightfoot, *History and Interpretation in the Gospels* (1935).

The eucharistic texts (see 7 IV 4) raised the question: in what way does the kerygma go back to the historical Jesus?[1]

It was argued earlier that the report of the historical career of Jesus was outlined in the kerygma; cf. Acts 2.22: Jesus is ἀνὴρ ἀποδεδειγμένος ἀπὸ τοῦ θεοῦ εἰς ὑμᾶς δυνάμεσι καὶ τέρασι καὶ σημείοις. The question with which we are concerned is therefore that of the eye-witnesses of the events and of the further tradition up to the time of the composition of the gospels. The stages in the process of tradition can still be recognized in the prologue to the gospel of Luke: (*a*) eye-witnesses; (*b*) written accounts, on which Luke can already look back. He himself is therefore in third or even fourth place in the chain of tradition.

Form criticism shows that at the beginning, only individual narratives and words were handed down. Each piece of tradition has independent christological significance: it sets out to establish or explain belief in Jesus. Jesus is represented as a miracle-worker in whom divine power is made manifest, in such a way that his outward appearance is not only that of a figure of power but also of the 'saviour' who drives out demons, sicknesses, sin (Acts 10.38). Furthermore, Jesus is the teacher – in conversations, parables, logia. At the next stage of the tradition, the first collections can be seen, above all the source Q. True, Q predominantly contains sayings of Jesus (there is still no kerygma of the passion); nevertheless, the significance of the whole collection is a christological one.[2]

[1] Literature: R. Bultmann, 'The Primitive Christian Kerygma and the Historical Jesus' in: Carl E. Braaten and Roy A. Harrisville (eds.), *The Historical Jesus and the Kerygmatic Christ* (1964); H. Ristow and K. Matthiae (eds.), *Der historische Jesus und der kerygmatische Christus* (1960).

[2] This is shown by H. E. Tödt, *The Son of Man in the Synoptic Tradition* (1965).

The gospel as a literary form was created by Mark.[1] Also at this stage, a christological significance in the overall presentation of the book appears. Mark's theological achievement lies in the way in which he makes explicit a recognition that had hitherto still been latent: the total tradition may be extremely varied in form, but there is an over-riding material unity: in all its forms (confession of faith, narrative about Jesus, words of Jesus) it depicts the Christ of faith. Thus despite the extreme simplicity of its literary means, Mark's book is a landmark in the history of theology.

According to Bultmann's concept of theology, one cannot speak of theology as early as the synoptic gospels. Theology only comes with the conceptual elaboration of the kerygma by Paul and John. But this approach does not do justice to the historical facts. The kerygma is expounded not only by a conceptual exposition but also through historical narration. Moreover, each of the synoptists puts forward a developed overall theological conception. Bultmann is still dominated by the original perspective of form criticism, which primarily investigated the individual pieces of tradition and their significance. There is truth in this approach, but it needs to be supplemented by the interpretation of each gospel as a whole.

The task of exegesis is threefold:

1. Interpretation of the gospels in their present form;
2. Interpretation of the tradition which underlies them;
3. Reconstruction of the proclamation of Jesus.

It is possible to follow the same method as Bultmann. He offers the result of his reconstruction in a short space, and refers to his *History of the Synoptic Tradition* for the analyses that underlie it. It is, however, also possible to depict the synoptic kerygma as a product of the history of the tradition and then to ask in particular instances what the authentic basic material is. We choose the second approach, because it offers a better view of the material.

The arrangement follows from the material itself. There are three distinct themes which can be presented in relative independence: eschatology, ethics and christology. The basis common to them all is the idea of God.

LITERATURE ABOUT JESUS

H. Conzelmann, 'Jesus Christus', *RGG*[3] III (1959), 619–53 (further literature there); A. Vögtle, 'Jesus Christus', *LThK*[2] V (1960), cols. 922–32; A. Schweitzer, *The Quest of the Historical Jesus* (1910;1954[3]). Outside form criticism: R. Otto, *The Kingdom of God and the Son of Man* (1938); R. Bultmann, *Jesus and the Word* (1958); M. Dibelius, *Jesus* (1963[2]); E. Käsemann, 'The Problem of the Historical

---

[1] H. Conzelmann, 'Gegenwart und Zukunft in der synoptischen Tradition', *ZThK* 54 (1957), p. 293.

Jesus', in: *Essays on New Testament Themes*, SBT 41 (1964), pp. 15–47; G. Born-kamm, *Jesus of Nazareth* (1960); E. Fuchs, 'The Quest of the Historical Jesus', in: *Studies of the Historical Jesus*, SBT 42 (1964), pp. 11–31; G. Ebeling, 'Jesus and Faith', in: *Word and Faith* (1963), pp. 201–46; id., 'The Question of the Historical Jesus and the Problem of Christology', *Word and Faith*, pp. 288–304; H. Braun, 'Der Sinn der neutestamentlichen Christologie', *ZThK* 54 (1957), pp. 341–77 (=*Gesammelte Studien zum NT*, pp. 243–82); J. M. Robinson, *A New Quest of the Historical Jesus*, SBT 25 (1959); R. Bultmann, 'The Primitive Christian Kerygma and the Historical Jesus', in: Carl E. Braaten and Roy A. Harrisville (eds.), *The Historical Jesus and the Kerygmatic Christ* (1964), pp. 15–42; W. G. Kümmel, *Promise and Fulfilment*, SBT 23 (1957); id., *Heilsgeschehen und Geschichte* (1965), *passim*; W. Grundmann, *Die Geschichte Jesu Christi* (1957); J. Jeremias, *The Problem of the Historical Jesus*, Facet Books, Biblical Series 13 (1964); W. Manson, *Jesus the Messiah* (1943); T. W. Manson, *The Servant Messiah* (1953); X. Léon-Dufour, *The Gospels and the Jesus of History* (1968); N. Perrin, *Rediscovering the Teaching of Jesus* (1967); J. Reumann, *Jesus in the Church's Gospels* (1968). See also H. Ristow and K. Matthiae (eds.), *Der historische Jesus und der kerygmatische Christus* (1960); on the Catholic side: K. Schubert (ed.), *Der historische Jesus und der Christus unseres Glaubens* (1962).

13 · THE IDEA OF GOD

I Jesus' Belief in God

It is not Jesus' intention to teach a new idea of God, but to make it clearer who the God of Israel, the creator, ruler of the world, law-giver, is – not in his metaphysical aseity (there is no question of that), but in his significance for the individual.

Of course, Jesus also speaks of the attributes of God: God is good, indeed he is the only one to whom the title 'good' can be applied (Mark 10.18). But even that is a definition of his relationship to the world.

Only in a qualified sense can one describe Jesus' idea of God as eschatological. The concept of the kingdom of God is eschatological. But the idea of God is not exhausted in statements about the coming kingdom of God. Alongside it stand statements about God's present rule which do not look for an imminent end of the world. The reasons Jesus gives for his demand, 'Take no thought for the morrow', are not eschatological: 'for soon the evil world will be at an end'; in justifica-tion, he refers to God as the Father: 'for he cares for you'. God makes his sun rise on good and bad alike. In sayings like this, the world is not seen as hastening towards its end, but simply as creation, as the sphere of the rule and providence of God.

Bultmann notes the tension between the two sets of statements, the cosmological and the eschatological, in formulating the theme of Jesus' doctrine of God: the God who is far and near. But he makes too close a connection between general considerations about the world, in the style of 'Take no thought . . .', and eschatology. The exegetical problem consists primarily in the fact that these two sets of statements are *not* linked. In that case, of course, we must ask whether there are material reasons for the juxtaposition.

The reason for the juxtaposition of the two sets of expressions is a historical one. Jesus begins from the teaching of Judaism. He often uses it as a starting point. First, he takes up the Old Testament, Jewish doctrine of God, the idea of God as creator and ruler. On another occasion, he begins with the teaching of the law, and yet elsewhere with the Jewish view of the last things. He is not concerned to bring the individual doctrines into a system, but each time takes his thought to the point where its actual significance for the present can be recognized. His aim is to bring about an immediate, present confrontation between man and God.

God is the Father. This teaching is not new. But the way in which it is presented is new. God is the creator. Here, however, there is no derivation of the metaphysical statement that there 'is a God' from a theoretical observation of the world. There is no question of that. Because a man acknowledges God as the creator, he can understand the world.

Understanding does not take place theoretically, in the Greek style, as an elucidation of the context of being. There is no causal explanation of the world, no concept of nature. The world is not regarded as something to hand. It is world, in that man acts in it, towards it. The world is disclosed when a man perceives the word of God and understands the world as God's world. In so doing, he understands himself and realizes this knowledge in the ascent from care to freedom.

The creator is at the same time the lawgiver and thus the judge. Jesus does not replace the picture of the righteous God with that of the kindly one. He does not exclude the idea of judgment.

II   The Designations of God in the Synoptic Gospels

H. Weinel, *Biblische Theologie des NT* (1928[4]), pp. 122ff.

(ὁ) θεός occurs most frequently.[1] There is no reluctance to use the

[1] For the use of the article see Blass-Debrunner-Funk, *A Greek Grammar of the New Testament and other Early Christian Literature* (1961), §254, 1.

word 'God', as there is in Judaism. There is only one instance of θεός being replaced by a periphrasis in Jewish style: Matthew prefers to say ἡ βασιλεία τῶν οὐρανῶν instead of 'kingdom of God'.

This periphrasis occurs elsewhere only in Mark 11.30: was the baptism of John from heaven or from men?

The title 'the most High' is rarer (Mark 5.7 par. Luke 8.28; Luke 1.32, 35, 76; 6.35).

In view of the frequent mention of God's βασιλεία, it is striking that God is only rarely designated βασιλεύς. His βασιλεία and his being βασιλεύς[1] are not linked together conceptually.

The reason for this is that Jesus and primitive Christianity did not derive the expression βασιλεία τοῦ θεοῦ from God's title 'king', but found it already in existence as a stereotyped phrase, filled with a specifically eschatological meaning. The title 'king', on the other hand, designates God's continuing rule. Cf. the doxologies: τῷ δὲ βασιλεῖ τῶν αἰώνων, ἀφθάρτῳ ἀοράτῳ μόνῳ θεῷ, τιμὴ καὶ δόξα εἰς τοὺς αἰῶνας τῶν αἰώνων (I Tim. 1.17; similarly I Tim. 6.15f.).

βασιλεύς occurs in Matt. 5.35; cf. 18.23.[2] κύριος occurs in the synoptic gospels as a designation of God[3] only in quotations and in ceremonial phrases (Luke 10.21 par. Matt. 11.25).

The evidence for the title 'Father' is important, and in some respects striking.

The word contains elements of power and protection. God is called 'Father' in the Old Testament in respect of the chosen people (Deut. 14.1). The suppliant calls upon him as 'Father' (Ps. 89.27). Philo uses the title in both a cosmological and a genealogical sense. The way from collective to individual piety is shown by passages like Wisdom 2.16; 14.3; Ecclus. 23.1; Tobit 13.4; III Macc. 5.7. The mode of expression:[4] the expression 'Father in Heaven' (Matthew; Mark 11.25) occurs in the Palestinian synagogue after the end of the first century AD. It is absent from apocalyptic and the pseudepigrapha.

If one considers the synoptic evidence without taking account of the question of authenticity, the following themes appear: Matt. 23.9: 'Call no man your father on earth, for you have one Father, who is in heaven.' 'Father' thus describes the being of God so exactly that the title is really his due alone. Matt. 6.25ff.: 'Do not be anxious . . . your heavenly Father knows that you need all these things.' Matt. 7.7–11 par. Luke 11.9–13: the Father gives good things to those who

[1] אל is frequent at Qumran.
[2] On the other hand, the saying in Matt. 25.40 is only used as a metaphor.
[3] On the question of the LXX evidence, see 10 IV above.
[4] Cf. Bill I 392ff.

ask him. And: 'Fear not, little flock, for it is your Father's good pleasure to give you the kingdom' (Luke 12.32).

There is a widespread view that the really distinguishing feature in Jesus' idea of God is his use of the title 'Father' for God: on the one hand, Jesus uses this title to express his own special consciousness of mission (as 'the Son'); on the other, he shows men that they are children of God and may regard God as their Father.

Thus whenever the designation 'Father' for God appears, we must always ask whether it means the general Fatherhood of God ('sons of your Father who is in heaven': Matt. 5.45) or the specific designation of God as the Father of Jesus.

This distinction is expressed in the terminology: the Jesus of the synoptic gospels says 'my Father' on the one hand and 'your Father' on the other. But he never takes himself and his disciples together and speaks of 'our Father'.

Even the 'our Father' at the beginning of the Lord's Prayer is no exception. Luke 11.2 has a simple πάτερ. In Matthew, Jesus does not include himself with the disciples, but gives them the instruction that they are to speak to God in the way that he shows them.

Now does this linguistic usage go back to Jesus himself?

SURVEY[1]

A number of passages can be excluded on the basis of a comparison of the synoptic gospels. The word 'Father' occurs far less frequently in the ancient sources Q and Mark than in the latest stratum, the redaction of Matthew and Luke.

Cf. Mark 3.35: 'Whoever does the will of God', with Matt. 12.50: 'Whoever does the will of my Father'. Matt. 7.21; 20.23; 26.29, 42 (repetition of v. 38 par. Mark 14.36) are Matthaean additions.

(a) The Father

1. Mark has only one passage, 13.32 par. Matt. 24.36: 'But of that day or that hour no one knows, not even the angels in heaven, nor the Son, but only the Father.' The absolute use of 'the Son' is a mark of the language of the community.[2] It follows that the phrase 'the

---

[1] H. Braun, Spätjüdisch-häretische und frühchristliche Radikalismus II, BHTh 24 (1957), pp. 127f.; J. Jeremias, 'Abba', in: The Prayers of Jesus, SBT II 6 (1967), pp. 29ff.

[2] W. G. Kümmel, Promise and Fulfilment, SBT 23 (1957), pp. 42f.

Father' at this point is also a formulation by the community.

2. Similarly, there is only one passage in Q: Matt. 11.27 par. Luke 10.22: 'No one knows the Son except the Father'. The same verdict must be given here. The whole passage is a Hellenistic construction.[1]

3. There is no absolute use of 'Father' in the Lucan special material.

4. In the Matthaean special material, it occurs only at 28.19, in the triadic baptismal formulation, a construction by the community.

5. There remains Luke 9.26: the Son of Man (!) is coming ἐν τῇ δόξῃ αὐτοῦ καὶ τοῦ πατρός. This is a Lucan alteration of Mark 8.38: ἐν τῇ δόξῃ τοῦ πατρὸς αὐτοῦ.

Even if this saying is taken to be genuine, the problem of the eschatological Son of Man sayings remains: does Jesus regard himself as the coming Son of Man (see 16 IV below)?

(b) My Father

In the prayer in Gethsemane, where Jesus addresses God (i.e. not as in Matt. 6.9ff., where he is speaking to a man), he says: ἀββὰ ὁ πατήρ (Mark 14.36). This is a community construction: no one could have heard the prayer.

The word ἀββά has provoked a special discussion.[2] There is no ancient rabbinic evidence for this form of address to God. The form ἀββά is a vocative,[3] and may be used familiarly: 'Daddy'. Such an address to God, it is argued, can only go back to Jesus himself. It is a new way of speaking with God. It can be explained from Jesus' special awareness of himself as Son. But, in the first place, the word need not have had a connotation of familiarity. Secondly, even if it were certain that Jesus spoke in this way, the main question is whether he distinguished himself from his disciples with this form of address, and kept it to himself in order to show his special consciousness of being Son. The answer is clear: two passages in Paul show that ἀββά is the word generally used by the community in prayer: Gal. 4.6; Rom. 8.15. If the form of address goes back to Jesus himself, then it can be shown that he did not keep it to himself.

Furthermore, it is not the case that the Jews could not speak in this way to God.

[1] R. Bultmann, History of the Synoptic Tradition (1968²), pp. 166f., 174; M. Dibelius, From Tradition to Gospel, pp. 245, 279ff.
[2] G. Schrenk, πατήρ, TWNT V 981ff.; Jeremias, 'Abba', pp. 29ff.
[3] Not emphatic: see TWNT V 984 against TWNT I 4, line 26 and Bill. II 49f.; J. Jeremias, loc. cit.

Rabbis do in fact say 'my Father'. There is no essential difference between that and ἀββά. And the absolute use of πάτερ is also to be found in III Macc. 6.3, 8.

Are there passages in which Jesus says 'my Father' in the presence of men?

1. Mark: no instance.

2. Q: one passage, the Hellenistic construction Matt. 11.25–27 par. Luke 10.21f., mentioned above. Matt. 10.33: 'Who ever denies me before men, I also will deny before my Father who is in heaven', also comes from Q. In the (original) parallel version, Luke 12.9, we find: 'before the angels of God'. – The evidence in the ancient sources for the words 'my Father' used in conversation with a man is therefore negative.

3. Luke 22.29: 'As my Father appointed a kingdom for me . . .' This is a late construction within the Lucan dialogue at the Last Supper. Luke 24.49, a saying by the Risen Lord, is also late.

4. Matt. 16.17; 26.53 are two secondary sayings, one to Peter, the other to an unnamed disciple. In all the other passages in Matthew, the phrase probably goes back to his redactional work: 15.13; 18.10, 19, 35; 25.34.

(c) *Your Father*

1. Mark: one passage, 11.25 par. Matt. 6.14f. From the point of view of tradition, this is a saying concerned with the practice of the community.[1]

2. Q: Matt. 5.48 par. Luke 6.36: 'You, therefore, must be perfect (merciful) as your Father'. This passage may be primary. Matt. 6.32 par. Luke 12.30: 'Your Father knows that you need them all'. This saying may also be primary.

Matthew and Luke diverge in a number of Q passages. Here the verdict is, of course, quite uncertain. Cf. Matt. 7.11 with Luke 11.13; Matt. 6.26; 10.29 with Luke 12.24, 6; Matt. 5.45 with Luke 6.35; Matt. 10.20 with Luke 12.12; Matt. 18.14 with Luke 15.7.

3. Luke 12.32 is a typical community-saying.[2]

4. Matthew: 5.16 is perhaps a construction by the evangelist; 6.1 is redactional; 6.8 is an anticipatory doublet of 6.32 (see above); 23.9 ('you have one Father, who is in heaven') may be genuine.[3]

[1] R. Bultmann, *History of the Synoptic Tradition*, pp. 146f.
[2] H. Braun, *Radikalismus* II, p. 102, n. 1.
[3] R. Bultmann, *History of the Synoptic Tradition*, pp. 144f.

'Your (singular) Father' also occurs in Matthew (6.4, 6, 18); 'their Father' in the redactional interpretation of the parable of the wheat and the tares (13.43).

Result

There is no doubt that Jesus designated God as 'Father'. But the basic difference between 'my Father' and 'your Father' is a matter of the christological style of the community. A further tendency appears, which is typical of the church: in the ancient sources, Jesus says 'your Father' to all his hearers. That is, in preaching to them he declares that they are the children of God. In the tradition, however, there is a tendency to limit this 'your Father' to the disciples. This indicates the perspective of the church: it makes it clear that not simply anyone is a child of God, but that being a child of God includes discipleship and faith.

Of course, Jesus does not also mean that man is God's child as it were by nature. He becomes a child of God by understanding that God treats us as his children; he becomes a child of God by accepting God's gift 'as a child', i.e. without reservations. The condition of being a child of God is thus simply trust in God. With the death of Jesus, the situation changes. It must now be made clear that it is impossible to have the word of Jesus, the promise of becoming a child of God, without taking up a particular standpoint towards Jesus himself – and that involves the church. The church is the place where Jesus is present as the one who is preached. This relationship between being a child of God and the church is legitimate as long as the church understands itself as the church of the word, and not as a saving institution, as an intermediate authority between God and man, with its own power to save.

Understanding of human existence stems from man's relationship to God. There is no theoretical doctrine of God's omnipotence, no doctrine of general determinacy. God's providence is demonstrated in the act: no sparrow falls from the rooftop against his will. This shows man that in the world he need have no fear. God's authority and human freedom are not balanced against each other. For a man to suppose that he had to guard his freedom over against God would be to misunderstand him. By making himself care, he becomes free and reaches a position in which the world cannot harm him, and with it the privilege of turning directly to God. Jesus makes the way clear for unconstrained address towards God, without any other condition than is laid down in the relationship with God itself: when you pray, forgive.

In this living relationship with God, problems which Judaism could never settle, guilt and fate, theodicy, the origin of evil, are superseded. Evil is not explained, but unmasked. Jesus does not develop a concept of sin; Paul is the first to do that. But in hearing the demand of God, man is in the position of having to ask God for forgiveness. God does not justify his action. Man must not summon God to combat; otherwise he will provoke God's vengeance. But he can reach God at any time. God is no oracle, giving information in answer to general questions about the meaning of life, or of the world. Rather, this question of meaning is superseded in man's possibility of understanding himself as the child of God.

14 · THE KINGDOM OF GOD

See the literature mentioned before section 13. K. L. Schmidt, βασιλεία, TWNT I 579–92; E. Grässer, Das Problem der Parusieverzögerung in den synoptischen Evangelien und in der Apostelgeschichte, BZNW 22 (1960²); P. Vielhauer, 'Gottesreich und Menschensohn in der Verkündigung Jesu', Festschrift für Günther Dehn (1957), pp. 51–79 (=Aufsätze zum NT, ThB 31 (1965), pp. 55–91); H. Conzelmann, 'Gegenwart und Zukunft in der synoptischen Tradition', ZThK 54 (1957), pp. 277–96; H. E. Tödt, The Son of Man in the Synoptic Tradition (1965); R. Schnackenburg, God's Rule and Kingdom (1963); E. Lohse, 'Die Gottesherrschaft in den Gleichnissen Jesu', EvTh 18 (1958), pp. 145–57; H. Schürmann, 'Das hermeneutische Hauptproblem der Verkündigung Jesu', in: Gott in Welt (Festschrift für Karl Rahner) I (1964), pp. 579–607; S. Aalen, '"Reign" and "House" in the Kingdom of God in the Gospels', NTS 8 (1961/2), pp. 215–40. Cf. the articles 'Eschatologie', 'Jesus Christus', 'Reich Gottes', in RGG³.

I Problems

Is the kingdom of God future, or is it already present? And if it is already present, in what way is this so?

Widely differing answers have been given to these questions. The gospels contain some sayings which suggest that the kingdom is still to come (cf. the petition in the Lord's Prayer, 'Thy kingdom come'), and others which suggest that it is already here. The usual explanation is that the relationship between the two sets of expressions is a 'both – and'.[1] But in that case how did Jesus regard the juxtaposition of present and future?

[1] W. G. Kümmel, Promise and Fulfilment, pp. 141ff.

Is it that the kingdom of God must still develop to its full extent, like the seed, the grain of mustard? Or that it is already present in the person of Jesus and will dawn openly in the future? But what does 'present in the person of Jesus' mean? Karl Ludwig Schmidt (*TWNT* I 590f.) takes up the word αὐτοβασιλεία, coined by Origen of Jesus: Jesus himself is the kingdom in his person. If that is to mean anything it can only be in a spiritual sense (Origen!).

Or does one group of sayings come from Jesus himself and the other from the community? But which comes from which? In what direction was the development? Was Jesus' preaching more apocalyptic and that of the community more spiritual – or *vice versa*?

The most important hypotheses are:

1. Jesus spoke only of the kingdom in the future: it is near, but still not present. In that case, the sayings which assert that it is here are to be regarded as constructions of the community.

Thus A. Schweitzer, R. Bultmann. True, both recognize eschatology as the means of Jesus' teaching. But they evaluate this position in completely different ways. Schweitzer wants to exclude the eschatology as a view of the world determined by the environment in which Jesus lived: Bultmann wants to interpret it, asking, What understanding of God and the world is expressed here? The two also understand the relationship between the kingdom of God and the person of Jesus quite differently. According to Schweitzer, Jesus hopes that he will be transformed into the Son of Man. Bultmann argues that Jesus understands himself to be the sign of the imminent kingdom of God. He regards his call as God's last call before the dawn of the kingdom. He expects the Son of Man as a figure distinct from himself, who will come down from heaven.

2. Jesus teaches that the kingdom of God is already present in his person.[1] According to C. H. Dodd, ἤγγικεν means 'has come' ('realized eschatology', changed by J. Jeremias to 'eschatology in process of realization'). That the kingdom is coming in the future is a secondary idea which only arose in the community.

What criteria are there? There is the methodological principle: we cannot determine with certainty that Jesus uttered this or that saying. In particular instances it can be demonstrated with considerable certainty that we have a community construction. Nevertheless, we cannot deny that there is a firm basis of authentic tradition. The majority of the parables belong here. In form and content they cannot be derived either from Judaism or from the post-Easter community. They reflect a specific understanding of the situation before Easter. Consequently, sayings which announce the nearness of the kingdom

[1] C. H. Dodd, *The Parables of the Kingdom* (1936); T. W. Manson, *The Servant Messiah* (1953).

and its presence in a situation which can only be dated before Easter are also authentic. The expression 'kingdom of God' is not defined. Jesus takes it over from Judaism, but determines its meaning in an entirely new way by his actualization of the message of the kingdom. One rule of thumb can be made: in Judaism, the expression means the act of God's rule: with Jesus, it means God's kingdom.[1]

II Terminology

The two expressions 'kingdom of God' and 'kingdom of heaven' are synonymous.

The latter occurs almost exclusively in Matthew. 'Heaven' is simply a periphrasis of the divine name in Jewish style; it is secondary, cf. Mark, Q.

βασιλεία also occurs on its own.

This is without precedent in Judaism. There, מַלְכוּת by itself means the Roman Empire (Bill. I 183).

History of the Concept

In the Old Testament, the phrase מֶלֶךְ יהוה plays a special role (royal psalms).

The rabbis avoid using sentences with God as subject, just as they avoid the divine name. They therefore no longer say מֶלֶךְ יהוה, but speak of his מַלְכוּת.[2] This expression does not mean God's kingdom, but the fact that God reigns. It is simply an abstract form of the sentence 'God is king', and should be translated 'rule of God'. There are two significant elements.

1. God's rule is understood eschatologically, as something that is to come.

2. The individual has to come to a decision in the face of the kingdom of God. There is still an opportunity for this. But the time is limited. In this group of ideas, the people play no part; there is simply the individual, who is summoned to make a decision. The idea of God as king of Israel stands alongside this, but is not connected with it. Nor is there any link with the expectation of the Messiah.[3]

On the basis of the verbal significance of the expression, we can understand why it is rare in apocalyptic literature. Here the new aeon

---

[1] S. Aalen, *op. cit.*

[2] K. G. Kuhn, *TWNT* I 570ff.

[3] K. G. Kuhn, *TWNT* I 573; P. Vielhauer, *Aufsätze*, pp. 175ff.

of the Son of Man is expected. Only in the book of Daniel is there a connection between the two.[1]

The future world is described as 'kingdom' only in the following passages:

Dan. 2.44: στήσει ὁ θεὸς τοῦ οὐρανοῦ βασιλείαν ἄλλην, ἥτις ἔσται εἰς τοὺς αἰῶνας . . . There is no messianic figure.

Dan. 3.33: מַלְכוּתֵהּ מַלְכוּת עָלַם = 4.3 Θ: ἡ βασιλεία αὐτοῦ βασιλεία αἰώνιος.

Dan. 7.13f.: . . . καὶ ἰδοὺ ἐπὶ τῶν νεφελῶν τοῦ οὐρανοῦ ὡς υἱὸς ἀνθρώπου ἤρχετο . . . καὶ θη ἐδόαυτῷ ἐξουσία . . . καὶ ἡ ἐξουσία αὐτοῦ ἐξουσία αἰώνιος . . . καὶ ἡ βασιλεία αὐτοῦ.

Assumption of Moses 10.1: 'And then his kingdom shall appear throughout all his creation'.

Sibylline Oracles III 767: 'And then indeed he will raise up his kingdom for all ages'.

It is clear that the history of the concept is not very helpful. The most important element is its eschatological significance.

If the rule of God or the kingdom of God is said to be future, then a number of questions arise: is God without a sphere of rule in the present? What sort of a God could this be? Does the idea of the futurity of his reign not take us into the realm of mythical ideas of the arrival of a God? An answer can only be given if we go back to the further question of the existential significance of the idea of the kingdom of God in the teaching of Jesus and in the synoptic tradition. Of course, the meaning is not that God's rule is temporally suspended – cf. the uneschatological sayings about God's authority: without his will no sparrow falls to the earth (Matt. 10.29). Finally, 'kingdom of God' does not mean a metaphysical state which is open to analysis; it means that man has God before him, that God is not presented to him as an object, or even as an idea. The fact that God is coming does not exclude, but includes the fact that he is God now. This is thought out consistently to the end through the announcement of his coming. Men can be sure of his coming precisely because he is already the ruler. This meaning is already present in the pictures of the future drawn by the Old Testament prophets in their expectations: of the saviour king (Isaiah), the new covenant (Jeremiah), the restoration of temple and cult. The view common to these hopes is the faith that God is the one who brings salvation, that man is therefore radically directed towards him, and that *this* is the most hopeful thing of all. In the prophets, the expectation of salvation is bound up with the people of Israel. But the real point is that the hope is not grounded in Israel, but in God's saving act.

III The Material

One of the best-known passages, Mark 1.14f., can only be used with care. It is a thematic summary of the preaching of Jesus as Mark understands it: (a) announcement: πεπλήρωται ὁ καιρὸς καὶ ἤγγικεν ἡ

[1] See P. Vielhauer, *Aufsätze*, pp. 8off.; W. Bousset, *Die Religion des Judentums*, pp. 213ff.

βασιλεία τοῦ θεοῦ (b) summons: μετανοεῖτε καὶ πιστεύετε ἐν τῷ εὐαγγελίῳ. This formulation has its setting in the Hellenistic community, which makes Jesus himself the proclaimer of the christological kerygma of both 'gospel' and 'faith'. The announcement corresponds with the historical preaching of Jesus in saying that the kingdom of God is near. It also occurs in Mark 13.29 and in Q: Matt. 10.7 par. Luke 10.9 (mission speech).[1]

The kingdom 'comes' – it is not created. It is itself the subject of movement, not the culmination of our movement. We cannot bring it in, but must be ready for its dawning.

But how near is it?

The question cannot be answered from an analysis of the meaning of ἐγγύς/ ἐγγίζειν. It is, however, clear that Dodd's interpretation ('has come') goes too far.[2] ἐγγύς primarily means 'near in space' and then 'near in time'; ἐγγίζειν does not mean 'to come', but 'to approach' (Matt. 26.18, of the hour of death). ὁ κύριος ἐγγύς (Phil. 4.5) cannot mean 'is here'. Cf. Mark 13.29: ἐγγὺς ἐπὶ θύραις; Rev. 1.3; 22.10: ὁ καιρὸς ἐγγύς.

The kingdom is still not visibly present; it can and must be announced. But it is so near that it can be announced with certainty. It will be brought in by God himself. So men may pray, 'Thy kingdom come'. This hope is based on the fact that men cannot hinder the coming of the kingdom.

But can they hasten it? Yes, through prayer. There is apparently a contradiction: God alone acts, yet man can intervene and influence God. This is the apparent contradiction of prayer in general, which disappears in the act of prayer. For the confession of God as sole agent and the petition to him are a realization of the complex relationship between men and God, the Father.

The kingdom breaks in suddenly, like lightning, the flood, fire on Sodom and Gomorrah (Luke 17.20ff.). There can be no escape; it will be everywhere (Luke 17.37). The kingdom brings division. Everything will depend on the condition in which it finds a man. Judgment, which comes upon man either as wrath or salvation, is part of the idea of the kingdom.

So how near is the kingdom?[3] What is the relationship between the sayings in which it seems to be already present and those which

---

1 The church then says ὁ κύριος ἐγγύς (Phil. 4.5).
2 Cf. W. G. Kümmel, *Promise and Fulfilment*, pp. 19ff.
3 W. G. Kümmel, 'Die Naherwartung in der Verkündigung Jesu', *Zeit und Geschichte* (Bultmann Festschrift), pp. 31–46 (= *Heilsgeschehen und Geschichte*, pp. 457–470); O. Cullmann, *Salvation in History* (1967), pp. 193ff.

still presuppose a certain intermediate period before its arrival? If both are regarded as genuine (Kümmel), this evidence must be explained.

We must, however, examine the way in which the question is put: Jesus is not interested in the question of the interval of time in itself. If the expectation of the kingdom is understood radically, then ἤγγικεν does not represent a primarily neutral statement about the length or brevity of an interval of time, but a fact which determines human existence: man has no more time left for himself. He must respond to the kingdom in the present moment. It is still not there; otherwise the opportunity for this response, for repentance, would be past. The kingdom would no longer be preached. But it is so near that a man can no longer ask, 'For how long can I postpone repentance?' There is no more time. Now is the last moment for those who are addressed. For this reason, the question of time cannot be put in neutral terms. Jesus' perspective is not that of apocalyptic contemplation.

Thus the kingdom is still to come. On the other hand, we cannot simply say that it is not yet there; we must recognize the connection between the coming of the kingdom and the present: the signs of the kingdom are already visible.

Jesus' understanding of himself can be seen in this connection: 'Blessed are the eyes which see what you see' (Luke 10.23f.). 'Blessed are you poor, for yours is the kingdom of God' (Luke 6.20). The kingdom is not yet there – there are still the poor. But it is manifesting itself: not only are the poor promised a better future, but the present announcement transforms them into those who are blessed. So we have the rule of thumb: the kingdom is imminent, the signs are there. On the other hand, the present or apparently present sayings seem to tell against this. The following passages are involved:

1. The sayings which talk about 'entering into' the kingdom do not demonstrate the presence of the kingdom.[1] Mark 10.23–25: it is hard for the rich to enter the kingdom of God. Mark 10.15: anyone who does not receive it like a child will certainly not enter into it. These sayings are not meant to give any indication of the time of the arrival of the kingdom; they describe the conditions of accepting it. Cf. Mark 9.47: anyone who is not allowed in will be thrown into hell. Matt. 21.31: the publicans and sinners enter before you. The kingdom can be taken away (Matt. 21.43). A man can be unfit for the kingdom

[1] H. Windisch, 'Die Sprüche vom Eingehen in das Reich Gottes', *ZNW* 27 (1928), pp. 163–92; W. G. Kümmel, *Promise and Fulfilment*, pp. 52, 127.

of God (Luke 9.62). Mark 12.34: you are not far from the kingdom of God, i.e. you are fulfilling the conditions of acceptance. Luke 12.32: it pleased the Father to give you the kingdom – not as an inner possession, but as hope.

2. The saying about 'storming the kingdom', Matt. 11.12, is an obscure one: from the days of the Baptist until now, ἡ βασιλεία τῶν οὐρανῶν βιάζεται καὶ βιασταὶ ἁρπάζουσιν αὐτήν. We might conclude from this that the kingdom suffers violence, and so it must be present. But quite apart from the fact that the sense is obscure, we must ask whether Matthew has understood the words of the tradition properly. The parallel Luke 16.16 points in a different direction. Perhaps the saying means that people attempt to bring in the kingdom with force: that is reprehensible. In that case, it would in fact presuppose that the kingdom had yet to come.[1]

3. Mark 3.27: the strong man cannot be robbed unless he has first been bound. The saying is wholly keyed to victory, but spoken in the situation of the struggle. We find the Q version (Matt. 12.28 par. Luke 11.20), εἰ ἐν δακτύλῳ (Luke)/ἐν πνεύματι θεοῦ (Matt.) ἐκβάλλω τὰ δαιμόνια ἄρα ἔφθασεν ἐφ'ὑμᾶς ἡ βασιλεία τοῦ θεοῦ.

The word φθάνειν means 'to arrive'. But we do not know the Hebrew equivalent. This word, too, might point to the present sign of the coming kingdom.

4. Luke 17.21: the kingdom of God is ἐντὸς ὑμῶν. The meaning can be: (a) indwelling in you; (b) in your midst; (c) is in your hand (when it comes).[2] Here, too, final certainty is impossible, as we do not possess the original version of the saying.

5. The parables (especially the 'parables of growth').[3] In a number of parables nothing is said about the time of the kingdom, but only about its value: the treasure in the field, the pearl of great price (Matt. 13.44–46), the finding of what is lost (Matt. 18.12–14, Luke 15.1–10). Significantly enough, the time factor lies in another place: the parable itself is now meant to induce a frame of mind towards the kingdom.

[1] G. Braumann, ' "Dem Himmelreich wird Gewalt angetan" (Matt 11, 12 par)', ZNW 52 (1961), pp. 104–9, explains the word as an apologetic construction by the community. It is not Jesus and the Christians who snatch the kingdom of heaven for themselves, but persecutors.

[2] A. Rüstow, ZNW 51 (1960), p. 197.

[3] Literature: C. H. Dodd, The Parables of the Kingdom (1936); J. Jeremias, The Parables of Jesus (1963²); N. A. Dahl, 'The Parables of Growth', StTh 5 (1951), pp. 132–66; E. Linnemann, The Parables of Jesus (1966).

The futurity of the kingdom is clearly presupposed in the parable of the net (Matt. 13.47–50).[1] Its futurity is also the point of the parable of the wheat and the tares (Matt. 13.24–30). The picture of the seed growing secretly (Mark 4.26–29) does not mean that the kingdom is already there and is unfolding in the world, but that it comes 'of itself'. In the picture of the grain of mustard (Mark 4.30–32), the stress is not on the process of growth but on the contrast (cf. the parable of the leaven; Matt. 13.33).

The intention is always to depict the relationship between the coming kingdom and the present activity of Jesus and thereby to bring about a decision in face of the present offer of salvation.

The form of the announcement is not: there is salvation and damnation, but: Here is salvation! Not to accept it means that a man is lost.

The kingdom of God is salvation. Thus the phrases 'to enter the kingdom of God' and 'to enter life' can alternate without a change in the meaning: cf. Mark 9.47 with vv. 43, 45.

'Life', too, has not only a formal sense, that man will exist again after death, whether in salvation or in damnation, but also the positive meaning of being in salvation. It can be depicted in the imagery of a feast.

Salvation is offered unconditionally: the poor are called and – to heighten the point further – so are sinners (cf. the parables of the lost sheep and the lost coin, the great feast; and the beatitudes).

The idea of compensatory righteousness appears in one place, in the parable of Dives and Lazarus. This corresponds to the apocalyptic statement: 'the first will be last'. But that is said with a purpose, as an offer and an appeal. Poverty is neither an ideal nor a means of becoming blessed, but simply a natural ill. But anyone who is poor experiences the gospel, and in so doing undergoes a transformation of his situation that very day.

Acceptance of the message is the sole condition of blessedness.

A condition? Of course. A man is not automatically transported into the kingdom of God. The fact that a man enters it is an offer of grace, a miracle, possible only through God (Mark 10.24–27). This is expressed in a picture: the gate is narrow (Matt. 7.13f.). Many are called, but few are chosen (Matt. 22.14).

As salvation is a pure gift, there is no worldly status which gives precedence, not even membership of the chosen people. Many will come from east and west and sit with the patriarchs, but the sons of the kingdom will be cast out (Matt. 8.11f.). The Queen of the South, the people of Nineveh, will rise up against them (Luke 11.31f.).

---

[1] It is irrelevant whether the interpretation (vv. 49f.) is original or not.

The individual is at risk: who ever loses his life will gain it (Matt. 10.39; Luke 9.24; 17.33). Now is the moment to let the dead bury their dead (Luke 9.60). In a word, the condition is repentance. It is integral to the matter itself that it cannot be postponed.

Is the message of Jesus 'universalistic'?[1] If the only important thing is to accept the offer, to repent, if there is no longer any advantage in belonging to a particular people, then is that not the end of the idea of Israel as the people of God? The point in the passages quoted is not primarily salvation for the Gentiles, but rather the threat of judgment for the Jews, if they refuse to repent. Jesus does not go beyond the idea of the Jewish people: the Jews are the chosen people. But this is no guarantee for the individual; it is rather a demand. Jesus develops no programme of Gentile mission. But universalism is in fact already present in his offer of unconditional salvation.

The contradiction between the 'present' and the future sayings is only an apparent one. The two have the same significance for human existence: man's attitude of the moment towards the coming kingdom. Once this point has been recognized, then another apparent contradiction also resolves itself. On the one hand, it is said that the kingdom dawns suddenly, without warning. On the other hand, there is a summons to understand the signs which precede it (the parable of the fig tree, Mark 13.28f.). The two motifs (the suddenness of the coming and the signs preceding) are already combined in Jewish apocalyptic. As long as the hope is dependent on the apocalyptic picture, the contradiction remains. But it vanishes in Jesus' preaching, because he concentrates the statements made in this imagery on their meaning for existence. Now both the announcement of the suddenness of the kingdom and the preceding signs require the same situation: an immediate reaction. For the signs are mentioned in such a way that they cannot be noted at a neutral distance. They are quite simply Jesus' activity itself.

Nor is the idea of judgment developed by Jesus in a speculative way: it is fully directed towards the situation of the offer of salvation. It serves to make salvation understandable as promise. The ideas can be varied, and are taken out of the tradition quite arbitrarily. The Old Testament idea of guilt and retribution is taken up (Luke 13.1ff.). But the dominant idea is that of judgment in the world to come. The

[1] J. Jeremias, *Jesus' Promise to the Nations*, SBT 24 (1967[2]).

world's history is not the world's judgment. Rather, the world's judgment is the world's end.

There are also two groups of sayings about the judgment:

1. The coming of the kingdom is itself the judgment, i.e. the division (Luke 17.34f.). Faith is the criterion at the moment of the onset of the kingdom, with whose coming man is immediately confronted. Penitence is required, and in return man receives forgiveness.

2. The judgment is described as a legal judgment in which a verdict is passed on man's works. They are the criterion. Fulfilment of the commandments is required. Life is determined by obedience or disobedience. Each man receives his due reward.

Is this, then, justification by works? Once again, it is important to see how Jewish ideas are heightened by Jesus. The paradigm is the (redactional) picture of judgment in Matt. 25.31ff.: we do not know our works. We only learn of them by the pronouncement of the judge. That means that men cannot play them off against God or appeal to them in the face of God. Cf. the parable of the Pharisee and the publican!

The announcement of the kingdom inevitably raises the question: what must I do to gain eternal life (Mark 10.17)? The answer consists in a reference to the commandments. But that was precisely the Jewish problem: what does God want, and how can man fulfil his demand? How are we to understand the relationship between God's demand and its fulfilment by man?

15 · THE DEMAND OF GOD

R. Bultmann, *Theology of the New Testament* I, pp. 11–22; W. Pesch, *Der Lohngedanke in der Lehre Jesu*, MThS I 7 (1955); H. Braun, *Spätjüdisch- häretischer und frühchristlicher Radikalismus* II, BHTh 24 (1957) (see the index); R. Schnackenburg, *The Moral Teaching of the NT* (1965); E. Neuhäusler, *Anspruch und Antwort Gottes – Zur Lehre von den Weisungen innerhalb der synoptischen Jesusverkündigung* (1962); C. Spicq, *Théologie morale du NT* (2 vols.) (1965).

I General Problems

The form of ethical teaching in the synoptic gospels corresponds with Jewish tradition. This already indicates a general understanding of ethics: there is no 'system', no derivation of individual demands from a systematic principle, no 'formal' ethics.

True, in one place there is a summary of the demand in a formal definition, the 'golden rule' (Matt. 7.12; see II below): 'Whatever you wish that men would do to you, do so to them'. This, however, is no 'categorical imperative' from which a man could derive all concrete demands. For this rule does not take into account the disposition in which an action is performed or a man's attitude towards God (fasting, praying).

Jesus' ethics are not 'dispositional ethics'. Of course, Jesus speaks of man's inwardness, of the heart. But that does not mean that actions are of no importance. On the contrary, God demands actions, and even man's disposition is an action which must be answered for. Is then Jesus' ethical view (and also that of the synoptic gospels) concerned with material values? That is hardly the case, for there is no definition of a highest good and no construction of a table of values.

Occasionally the concept of righteousness seems to function as the supreme good (Matt. 6.33). But this concept does not occur in the authentic teaching of Jesus; only in Matthew's redaction. It occurs alongside other equally general summaries. There is no question of a systematic comparison. Cf. Matt. 5.48 with Luke 6.36. Even the concept of the kingdom of God cannot be designated a supreme value. For no concrete demands are based on references to the kingdom of God; they are based on God's continuing attitude, on his will. The whole demand can also be summed up in the commandment to love. But the concept of love cannot be understood either as a formal principle or as a supreme good. Love always proves itself to be an expression of an attitude to the world in general, 'freedom from care'.

Furthermore, there is no question of a principle or a supreme good, because no completeness is sought after. Considerable areas are excluded: the state almost entirely, society, culture, education, personal life.

As a result, the question whether a material unity can be detected in the background becomes all the more pressing. For the time being, it can be pointed out that Jesus' ethical teaching is meant as an exposition of the will of God; the starting point is the revealed law, laid down in the Old Testament. The 'open' character of this ethical approach is matched by its form: the individual sayings,[1] doctrinal discussion,[2] parables.[3] However, we have only a revised form of the

[1] R. Bultmann, *History of the Synoptic Tradition*, pp. 69ff., 130ff.; M. Dibelius, *From Tradition to Gospel*, pp. 233ff.
[2] R. Bultmann, *History of the Synoptic Tradition*, pp. 12ff., 39ff.
[3] *ibid.*, pp. 166ff.

tradition, so that in each individual instance we have to investigate
(a) the original form and (b) the question of authenticity.

One example is the two traditions of the saying about divorce, Mark 10.11f.
par. Matt. 19.9; Matt. 5.31f. par. Luke 16.18. The commandment is absolute in
Mark and Luke. In both versions, Matthew has inserted 'except on the grounds
of unchastity' (or 'except for unchastity'). In doing this he makes the absolute
statement about marriage and God's will into a casuistic rule about how one
should act in the community in the case of a marriage judgment. This is a question
with which Jesus did not concern himself, simply because he organized no community. Particularly vivid examples of the tendency of the tradition to use the
Jesus tradition in a paraenetic way are to be found in the parables and the redactional work done upon them (J. Jeremias).

The ethical tradition has been collected to form a larger unit in
the 'Sermon on the Mount' (on the basis of the 'Sermon on the Plain'
in the Q source; see Luke 6.20ff.).[1] Here there are several strata in
succession: early traditional material about Jesus, and its appropriation by the church in several stages (oral tradition, Q, Matthew).
Matt. 5.38f.: 'You have heard that it was said, "an eye for an eye and a
tooth for a tooth". But I say unto you, Do not resist one who is evil.
But if anyone strikes you on the right cheek, turn to him the other
also.' Can this demand be fulfilled: not only to offer the cheek but
still to love one's 'enemy' in so doing? Anyone who is angry with his
brother is liable to the judgment. Anyone who looks at a woman
lustfully has already committed adultery with her. How can a man
be perfect?

The command is not 'Strive for perfection', keep down anger and desire. At the
very moment when I have to fight, I already find myself angry, covetous. I am to
be in a position in which I no longer have to overcome, but am like the tree which
brings forth good fruit of itself. How is that possible?

Is not 'You shall – love' a contradiction in itself?

Is this command an illuminating human, moral ideal? Does it not already
contradict the demand by the impossibility of its fulfilment, even in the social
sphere? One cannot use it to run a state or a factory, or even to live together in a
family. Church history offers a long list of attempts to come to terms with the
Sermon on the Mount. The worst is the commonest, to praise the Bible and ignore
it in practice.

The catholic attempt is self-consistent. It distinguishes two ethical levels: the
minimal demand of the Decalogue, which is binding on every man, and in ad-

---

[1] M. Dibelius, 'Die Bergpredigt', in: *Botschaft und Geschichte* I, pp. 79–174; W. D.
Davies, *The Setting of the Sermon on the Mount* (1964); for the history of its exposition
see G. Bornkamm, *Jesus of Nazareth*, pp. 221–25.

dition, the higher level of 'better righteousness' as the possibility of acquiring merit. In this way, a practical rule can be offered, together with an incentive to strive for higher things. The price is, of course, that the meaning of Jesus' demand is destroyed; the consequence is that certainty of salvation is impossible.

The Reformation protested against this solution. The 'enthusiasts' aimed at literal fulfilment, even in politics, but became involved in the contradiction of having to carry through the renunciation of authority by authority. Luther recognizes that they are once again making the Sermon on the Mount into a law. His solution is to argue that the Sermon on the Mount is not to be turned into a legalistic, bourgeois ordinance. It is to be fulfilled in faith. Jesus does not teach a new law, but renunciation of retributory justice in the particular instance.

More recent attempts at a solution: Tolstoy again required consistent fulfilment, renunciation of force, of sexual intercourse. He, too, becomes involved in the same contradictions as the enthusiasts. Thurneysen[1] revived the orthodox thesis, that the Sermon on the Mount cannot be fulfilled in principle and indeed is not meant to be. Its aim is to convict man of his sinfulness. It is not to be fulfilled by our efforts, but to be understood as in Christ, and to be fulfilled through the saving act. This solution fails to answer the question, what shall I do? Albert Schweitzer[2] declared that the demand of the Sermon on the Mount was an 'interim ethic'. In his view, it was developed in the context of an acute expectation of the end of the world, and could only be fulfilled for this brief period. But the thesis of interim ethics cannot be justified from the texts. True, Jesus believes that the kingdom of God is coming soon, and enjoins repentance with a reference to the fact. But the content of his demands is not to be derived from the imminence of the end of the world, and is not justified by Jesus on this basis, but through the example and will of God. 'Love one another' is no special commandment for the last time. It always has been God's will and therefore holds true independently of the world situation.

But what about the fulfilment of this demand? Is it possible? Jesus does not ask theoretically about man's general capability. His presupposition is that God makes fulfilment possible by making known the demand. The one who commands is at the same time the one who cares and the one who forgives. Precisely because his demand is absolute, it is liberation. The exclusiveness of the orientation to the kingdom of God removes care, because God gives all that is needful.

The commandment can be understood precisely because it is absolute. I can very well understand that God cannot content himself with half-hearted obedience, that he does not claim *something*, but *me*. All the individual instructions carry through this basic idea. The concept of repentance is concerned with this: it means the totality of conversion, a new orientation. The demand for penitence discloses to me that I am not what I should be. The fact that I am told to repent is strictly a verdict on my standing before God. This is not to be con-

---

[1] E. Thurneysen, *Die Bergpredigt*, ThExH NF 105 (1963).

[2] A. Schweitzer, *The Mystery of the Kingdom of God* (1925), pp. 96–98; *The Quest of the Historical Jesus* (1954³), pp. 353f.

fused with moral pessimism, the view that all men are evil and corrupt. Jesus speaks freely of good and evil. The important thing is what I can say to God face to face, when I am confronted with him.

In the well-known parable, the Pharisee does not lie when he enumerates his good works. But he brings them before God, i.e. he brings himself forward as a man who does not need God, or rather can treat with him on the basis of his own rights.

The general call to penitence is grounded on a reference to the nearness of the kingdom of God, but this is not the case with the individual, concrete commandment. In the synoptic tradition, the call to penitence and the exposition of the law stand side by side, with relatively little connection between them. Conversion is not defined as a return under the law.[1] This direct connection is lacking. Rather, the view of conversion already existing in Judaism and the regulation of life by the commandments are each made more radical in themselves.

Jesus' criticism is not of the law, but of legalism. For this prevents fulfilment. Nor does he set out to supplement the law with additions; his aim is to bring it into the open after its concealment under the commentaries of tradition. One can speak of Jesus' 'exposition' of the law only in a dialectical sense. For him the law is understandable in itself, its exposition is nothing but the opening up of this understandable sense. I can understand not only what God wills but also why he wills a particular thing: love, renunciation of law instead of retribution. The understanding of the commandment is indissolubly connected with obedience. Formal obedience would not be real obedience. In the demand I can understand God, and myself as his child. In forgiving at the same time as the demand, I experience God's forgiveness (the parable of the unmerciful servant). The integral meaning of the individual commandments lies in the fact that I am freed from care, for love. They are limited as principles in the light of the commandment of love. Indeed, in individual instances they are transcended.

The sabbath rest is not done away with. But Jesus questions whether a conflict can arise between the sabbath commandment and the commandment of love. No regulation about the sabbath can prevent the doing of whatever good may be enjoined in a particular case. The Jewish cult is not abolished. But no prescription for sacrifices removes the duty of reconciling oneself instantly with one's brother.

---

[1] Thus in Qumran: cf. H. Braun, *Radikalismus* I 25, II 17.

Hence Jesus' ethical view does not know the problem of the conflict of duties, which only arises through a legalistic misunderstanding of the commandments.

II   The Material

A considerable part of the ethical teaching of Jesus consists in wisdom rules which have parallels in the sayings of Jewish wisdom literature and the rabbis.[1]

Examples: (a) Matt. 7.2: 'The measure you give will be the measure you get'; cf.: 'Man is measured by the measure with which he measures'. (b) 'Do not be anxious about tomorrow, for tomorrow will be anxious for itself. Let the day's own trouble be sufficient for the day.' Cf.: 'Do not be anxious about tomorrow's anxiety, for you do not know what the day will bring forth. Perhaps you will not be here tomorrow . . . The need is sufficient for its hour.'

Where is the difference? It is perverse to want to prove Jesus' 'superiority' in apologetic terms. It is rather the case that if a Jew thinks through these ideas he is not far from the kingdom of God. The difference lies in the understanding of law and salvation.

One example is the 'golden rule' (Matt. 7.12).[2] Hillel knows it in the version: Do not do to your neighbour what you would not have done to yourself.[3] A favourite argument is that Judaism knew only the negative version and that Jesus formulated it in positive terms. But quite apart from the fact that the positive formulation can also be found in Judaism (*Letter of Aristeas*, 207), there is in fact no real difference between the two forms. Taken by itself, the rule can be understood in the sense of a naïve egoism in both versions: I am friendly in order that other people may be friendly to me. I do not require much of them, so they cannot require much of me. What matters is thus the total understanding of man and his neighbour. If we look at the rule in the context of the whole of Jesus' proclamation, what it is intended to mean is clear: make what you would ideally demand of the other man the standard of your real conduct towards him.

THE ANTITHESES OF THE SERMON ON THE MOUNT[4]

Literary criticism: three of the six antitheses are 'genuine'. 'Genuine' does not mean that they are authentic words of Jesus, but that the antithesis is strictly related to the thesis: 'But I say to you that every one who looks on a woman lustfully . . .' The genuine antitheses are the first, second and fourth. They have no parallel in Luke, and therefore did not stand in Q. The three other antitheses are

---

[1] Bill. *ad loc.*; cf. R. Bultmann, *History of the Synoptic Tradition*, pp. 73ff.
[2] A. Dihle, *Die Goldene Regel, Aus Griechentum und Judentum* (1962).
[3] Shab. 31a; cf. Bill. I 460.
[4] H. Braun, *Radikalismus* II 9.

formed from sayings which were also transmitted by Q, but not in an antithetical version. This form was only given to them by Matthew. Their characteristic mark is that the antitheses can be understood by themselves, without the preceding theses: 'But I say to you, "Love your enemies".'

It is often said that Jesus appears here as the bringer of the 'messianic Torah'; he puts himself above Moses. But no 'messianic Torah' is to be found in Judaism. It is at least questionable whether the antithetical form goes back to Jesus.

Braun asserts that the secondary antitheses are the sharper and contain primary material: 'Where the intensification of the demand signalizes a genuine saying of Jesus, the ἐγὼ δὲ λέγω ὑμῖν is the work of Matthew; where ἐγὼ δὲ λέγω ὑμῖν is a primary literary element, it introduces no sharpening of the Torah.'

The significance of the antitheses does not depend on a formal authority of the speaker, but on the absoluteness of the commandment through which this becomes understandable. I can no longer ask whether 'I must' offer the other cheek. In that case, the further question, when I need not do so, would be in the background. This casuistry does not bring one to the matter itself, to what has been enjoined. Offering the cheek is not an attitude; it can be meaningful only in the act. When this case arises cannot be discovered from the Bible, but I will know when it comes. Then I shall not need any more research work.

The same actuality is operative in the case of the renunciation of law and property (Matt. 10.17ff.). Of course, the question will arise again and again: must I, can I, forgive? I cannot go beyond it unless I begin at the point at which Jesus' demand itself begins: God has first forgiven me, and thus given me the possibility of living in freedom, without worldly assurances. Proving this freedom in life together is the essence of Christian morality.

In its absoluteness, the commandment of love thus does away with casuistry. The individual ethical regulations are not intended to regulate individual instances, but to disclose the immediacy of acting in the moment. This is at the same time a transcending of ethical rigorism. Rigorism and casuistry belong together (Qumran texts). If God's forgiveness comes first, then I must no longer seek to obtain my salvation by the rigorous fulfilment of individual precepts. Because God assures me of salvation, I am free to put myself beyond the individual precepts of casuistry in each individual case. Because the presupposition of rigorism is done away with by Jesus, he does not practise and demand ascesis (Luke 7.33f.; Mark 2.18f.). Words of Jesus which sound ascetic do not in reality demand ascesis, but sacrifice, in a particular instance. Jesus does not develop any ideal of poverty. He does not demand renunciation of property in general, but its surrender by anyone who is called to discipleship (Mark 10.17ff.). Moral effort does not bring a man into relationship with God; the relationship with God is given by God himself. Only then is the possibility for moral action opened up. This should be noted if we want to assess a point which represents the severest stumbling block to modern philosophical ethics: the fact that Jesus openly points to rewards and punishments for action.[1]

Two principal objections are raised: 1. Theological: is there not a contradiction here between Jesus and the Pauline doctrine of justification by grace alone? 2. A general point: does not expectation of reward corrupt the motive for morality? Is a good act done for the sake of reward really good? Must we not do good for the sake of the good itself (Lessing, Kant)?

In fact, action for the sake of one's own advantage is human enough, but not moral. How then are we to assess the ethics of Jesus, in view of the fact that the idea of reward cannot be dissociated from them?

Matt. 5.44f., 46; Mark 10.21. These passages will be basically authentic (cf. Braun II, p. 54, n. 1). True, the accents have been shifted in the course of tradition.[2] Nevertheless, the idea of reward remains constitutive even for the ethics of Jesus.

We must ask what function the idea of reward has. Is it a Jewish relic?[3] Not at all![4] It is presented along with the rest of Jesus' proclamation. It is not a support, to be tolerated with difficulty, but an original element of the message, in so far as this is a message of good news. It stems from the offer of God the Father, the promise of his kingdom. The idea of judgment is the other side of the picture, and cannot be separated from it: anyone who does not accept salvation is damned (Matt. 10.28; Mark 9.42, 47).

From this starting point (God and the kingdom of God), it is quite clear that there can be no claim on God, that man cannot rely on merit. For it is by grace that I am what I am. The reward is

---

[1] W. Pesch, op. cit.

[2] H. Braun, Radikalismus II 34ff., esp. pp. 55f., note. E. Haenchen, Gott und Mensch, Gesammelte Aufsätze (1965), pp. 6ff., points particularly to Luke: 14.12–14; 12.33; 6.24–26, 32–35; 18.18–30.

[3] This is Braun's inclination; see below.

[4] With G. Bornkamm, 'Der Lohngedanke im NT', Studien zu Antike und Urchristentum, Gesammelte Aufsätze II, pp. 69–92.

promised and given, not 'earned' (Matt. 20.1–15).[1] In the relationship between father and child, considerations of reward become 'harmless': because God shows himself to be my Father, I can expect good of him. Unless I do, I am not doing him justice. In this respect it is clear that to do good for the sake of the Father who is good to me is to do it out of gratitude, in freedom. The idea of reward means that man is put before abstract definitions of the Good, that man is God's real goal, by grace alone.

Bultmann, *Theology of the New Testament*, I p. 14: 'The motive of reward is only a primitive expression for the idea that in what a man does his own real being is at stake . . . To achieve that self is the legitimate motive of his ethical dealing and of his true obedience.'

Survey of the Development of the Tradition:

After the death of Jesus, ethics have to be adapted to the nature of the church. That means that the accent must be shifted. But we must beware of unhistorical value judgments. Matthew, in particular, is criticized: he narrows the demand to an esoteric ethics for the disciples and introduces a new legalism. According to Matt. 5.1, the Sermon on the Mount seems to be directed only to the disciples. At the end of the Sermon on the Mount, however, in Matt. 7.28, the people is presupposed as the audience. Matthew's understanding of the church accords with this duality. Jesus' teaching was public. He organized no group of the elect. The judgment is exclusively God's concern. After Jesus' death, on the other hand, outward membership of the visible group of believers is also demanded through preaching and confession. Now everything will depend on how the church understands itself. Will it become an end in itself, a sect, or will it constitute itself in the light of the freedom of God's election? Will the ethic of the disciples be understood as a saving work or as its concretion? True, certain 'legalistic' features are evident in Matthew. There is no pure, distilled Christian thought. But acceptance of the situation must take the place of catch-phrases. In no case can one say that Matthew teaches a double standard, normal righteousness and the better righteousness of the disciples. Matt. 5.17–20, which is in fact to be taken as the evangelist's programme, means rather that anyone who does not fulfil the better righteousness will not enter into the kingdom of heaven. Furthermore, in Matthew above all, all

[1] On this see G. Bornkamm, *op. cit.*, pp. 81ff.; H. Braun, *Radikalismus* II 41, note 1.

precepts are concentrated on the commandment of love. In the light
of this he does away with casuistic observance (Matt. 23). Matthew
maintains what the double standard surrenders, the indivisibility of
the will of God which faith acknowledges.

PROVISIONAL SUMMARY

We have attempted to obtain an overall view of three areas of the
synoptic tradition, and in so doing have from time to time returned
to the teaching of Jesus: God, his kingdom and his will. Each time we
came up against Jewish presuppositions and recognized how these
were taken up and at the same time made more radical, concentrated
on their significance for existence. There remains one further area,
the one that is most disputed – synoptic christology. Our next question
must be: how did Jesus understand himself? What did he teach about
himself?

What is the relationship between the areas discussed so far: the
doctrine of God, eschatology and ethics?

It will become clear that christology does not simply stand alongside these as a
fourth area. At least with Jesus himself, it stands behind them. It is not a doctrine
alongside other doctrines, but the key to understanding the material of the other
three complexes.

The evidence is quite remarkable: the three areas stand side by
side with a striking lack of connection.

1. When Jesus teaches about God, the Creator, the Father, the
Ruler, his attention is clearly also directed immediately to the world,
to its limitations, which are expressed in care, and to the wickedness
of men ('You who are evil'). But in the context of the idea of God there
is no thought of an imminent end to the world. The world is rather
accepted quite simply as being to hand: count the lilies of the field,
the birds under the heavens! God makes his sun rise on evil as well as
good. Thus when Jesus heals the sick, he is not acting towards a
world which will only last a short time. Here is a world that is God's
creation, which is perishing and needs to be healed.

Jesus does not heal the sick to prepare them for the kingdom of God: healing
stories are not conversion stories.

An eschatological link becomes apparent only in the exorcisms:
'If it is by the finger of God that I cast out demons, ἄρα ἔφθασεν ἐφ᾽ὑμᾶς
ἡ βασιλεία τοῦ θεοῦ' (Luke 11.20).

2. The connection between eschatology and ethics is analogous. Albert Schweitzer wanted to derive an interim ethic immediately from the expectation of the end. On the other hand, we had to point out that this theory does not fit the texts. The content of the demand – loving one's enemy, etc, is not derived from the nearness of the kingdom of God, nor is its validity restricted to a last, brief period. On the contrary, in ethics, as in the doctrine of God, there is no limit to the duration of the world. Jesus believes that the demand of God is understandable and possible in itself, not only by way of apocalyptic expectation.

There is an abstraction which is quite dominant in theological discussion of the question of the possibility of fulfilling the law: 'Can "man" fulfil it?' This question is quite alien to Jesus. The 'man' in it is an abstraction. The question of 'man's' ability in respect of God's command is in itself a meaningless one, as in this command man is always already particularized as God's man. The question is, what is the command, in the light of God's declaration that he accepts me as his child?

The evidence can be made more precise in the following way: whereas ethics and the idea of God are associated, there is no immediate connection between these two complexes and eschatology. In that case, are we not to posit some notional unity between them in the case of Jesus?

Bultmann finds this unity in the fact that all three complexes of expressions are controlled by the same understanding of existence: on each occasion man is related to God in the same way: eschatology is to be understood existentially and ethics are to be understood as eschatological ethics: 'Now is the last hour; now it can be only: either-or! Now the question is whether a man really desires God and his Reign [sic!] or the world and its goods; and the decision must be drastically made.'[1] Ethics are eschatological, in that Jesus' teaching 'does not envisage a future to be moulded within this world by plans and sketches for the ordering of human life. It only directs man into the Now of his meeting with his neighbour. It is an ethic that, by demanding more than the law that regulates human society does and requiring of the individual the waiver of his own rights, makes the individual immediately responsible to God'.[2] Now Bultmann can examine the connection between eschatology, ethics and the idea of God: 'Once one has understood the unity of the eschatological and the ethical preaching of Jesus, one also has the answer to the real meaning

[1] R. Bultmann, *Theology of the New Testament* I, p. 9.
[2] Bultmann, *op. cit.*, p. 19.

of the eschatological message, namely: the answer to the question, what idea of God is at work in it'.[1] The conclusion is: 'For Jesus . . . man is taken out of the world by God's direct pronouncement to him, which tears him out of all security of any kind and places him at the brink of the End. And God is taken out of the world by understanding his dealing eschatologically: he lifts man out of his worldly ties and places him directly before his own eyes. Hence the way in which both God and man are taken out of history and taken out of the world is to be understood in dialectic terms: precisely that God, who stands aloof from the history of nations, meets each man in his own little history, his everyday life with its daily gift and demand; de-historicized man (i.e. naked of his supposed security within his historical group) is guided into his concrete encounter with his neighbour, in which he finds his true history'.[2]

Criticism: We can agree with Bultmann that a unity of content is to be found. But the way by which he has reached it is too abrupt, in that he has made direct connections between the three areas. This course does not overcome the real difficulty, the striking lack of connection in the texts. The unity is only visible if we recognize the common starting-point of all three outlines. To do this, we have to look back to Jesus' understanding of himself, as it can be detected in the texts. The fact that Jesus speaks now of God's rule, and now of his coming, in so disconnected a way, is to be explained from the fact that he does not construct his doctrine freely, but takes up and presupposes existing Jewish religion, its concept of God, etc. and takes it for granted that the Old Testament teaching about God and his commands is true. He does not outline a new religion, but sets out to elucidate the significance of Judaism. In the latter, the three areas are developed in relative independence from each other: the idea of God in piety, and in prayer; ethics in the exposition of scripture; eschatology in the free outlines of apocalyptic. Jesus takes up what already exists and particularizes it in relation to existence. He does this by incorporating his own person each time as a factor in the matter.[3]

We cannot understand Jesus' eschatology without him as proclaimer; we cannot understand his talk of God without him as the

---

[1] Bultmann, *op. cit.*, p. 22.

[2] Bultmann, *op. cit.*, pp. 25f.

[3] Bultmann himself gives the most important indication: 'But what are the "signs of the time"? He himself!' (*op. cit.*, p. 7).

one who makes clear the relationship to God; we cannot understand his ethics without him as the one who expounds them. All parts of Jesus' teaching are stamped with an indirect christology. Jesus does not teach expressly who he is. But he acts in his proclamation as one who opens up immediacy to God in every relationship. After his death, this indirect christology is transposed into the direct christology of the community's faith.

16 · THE QUESTION OF JESUS' UNDERSTANDING OF HIMSELF

O. Cullmann, *The Christology of the New Testament* (1959); F. Hahn, *Christologische Hoheitstitel*, FRLANT 83 (1963); H. R. Balz, *Methodische Probleme der nt. Christologie*, WMANT 25 (1967).

The synoptic tradition presents its conception of the person of Jesus by bestowing titles upon him and making Jesus himself use these titles. But how much of this is historical? What does it tell us about Jesus himself? In the earlier part we were concerned with the question whether Jesus described God as his Father in an exclusive sense, and consequently himself as the Son. Now we have to make soundings from the other side.

I The Son

A distinction should be made between 'the Son' in the absolute and 'the Son of God'. 'The Son' is expressly related to 'the Father'. The decisive feature of the title is subordination, the revelation of the Father to the Son, obedience.[1] The only two passages which speak absolutely of 'the Father' (Mark 13.32; Matt. 11.27 par. Luke 10.22) are demonstrably community constructions. The same is true of the parable of the wicked husbandmen (Mark 12.1ff.). This is an allegorical account of the saving history which presupposes the death of Christ.[2] All the passages with the title 'the Son' are thus demonstrably community christology.

[1] F. Hahn, *Hoheitstitel*, pp. 319–33.
[2] W. G. Kümmel, 'Das Gleichnis von den bösen Weingärtnern (Mark 12.1–9)', in: *Aux sources de la tradition chrétienne* (Mélanges M. Goguel) (1950), pp. 120–31 (= *Heilsgeschehen und Geschichte*, 1965, pp. 207–17); F. Hahn, *Hoheitstitel*, pp. 315f.

II   The Son of God

O. Cullmann, *Christology*, pp. 270–305; F. Hahn, *Hoheitstitel*, pp. 280–346; B. M. F. van Iersel, *'Der Sohn' in den synoptischen Jesusworten*, SupplNovTest 3 (1964²).

Does this title go back to Jesus himself? A number of passages can be shown to be secondary by comparison with the other synoptic gospels: Matt. 14.33; 16.16; 27.40, 43.[1]

The title does not occur in narrative.[2] Its place is in the confession. This is clear from the usage:

1. It occurs in the confession of the Gentile centurion beneath the cross (Mark 15.39). This utterance is not historical, but a symbolic representation of the Gentile church's confession of the Crucified One.[3]

2. It occurs in epiphanies. (*a*) The baptism: Jesus is declared to be Son of God by a heavenly voice (in the words of Ps. 2.7 and Isa. 42.1). The incident described cannot be understood as a historical event. Cullmann[4] speaks of 'Jesus' baptism experience' but the texts contain no trace of any reference to a vision. Furthermore, Jesus would have had to have spoken of it for the tradition to have arisen at all; and in that case it would have taken the form of a saying of Jesus.[5]

(*b*) The transfiguration (Mark 9.1ff. par.): The same might be said of this story. The narrative contains a whole series of epiphany motifs. As an action it is inconceivable. Here, too, we have an account of a first appointment of Jesus to the rank of Son of God; the story originally competed with the narrative of the baptism. In the present context, it is the heavenly confirmation which follows the confession of Peter and the prophecy of the passion.[6] In both passages, the status of the Son of God is understood in legal terms. The idea of the pre-existence of Jesus is very remote.

3. It occurs in the cries of the demons (Mark 3.11; 5.7): the key to understanding this is in Mark 3.27: no one can enter a strong man's house and plunder his goods, unless he first binds the strong man. The demons recognize Jesus' authority, i.e. the reader understands it.

---

[1] For the historical question whether this title was used in Judaism, see p. 76.

[2] We never find, for example, 'The Son of God went along the lakeside'.

[3] M. Dibelius, *From Tradition to Gospel*, p. 195.

[4] O. Cullmann, *Christology*, p. 284.

[5] M. Dibelius, *From Tradition to Gospel*, p. 272.

[6] R. Bultmann, *History of the Synoptic Tradition*, p. 259, regards it as originally an Easter narrative. No!

4. It occurs in the story of the temptation of Jesus (according to Q): this is a legend, which rejects the transference of the popular θεῖος ἀνήρ conception to Jesus.[1]

5. It occurs in the Matthean and Lucan birth narratives. They combine the motif of the Son of David and the Son of the Virgin as the Son of God. This association is secondary. Whereas in the stories of the baptism and the transfiguration the status of 'Son of God' is understood in legal terms, here the understanding is more or less physical: Jesus is Son of God through his miraculous birth (Luke 1.35). Here, too, the idea of pre-existence is absent. If this narrative is made to precede the baptism and the transfiguration in the gospel narratives, the latter lose their significance: they become a subsequent confirmation of the fact that Jesus is Son of God, a status which he already has.

Hahn (p. 308) assumes that it was Hellenistic Jewish Christianity which first transferred the title 'Son of God' to the earthly Jesus. This is true in the case of the birth narratives, but not for the accounts of the baptism and transfiguration.

6. It occurs a single time in the mouth of Jesus (Mark 14.61f.): only this last passage can possibly be taken to be historical material. It deals with the trial of Jesus before the Sanhedrin: 'Are you the Son of the Blessed?' But the report is not historical; the passage offers a compendium of christology as Mark understands it (cf. the context!).

The conclusion therefore is that, according to the texts we have, Jesus did not use the title 'Son of God'.

III The Messiah

O. Cullmann, *Christology*, pp. 111–136; F. Hahn, *Hoheitstitel*, pp. 133–241.

In the creed, the chief aspect of the title Messiah is clearly the saving work, i.e. the past.[2] Did Jesus use this title? We must exclude all passages in which Christ is a name (Mark 1.1); further, those in which comparison with the other synoptic gospels shows the use of the title to be secondary: Matt. 11.2 (cf. Luke 7.18); Matt. 24.5; 26.68; Luke 3.15; 23.2, 39. The title Messiah does not occur in the source Q.

Mark: the occurrence in the trial before the Sanhedrin (Mark 14.61f.) is redactional. The same is true of the apocalyptic discourse

---

[1] F. Hahn, *Hoheitstitel*, p. 303.
[2] Cullmann interprets this otherwise: the title, which Jesus uses with the utmost restraint, is directed towards the future.

(Mark 13.21f.), where there is an expectation of the appearance of false Messiahs in the last days. This is a picture of the future drawn by the community. Mark 9.41:[1] this saying has been formulated at a time when a man can only serve Jesus indirectly, by serving his followers.[2]

Special Matthean and Lucan material: Matt. 23.10 is a redactional conclusion after the polemic in 23.8f. Luke 24.26, 46 gives the Lucan pattern of scriptural proof (cf. Acts 17.3).

There remain two passages whose authenticity must be examined.

1. Mark 8.29, the confession of Peter: at present there is again a certain tendency to assume a historical nucleus for this scene: Jesus refused to have himself designated Messiah.[3] But any assumption of a historical nucleus makes the texts incomprehensible. The scene is not a story, but a piece of christological reflection given the form of a story. Peter utters the creed of the community, 'You are the Messiah'.

2. Mark 15.32, the mocking of the crucified Jesus: the Messiah, the king of Israel, is to descend from the cross. The formulation pre-supposes the famous *titulus* in Mark 15.26: ὁ βασιλεὺς τῶν Ἰουδαίων. This inscription is regarded as genuine: it cannot have been invented. But we must note the thoroughgoing christological interpretation of the passion. The use of the title 'king' in this connection seems to be completely redactional.[4]

Son of David

The genealogies have no relevance to the historical question. There remain: Mark 10.48: the call of the blind Bartimaeus; Mark 11.10: in the entry into Jerusalem, people hail the coming of the kingdom of David. We have an epiphany legend here. Mark 12.35–37: can the Messiah be David's son? This passage expresses the two-stage christology of the community (see p. 74); cf. Rom. 1.3f.

The conclusion must be that in the case of the title 'Messiah', too, the evidence is negative.

---

[1] The title does not occur in the variant Matt. 10.42.

[2] The article is absent; cf. Hahn, *Hoheitstitel*, pp. 223f.

[3] F. Hahn, *Hoheitstitel*, pp. 226–30; E. Dinkler, 'Petrusbekenntnis und Satans-wort', *Zeit und Geschichte* (Bultmann Festschrift) (1964), pp. 127–53.

[4] According to R. Bultmann, *History of the Synoptic Tradition*, p. 284, Mark 15.2 is a secondary expansion, in competition with vv. 3–5; thus v. 2, with its companion v. 26, is also secondary.

IV   The Son of Man

O. Cullmann, *Christology*, pp. 137–92; W. G. Kümmel, *Heilsgeschehen und Geschichte* (1965), *passim*; P. Vielhauer, 'Gottesreich und Menschensohn in der Verkündigung Jesu', *Festschrift für Günther Dehn* (1957), pp. 51–79 (=*Aufsätze zum NT*, ThB 31 (1965), pp. 55–91); E. Schweizer, 'Der Menschensohn', *ZNW* 50 (1959), pp. 185–209 (=*Neotestamentica* (1963), pp. 56–84); H. E. Tödt, *The Son of Man in the Synoptic Tradition* (1965); F. Hahn, *Hoheitstitel*, pp. 13–53; P. Vielhauer, 'Jesus und der Menschensohn. Zur Diskussion mit H. E. Tödt und E. Schweizer', *ZThK* 60 (1963), pp. 133–77 (=*Aufsätze*, pp. 92–140); id., 'Ein Weg zur nt. Christologie? Prüfung der Thesen F. Hahns', *EvTh* 25 (1965), pp. 27f. (*Aufsätze*, pp. 145ff.); id., 'Zur Frage der christologischen Hoheitstitel', *ThLZ* 90 (1965), cols. 569–88; C. Colpe, *TWNT* VIII, 430ff.

Meaning: the expression is not a Greek one. It is to be derived from בַּר־אֱנָשׁ, determinative אֱנָשָׁא or נָשָׁא,[1] and primarily denotes the individual man; it is not, therefore, a title.

Wellhausen[2] argues that ὁ υἱὸς τοῦ ἀνθρώπου could not possibly be a title. Aramaic could not distinguish between ὁ ἄνθρωπος and ὁ υἱὸς τοῦ ἀνθρώπου. Matt. 8.20 is therefore to be translated: '. . . but man has nowhere to lay his head'. The expression became a title only when it had been translated into Greek, and that was because of a misunderstanding caused by Dan. 7.13: καὶ ἰδοὺ ἐπὶ τῶν νεφελῶν τοῦ οὐρανοῦ ὡς υἱὸς ἀνθρώπου (כְּבַר־אֱנָשׁ) ἤρχετο (a man – as distinct from the beasts of Daniel's vision). This passage was interpreted contrary to its original meaning, to refer to the Messiah. But it is doubtful whether such an idea comes from a mere misunderstanding.[3]

The Linguistic Evidence

Dalman[4] explains (against Wellhausen) that Aramaic can indeed differentiate between ὁ ἄνθρωπος and ὁ υἱὸς τοῦ ἀνθρώπου. In the time of Jesus and in the dialect which he spoke, בַּר־אֱנָשׁ was not a usual expression in colloquial speech. The expression was only used as a biblicism, in imitation of the biblical text (i.e. Daniel and Ezekiel). On the other hand, J. Jeremias and M. Black[5] state that it was even used in colloquial language. The meaning, however, is disputed. Black explains that it was a substitute for 'I', an effacing self-designation. Jesus, too, used it in this way. This thesis cannot,

[1] בֶּן־אָדָם is never determinative in the OT.

[2] J. Wellhausen, *Einleitung in die drei ersten Evangelien* (1911²), pp. 123–30.

[3] W. Bousset, *Die Religion des Judentums*, pp. 265ff.

[4] G. Dalman, *The Words of Jesus* (1902), pp. 234ff.; see further: id., *Die Worte Jesu* I (1930²), pp. 191–219, 383–97.

[5] J. Jeremias, *ThLZ* 74 (1949), cols. 528f.; M. Black, *An Aramaic Approach to the Gospels and Acts* (1954²), pp. 246f.

however, be substantiated. There is no Jewish analogy to the definite statement, 'the Son of Man has come', or, 'Whoever blasphemes the Son of Man'.[1] So the Aramaic evidence only allows limited conclusions. The language of the gospels themselves is decisive. If בַּר־אֱנָשׁ can mean 'the man', the possibility of its use as a title cannot be excluded.[2]

Ezekiel is irrelevant for the question of the historical derivation of the title.[3] Only three passages (or groups of passages) have a bearing on the issue:[4] 1. Dan. 7.13: the phrase is not used as a title here. 2. Eth. Enoch 37–71 ('Similitudes'): here the Son of Man is an individual figure. The expression 'Son of Man' is used in a quasi-titular sense, even if it is not actually a title. 3. IV Ezra 13: here, too, the Son of Man is an individual figure.

Thus in certain apocalyptic groups there was an eschatological figure, the 'Son of Man'. The primitive Christian title took its point of departure from there, and its apocalyptic derivation is in fact clear: the Son of Man will come on the clouds of heaven (an explicit borrowing from Daniel). Unlike Jewish apocalyptic, however, the synoptic gospels know nothing of a heavenly pre-existence of the Son of Man (John is different, see below).

Are the Son of Man sayings authentic? The following reasons are given to support their authenticity: 1. The expression must be ancient, as it can only have arisen in an Aramaic-speaking context. It disappears in the Hellenistic milieu. But extreme antiquity is still no proof of its authenticity. 2. The title occurs only on the lips of Jesus.[5] But a number of passages can be demonstrated to be secondary in a comparison of the synoptic gospels: Luke 6.22 in comparison with Matt. 5.11; Luke 12.8 in comparison with Matt. 10.32. On the other hand, Matthew is secondary in the following passages: Matt. 16.13 in comparison with Mark 8.27; Matt. 16.28 in comparison with Mark 9.1; Matt. 26.2 in comparison with Mark 14.1; Matt. 19.28 in comparison with Luke 22.28–30. Matt. 13.37; 24.39 (repetition of v. 37); Luke 18.8; 21.36; 22.48 are redactional.

[1] The Jewish instances use the expression more in an undetermined way in the sense of the English 'someone' or 'one'.

[2] F. Hahn, Hoheitstitel, pp. 15f.

[3] In Ezek. 2.1 the prophet is addressed as 'Son of Man'. But the messianic title cannot have arisen from this. The prophet is addressed as being a man.

[4] Survey in Vielhauer, Aufsätze, pp. 8off.

[5] There are, however, exceptions: Acts 7.56 and Hegesippus in: Eusebius, HE II 23.13; Barnabas 12.10 rejects the title.

Three groups of sayings remain: 1. The Son of Man must suffer many things. 2. (*a*) The Son of Man has come to seek what is lost; (*b*) The Son of Man has nowhere to lay his head. 3. The Son of Man will come on the clouds (Mark 13.26).

1. *The sayings about the 'necessary' sufferings of the Son of Man.* Neither these, nor the title 'Christ', occur in Q. Special mention should be made of the three prophecies of the passion in Mark 8.31; 9.31; 10.33f.; also Mark 14.21, cf. v. 41. These are all *vaticinia ex eventu*: not prognoses for the further development of the situation, but dogmatic assertions. Mark 9.9, 12 is redactional, as is shown by the motif of the messianic secret.[1]

Conclusion: this group of Son of Man sayings is not historical.[2]

2. *The activity of the Son of Man on earth.* The material occurs in Mark, Q and Luke.

Mark 2.10 par.: the Son of Man now has authority on earth to forgive sins. Whether this is an originally independent saying or not,[3] we have a dogmatic statement which was formulated in the community.

Mark 2.28 par.: the Son of Man is Lord of the sabbath. The same assessment is to be made of this saying as in the case of the previous one.[4]

Matt. 8.20 par. Luke 9.58: the Son of Man has nowhere to lay his head. E. Schweizer[5] thinks that the saying could not have been shaped by the community; on the other hand, P. Vielhauer[6] objects that on the lips of Jesus the saying would be an unjustifiable exaggeration. According to Tödt,[7] it does not speak of Jesus' humiliation, but of his exalted state; it is an authoritative call to discipleship. But the

---

[1] E. Schweizer, *Neotestamentica*, p. 69: Mark 9.12 is an isolated logion; the Son of Man was originally the new Elijah. P. Vielhauer, *Aufsätze*, p. 118, disagrees: he regards Mark 9.12 as a construction by a scribal element in the primitive community.

[2] In prospect: it deals with the resurrection and not with the parousia. This matches the situation in the creed.

[3] According to E. Schweizer, *Neotestamentica*, p. 70, Mark 2.10 could be an authentic independent logion; P. Vielhauer, *Aufsätze*, p. 121, regards this as a serious possibility.

[4] Cf. P. Vielhauer, *Aufsätze*, pp. 122f.; E. Lohse, 'Jesu Worte über den Sabbat', BZNW 26 (Jeremias Festschrift) (1960), pp. 82f.; Vielhauer wonders whether any titular usage is present here at all. But this is surely the case.

[5] E. Schweizer, *Neotestamentica*, p. 72.

[6] P. Vielhauer, *Aufsätze*, pp. 123f.

[7] H. E. Tödt, *The Son of Man in the Synoptic Tradition*, pp. 120ff.

saying only becomes a call in the context (v. 19), which Schweizer regards as original; the scene is historical. – The saying is only comprehensible as a summary survey of the whole of Jesus' activity, and thus as a dogmatic statement.

Matt. 11.18f. par. Luke 7.33f.: John came and did not eat and drink . . . The Son of Man came eating and drinking. This saying, too, is not 'uninventable'. It is again a summary characterization of the whole of Jesus' activity.

Luke 11.30 (Q): the sign of Jonah. The saying is given with considerable variations in Matt. 12.40. If it is an isolated logion it cannot be interpreted. If the connection with v. 29 is original, it is uncertain whether the reference is to the present or the future Son of Man. In either case, it is impossible to make historical use of the saying.

Mark 10.45 par. Matt. 20.28: this, too, is a general dogmatic interpretation of the career of Jesus.

Matt. 12.32 par. Luke 12.10: the saying presupposes a division of periods of salvation history on the basis of Easter. It occurs without the title Son of Man in Mark 3.28f.

Luke 19.10: this is a variant of Mark 2.17. Here, too, there is a generalized interpretation by the community.

Conclusion: Bultmann continues to assume that this group of words originally spoke of 'man' in general terms. But its significance as a title cannot be questioned. In every case, therefore, we have formulations of community doctrine.

E. Schweizer[1] would find the authentic nucleus of material precisely in this group, i.e. in the idea of the humiliation and exaltation of the righteous man, which Jesus refers to himself. Neither Judaism nor the community know the rejected Son of Man, living on the earth. Jesus takes up the Jewish theme of the suffering righteous man (Wisdom of Solomon). But the suffering righteous man is not called 'Son of Man', but 'Son of God'. Moreover, the Jewish Son of Man is an apocalyptic figure. 'Son of Man' is not a self-designation. Above all, the sayings about the present Son of Man nowhere contain the idea of exaltation. Schweizer has to introduce this from John.

3. *The coming Son of Man.* Material: Mark, Q, special material. There is no reference to the suffering and resurrection in this group. In it, Jesus speaks of the Son of Man as though he were another person. Mark 13.26 par.: the saying comes from Dan. 7.13.

---

[1] E. Schweizer, *Neotestamentica*, pp. 74f.

Mark 14.62: Dan. 7.13 is combined with Ps. 110.1 in the framework of a compendium of christological titles.[1]

Matt. 10.23 (Jesus' sending out of the disciples, special material) is an apocalyptic word of comfort in view of the persecution of the church, and therefore arose after Easter. Jesus is identical with the Son of Man. The same situation (persecution of the church) is reflected in Luke 6.22; cf. Matt. 5.11.

Luke 17.22ff.: the basic theme of the 'Logia apocalypse' is the sudden onset of the end.

Luke 17.22 is a redactional introduction, which does not fit with v. 26. The same expression occurs in both verses, but with different senses. The interpretation of the 'days of the Son of Man' to refer to the days of the earthly Jesus is impossible. The authenticity of vv. 23f. is debated. Vielhauer[2] finds the expectation of the Messiah in v. 23 and the expectation of the Son of Man in v. 24. In that case, the combination would be secondary, anyway.

As a nucleus there remains Mark 8.38 par.[3] The saying also occurs in Q: Matt. 10.32f. par. Luke 12.8f. In Mark and Q there is originally a formal distinction between Jesus and the Son of Man: the future attitude of the Son of Man to men depends on the present attitude of men to Jesus. The Son of Man is the judge (not the witness before the judgment-seat of God). There is a wide-ranging consensus that this saying is authentic. The distinction between Jesus and the Son of Man cannot be explained as a community construction. The community identified the two, as Matthew's version shows. But on the lips of Jesus the saying becomes incomprehensible: there is no indication of the relationship in which Jesus himself stands to this Son of Man. There is no suggestion, for instance, that Jesus expects to be changed into the Son of Man. E. Schweizer[4] argues that Jesus did not expect the coming of the Son of Man, but his exaltation to being the Son of Man. This assumption is impossible (see above on Mark 14.62). The idea of exaltation is introduced from John. It occurs in Jewish literature only in Eth. Enoch 70f., which is an addition. Furthermore, the impression that Jesus and the Son of Man are differentiated in

---

[1] J. A. T. Robinson, *Jesus and his Coming* (1957), pp. 43ff.: the saying is concerned with the exaltation rather than the parousia. But this interpretation goes against the order: sitting at God's right hand, coming on the clouds.

[2] P. Vielhauer, *Aufsätze*, p. 75.

[3] E. Haenchen, 'Die Komposition von Mk VIII 27–IX I und Par.', *NovTest* 6 (1963), pp. 81ff.

[4] E. Schweizer, *Neotestamentica*, pp. 58f.

this saying rests on a confusion. The distinction is not between two persons, but between two periods in the activity of the same person.[1] The fact that the Son of Man is spoken of in the third person is in accord with the widespread evidence in all groups of sayings about the Son of Man. Therefore this saying has not been formulated on the basis of a general apocalyptic idea of the Son of Man, but is referred *a priori* to Jesus as the Son of Man, i.e., it arose after Easter. This is confirmed by the keywords ὁμολογεῖν (Luke 12.8), ἀρνεῖσθαι or ἐπαισχύνεσθαι: the situation of the confessing church in the world is presupposed. The time is one in which the whole relationship to Jesus is determined through confession of his person, a time in which a man can be summoned before a tribunal because of this confession. Finally, the point made by Vielhauer, that 'kingdom of God' and 'Son of Man' are consistently separated in the earliest strata, also tells against its authenticity.

The evidence in John is very different.[2] The Son of Man is the pre-existent revealer who descended from heaven (3.13) and lives in constant union with his Father (1.51). Even the suffering of the Son of Man is changed in the Johannine presentation: he will be 'raised up' on the cross (3.14). The cross and Easter are identical, as are Easter and the parousia. In the same way, his role as judge is determined by the Johannine eschatology (5.27). John has evidently taken up the title Son of Man from the community tradition and shaped it afresh along the lines of his theology.

Bultmann's interpretation differs: In his view, the Johannine Son of Man has a different origin in the history of religion from the Son of Man in the synoptic gospels. He does not derive from apocalyptic, but from gnosticism, and is identical with the mythical Anthropos. Against this, however, it must be affirmed that the Johannine Son of Man has the same apocalyptic derivation as the synoptic Son of Man. The deviations of John from the synoptic gospels can be understood as a deliberate revision by the author of the Fourth Gospel.

Summary

The unconnected juxtaposition of the three groups of sayings about

[1] Thus with Vielhauer, *Aufsätze*, p. 106, and G. Iber, to whose unpublished Heidelberg dissertation *Überlieferungsgeschichtliche Untersuchungen zum Begriff des Menschensohnes im NT* (1953), p. 55, Vielhauer refers.

[2] R. Schnackenburg, 'Der Menschensohn im Johannesevangelium', *NTS* 11 (1965), pp. 123–37; G. Iber, see previous note; S. Schulz, *Untersuchungen zur Menschensohnchristologie im Johannesevangelium* (1957); F. Hahn, *Hoheitstitel*, p. 39, n. 6.

the Son of Man can be explained from the structure of the christology of the early community. They believed in the death and resurrection of Jesus; they waited for the parousia. Both points are formulated independently, as the evidence of the confession shows. The one who was expected, and imagined with the help of the idea of the Son of Man, was identified with Jesus. So his appearance on earth was also interpreted with the title Son of Man.

V The Miracles of Jesus

A. Fridrichsen, *Le problème du miracle dans le Christianisme primitif* (1925). History of religions: O. Weinreich, *Gebet und Wunder* (1929); R. Bultmann, 'The Question of Wonder', *Faith and Understanding* (1969), pp. 247–61; H. Schlingensiepen, *Die Wunder des NT* (1933); R. Hansliek, 'Christus und die hellenistischen Wundermänner', *Theologie der Zeit* (1936), pp. 203ff.; R. M. Grant, *Miracle and Natural Law in Graeco-Roman and Early Christian Thought* (1952); K. Prümm, *Religionsgeschichtliches Handbuch für den Raum der altchristlichen Umwelt* (1954), pp. 442–64; G. Delling, 'Zum Verständnis des Wunders im NT', *ZSTh* 24 (1955), pp. 265–80; T. A. Burkill, 'The Notion of Miracle', *ZNW* 50 (1959), pp. 33–48; R. S. Wallace, *The Gospel Miracles* (1960); R. H. Fuller, *Interpreting the Miracles* (1963); H. van der Loos, *The Miracles of Jesus*, SupplNovTest 9 (1965).

The miracles said to have been performed by Jesus are also a factor of christology.

There will be no discussion of the scientific side of miracle here. This enquiry is limited to the New Testament understanding of miracle and is not concerned with reflection on natural laws. Of course, it is an exaggeration to say that during the New Testament period there was a general readiness for the occurrence of miracles. It is an integral feature of the concept of miracle that a miracle is 'impossible' and is surprising when it takes place.

Jesus sees his actions as signs of the coming kingdom of God. It is from them, and not from the christological titles, that his understanding of himself can be grasped – above all from his expelling of demons. The exorcisms seem to put Jesus on a par with contemporary exorcists, and he can in fact sometimes be compared with them (Matt. 12.27). In that case, how is his action different from magic? The texts also show attempts of the community, while asserting the miracles, to differentiate them from magic.[1]

This tendency becomes manifest in the story of the temptation and in the reflections of Mark, who makes the miracle stories an illustration of the power of

---

[1] M. Dibelius, *From Tradition to Gospel*, pp. 102f.; H. Windisch, *Paulus und Christus*, UNT 24 (1934), pp. 154f.

the teaching of Jesus (1.21ff.). The distinction in Acts, which shows the superiority of the Christian θεῖος ἀνήρ to the non-Christian (19.14ff.), is more primitive. Here the miracle appears once again as an expedient (13.6ff.).

Can belief in miracles really be shown to differ from magic, rather than this difference simply being asserted through the representation of the helplessness of the magician? According to Ernst Käsemann[1] the question is whether Jesus appears as a magician who believes that the world is bedevilled, or as one who knows the evil of the human heart and claims this heart for God. This is an important insight; but it is still insufficient. The decisive question is whether the community makes miracles the content of belief, whether the programme of the temptation narratives is maintained to its culmination on the cross.

The understanding of the miracles as a sign of the nearness of the kingdom produces a unitary standpoint from which to understand Jesus' words and actions.

VI   The Messianic Secret

W. Wrede, *Das Messiasgeheimnis in den Evangelien* (1901); H. J. Ebeling, *Das Messiasgeheimnis und die Botschaft des Marcus-Evangelisten*, BZNW 19 (1939); E. Sjöberg, *Der verborgene Menschensohn in den Evangelien* (1955); G. H. Boobyer, 'The Secrecy Motif in St. Mark's Gospel', *NTS* 6 (1960), pp. 225–35; T. A. Burkill, *Mysterious Revelation* (1963); G. Strecker, 'Zur Messiasgeheimnistheorie in Markusevangelium', TU 88 (*Studia Evangelica III*) (1964), pp. 87–104; U. Luz, 'Das Geheimnismotiv und die markinische Christologie', *ZNW* 56 (1965), pp. 9–30; G. Minette de Tillesse, *Le secret messianique dans l'évangile de Marc* (Paris, 1968).

The view that Jesus conceals his majesty determines the whole shape of the gospel of Mark; it is indicated in the following instances:

1. The demons know Jesus and call to him. But Jesus makes them keep silent, precisely because they know him (1.24f., 34; 3.11f.). This command for silence cannot be understood in biographical terms. It takes place too late; the secret has already been betrayed.

2. Healings of the sick: Jesus raises to life the dead daughter of Jairus and commands that no one shall be told what has happened. This is an impossible command: the house is full of mourners.

3. Jesus' work is not understood, even by his disciples (Mark 6.52).

4. He tells the parable of the sower. The disciples do not understand it and ask him the meaning of the parable. They are rebuked: 'Do you not understand this parable? How then will you understand all the parables?' Jesus then explains that the parables are disclosed only to faith. They are told to those outside in order that they shall not be understood (Mark's 'parable theory', 4.10–12). It is clear that

---

[1] E. Käsemann, *Essays on New Testament Themes*, pp. 39f.

this theory is secondary. That makes the question what the evangelist means by it all the more urgent.

5. Jesus goes with his disciples into a lonely place and asks them whom people say that he is, then, whom the disciples say that he is. Peter replies with the confession: 'You are the Messiah'. Jesus forbids him to mention this further. There then follows the first prediction of the passion. Peter protests against it. He has thus not understood what he has said. Cf. Mark 9.32. The misunderstanding of the disciples continues, since they have not understood even after the transfiguration.

Wrede attempted to interpret these observations in a comprehensive way: that Jesus concealed his Messiahship does not accord with historical reality. It is rather a view of the community after Easter. Jesus did not regard himself as Messiah. He only became Messiah in the belief of the community. This raises a difficulty: the tradition of the deeds and actions of Jesus says nothing about his Messiahship. The imbalance between faith after Easter and the tradition before Easter drove the community to the explanation that Jesus knew he was Messiah, but kept the fact secret. Wrede's observations are brilliant. His explanation is, of course, a speculative historical construction. Certainly Jesus did not regard himself as Messiah, and the messianic secret is a theological construction of the community.[1] But it did not arise out of the working over of originally un-messianic material. Rather, the whole Jesus tradition already had a messianic stamp at the time when this theory was first developed (presumably by Mark himself). It is not a laborious apologetic expedient, but a positive account prompted by an understanding of revelation. Wrede's explanation is much too modern by the standards of early Christian thought. This can be seen from the passages where the theory of the secret and the tradition clash most sharply. Here the tradition is certainly not un-messianic, but expressly and thematically messianic: the confession of Peter, the conversation after the transfiguration. The theological construction is to be understood in the context of the whole christological development of the tradition about Jesus. It does not simply serve to overcome an individual problem. The tenor is not apologetic. The stress is on the irresistible way in which the call of Jesus is passed on – despite commands to keep silence. The theory becomes clear when we realize that here the evangelist represents the paradoxical character of the revelation: the faithful – i.e. the readers of the book – are shown the mystery in such a way that it remains veiled from the world even after Easter. It can only be grasped through faith, i.e. in the church. To those without it remains hidden. The misunderstanding of the disciples means that Jesus' work can be understood only after Easter.

This theory made it possible for Mark to collect the different groups of traditional material under a single viewpoint and thus to create the form of the 'gospel'.

---

[1] See Bultmann, *Theology of the New Testament* I, p. 32, against J. Schniewind, 'Messiasgeheimnis und Eschatologie', in: *Nachgelassene Reden und Aufsätze* (1952), pp. 1–13: it is not in the substance of the traditional stories, but in the redactional work.

How then did Jesus regard himself? The answer cannot be given by a christological concept. It must come through a demonstration of how Jesus associated the announcement of the kingdom of God with himself as its sign. Of course a christology is implied here.[1] It will have to be developed after Easter.

17 · THE THEOLOGY OF THE THREE SYNOPTIC GOSPELS

S. Schulz, *Die Stunde der Botschaft* (1967); J. Reumann, *Jesus in the Church's Gospels* (1968).

In the period before the emergence of form criticism, the gospels were regarded predominantly as sources for the historical reconstruction of the life and teaching of Jesus. Form criticism showed that each individual piece of tradition had christological significance in itself. It left the literary framework, which it demonstrated to be secondary, relatively untouched. As the evangelists had only primitive literary means at their disposal, they were not rated very high as theologians. On the other hand, form criticism had created the presupposition for recognizing and interpreting the literary framework. If we investigate this, we shall recognize that we are using the evangelists as a means of depicting their theology.

I   Mark

In addition to the literature mentioned in section 16 VI, see: E. Lohmeyer, *Galiläa und Jerusalem*, FRLANT NF 34 (1936); C. H. Dodd, *The Apostolic Preaching and its Developments* (1956[8]); R. H. Lightfoot, *Locality and Doctrine in the Gospels* (1938); id., *The Gospel Message of St Mark* (1950); J. M. Robinson, *The Problem of History in Mark*, SBT 21 (1957); T. A. Burkill, 'St. Mark's Philosophy of History', *NTS* 3 (1956/7), pp. 142–48; id., 'The Cryptology of Parables in St. Mark's Gospel', *NovTest* 1 (1957), pp. 246–62; id., 'St. Mark's Philosophy of the Passion', *NovTest* 2 (1958), pp. 245–71; id., 'Anti-Semitism in St. Mark's Gospel', *NovTest* 3 (1959), pp. 34–53; W. Marxsen, *Der Evangelist Markus*, FRLANT 67 (1959[2]); E. Schweizer, 'Anmerkungen zur Theologie des Markus', SupplNovTest 6 (Cullmann Festschrift) (1962), pp. 35–46 (=*Neotestamentica* (1963), pp. 93–104); id., 'Die theologische Leistung des Markus', *EvTh* 24 (1964), pp. 337–55; E. Haenchen, *Der Weg Jesu* (1966); P. Vielhauer, 'Erwägungen zur Christologie des Markusevangeliums', *Zeit und Geschichte* (Bultmann Festschrift) (1964), pp. 155–69 (=*Aufsätze zum NT*,

---

[1] Bultmann, *op. cit.*, p. 43; *Faith and Understanding* (1969), p. 237; H. Conzelmann, *RGG*[3] II 667f.; III 633f.

ThB 31 (1965), pp. 199–214); A. Suhl, *Die Function der at. Zitate und Anspielungen im Markusevangelium* (1965); J. Schreiber, *Theologie des Vertrauens* (1967); S. Schulz, *op. cit.*, pp. 9ff.

Dibelius described the gospel of Mark as the 'book of secret epiphanies'. This characterization is apt and has not been superseded by more recent attempts to air the messianic secret.

E. Sjöberg wants to derive the secret from Jesus himself by an investigation of themes in the history of religion. This attempt fails because the secret does not have its place in the early parts of the tradition, but in the framework. There is only one apparent exception: the command to the demons to keep silent (1.24). But this is not historical: it represents the pre-Marcan form of the secret-theory.[1]

Mark's understanding of revelation is clear from the structure of his book. In literary terms, its shaping is primitive. But from a theological point of view it proves to be astonishingly well thought out. This is already clear as early as in the introduction, which is a title: ἀρχὴ τοῦ εὐαγγελίου ᾽Ιησοῦ Χριστοῦ.[2] By opening his report with John the Baptist, Mark (like Q) constructs a framework of saving history round the work of Jesus. Mark does not follow Matthew and Luke in claiming the history of Israel as the early history of the church. Israel is presented only in contrast to Jesus: the Old Testament is not understood in respect of its immanent meaning, as the history of Israel, but as a prophecy of the Baptist, who prepares the way for Jesus.[3] The strict limitation of perspective at the beginning is matched by the limitation of eschatological prospect at the end: it points towards the parousia, but not beyond. This time between resurrection and parousia (Mark 13.10) is usually called 'the time of the church'. But care should be exercised in the use of this expression. It is appropriate for Luke, but only with qualifications for Mark: true, he already reckons on a lengthy period between present and parousia.[4] But he still does not develop the notion of the church positively into a theological concept. He defines the church only in terms of the one task of preaching the gospel throughout the world. Above all, as yet, he does not grasp the connection in thought between christology and the intermediate period. What does the Exalted One do in the intermediate period? He strengthens those who confess him under persecution.

[1] U. Luz, *op. cit.*
[2] Haenchen, *ad loc.*
[3] Suhl, *op. cit.*, pp. 133–37.
[4] Against Marxsen, *op. cit.*, with E. Grässer, *Das Problem der Parusieverzögerung*, BZNW 22 (1960²).

But ideas about the present activity of the Exalted One are not yet systematized. In this respect, Mark represents an intermediate stage of reflection between the oral tradition and Luke, or Matthew.

After the introduction, concerned with John the Baptist, there are two distinct blocks which describe two different epochs of Jesus' ministry:

1. Galilee. Jesus preaches and heals; he is surrounded by mystery. He does miracles; but not once do the disciples understand them or Jesus on the basis of them (6.52; 8.17ff.). The sphere of his authority is first the district round the Sea of Galilee. Then he extends it, to Phoenicia, to the land east of the Jordan. Finally Jesus goes with his disciples to the north, to the neighbourhood of Caesarea Philippi. The noose tightens, the events reach a dramatic climax. The mystery is penetrated in the circle of disciples, by Peter's confession. But his recognition that Jesus is the Messiah may not be made public. The announcement of the nature of Jesus and his mystery are still more intensively related in the transfiguration scene. But in both cases the revelation comes up against a failure to understand. The Christian reader knows that Jesus cannot yet be understood; this will only be possible through the resurrection. Peter's confession and the transfiguration usher in the period of the passion, rather than that of open messianic proclamation.

Attempts are still continually made to maintain that Jesus' 'withdrawal' after Caesarea Philippi is historical, and to give it a pragmatic explanation: Jesus had no success with his preaching, therefore he wanted at least to assure himself of his last faithful followers. This theory of a failure in Galilee is exclusively the result of an unhistorical combination of the Marcan and Johannine accounts (John 6.66–71). The motive for the 'withdrawal' is rather the messianic secret. This is shown by the link between Peter's confession and the prophecy of the passion and Peter's reaction to it. Mark's intention is demonstrated in the threefold repetition of the prophecy of the passion at the climax in chs. 8, 9 and 10.

2. With the presentation of the true nature of Jesus by confession and transfiguration, and the announcement of his destiny in the prophecy of the passion, the first epoch, the time of preaching in Galilee, is at an end. Now Jesus must set out for his divinely appointed goal, for Jerusalem (ch. 10). Here he reveals his nature in public by entering the city as Son of David, i.e. as Messiah. Events at Jerusalem are compressed into a few days. He still preaches, even now, but his

teaching is limited to a few themes, above all the doctrine of the last things (ch. 13). Then follows the passion in Jerusalem.

Lohmeyer and Lightfoot and, following them, Marxsen, have shown that in Mark the districts of Galilee and Judaea designate more than geographical areas. They have a theological quality. The despised Galilee, the land of the Gentiles, is the place in which salvation appears. In this way the paradoxical character of revelation as concealed revelation, the choice of the lowly ones, despised by official Israel, is shown. On the other hand, the centre of religion, Jerusalem, is portrayed as a place of extreme hostility. Salvation by means of Galilee and the rejection of Jerusalem both come about in the activity of Jesus: the former by his concealed epiphany, the latter in his public passion. After the crucifixion, the risen Messiah leaves the city. He goes to Galilee and summons his people to follow him (Mark 16.7). Here the final verdict on Jerusalem and its worship takes place.[1]

The division of the gospel of Mark into two epochs, two areas, is of a theological nature. Mark presents no psychological development of the personality of Jesus and no biographical association of events, but depicts the twofold way in which the revelation is presented to the world, first by means of the proclamation. This is directed towards a public. But its meaning, i.e. its truth, remains concealed to some extent even after Easter. For even after Easter, the Exalted One is visible only in such a way that he is also recognized at the same time as the Earthly One, and that means as the Crucified One. The account of this event itself becomes an ingredient of the saving event, as it discloses the mystery of the kingdom of God. The whole book is thus shaped by the Easter faith. It is quite simply a commentary on the kerygma. This is already clear from the external extent of its two main sections.

The fact that the account of the last weeks of the life of Jesus occupies almost as much room as that of the whole of his public ministry represents an imbalance from the biographical point of view. But this proportion becomes clear from the kerygmatic division which can be recognized, e.g. in Acts 2. 22–24: 1. God showed wonders through Jesus. 2. According to God's plan you nailed him on the cross, but God has raised him up.

Lohmeyer derives the Marcan view of Galilee from a primitive community in Galilee which existed alongside that of Jerusalem. In this way he tries to assign two types of christology to the two communities: Galilee reveres the Son of Man, Jerusalem the Messiah (Luke). He also sees two types of eucharist: Galilee celebrates the breaking of the bread, Jerusalem the memorial meal. But Son of Man and Messiah cannot be assigned to two different groups.[2] (For the eucharist, see

---

[1] For a criticism of Lohmeyer see R. Preuss, *Galiläa im Markusevangelium*, Diss. Göttingen, 1967.

[2] Bultmann, *Theology of the New Testament* I, pp. 52f.

section 7 IV 3 above.) Marxsen assumes that the gospel of Mark was composed at the beginning of the Jewish war, c. AD 66, not in Galilee, but in Jerusalem, with an eye to Galilee. It represents a topical programme, brought out in the expectation that the approaching war was bringing the end of the world and the parousia. It therefore summons the community to flee from Jerusalem to Galilee, where the Lord will appear (Mark 13.14; 16.7). This assumption can be refuted by an analysis of Mark 13 alone – quite apart from the improbability that anyone who saw the catastrophe on the way would calmly write a book to prompt immediate flight. Vielhauer discusses the Marcan type of christology.[1] He rightly asserts that Mark has no pre-existence. The essential christological title is Son of God. He designates the nature of Jesus as that of a θεῖος ἀνήρ (miracle stories!). The significance of the title as a designation of Jesus, however, emerges more strongly: Jesus is the king of the eschatological time of salvation. This status is developed in three related stages in accordance with the scheme of progressive enthronement: baptism, transfiguration, crucifixion. The characterization of the Marcan theology as a *theologia crucis* is apt. This also governs the messianic secret.

II Matthew

K. Stendahl, *The School of St Matthew* (1954); G. Bornkamm, G. Barth, H. J. Held, *Tradition and Interpretation in Matthew* (1963); W. Trilling, *Das wahre Israel* (1964³); G. Strecker, *Der Weg der Gerechtigkeit*, FRLANT 82 (1962); R. Hummel, *Die Auseinandersetzung zwischen Kirche und Judentum im Matthäusevangelium*, BhEvTh 33 (1963); R. Walker, *Die Heilsgeschichte im ersten Evangelium*, FRLANT 91 (1967); S. Schulz, *op. cit.*, pp. 157ff.

Matthew takes up Mark's idea of Galilee as the chosen district and emphasizes it further by introducing a scriptural proof showing Galilee as the promised land of fulfilment (Matt. 4.15f.). This passage illustrates Matthew's tendency to clarify the paradox of revelation: it appears in the form of lowliness, it is intended for the poor and those of no account (10.42; 18.6, 10). Thus the entry into Jerusalem is illuminated by a quotation from Isa. 62.11; Zech. 9.9. The natures of the revealer and the receiver of revelation correspond.[2] This is set out in almost tabular form in the beatitudes (5.3ff.). They certainly go back to tradition (Q, cf. Luke), but have been extended and modified by Matthew: Matthew interprets the phrase 'Blessed are the poor' by the addition 'in spirit'[3]; 'those who hunger and thirst' by

[1] P. Vielhauer, *Aufsätze*, pp. 199ff., against J. Schreiber, 'Die Christologie des Markusevangeliums', *ZThK* 58 (1961), pp. 154–83.

[2] G. Barth, 'Matthew's Understanding of the Law', in: Bornkamm, Barth, Held, *Tradition and Interpretation in Matthew*, pp. 129ff.

[3] There is now evidence for the expression 'poor in spirit' in the Qumran writings; cf. H. Braun, *Qumran und das NT* I (1966), *ad loc*. That does not mean that Matthew is original in comparison with Luke.

'after righteousness'. See v. 10, a redactional creation by the evangelist: 'who are persecuted for righteousness' sake'.

The word δικαιοσύνη plays no role in the teaching of Jesus. In Matthew it becomes an ethical principle (5.20; cf. 6.33). A further key word of Matthew is 'perfection'. Among the synoptic gospels, it occurs only in his work (5.48; 19.21).

These words have led scholars to talk of Matthew's 'legalism' and to explain it from his Jewish background. But a verdict of this kind is a superficial one. The mere fact that Matthew presents a universalistic idea of the church should prompt reflection (28.16–20.)[1] The situation in which Matthew thinks and writes must be kept in mind. His community is involved in an actual controversy with Judaism – evidently in connection with the Jewish war and the Jewish restoration movement which began after it, in which the Pharisaic rabbinate came to the fore. The acuteness of the controversy can be seen in Matthew's basic idea, which involves the saving history: the church is the true Israel. The empirical Israel has misunderstood its commission to be a light to the nations and therefore lost its election (in a metaphor: the vineyard has been given to another people). The church has taken the place of Israel; but it must maintain continuity. The Jewish-Christian community to which Matthew belongs withdraws from the Jewish alliance and the law, but struggles with it over the claim to be the true people of God (Matt. 23.1ff.). This tie with Israel does not lead Matthew to limit the church to Jewish Christianity; on the contrary, the task of Israel was always a universal one. This is the origin of Matthew's notion of the church made up of all nations (Trilling).

The theological principle at work here is that of promise and fulfilment. It permeates the whole book, noticeably in the 'formula quotation'. The existence of Jesus in lowliness and persecution, determined by the salvation history, is the pattern for the present relationship of the church to Judaism. Thus the fulfilment of the promise results in the sharpest of antitheses between the Israel which refused the message of faith and the Israel who will be blessed with its righteousness (5.17–20).[2] Matthew uses a logion from Q (Luke 16.17) about the abiding of the law. He makes this into a statement of

[1] G. Bornkamm, 'Der Auferstandene und der Irdische. Mt. 28.16–20', *Zeit und Geschichte* (Bultmann Festschrift) (1964), pp. 171–91.

[2] E. Schweizer, 'Matt. 5, 17–20', *ThLZ* 77 (1952), cols. 479–84 (= *Neotestamentica*, 1963, pp. 399–406); G. Barth, *op. cit.*, pp. 64–73; W. Trilling, *op. cit.*, pp. 167–86; G. Strecker, *op. cit.*, pp. 143–47.

principle about the law, righteousness and the way of salvation. Jesus has not come to destroy, but to fulfil, i.e. to assert as valid (in the sense of the 'exposition' which follows). Here Jesus seems to enter into competition with the rabbis: Christian exposition of the law is set against that of the rabbis. In reality, however, Matthew does not think of a quantitatively definable number of regulations in the law which are to be carried out. He is concerned rather with exposition of the law as a whole through the commandment of love. On the other hand, the Jewish tradition is seen not as practice, but as avoidance of the commandment. Its representatives separate the outward and the inward. They sieve out flies and swallow camels. They are hypocrites and lead men astray: they shut up the kingdom of heaven. The Sermon on the Mount and the address to the Pharisees (Matt. 23) illustrate the way in which they set the commandment at naught with their precepts. Their conduct serves for them to assert themselves. Therefore they persecute the faithful and thus document the fact that Israel has lost its nature as a people of God. So the church, because it is the true Israel, is handed over to suffering. The commandment to love one's enemy gains its concrete significance in persecution (5.44).

In the train of Israel, the church shapes its inner ordering as an eschatological brotherhood which deliberately sets itself apart from the Jewish form of the synagogue (Matt. 23.8–12).

Here we have the factors of the idea of the church: Israel, the law, a particular christology, eschatology, which is given a new intensification in Matthew's work. The relationship to the Jews on the one hand, and the necessity to make long-term arrangements in the world on the other, lead to the setting up of both teaching ordinances and discipline (Matt. 18).

After the baptism and temptation, Mark begins Jesus' ministry with a series of miracles (Mark 1f.). Instead, Matthew puts the great sermon (Matt. 5–7) at the beginning and the miracles only after that (Matt. 8f.). As a result of this construction the miracles appear in another light: they support doctrine, which is the main thing.

Matthew distinguishes Jesus' public teaching from the special instruction to the disciples. He did not invent this esoteric teaching. It is already to be found in Mark (the key to the parables, Mark 4.10–12; the eschatological speech, Mark 13). But Matthew takes it far beyond these early beginnings. Esoteric is in itself a characteristic of a sect. But although there is esoteric teaching in Matthew, he knows of no instructions, unlike the sect, to keep it secret. The special instruction of the disciples is merely to show the community the origin of their public proclamation (cf. 10.26f.). Esoteric is thus associated with the period before Easter. From then on everything is public.

Even the teaching about the end of the world is not secret. The only question is whether it is heard and understood. Apocalyptic features are more pronounced in Matthew than with Jesus. But there is a counterbalance against speculations: where Matthew develops his picture of the judgment (Matt. 25), it is not an end in itself. From the judgment, one learns only one thing, that one must know how to stand in it; that judgment is exclusively according to works.

Judgment by works is the standard of the whole New Testament, even in Paul. This is only surprising if one begins from a restricted concept of justification. Both Paul and Matthew show the critical significance of the principle: the end of all human assurance. It is no advantage for the Jew to be a Jew – or for the Christian to be a Christian. The idea of justification only by works corresponds to the universality of the offer of salvation. It prevents calculation of merit. The antitheses of the Sermon on the Mount with their radical quality and demand for perfection leave no room for this. In the judgment (Matt. 25.31) the elect do not know beforehand what they have contributed. Cf. also the stress on discipleship, humility. Discipleship is not the way to perfection, but the very perfection that is demanded.[1]

The church distinguishes itself from an apocalyptic sect by not isolating itself from the world. The world is not demon-ridden, but reclaimed as the kingdom of Christ (13.37ff.). Therefore the church does not attempt the eschatological separation of righteous and unrighteous in the world. The separation is reserved for God; it lies in the future (13.24ff.).[2]

It is illuminating to see how Matthew brings each of his teaching discourses to a climax in an eschatological prospect.[3] From time to time he introduces this from the idea of the church: the church is threatened in the world by persecution from outside and by heresy within. Warnings can also be found in these discourses in the fixed passages which precede the eschatological prospect. In accordance with this idea of the church, the disciples are instructed about the commandments and a church order arises. But neither the law nor the ordering of the church lead to the formation of the church along

[1] G. Barth, *op. cit.*, pp. 95ff., esp. p. 101.

[2] The parable of the wheat and the tares can lead to a differentiation against either the conception of the church as a *corpus mixtum* or the idea of an *ecclesia invisibilis*.

[3] G. Bornkamm, 'End-Expectation and Church in Matthew', in: Bornkamm, Barth, Held, *Tradition and Interpretation in Matthew*, pp. 15–51.

the lines of a sect. The law is not understood as a regulating ordinance through which the elect incorporate themselves, by giving themselves a special ordering of life. What is demanded applies to every man.

We cannot simply measure Matthew's teaching on the law against Paul and argue that Matthew represents the law.

Strecker falls victim to this tendency: the presupposition of the ethical imperative is not, in his view, the offer of salvation (the indicative). On the contrary, the ethical demand marks the beginning and forgiveness of sins is the goal. This is to misunderstand the situation in which Matthew writes: (a) he writes after Easter; i.e. the existence of the church, baptism, the forgiveness of sins are the presuppositions of his theological thought. Strecker is wrong in pointing to the Lord's Prayer as a basis for his interpretation of Matthew: 'And forgive us our debts, as we forgive our debtors'. This is an address to God in prayer. One need only think of the reverse of the remark: 'O God, forgive me first and then I will forgive, too.' No, I turn to God for forgiveness, and the declaration of my own readiness to forgive makes it clear that I cannot behave like the unmerciful servant. (b) Matthew presupposes the existence of Israel, where the law is an entity which is taken for granted. In this situation, Matthew has to make a critical use of faith; against the use of the law for self-assertion, against hypocrisy, against casuistry which in truth means avoidance of the will of God. This all-embracing protest against legalism governs his outward polemic against the Jews and the inner life of the community. Just as in the outside world the commandment of love applies without qualification, so in the community the stumbling block to the 'little ones' is to be avoided. The teaching ministry is the only legitimate one.

The assembly of the community has the power to bind and to loose, i.e. authority in teaching and in discipline. Its decisions will hold in heaven.[1] It is clear that this is no doctrinal and disciplinary authority in the sense of the catholic concept of the church. It is not irrevocably delegated to any particular authority; the church is not an intermediate authority with its own power of communicating salvation. Its authority to divide is achieved in the administration of the word, the distinction between true and false teaching, order and disorder in the church.

It cannot be disputed that it is possible for a development to lead from Matthew to a new legalism. This happens as soon as his thought is detached from its historical context and regarded as abstract teaching about the way of salvation.[2] Even in Matthew, the dialectic of

---

[1] According to Matt. 16.19, this authority is given to Peter; according to Matt. 18.18 it is given to the community.

[2] The exact church in which Matthew came into being and the situation towards which it is directed are both disputed. Strecker argues that it is Gentile-Christian, Bornkamm (in *Zeit und Geschichte*, pp. 171ff.) that it combines law and

present and future is dominant, particularizing itself in the imperative and following from the indicative of the promise of salvation. In the context of systematic theology, there is no correspondence between righteousness in Paul and righteousness in Matthew; the parallel is between righteousness in Paul and the kingdom of God in Matthew.

III   Luke

P. Vielhauer, 'Zum "Paulinismus" der Apostelgeschichte', *EvTh* 10 (1950/51), pp. 1–15 (=*Aufsätze zum NT*, ThB 31, 1965, pp. 9–27); H. Conzelmann, *The Theology of St Luke* (1960); E. Lohse, 'Lukas als Theologe der Heilsgeschichte', *EvTh* 14 (1954), pp. 256–75; U. Luck, 'Kerygma, Tradition und Geschichte Jesu bei Lukas', *ZThK* 57 (1960), pp. 51–66; J. C. O'Neill, *The Theology of Acts in its Historical Setting* (1961); U. Wilckens, *Die Missionsreden der Apostelgeschichte*, WMANT 5 (1961); H.-W. Bartsch, *Wachet aber zu jeder Zeit!* (1963); W. C. Robinson, *Der Weg des Herrn*, ThF 36 (1964); H. Flender, *St Luke, Theologian of Redemptive History* (1967); W. Ott, *Gebet und Heil*, StANT 12 (1965); G. Voss, 'Die Christologie der lukanischen Schriften in Grundzügen', in: A. Descamps and B. Rigaux (eds.), *Studia Neotestamentica* II (1965); S. Schulz, *op. cit.*, pp. 235ff.

Luke's theology represents an average type.

His thought is often characterized as 'early catholic'. In fact the idea of tradition is strengthened in it. It is guaranteed by the concept of the apostle, which is limited to the twelve. The church no longer looks forward to an imminent end, but comes to terms with the world. This characterization is not, however, enough. The presence of the idea of tradition is not in itself an indication of early catholicism. An idea of tradition is there from the beginning. It is given with the relationship of faith to historical revelation, with the creed itself. It becomes 'catholic' only when the tradition is guaranteed in an institutional way, by teaching ministry and church ordinances, and above all by a succession in ministry; when the spirit and the sacraments are bound to an institution, when the church makes itself the legally constituted form of salvation. Luke knows the office of the apostle, but has no idea of succession; he knows the tradition, but has no legally constituted organization to hand it on.

Even the relaxation of eschatology, which is certainly to be noted, proves to be a positive result of theological reflection. Luke has understood that the expectation of an imminent end cannot be continued.

---

christology as a corrective against a Hellenistic Christianity. Cf. G. Barth, *op. cit.*, pp. 64ff., 125ff. On the other hand, W. G. Kümmel, *Introduction to the New Testament* (1966), p. 83, objects that there is no polemic against antinomianism. Hummel's view is that it is Jewish-Christian; Trilling's, that a Jewish-Christian stratum has been worked over in a Gentile-Christian direction by a final redaction.

That he works deliberately is clear from the fact that not only does the expectation of an imminent end simply disappear, but it is also replaced by a picture of salvation history. Cf. the programme in Luke 1.1–4.[1]

The 'internal' account of the life of Jesus and its 'external' insertion into a framework of salvation history, in the centre of this history, correspond.[2] In this interplay we have evidence of the single understanding of eschatology and history.

Theology is acquainted with salvation history and its course from the beginning. This is a Jewish heritage: the church is the true Israel (Paul: Rom. 9–11). Its place is determined in terms of salvation history by its position between the resurrection and the parousia. But the question is how it understands this intermediate period, or itself in this intermediate period.

Paul: We are justified, a new creation. The spirit has been given to us as a pledge. We live in the flesh; no longer, however, κατὰ σάρκα but rather κατὰ πνεῦμα; we live in Christ and Christ in us. The end of the world is documented as freedom from sin and death, as freedom by acquittal, which we gain through faith.

For Luke's salvation-historical conception, too, the foundations are: Israel, the church as a church between resurrection and parousia. But the horizon is different. The church does not see itself immediately confronted with the end of the world; the new world lies much further away. So arrangements must be made for the long period before the end comes. With his picture of history, Luke prevents this attitude being primarily a negative one, one of resignation. The time leading up to the parousia is built into God's saving plan as the time of the church. Luke does not stress that the kingdom is near, but that it already exists beyond time and that it will surely come. When, we do not know. Even that is given a positive aspect: we are not meant to know, indeed, we need not know. For it is certain that the kingdom is coming and we know what it is.

Luke associates the historical prospect of the parousia with a retrospect to Jesus. This retrospect provides the certainty that Jesus announced the kingdom: the truth is guaranteed by Jesus himself, by his miracles, his resurrection and ascension and the sending of the spirit. We can also read what the kingdom is in the person of Jesus.

---

[1] G. Klein, 'Lukas 1.1–4 als theologisches Programm', *Zeit und Geschichte*, pp. 193–216.

[2] This centre is not to be calculated in chronological terms.

Therefore the historical appearance of Jesus is made by Luke into a picture of the condition of salvation. In this way we have a twofold assurance: a mediated one through the picture of Jesus and an immediate one through the rule of the spirit.

Whereas in Paul the spirit is the sign of the end, in Luke it is a substitute for the time of salvation, given for the time between resurrection and parousia. It is the sign of the third epoch of salvation history. Common to both is the view that the spirit gives power to withstand persecution.

The work of the spirit in the three epochs of salvation history is characterized differently:[1] (a) in Israel it brought about individual inspirations; (b) in the time of Jesus, Jesus himself is the only bearer of the spirit; (c) in the time of the church, God gives the spirit to all believers, but in a qualitatively different way from that in which it was given to Jesus. Jesus has control over the spirit; the believers are led by the spirit.

The continuity of the salvation history is clear from the law: the first age is the time of the law and the prophets. Then Jesus develops the law by his preaching of repentance and his commandments. These remain in force for the church, but now it is given in addition the preaching of the kingdom of God (Luke 16.16) and the spirit.

This view of history governs the whole of Luke's formation of concepts and ideas. The election is related to a collectivity, the church. The picture of Jesus is adapted to this framework. The time of Jesus is now extended into an epoch. The idea is no longer punctiliar as in Mark, but achieves a temporal dimension. The confrontation of Galilee and Jerusalem is replaced by the division of Jesus' career[2] into three stages. These are matched by three stages in Jesus' understanding of himself: of his Messiahship, of his passion and of his kingship. Within this period, the time between the temptation and the passion is stressed: Satan is driven out (cf. 4.13 with 22.3); salvation can present itself in its purity.

The picture of Jesus is not presented as a timeless, ideal pattern. Jesus cannot indeed be imitated. His work is historically unique. After his departure, there are new conditions for the existence of the church in the world (22.35f.). Luke's picture of salvation history also determines his understanding of the church. It is the true Israel. This is clear from the way in which the Risen One appears in Jerusalem and provisionally restricts the apostles to this city. Here the spirit is

[1] H. von Baer, *Der Heilige Geist in den Lukasschriften*, BWANT III 3, (1926).

[2] For this concept see W. C. Robinson, *op. cit.*, but he disputes the possibility of distinguishing three stages in the self-understanding of Jesus.

poured out. The Gentile-Christian church, too, is related to Jerusalem (Apostolic council; the despatch of Paul in Acts 22.17ff.; Paul's travels to Jerusalem). The mission is always directed first to the Jews; only when they have rejected salvation does it go to the Gentiles (conclusion of Acts).

PART THREE

THE THEOLOGY OF PAUL

18 · PROBLEMS OF SCHOLARSHIP

For literature, see R. Bultmann, *Theology of the New Testament* I, p. 362; G. Bornkamm, 'Paulus', *RGG*[3] V 166–90. As a first introduction, see M. Dibelius – W. G. Kümmel, *Paul* (1953); A. Descamps (ed.) et al., *Littérature et théologie pauliniennes*, Recherches Bibliques 5 (1960); B. Rigaux, *Saint Paul et ses lettres*, Studia Neotestamentica (1962); A. D. Nock, *St Paul* (1938).

I The Sources

Only the letters of Paul can be used as sources (not Acts; its picture of Paul's theology is not authentic). For reasons of method, only the undisputedly authentic letters are to be used: Romans, I and II Corinthians, Galatians, Philippians, I Thessalonians, Philemon.

Colossians and II Thessalonians are also usually accepted as authentic; Ephesians is more strongly disputed. The Pastoral Epistles are usually taken to be inauthentic. All these letters show ideas from the genuine Pauline epistles in a particular transformation and therefore occupy a special position. For reasons of exactness, they must therefore be excluded to begin with.

II The Problems

It would be quite wrong to try to explain Paul's theology psychologically, in terms of his personality. For we only have his personality as presented in his work. An earlier stage of scholarship looked for the 'religion' behind his theology. But in Paul's view, theology is not the foreground, but the description of the thing itself.

III The History of Pauline Scholarship

A. Schweitzer, *Paul and his Interpreters* (1912); R. Bultmann, 'Zur Geschichte der Paulus-Forschung', *ThR* NF 1 (1929), pp. 26–59; W. G. Kümmel, *Das Neue Testament, Geschichte der Erforschung seiner Probleme* (1958); K. H. Rengstorf (ed.), *Das Paulusbild in der neueren deutschen Forschung* (1964).

The interpretation of Paul reflects the phases of the more recent history of theology. During its course we find the problems of Paul's thought in a sequence which matches the subject-matter itself.

Since the Reformation, scholars have been convinced that the doctrine of justification by faith alone is the centre of New Testament doctrine and therefore also of Paul's theology. Of course, Protestant orthodoxy, following Luther, saw a shift in the understanding of justification. Luther's view was that God declares sinners righteous. Thus man is righteous and becomes righteous before God by believing in God's justifying word – against all appearances. The hearer's attention to the message is not concerned with his own condition – empirically, he remains a sinner as he was before – but with what God communicates as affecting him: that he is righteous. His righteousness is promised, alien righteousness. The justified one cannot therefore allude to his own deserts, establish himself as righteous. He can only believe. Luther recognized the forensic sense of the Pauline concept of δικαιοσύνη, and saw that justification represents a judgment on all of man's being. A narrowing takes place in Protestant orthodoxy. The forensic sense is indeed maintained, but it is understood in a different way: I am a sinner; but God regards me on the basis of the saving work of Christ as though I were righteous. Here the communication of righteousness in the justificatory word becomes the theory of 'imputation'. Thus justification is now understood in a predominantly negative way. The external act of justification and the inner working of God are distinguished. Justification is no longer the whole of the work of salvation. It must be supplemented by sanctification.

Modern scholarship discovered, first, that the doctrine of justification does not dominate the whole of the New Testament; secondly, that there are differences between Paul and Jesus; and thirdly, that it is doubtful whether the doctrine of justification occupies a central position even in the writing of Paul himself.

The pioneer of modern scholarship is Ferdinand Christian Baur. He interprets Paul with the basic concepts of Hegel. Flesh stands in antithesis to spirit; the antithesis is sublimated in 'reconciliation'. Righteousness is defined as an adequate relationship to God.[1] Here scholarship is set the problem of antithetical conceptuality: righteousness – sin; life – death; freedom – slavery; spirit – flesh, etc. In the time after Baur, attempts were made to define the conceptuality more exactly and the discovery was made that it is not homogeneous. Alongside a group of 'juridical' concepts: law, righteousness, sin, etc., stand terms of quite a different kind: spirit and flesh, life and death. The conclusion was reached that two different doctrines of redemption

[1] P. Stuhlmacher, *Gerechtigkeit Gottes bei Paulus*, FRLANT 87 (1965), pp. 29ff.

are juxtaposed in Paul: 1. the juristic: men do not fulfil the law; they are sinners. But God reckons to them the saving act of Christ through which they are redeemed. The question is, whether an account of religious and moral life is possible on the basis of this theory of redemption. 2. The nature of the second doctrine of redemption is more strongly disputed. Some characterize it in almost physical terms: man lives in the flesh, and he is redeemed by the pouring out of the spirit; others see it as physico-ethical: Paul speaks of walking in the spirit. Some describe it as mystical ('being in Christ') or as mystico-ethical. In this group of ideas the new life of the redeemed is depicted. But what is the link here with the past Christ and his saving work? Scholarship comes up against a brick wall. The conceptuality which is meant to explain Paul is not itself clarified. What does, for example, 'physico-ethical' mean? Nevertheless, one concrete contribution was an advancement of observations in the various areas, above all those of anthropology and eschatology.

The next step forward was the question of the origin of Paul's concepts. This was worked out systematically by the history of religions school. Hitherto, for example, Pauline dualism had been associated with Plato. Now there was a recognition of the change of style in philosophy and religion in the time of Hellenism. As a result, investigations were made into the necessary intermediate stages: on the one hand Hellenism and, above all, its pneumatic character (Gunkel, Weinel), and, on the other Judaism, and above all its apocalyptic. Since then it has been possible to distinguish two types of interpretation of Paul; 'Hellenistic' (Reitzenstein, Bousset) and 'Judaistic' (in different forms, e.g. Schweitzer). For the 'Hellenists', Paul is a pneumatic (II Cor. 3.17), a mystic, a gnostic. He is alien to modern sensibilities. His significance is seen in his being a type of *homo religiosus* who transformed the mysticism of the Hellenistic, pre-Pauline Christianity 'in the glow of experience into an individual mysticism, ethicized it and transposed it from the cult into the whole of personal life'.[1] Wrede, on the other hand, objected that Paul was essentially a theologian. His religion could not be separated from his theology (a fact which Wrede himself regretted).

In sharp antithesis to the 'Hellenistic' interpretation, Albert Schweitzer derived the thought of Paul exclusively from Jewish apocalyptic.[2] Paul was not an exuberant enthusiast, but a consistent

[1] W. Bousset, *Kyrios Christos*, p. 107.
[2] 'Thoroughgoing eschatology' even here!

thinker; a mystic, but a mystic in thought. His problems were pre-
scribed by apocalyptic, by the necessity of describing the appearance
of Jesus in the framework of the apocalyptic outline of history: what
does it mean that the Messiah has already been here without the
world being visibly changed? Paul solves the problem by developing
his own mysticism: the forces of the new age are already effective
among believers. Of the three doctrines of redemption which are to
be found side by side in Paul, the eschatological, the juridical and the
mystical, the mystical is the one that is authentically Pauline. The
doctrine of justification, only worked out in fragmentary fashion,
merely represents a 'subsidiary crater'. Paul's mysticism, on the other
hand, encompasses not only subjective salvation but also a historical,
cosmic event: it is an 'objective mysticism of facts'.[1]

Criticism: It is much to Schweitzer's credit that he has energetically sought the
unity of Paul's thought and attempts to explain its historical form without concern
for its value for the present. But to dispute its Hellenistic elements is to do it violence.
Paul's doctrine of the sacraments, his Kyrios christology and his pneumatism,
cannot be derived from Judaism. The doctrine of justification is not forced aside by
exegetical arguments, but on the basis of the theology of the exegete. Schweitzer,
moreover, misunderstood this doctrine, as he overlooked the difference in the
primitive Christian doctrine of the forgiveness of sins. The doctrine of the double
resurrection and the fixed number of the predestined has been forcibly read into
the text.

The contribution of the history of religions school lies in its
clarification of the context of Paul in the history of religions and of the
significance of concepts and ideas, as in the recognition of the importance of eschatology. But historical derivation falls short of being
real understanding. The question remains: what is Paul saying?
What is the relationship between his different ideas? What is his aim?
What, for example, is the significance of his identification of the Lord
and the spirit? Karl Barth raised these questions. He did not dispute
the results of historical investigation, but went beyond historical insights to ask about the message of Paul. He did not look only for his
view of God and the world but also for how God and the world,
Christ and faith, are related. Exegesis is now indivisibly bound up
with the question of the authority of Paul's statements, an authority
which has to be demonstrated by means of the subject-matter which
is presented.

Paul Wernle confronted Barth with everything that was a product of Paul's

---

[1] A. Schweitzer, *The Mysticism of the Apostle Paul* (1931), p. 100.

time, therefore inexplicable and therefore finished with: his scant concern with the historical Jesus, his doctrine of Christ as the Son of God, his doctrine of reconciliation through the blood of Christ; his contrast of Christ and Adam, his argument from scripture, baptismal sacramentalism, double predestination, attitude to authorities. In reply, Barth observed: 'Now, imagine a commentary on the Epistle to the Romans which left these eight points unexplained; which allowed them to remain "uncomfortable points"; and in which a maze of contemporary parallels did duty for an explanation of them!'[1]

At about the same time, Karl Holl, from a background of Luther scholarship, asserted that the doctrine of justification was the centre of Paul's theology. Nearer to Karl Barth stands Bultmann, who develops his account of Paul on the basis of the concept of faith. The doctrine of justification is not regarded as one dogma among others, or even as the central dogma in Paul, but as an account of man. Bultmann asks not only after the doctrine or doctrines of Paul, but also about how this doctrine interprets man. In a programmatic way, he presents Paul's theology as anthropology and can thus outline an attractively homogeneous picture in which historical analysis and the development of systematic significance form a unity.

Bultmann develops his account in two parts:

A. Man prior to the revelation of faith;
B. Man under faith.

This looks like a pietistic scheme. But for Bultmann, faith, and therefore the man of faith, is not a tangible phenomenon. He does not describe the man of faith and the man outside faith in psychological terms, but – in agreement with Paul – describes existence before and in faith as it is disclosed objectively, through revelation. A notional interpretation of self-understanding in faith does not mean a self-illumination of the believer, consideration of his own religious state, but on the contrary, understanding the kerygma as the determining factor. Faith is not a subjective condition. It is simply the acceptance of the message which comes from outside. Theology is anthropology, as this message does not speak about this and that, about God, the world and man, but concerns me. Existence outside faith is understood in a similar way: faith looks through the past. It discloses to me what I was, namely, a sinner.

How can the truth of this message be shown? It becomes clear exclusively through itself by my coming to know myself through it. The programme is one of 'faith and understanding'. Faith does not bring about any ontological transformation. The ontological structures are neutral and are identical for existence before faith and in faith. This neutrality stems from the nature of faith. It makes it possible for Bultmann to use Heidegger's analysis of existence.

Questions for Bultmann: 1. Are the accents rightly placed? Is not man before faith given a significance which he does not have in Paul? He becomes an explicit

---

[1] K. Barth, *The Epistle to the Romans* (1933), p. 12.

theme only twice, though in key passages: Rom. 7 and Phil. 3. Is there not a danger that Bultmann's description may be understood as an objectifying account so that once again man, instead of faith, becomes the subject of theology? 2. The temporally conditioned form of Paul's thought is dealt with too briefly. Bultmann gives so to speak a chemically purified distillation. There is too little attention to: the sacraments, the idea of the parousia and the end of the world, the theme of the Old Testament, Israel and salvation history, predestination.

Bultmann's presentation has been followed by the general account by H.-J. Schoeps.[1] The latter hardly represents progress in scholarship but account must be taken of it. In contrast to the 'theologians', Schoeps seeks to unravel the mystery of Paul as an independent historian of religion: 'From Marcion to Karl Barth, from Augustine to Luther, Schweitzer or Bultmann, he has always been either misunderstood or only partially understood.' For, 'he had a contradictory nature'. And he 'fell into the hands of the professional theologians of all ages'. But the solution to the riddle has been found. Paul is now understood in terms of 'the history of his life'. The most profound reason for the misunderstanding of him is that no one recognized that all his theology itself rests on a tremendous misunderstanding: the Jew Paul misunderstood the essence of Judaism, in his conception of the law (one might recall the arguments of the catholic theologians in their controversy with Luther). Paul grew up in Hellenistic Judaism. According to Schoeps, this had lost a true understanding of the law. Originally the law was the sign of election for Israel. But in Hellenistic Judaism, this had been concealed in a legalistic fashion. Here Paul develops his view of the law. And he fights against this legalism after his conversion. Hence his polemic against the law does not apply to Judaism proper. Paul is instrumental in spreading a caricature of Judaism throughout the world.

The fight for the basis of Jewish existence carried on by the Jewish scholar Schoeps commands respect. But in terms of the history of Pauline scholarship his book is a retrograde step, a relapse into psychologism and causal explanations. Schoeps measures Paul onesidedly by a particular Jewish view of the law, the rabbinic one. But it is not the only one that there was. In addition, it should be pointed out that whatever specific type of Judaism Paul had in mind is not decisive, in view of the radical nature of his criticism of the law. He is not concerned with a particular understanding of the law; he does not

[1] H.-J. Schoeps, *Paul. The Theology of the Apostle in the Light of the History of Jewish Religion* (1959). The following quotations are on p. 13.

fight against legalism, but against the law as a whole. For him, the law is a whole view of the world. The struggle applies to the law in any form, as long as it serves as a way to salvation. He is concerned with the absolute alternatives: salvation through fulfilment, or through faith alone.

IV Paul's Position in the History of Theology

J. Schniewind, 'Die Botschaft Jesu und die Theologie des Paulus' (1937), in *Nachgelassene Reden und Aufsätze* (1952), pp. 16–37; W. G. Kümmel, 'Paulus und Jesus', *ThBl* 19 (1940) pp. 211–31 (=*Heilsgeschehen und Geschichte* (1965), pp. 81–106); id., *Judaica* 4 (1948), pp. 1–35 (=*Heilsgeschehen*, pp. 169–91); id., *NTS* 10 (1963/4), pp. 163–81 (=*Heilsgeschehen*, pp. 439–56); M. Goguel, 'De Jésus à l'apôtre Paul', *RHPR* 28/9 (1948/9), pp. 1ff.; E. Jüngel, *Paulus und Jesus* (1962).

Paul already stands in a Christian tradition and receives the material for his theology from it. What does he find, and how does he develop what he has found? The significance of this question can be made clear from a theme which formed the focal point of the discussion of Christianity's claim to truth at the turn of the century: Jesus and Paul. For a long time, the view prevailed that the rabbi Paul had transformed the simple teaching of Jesus into a complicated theology in Jewish style. He ignored the historical person of Jesus and replaced him by a mythical figure. This transformation did in fact take place, but it is not the work of Paul. It had already happened before the conversion of Paul. He himself learned Christianity as faith in the exalted Lord Jesus. His contribution consists in the way in which he thought through the faith theologically. He did not invent either christology or the doctrine of the sacraments, but interpreted what he found. His relationship to Jesus can only be described properly if the intermediate stages between the two are remembered: the primitive community and the Hellenistic community, and above all the latter. Where there are Jewish ideas in Paul they are predominantly those of Hellenistic Diaspora Judaism: the idea of God (Rom. 1), the basis of ethics (Rom. 2), methods of interpreting the Bible (I Cor. 10), use of the Septuagint, etc. Paul's origin in the Hellenistic community makes it clear why he ignores the historical activity of Jesus (for example, he says nothing of the miracles of Jesus and takes only a few of Jesus' sayings from the synoptic material). All that matters to him about Jesus is his saving work, the cross and resurrection. He does not have Jesus' preaching before his eyes, but his present position and the founding of the church. Thus faith in the Exalted One is asserted as the only way to salvation, and the law is ruled out as a possible course.

Bultmann, *Faith and Understanding*, p. 234: 'Jesus preaches the law and the promise; Paul preaches the Gospel in its relation to the law. Law and Gospel together form a unity. The law is rightly understood only together with the promise; the Gospel only together with the law.'

If one were merely to reproduce the teaching of Jesus, it would automatically be turned into a new law. The question of the historical Jesus should not turn on whether Paul considers the earthly career of Jesus or not, but on the theological question whether Jesus himself has his proper place in faith, whether he is understood as the end of the law, whether 'Jesus' means that salvation is won in the immediacy of faith in God.

Once the old, orthodox authority of scripture had been lost, there was concern for its vindication by historians. But the historian cannot provide a basis for certainty. On the contrary, Paul asserts the immediacy of faith to its object, the exalted Lord, who makes himself the subject of faith today by being preached. In this way, and only in this way, is his resurrection saved from being isolated as a 'historical fact'. It is particularized in the present witness to itself. The preaching of reconciliation in Christ is present proof for the truth of faith in Jesus as the Risen One. There is no other. For only the cross can be seen. We have the Risen One only as he is preached, as the Crucified One. Where attempts are made to gain direct control over the revelation of God in Christ, by means of a *theologia gloriae*, an ontology of revelation, the place of the reconciling word is inevitably taken by the ontology of the reconciled man, and the picture of the historical or mythological Jesus takes the place of the λόγος τῆς καταλλαγῆς.

V   The Significance of Paul's Conversion

R. Bultmann, 'Neueste Paulusforschung', *ThR* NF 6 (1934), pp. 229–46; W. G. Kümmel, *Römer 7 und die Bekehrung des Paulus*, UNT 17 (1929); H. G. Wood, 'The Conversion of St Paul: its Nature, Antecedents and Consequences', *NTS* 1 (1954/5), pp. 276–82; U. Wilckens, 'Die Bekehrung des Paulus als religionsgeschichtliches Problem', *ZThK* 56 (1959), pp. 273–93; H. Grass, *Ostergeschehen und Osterberichte* (1962²), pp. 207–26.

Attempts have continually been made to derive Paul's theology from the experience of his conversion, i.e. from personal experience. He himself declares that his gospel has been revealed to him. But in what sense is that to be understood? We can get an answer only when we put the question in terms of the history of religions, and not in psychological terms. For 'inner experience' explains nothing: it is an *x* which itself needs to be explained. Attempted reconstructions of the experience of conversion are useless, as the sources simply are not there. Just as Paul has visions without making personal use of them (II Cor. 12), so he never speaks of the inner event of his conversion but only of its theological content: his commission to preach the gospel to the Gentiles. This includes the consequence that the law is finished as a way to salvation. What are the presuppositions, from the point of view of the history of religions, by which Paul came to this theological insight?

Our material is limited. The threefold report of the conversion in Acts is no use as a source, as it is legendary. It is impossible, too, to exploit another text, Rom. 7.7ff., which has long been regarded as an authentic document about Paul's conversion. Here Paul is describing man in revolt, and makes his account end in the thanksgiving of the redeemed. He is not, however, picturing his feelings before his conversion, but the way in which he later came to know himself through faith. Only faith shows me that without faith I was objectively in despair. As Paul says in Phil. 3, he did not feel this in subjective, psychological terms. Nor does Acts 26.14, the saying about the goad which it is impossible to kick against, tell us anything about inner struggles. In the first place, it is not one of Paul's own statements. But even Luke does not intend the saying in a psychological way. He uses a proverbial phrase which asserts the impossibility of fighting against God. It already has this sense in Euripides.

Paul's own statements are brief: 1. Phil. 3.4–9: through his conversion, Paul does not surrender an inner misery, but his pride: 'Whatever gain I had, I counted as loss'. How does this come about? 2. Gal. 1.11f. gives the answer. Here Paul is fighting for his authority as an apostle (cf. I Cor. 15.8–11), through the demonstration that his gospel is not κατὰ ἄνθρωπον. 'But when he who had set me apart before I was born, and had called me through his grace, was pleased to reveal his Son to me, in order that I might preach him among the Gentiles, I did not confer with flesh and blood.' Does that mean that Paul thought out his teaching in a purely speculative way? No! Of course Paul had a knowledge of Christian teaching even before his conversion. That is why he became a persecutor. The external extent of his knowledge of the faith was still small. It consisted of only a few statements. Paul in fact declares that he persecuted Christians out of zeal for his ancestral traditions, i.e. for the law. It is often said that Paul was offended at the cross. True, but that is still no reason why he persecuted Christians; it simply shows why he despised them. Paul must have had before him a Christianity which already derived freedom from the law from faith. Now the Lord himself came to him, while he was persecuting this Christianity; i.e., simply by appearing to him, the Lord himself declared that the way of salvation was the end of the law. Hence it is 'only through faith'. Thus Paul's conversion in fact represents a decision between the alternatives of salvation from works or salvation from faith alone. This makes a mission to the Gentiles not only possible, but even necessary. The universal dominion of the Lord must be made known universally. The psychological interpretation cannot explain why Paul, despite his insight that the law is not the way to salvation willed by God, maintained that it is God's will. The line from Paul's conversion to his theology does not lead to the mysticism of being in Christ, but to thinking through the election, to 'from grace alone' and 'from faith alone', to the righteousness of faith and thus the end of man's own righteousness.

VI Problems of Presentation

The difficulty of presenting Paul's theology stems first from the state of the sources. It has to be taken from occasional writing in which it appears for the most part only indirectly, in application to concrete problems. Paul offers no systematic account, because he can simply presuppose certain areas of doctrine, e.g. the doctrine of God as Creator. Nevertheless, we have a fairly extensive thematically presented survey in the epistle to the Romans, though that was, of course, written in controversy with Judaism: the account of justification by faith. We cannot, however, simply use the epistle to the Romans as a basis for working out the whole of Pauline theology, supplementing it if need be from other epistles; for even the account in the epistle to the Romans is from a particular perspective. Such a method is quite impossible, because it comes up against a difficulty of fundamental significance. The fact that Paul does not present a system is not a coincidence, something that can be explained in psychological terms – it is determined by his position. His theology is not a theoretical outline, but is always expressed in application, in reference to a particular pronouncement. Thus on each occasion, the total understanding of the saving event is kept in view in the discussion of a particular theme. How can we understand this character of Paul's theology in order to present it? Perhaps taking: (a) the saving event and its relationship to us; (b) the reference of the saving event to us (or, the relationship of the *extra nos* and the *pro nobis*), the unity of the *fides quae* and *fides qua creditur*? How do we avoid the Scylla of objectifying faith into a doctrine to be believed and the Charybdis of making faith subjective, a subjective view and self-consideration? The problem can never be seen clearly if we start from the content, the communication of the gift of an alien righteousness by God. This communication cannot be experienced, but only heard and believed. Theology is the understanding of this event.

19 · THE METHOD OF WORKING

I   Paul's Use of Christian Tradition

K. Wegenast, *Das Verhältnis der Tradition bei Paulus und in den Deutero-paulinen*, WMANT 8 (1962).

Pauline interpretations become visible in the reconstruction of pre-Pauline formulas. As they show the way in which Paul takes over the tradition, they must now be investigated more closely.

Examples: 1. *I Thess. 4.13ff.*: Paul is asked whether the dead, too, will enter into life. He replies by quoting the creed: Jesus died and is risen. He does not mean to prove that Jesus rose, but presupposes that as 'the faith'. He then quotes a saying of the Lord and attaches a catechetical passage about the last things (5.1ff.). Here the question of the date of the parousia leads back to the definition of what we are in the world: sons of the day. Finally, in 5.9f., he returns to the creed. By this description, Paul makes it clear that the creed has only been understood when the believer has grasped what he is under the determination of the saving event. When that has happened, apocalyptic concern is done away with, questioning about dates is a thing of the past. Our physical state is immaterial for the saving event, because our existence is determined by Christ: ἵνα εἴτε γρηγορῶμεν εἴτε καθεύδωμεν ἅμα σὺν αὐτῷ ζήσωμεν. The εἴτε—εἴτε shows the problem of the world-view to be irrelevant; cf. II Cor. 5.9 and Phil. 1.21.

2. The same kind of argument prevails in *I Cor. 15*. First the creed is cited and then the consequences are drawn: if Christ is risen, then our future is determined, i.e. the hope has a christological base, not one in speculative cosmology or psychology.

3. *I Cor. 8.1–6*. Here Paul takes up the Corinthian slogan: we all have knowledge. The Corinthians derive a particular view of the world from it. Paul criticizes them by turning the creed against them. He contrasts knowledge and love and makes it clear that objective knowledge about God is no real knowledge. The theme of God is not a question of a view of the world. The same is true in respect of the pagan gods. The question is not whether there are gods (as the Corinthians put it); the dispute is over traffic with the gods as powers. There is no rational dispute over their existence; Paul is concerned with the way in which they have been disarmed through faith.

4. The Pauline appropriation of tradition can best be seen in the *Epistle to the Romans*. In Rom. 1.3f., Paul relates the creed to his ministry. In Rom. 3.24–26, he interprets a credal formula about God's righteousness in terms of the righteousness of faith. In Rom. 4.25, a confession forms the starting point for the comprehensive analysis of existence in chs. 5–8. In Rom. 10.9ff., it is expounded in relation to faith, preaching and righteousness. In Rom. 14.9, it again serves as a basis for the interpretation of existence.

II Paul's Use of the Old Testament

A. von Harnack, *Das AT in den paulinischen Briefen*, SAB 1928, pp. 124–41; O. Michel, *Paulus und seine Bibel*, BFChTh II 18 (1929); H. Lietzmann, Excursus on Gal. 4.31 in HNT; J. Bonsirven, *Exégèse rabbinique et exégèse paulinienne au temps de Jésus Christ* I, II (1934, 1935); P. Bläser, 'Schriftverwertung und Schrifterklärung im Rabbinentum und bei Paulus', *ThQ* 132 (1952), pp. 152–69; C. H. Dodd, *According to the Scriptures* (1952); C. Smits, *Oudtestamentische Citaten in het Nieuwe Testament* I–IV (1952–63); E. E. Ellis, *Paul's Use of the Old Testament* (1957); H. Müller, *Die Auslegung alttestamentliches Geschichtsstoffs bei Paulus*, Diss. Halle 1960 (cf. *ThLZ* 86 (1961), cols. 788f.); B. Lindars, *New Testament Apologetic* (1961), pp. 222–50; C. K. Barrett, *From First Adam to Last* (1962); H. Ulonska, *Paulus und das AT*, Diss. Münster, 1963; U. Luz, *Das Geschichtsverständnis bei Paulus* (1968).

Schoeps remarks:[1] 'For all Saul's life, scripture was the supreme norm for all thought and action, so that even the Christian Paul does not advance an argument which he is not concerned to justify on a biblical basis: this applies especially to the Messiahship and the soteriological role of Jesus.' It should, however, be said in reply that Paul never uses a scriptural argument to show that Jesus is Messiah (contrast Luke, Acts 17.2f.). The Old Testament plays no role in I Thessalonians, Philippians and long stretches of I and II Corinthians.

[1] H.-J. Schoeps, *Paul*, p. 38.

Schoeps notes that Paul seeks to demonstrate even his doctrine of the end of the law from scripture. But this is precisely the point. The Old Testament comes to the fore where Paul is arguing thematically with Jews and Judaizers: in Galatians and Romans (though here only in particular parts; frequently in the latter). It again plays a role in the controversy with the Jewish-Christian enthusiasts of II Corinthians.[1] From this evidence, Harnack concluded that the Old Testament only provides Paul with external arguments and does not serve as a book of instruction. The evidence of e.g. I Cor. 10 is striking: Paul teaches the Corinthians about the Old Testament as though they had never heard of it: and Paul taught for at least eighteen months in Corinth. What, then, did he teach about?

Harnack's line is taken further by H. Ulonska: the Old Testament is only used by Paul when he is driven to do so by his opponents in actual controversy. This account is too simple.

Paul certainly uses the Old Testament to argue from. But the fact that he can and does do this presupposes that for him, too, it is revelation, a document not only of commandment, but also of promise.

Ulonska: the pattern of promise and fulfilment does not occur in Paul; there is no extended perspective of salvation history, no retrospect to a past which determines the present by the events which took place in it. Nor is the Old Testament a sacred document in the sense of a formal authority. What Paul cites from the Old Testament is not authoritative by virtue of the fact that it appears in Scripture, but by virtue of its content, as immediately convincing address, like 'golden words' in paraenesis. The latter is true, but these are words of scripture. And in fact, while Paul indeed knows no extension of salvation history in time, no isolated past, he still recognizes fulfilment: Gal. 4.4. Paul does not assert this fulfilment on the basis of Old Testament events but on the basis of the fulfilment in Christ: cf. Luther: *non enim tempus fecit filium mitti, sed econtra missio filii fecit tempus plenitudinis* (WA 57, 30.15f., on Gal. 4.4).

Paul does not keep to any particular pattern in his use of the Old Testament. There are literal quotations, free variations, allusions, references to the content: commandments, events, people. Paul usually uses the Septuagint.[2] He takes over Jewish citation formulas like כַּאֲשֶׁר כָּתוּב = καθὼς γέγραπται, etc. (Rom. 1.17; Dam. VII 19). Several passages can be strung together one after the other in

---

[1] D. Georgi, *Die Gegner des Paulus im 2. Korintherbrief*, WMANT 11 (1964), pp. 265ff.: for his opponents, the OT is the 'archive of the spirit'.

[2] For exceptions, see Lietzmann and E. E. Ellis, *Paul's Use of the Old Testament*, pp. 10ff.

such a way as to appear a single quotation: Rom. 3.10–18. Some exegetes assume that here Paul is deliberately assembling passages from the law, the prophets and the writings, after a Jewish pattern (thus Rom. 11.8–10). But he does not do this systematically: e.g. in Rom. 3.10–18 he assembles only passages from the writings. It is a disputed question whether he used anthologies, or worked with a relatively fixed supply of biblical proof texts which were already traditional in Christian apologetic (thus Dodd, Ellis, Lindars). Individual passages are used without concern for their original meaning in the Old Testament. A prophetic threat, Isa. 28.11f., becomes a prediction of speaking with tongues brought about through the spirit (I Cor. 14.21). Individual quotations are used in an isolated way, the Old Testament context is irrelevant.

Dodd assumes that the original context also has an influence. In the neighbourhood of a quotation there are sometimes allusions to the Old Testament context. But such allusions can only be detected by extremely artificial hypotheses. There is an example in Rom. 10.16, where Isa. 53.1 is introduced: in the context there is no trace of a servant of God christology.

The wording of the Old Testament can be varied in order to stress or obtain a particular sense. Examples are:

Lev. 18.5 â (referring to προστάγματα and κρίματα) ποιήσας ἄνθρωπος ζήσεται ἐν αὐτοῖς.

Gal. 3.12 ὁ ποιήσας αὐτὰ ζήσεται ἐν αὐτοῖς.

Rom. 10.5 (referring to righteousness from the law) ὁ ποιήσας ἄνθρωπος ζήσεται ἐν αὐτῇ.

There are contacts with rabbinic rules for the exegesis of scripture: the conclusion a minore ad maius (qal waḥomer: Rom. 5); the conclusion from analogy (gezera šawa: Rom. 4). In general, however, Paul works freely, following Hellenistic Jewish and pre-Pauline Christian exegesis. For the Christian exegetical tradition, cf. Rom. 9.33 with I Peter 2.6ff. Wisdom, Philo, etc. show how independently Hellenistic Judaism deals with the Old Testament. Paul can reject literal exegesis against the meaning of the Old Testament. In I Cor. 9.9 he quotes Deut. 25.4: 'You shall not muzzle an ox when it is treading out the grain', and explains, 'Is it for oxen that God is concerned? Does he not speak entirely for our sake?' But in the Old Testament God is in fact concerned with oxen. Paul once describes his exegesis explicitly as allegorical (Gal. 4.22ff.). But he does not allegorize systematically, even in this passage. He interprets Hagar as Mount Sinai, i.e. as servitude, the present Jerusalem, in contrast to Sarah, i.e. freedom, the Jerusalem that is above. The allegorizing is limited to this one feature. Paul does not, for example, narrate the Old Testament history itself as an allegory. In I Cor. 10.1ff., Paul describes Old Testament events as τύποι for us. The passage is regarded as a most important instance of Paul's typological method. But τύπος here simply means model, and a paraenetic model at that. The saying does not therefore describe a method of exegesis.

S. Ulonska, p. 113. Of course, a particular relationship between 'model' and 'us' is presupposed. It is obtained backwards, from the present. Paul does not think of a prefigurement which could be read methodologically from the Old Testament.

The following themes play a role: (a) the Old Testament contains prediction; it points forward to the gospel: Rom. 1.2; Gal. 3.8; (b) the Old Testament itself comes to a climax in the revelation of righteousness by faith: Rom. 1.17 (cf. Gal. 3.11; the foundation is Hab. 2.4: ὁ δὲ δίκαιος ἐκ πίστεώς μου (!) ζήσεται. Paul deletes the μου!). Here there is a hint at a salvation-historical perspective: Ἰουδαίῳ τε πρῶτον καὶ Ἕλληνι, but no programme of 'salvation history' is developed. The advantage of the Jew is discussed only in respect of its eschatological annulment; (c) the rule of sin since Adam: Rom. 5.12ff.; (d) the call of the Gentiles and Israel's attitude: Rom. 9–11; (e) the prefigurement of the sacraments: I Cor. 10.1ff; (f) teaching about eschatology: I Cor. 15 (but in I Thess. 4f. without the use of the Old Testament); (g) commandments: Rom. 12.9f. (but with only sporadic reference to the Old Testament).

Even when Paul sees the fulfilment of the promise, which was entrusted to Israel and recorded in the Bible, in Christ and the righteousness of faith, one should not describe his relationship to the Old Testament in terms of 'salvation history'. Of course, he stands in the tradition of the salvation-historical exegesis of Judaism (Rom. 9–11); but God's action in the history of Israel is not a theme in his doctrine.

Ulonska, pp. 188f.: 'The beginning of Paul's thought is not the concept of "Israel" but acceptance of the gospel'. He does not draw out any time-line, but merely refers to the points at which God has time and again freely chosen and rejected.

Paul can on occasion look back to the historical course of events – but look at the way in which this happens! Gal. 3: Abraham comes before Moses, so the promise comes before the law. The way in which he selects one thing or another at random is clear from Rom. 4: here he uses Abraham in an argument without noting his position in the course of history; he takes Abraham as an example of faith after the pattern of Jewish interpretation. This time Paul stresses the sequence within the life of Abraham, the priority of the promise to circumcision. In Rom. 5.12ff. he puts Adam, Moses and Christ together. Here, too, it is impossible to speak of typology; we have no more than a confrontation between different points of view. Adam and Christ are contrasted in I Cor. 15.21f., 45–49, without reference to Moses. Moses himself does not fit into the Adam-Christ scheme, as it was originally conceived in mythical rather than salvation-historical terms. Paul characteristically does not note historical and temporal periods and sequences; he jumps over periods in time. Rom. 1.18ff.: the time of the original knowledge of God and the time of sin or the wrath of God run side by side. Historically they are indistinguishable. Even after the point of the historical revelation of righteousness, the time of the knowledge of God and wrath continues. In Rom. 7.7 the history of Adam is projected into the present as 'my' history.

II Baruch 54.19: 'Adam is therefore not the cause, save only of his own soul, but each of us has been the Adam of his own soul.'

I Cor. 10.1ff.: time is bridged by the pre-existence of Christ. There is, however, no timelessness of a gnostic character in Paul. We should note, rather, the process of the concentration of time; see II Cor. 6.2 (=Isa. 49.8): καιρῷ δεκτῷ ἐπήκουσά σου καὶ ἐν ἡμέρᾳ σωτηρίας ἐβοήθησά σοι. ἰδοὺ νῦν καιρὸς εὐπρόσδεκτος, ἰδοὺ νῦν ἡμέρα σωτηρίας.

The characteristic Pauline νῦν describes the eschatological newness of the saving event. This is interpreted in II Cor. 3 as the new covenant which replaces the old. Here, too, the catchword 'salvation history' is not enough to interpret the evidence. For Paul defines the nature of the old and the new covenants by the timeless conceptuality of letter and spirit. The letter is the law, in so far as it is grasped and can be a means in man's hand.

How can Paul retain the Old Testament and reject the law as a way of salvation? He can do so because the law is good in itself (Rom. 7.7ff.), but is not a way to salvation. The law comes into effect in the establishment of righteousness by faith (Rom. 3.27ff.).

20 · ΠΙΣΤΙΣ

R. Bultmann, *Theology of the New Testament* I, pp. 314ff.; id., πιστεύω etc., *TWNT* VI 218ff.; A. Schlatter, *Der Glaube im NT* (1927⁴); E. Wissmann, *Das Verhältnis von Πίστις und Christusfrömmigkeit bei Paulus*, FRLANT NF 23 (1926); R. Gyllenberg, 'Glaube bei Paulus', *ZSTh* 13 (1936), pp. 612–30; O. Kuss, 'Der Glaube nach den paulinischen Hauptbriefen', *Theologie und Glaube* 46 (1956), pp. 1–26; H. L. Ljungman, *Pistis* (1964).

In the Septuagint, πίστις/πιστεύειν are the equivalent of אֱמֶת/הֶאֱמִין, what is fixed, valid and hence reliable.[1] This derivation gives the New Testament concept of faith its elements of trust (Rom. 4), obedience, hope (trust looking to the future). The essential element of the concept is not, however, to be seen in psychological terms, in terms of faith as an attitude, but in the connection of faith with its object, the kerygma. This is clear from the terminology: πιστεύειν εἰς . . . or ὅτι . . .[2] Man's relationship with God is grounded on the acceptance of this faith, i.e. by a decision (but not by a resolve, for in accepting the kerygma I cannot reflect on myself). Neither faith as an act nor faith as a condition are analysed in psychological terms,[3] because faith only exists in relation to its object. It cannot first be defined formally as a kind of conviction, the contents of which are only supplied later. The object of faith is not the man who is delivered, but the delivering word of God. The object is remembered even where it is not explicitly named, where πιστεύειν and πίστις are used absolutely, as the act of becoming a Christian (Rom. 13.11: salvation is nearer to us now ἢ ὅτε ἐπιστεύσαμεν) or the condition of being a Christian (II Cor. 13.5). This condition does not become an object of self-contemplation. The interchangeability of concepts is symptomatic of this: 'to stand in faith' is interchangeable with 'to stand in the Lord' (I Thess. 3.8); 'to stand in the gospel' (I Cor. 15.1); 'to stand in grace' (Rom. 5.2).

[1] For the link between primitive Christianity and Judaism see R. Bultmann, *TWNT* VI 205–8; for Paul and the general Christian concept of faith, see pp. 218–20.

[2] εἰς: Gal. 2.16; ὅτι: Rom. 10.9.

[3] Contrast Philo: Bultmann, *TWNT* VI 202f.

What has been said does not apply only to Paul, but to common Christian terminology. From the beginning, there is a unity between the *fides quae creditur* and the *fides qua creditur*. Can this unity be made understandable in theological terms? Yes, if faith is recognized as the only determining factor of existence.

The result is a radical individualization: the message encounters the individual and isolates him. We cannot hear it and believe it vicariously. Ernst Käsemann advances the thesis that the proclamation is not directed primarily as an address to the individual, but as a declaration of divine law to the world. In that case faith becomes a formal submission, a psychological act of decision. For primitive Christianity, the message communicates to the individual the decision made about him. This individualization makes the universality of salvation possible, because human conditions are now no longer required. Faith is acceptance in understanding, in so far as it becomes clear from the message. In that case, the unity between what happens for me (the objective saving act) and what happens to me or with me (appropriation) becomes comprehensible. The unity is constituted by the word that tells me what I have been made by God. Thus it is also clear that the self-understanding is not to be regarded in psychological terms. For what I am, I am not in myself, but in Christ. The nature of faith cannot be developed through self-analysis, but only through the description of its inner structure and external references. The following elements of the structure can be discerned: faith as knowledge, as obedience, as confidence, as hope. Each time, the starting point must be the connection with the object. Only in this way can the unity of objective and subjective faith be depicted.

Faith is *knowledge*. It has an understandable dogmatic content. The unity of objective and subjective faith is maintained in that this dogmatic content tells me something about myself and to that degree is comprehensible.

Faith is *obedience*, for the message of faith proclaims Jesus as the Lord. Faith and obedience are not therefore twofold, in the sense that faith first arises as the right religion and then obedience follows as the right morality. Faith is the obedience that God wills. And *vice versa*: obedience is simply believing God. It is therefore not even an achievement, but a refusal to calculate my achievements before God. In hearing the message, I can no longer reflect on myself as one who has his own achievements. Its content is the cross, the destruction of my boasting about my freedom. I need no longer consider how I can be pleasing to God. I am, and so I am obedient, because I let God prevail.

Of course, faith also has a personal side. Each one has his measure of faith (Rom. 12.3). Some are weak in faith (Rom. 14.1). People can grow in faith (II Cor. 10.15). But the experience that a man has with faith is not made the content of the message. It is merely seen under the perspective of being experience with this matter, with the cross. A man is not saved by strong faith, but by faith. Only in this way is the certainty of salvation possible.

The same thing applies when faith is described as trust. That, too, is not something alongside faith and obedience: the meaning is not that man must obey God, but he may also trust him; it is rather that man trusts God by trusting his word and understanding that his grace can be relied on. It can be understood from the object of faith that 'fear and trembling' correspond to trust. This has nothing to do with a tension of the *psyche* (rejoicing to heaven, oppressed to death). 'Fear and trembling' is a theological definition; it describes the relationship between God and man made and determined by God's choice in grace (Phil. 2.12f.). The idea of predestination is part of the understanding of faith: in faith I know that my salvation is exclusively brought about by God. That is the condition of the certainty of salvation.

21 · THE ANTHROPOLOGICAL (NEUTRAL) CONCEPTS

I World and Man

It would really make better sense if the description of the concept of hope, i.e. of eschatology, were to follow next. This concept will, however, become clearer with the help of the ideas and concepts which describe the world, i.e. cosmological and anthropological concepts. We therefore deal with them first: (a) cosmology: the end of the world, parousia, resurrection, judgment; (b) anthropology: transformation, new body.

R. Bultmann, *Theology of the New Testament* I, pp. 362ff., for literature; W. Gutbrod, *Die paulinische Anthropologie*, BWANT, 4 Folge, 15 (1934); W. G. Kümmel, *Das Bild des Menschen im NT*, AThANT 13 (1948); D. E. H. Whiteley, *The Theology of St Paul* (1964), pp. 17ff.; W. D. Stacey, *The Pauline View of Man* (1956); J. A. T. Robinson, *The Body* (1951); R. Scroggs, *The Last Adam* (1966). Cf. also the relevant articles in *TWNT*.

The cosmological (κόσμος) and anthropological (σῶμα) concepts are neutral in themselves. The σῶμα can be ψυχικόν or πνευματικόν. There is also an ambivalence in the meaning of σάρξ: (a) there is its qualified negative sense in antithesis to πνεῦμα: the σάρξ is the negative power (Gal. 5.17). (b) alongside this there is a neutral usage: ζῆν ἐν σαρκί

(Gal. 2.20; Phil. 1.22). Here σάρξ designates the human condition under the aspect of provisionality, transitoriness. In Philemon 16, Onesimus is no longer a slave, but a beloved brother καὶ ἐν σαρκὶ καὶ ἐν κυρίῳ, i.e. as a man and as a Christian. The Jew κατὰ σάρκα is a φύσει 'Ιουδαῖος (cf. Rom. 4.1 with Gal. 2.15). Paul can play on the double sense: ἐν σαρκὶ γὰρ περιπατοῦντες οὐ κατὰ σάρκα στρατευόμεθα (II Cor. 10.3).

There is a systematic background to the neutrality of cosmology and anthropology: faith is not a phenomenon which can be shown in a man. Existence in faith is not a being in new ontological structures. The believer is not a 'superman', but hears himself addressed in his humanity. That means that man does not become the subject of proclamation. The ontological structures are neither good nor bad, they are merely structures. In other words, the place of faith is the world; it can be, because it is God's creation.[1]

When Paul speaks of man in neutral terms, the aspects can change: sometimes they are more monistic, at others more dualistic. The nature of man as such is not the subject of his teaching. Therefore his remarks are sporadic. Paul has contacts with Judaism in not considering man in an objective sense, with a view to what he is in himself. Man is seen *a priori* in the circumstances in which he exists, primarily in the relationship of the creature to the creator and to the created world. Man's life consists in obeying God and being able to trust him.

These traits of existence can be envisaged as having a personal nature, along the lines of the apocalyptic picture of the world: as angels, good and evil. Paul, however, is not concerned with the way in which they are envisaged, but with their significance. He can replace the mention of the 'powers' with concepts of existence (Rom. 8.38f.). Paul has no fixed scheme for human nature. Sometimes he describes it in dichotomistic terms (I Cor. 5.3), and sometimes trichotomistically (I Thess. 5.23): ὑμῶν τὸ πνεῦμα καὶ ἡ ψυχὴ καὶ τὸ σῶμα.

It is wrong to conclude from this passage that Paul's (or the New Testament's) picture of man is trichotomistic. We have here what may be a pre-Pauline phrase, in liturgical style, with a tendency to be three-membered. Paul could just as easily have said: ὑμῶν τὸ πνεῦμα or ὑμεῖς. The three concepts are not defined but added together in an unreflective way. They designate the totality of human nature, in this passage from the perspective which Paul asks his community to maintain. Cf. his favourite alternation in the conclusions to his letters: the Lord be with you – or, your spirit.

II   The Concepts of Manifestation

Ancient Greek concepts of form already change their meaning in

---

[1] For this theme, see R. Bultmann, 'The Concept of Revelation in the New Testament', in: Schubert M. Ogden (ed.), *Existence and Faith* (1960), pp. 58–91.

Hellenistic Judaism. They become concepts of manifestation. One example is I Cor. 11.2ff. Here we find the cosmological-anthropological sequence, God – (Christ) – world – man.[1] The relationship between the individual factors is determined by the concepts εἰκών, κεφαλή, δόξα (radiance). They no longer describe the form, but the nature (homoousia).

At their root lies a mythical and emanationist picture of the world and of man, which in itself does not fit in with the Jewish idea of creation. It occurs, rather, in the Corpus Hermeticum (VIII: God – world – man; XI 15: God – aeon – world – sun – man). Philo took over this terminology and adapted it to the biblical account of creation (Op. Mund. 25: God – intelligible world (λόγος) – world of the senses). With this sequence, Philo overcomes the exegetical difficulties of Gen. 1 and 2: (a) the twofold account of creation; (b) the statement that God created man κατ' εἰκόνα θεοῦ. He finds two solutions:[2]

1. Gen. 1.27 describes how man is made 'after' the 'image' of the Logos.
2. Gen. 1.27 describes the creation of the idea-man, Gen. 2.7 that of the earthly man.

εἰκών has a christological sense in II Cor. 4.4; cf. Col. 1.15 (homoousia of God and the revealer). The same is true of κεφαλή. δόξα is understood in substantial terms, as the brilliance of light. In I Cor. 11, δόξα is in effect synonymous with εἰκών, but this sense is rare. 'Brilliance of light' is the nature (the substance) of the redeemed: II Cor. 3.18. Cf. Phil. 3.21.

The verbs μεταμορφοῦσθαι, μετασχηματίζεσθαι, used in the above-mentioned passages, lead to further, related concepts: μορφή, σχῆμα (Phil. 2.6ff.).[3]

Both the earthly and the heavenly body can be described as a 'garment' (II Cor. 5).

The finest pattern for this idea is provided by the Hymn of the Pearl:[4] 'Suddenly, as though I were encountering my reflection (the heavenly I), the garment became like myself.' Later we have 'the brilliance of light'.

The historical context extends still further. In I Cor. 15.44ff., Christ

---

[1] F.-W. Eltester, Eikon im NT, BZNW 23 (1958): J. Jervell, Imago Dei, FRLANT 76 (1960).
[2] See Jervell, op. cit., p. 53.
[3] E. Käsemann, 'Kritische Analyse von Phil. 2.5–11', Exegetische Versuche und Besinnungen I, pp. 65ff.; D. Georgi, 'Der vorpaulinische Hymnus Phil. 2.6–11', Zeit und Geschichte (Bultmann Festschrift), pp. 263ff. For μορφή cf. Corpus Hermeticum I 12; the word is synonymous with πνεῦμα in a Jewish prayer in Preisendanz, Zauberpapyri IV, 1167ff. 'ἐν μορφῇ': one 'wears' the form = the 'garment'.
[4] A. Adam, Die Psalmen des Thomas und das Perlenlied, BZNW 24 (1959), pp. 53f., lines 74 and 97.

is interpreted as the 'second Adam' (cf. I Cor. 15.21f.; Rom. 5.12ff.).[1]
True, Paul adduces evidence for this idea from the Bible, but he has
not taken it from the Bible.

It can only be found in the Bible once it has already been conceived. That is also
true of Philo's distinction between a first and a second man (but in Philo the first is
the higher).[2]

Adam is seen here not only as the tribal ancestor, but also as the
primal man who represents all humanity, i.e. sums it up in himself:
we were 'in Adam', and so under sentence of death. Now we are 'in
Christ', and we shall become like him (II Cor. 3.18).

These ontological concepts contain the same tendency as the ideas of emanation
and identity. They therefore acquired significance in gnosticism. In Paul, however,
no system of doctrine is built up on them. The tendency in the particular context
determines the meaning.

III   σῶμα

R. Bultmann, *Theology of the New Testament* I, pp. 192ff.; E. Käsemann, *Leib und
Leib Christi*, BHTh 9 (1933); J. A. T. Robinson, *The Body*, SBT 5 (1952); E.
Schweizer, *TWNT* VII 1057ff.; C. K. Barrett, *From First Adam to Last* (1962).

There is no exact Hebrew equivalent. Nevertheless, the meaning in
the Old Testament is not determined by the history of the Greek
word (trunk, body, person; visible form; soul-body antithesis). The
LXX occasionally uses the word for בָּשָׂר. From this, there develops
a certain affinity between σῶμα and σάρξ. But the two are not
synonyms. In Paul, σῶμα designates not only a part of a man, but the
whole man in so far as he is seen under a particular aspect.

There is no regular correlative concept. When Paul occasionally contrasts the
body and its members, they appear as virtually identical, as interchangeable:
Rom. 6.12f.; cf. I Cor. 6.13ff. σῶμα and πνεῦμα: I Cor. 5.3. The two together simply
designate the totality of humanity; cf. I Cor. 7.34 and the triad I Thess. 5.23.

Rule of thumb: it is not, 'I have a σῶμα', but, 'I am σῶμα, or, am in
the body'.[3]

We have to rid ourselves of the idea of the abstract subject and its works. The
two are not to be separated *a priori*: I achieve my existence in my works. I am the
sum of my actions. At every movement I do not consider 'something' – a possible

---

[1] E. Brandenburger, *Adam and Christus*, WMANT 7 (1962).
[2] Against H. Hegermann, *Die Vorstellung vom Schöpfungsmittler*, TU 82 (1961),
and H.-M. Schenke, *Der Gott 'Mensch' in der Gnosis* (1962).
[3] Bultmann, *Theology of the New Testament* I, pp. 195f.

act, a decision, an object – but myself, with the alternative of winning myself or losing myself.

Pauline anthropology is not dualistic. The place where God meets me is not the soul, but the body. This is the place of worship (Rom. 12.1; I Cor. 6.20). σῶμα designates the 'I' (I Cor. 13.3; 7.4), the I in so far as it can be grasped by itself and others as the possible object of action through others and through itself. I am σῶμα in so far as I can stand over against myself, govern myself and risk myself. I am σῶμα in so far as I desire (Rom. 6.12; cf. Gal. 5.16f.). σῶμα is thus the I as a subject which acts and an object which is acted upon, especially the I as one that acts upon itself. σῶμα thus designates man as the subject and object of sexual life (I Cor. 6.15f.; 7.4; Rom. 1.24).

Alongside the 'monistic' passages just quoted, there is a series of 'dualistic' passages in which a negative verdict is given on the body. The transition between the two groups can be seen in I Cor. 9.27: the demand for self-domination is based on the statement that I am alienated from myself in the world, fallen victim to the alien power of the σάρξ. Hence redemption is redemption from the body (Rom. 7.24). The body is dead; I must be saved by a new creation and encounter my body as a new man (Rom. 8.10–13). That I am free to stand over against myself and govern myself is a possibility given by the spirit.

This seems to be a contradiction to the assertion that the possibility of freedom and self-control is expressed in the concept of the σῶμα itself. In fact, σῶμα describes this aspect of being a man, but as a lost possibility. That, too, is already implied in the word σῶμα; the body is created – and, in so far as it is transitory, weak and exposed to temptation. Indeed, it has succumbed to it. I never experience myself as one who is still free and has his future in his hand, but as a fallen one, as σῶμα τῆς ἁμαρτίας Rom. 6.6; as σῶμα τοῦ θανάτου Rom. 7.24. In experiencing myself in this way, I also know that the fallenness is my own action, in which my freedom is perverted, and thus lost.

The two passages Rom. 6.6 and 7.24 offer a paradigm for the juxtaposition of ethical (or 'juridical') and 'physical' doctrines of redemption, i.e. for the terminology of 'justification' and 'redemption'. At first glance, the first passage seems to give a verdict on the moral and the second on the physical circumstances of man. Salvation in the first place would be the restoration of moral integrity or the gaining of recognition through God, in the second place the appropriation of the power of life, the spirit. These two patterns are, in fact, recognizable in the background. But Paul follows neither of them. For him, the characteristic element is the linking of death (in the physical pattern) and sin (in the ethical pattern). For the nature of sin is not realized if it is defined only as an ethical failure, if it is not seen to be fatal, a doom which man cannot avoid. And death is not understood if it is interpreted as a 'physical' event. Paul relates the two: death is the wages of sin. What that means is the theme of Rom. 5–8, especially ch. 5: original sin and original death (see section 23).

The difficulty in Paul's thought here is that he must, of course, also explain physical death. He presents the way in which this came to man in mythical terms; in Adam we all fell victim to death. The association of death, primal death, with sin, primal sin, suggests that death should be recognized as a historical power. But sin, too, is understood through this association as a trans-subjective power. This idea is further depicted by the relationship of sin to the σάρξ. That Paul's thoughts already go this far is shown by the theme of Rom. 5: not 'death', but the demonstration of the anticipatory freedom from death which I experience paradoxically in faith, which is shown precisely in the face of physical death. The power of death is transcended in faith. Faith opens up the possibility of resisting death (I Cor. 15.55f.).

Similar to this aspect of the σῶμα as having fallen victim to sin and death is another, that of the σάρξ (cf. the parallel formulations in II Cor. 4.10 and 4.11). The passage II Cor. 5.1ff. is put in the most strongly dualistic terms: the body is described here as σκῆνος and ἡ ἐπίγειος ἡμῶν οἰκία τοῦ σκήνους. It is therefore only the outer shell of the I, which is not appropriate to the latter. It is 'dissolved', 'put off'; this is dualistic symbolism. To be in the body is ἐκδημεῖν ἀπὸ τοῦ κυρίου; ἐκδημῆσαι ἐκ τοῦ σώματος over against ἐνδημῆσαι πρὸς τὸν κύριον. Redemption is freedom from the body (cf. Rom. 7.24). σῶμα and σάρξ can thus make contact. But they are not synonymous. σῶμα is man as the one who can fall, and in fact has fallen, victim to sin and death. σάρξ is man as the one who has fallen. This dialectic appears clearly in Rom. 8.10.

IV σάρξ

W. D. Davies, 'Paul and the Dead Sea Scrolls: Flesh and Spirit', in: Krister Stendahl (ed.), *The Scrolls and the NT* (1957), pp. 157–82; E. Schweizer, 'Die Hellenistische Komponente im nt. σάρξ-Begriff', *ZNW* 48 (1957), pp. 237–53 (= *Neotestamentica* (1963), pp. 29–48); id., σάρξ, *TWNT* VII 124ff.; H. Braun, *Qumran und das NT* II (1966), pp. 175ff.

We must start from the anthropological, partly neutral usage which continues the Old Testament line, 'All flesh is grass'. σάρξ is corporeality endued with life ('flesh and blood'; cf. I Cor. 15.50). πᾶσα σάρξ represents 'everyman' (Rom. 3.20); cf. πᾶσα ψυχή (Rom. 2.9; 13.1). τέκνα τῆς σαρκός are natural descendants (Rom. 9.8). Israel κατὰ σάρκα is the empirical people of Israel (I Cor. 10.18). In Gal. 4.13, ἀσθένεια τῆς σαρκός designates bodily weakness; the same expression in Rom. 6.19 describes human weakness. The line which leads from this neutral usage to a more pointed one can be seen in Rom. 2.28f.: σάρξ is the sphere of the visible, the transitory. Here Paul goes far beyond the Old Testament: σάρξ is the sphere in which I live and through which I am determined. Sphere in fact denotes power. It has its ἐπιθυμία and its ἔργα. The σῶμα is dominated by the σάρξ. If the σάρξ is finished, the σῶμα is freed from its prison (Rom. 8.9). We can thus see the line: σάρξ is (a) whatever is present to hand; (b) what is present to hand *coram deo*. As such it is marked by (a) transitoriness; (b) sin.

V ψυχή

The word plays no significant role. It is important to note that the Greek doctrine of the soul does not appear at any point. The Jewish origin of the word is determinative: נֶפֶשׁ is the living quality of the flesh. The soul belongs to man's earthly existence. It does not exist without physical life. It is not, say, freed by death, then to live in untrammelled purity. Death is its end. The word ψυχή can also mean the person, and this is related to σῶμα, σάρξ and πνεῦμα (Rom. 16.4: ὑπὲρ τῆς ψυχῆς μου 'For my life'). In the Old Testament, too, נֶפֶשׁ and רוּחַ can be associated.

II Cor. 12.15: ὑπὲρ τῶν ψυχῶν ὑμῶν 'for you'. Phil. 1.17; 2.2: μιᾷ ψυχῇ and σύμψυχοι 'of one mind' is synonymous with ἑνὶ πνεύματι and τὸ ἓν φρονοῦντες; cf. I Cor. 1.10: ἐν τῷ αὐτῷ νοΐ καὶ ἐν τῇ αὐτῇ γνώμῃ.

If a counterpart is used, it is not σῶμα, but πνεῦμα (despite the occasional affinity): compare the contrast of ψυχικός and πνευματικὸς ἄνθρωπος in I Cor. 2.10–16.[1]

In the Adam-Christ typology (I Cor. 15.45), ψυχὴ ζῶσα ('only alive on earth') is contrasted with πνεῦμα ζωοποιοῦν. The expression ψυχὴ ζῶσα derives from the Old Testament (Gen. 2.7), but there it has a positive meaning: man is made alive. Paul, on the other hand, gives it a negative sense by contrasting it with πνεῦμα.

---

[1] For the question how far the gnostic depreciation of the soul is a factor here, see R. Reitzenstein, *Die Hellenistischen Mysterienreligionen* (1927³), pp. 308ff., and E. Schweizer, *TWNT* VI 393f.; for gnosticism, not only the body but also the soul belongs in the cosmos; it is the factor which keeps men entrapped in the world. Both body and soul are contrasted with the un-worldly πνεῦμα. Cf. H. Jonas, *Gnosis*, I, pp. 212–4.

VI πνεῦμα (Anthropological)

πνεῦμα has a formal significance when Paul distinguishes between the human spirit and the spirit of God (I Cor. 2.11) or the (holy) spirit (Rom. 8.16). σῶμα and πνεῦμα together describe the whole person in I Cor. 7.34; 5.3. But πνεῦμα alone can also represent the person, as in the closing greetings; there we have without any differentiation in meaning: the Lord be 'with you' and 'with your spirit'. πνεῦμα, too, does not designate a metaphysical principle in man but the living 'I' which has a disposition: κοινωνία πνεύματος is concord in disposition (Phil. 2.1). In I Cor. 6.16f., we have rhetorically pointed expressions. What is meant is a body with the Lord, i.e. a spiritual one.

VII Further Anthropological Concepts

1. ὁ ἔσω ἄνθρωπος occurs twice, in Rom. 7.22 and II Cor. 4.16.

In Rom. 7.22, ὁ ἔσω ἄνθρωπος is man in so far as he acts as subject, the νοῦς which wills the good. It is, of course, no merit or excuse for man that he is still well-disposed. Willing the good is not a positive ethical value. Paul intends an ethically neutral condition, that man as such is concerned for what is good for him, but he goes on from there to conclude that man does not achieve it. In II Cor. 4.16, the meaning of ὁ ἔσω ἄνθρωπος is different: not the νοῦς as the natural, assertive I, but the new I, transformed through the spirit, which receives its life day by day, whereas the ἔξω ἄνθρωπος is exposed to death. The sense is therefore a purely formal one.

2. νοῦς: When man is described as subject, Paul can speak of the νοῦς. By that, he means above all the act of knowing, rational knowledge (cf. I Cor. 14.14f.: speaking ἐν νοΐ, comprehensible speech as opposed to glossolalia). God's peace surpasses the νοῦς, the human capability of understanding (Phil. 4.7). Here, theoretical thought is not to be separated from practical judgments, but should lead to them, to δοκιμάζειν (Rom. 12.2; cf. I Cor. 14.13ff.; Rom. 1.28). The verdict can be true or false. The guarantee of righteousness does not lie in the νοῦς as such, but in its illumination. This should be considered at the point where the supreme statement about the νοῦς is made, Rom. 1.20: it can understand God's invisible nature, and thus also his demand (Rom. 1.32; 12.2). But knowledge of God is not man's own possibility. It is possible, because God shows himself. Man is told here that he can understand what God lets him know. The conclusion is that man cannot excuse himself on the grounds of ignorance if he transgresses against God. If the νοῦς is ἀδόκιμος, that is man's fault.

There is apparently a contradiction between Rom. 1.28: the νοῦς has become ἀδόκιμος, and Rom. 7.23: the νοῦς wills the good (see above). But it does not come into play because an alien power, sin, which dwells in the body, prevents it. Can man then make the νοῦς responsible for his helplessness? Can it be called corrupt, if it is concerned for the good?

And must not the assertion be revised, that, according to Paul, man's inner nature is not free? In Rom. 7, Paul seems to give a good Stoic account: inwardly I am free and oriented to the good. But I am constrained from outside.[1]

It is a misunderstanding of Rom. 7 to read into it the usual view of the free subject and its will. Paul does not teach that the νοῦς is free and good. He merely asserts that it cannot do what it wills. This is demonstrated through the cleavage between willing and doing. It is wrong to read out of this that willing is nevertheless a positive contribution. Paul means to show only one thing, that this cleavage is something impossible. He does not divide man into a free part and an unfree part, but says that man exists in division, i.e. that he has totally lost his freedom. Rom. 1 and Rom. 7 agree completely in this: as a creature I am oriented to God, but I live contrary to my determination and thus to myself. Basically, the νοῦς cannot be described and defined directly as an anthropological factor. For man is not described as a timeless being. The νοῦς is the perception at any time of what encounters me. I experience myself as one who contradicts God and thus his own being as a creature, although I could know about my determination. The νοῦς is not an inner realm which remains intact, into which I might retreat from the realm of the σάρξ. The νοῦς is rather the indication that I have become alien to myself.

3. συνείδησις:[2] this concept does not derive from the Old Testa-

---

[1] Literature on Rom. 7: W. G. Kümmel, *Römer 7 und die Bekehrung des Paulus*, UNT 17 (1929): R. Bultmann, 'Römer 7 und die Anthropologie des Paulus', *Imago Dei* (Krüger Festschrift) (1932), pp. 53–62; G. Bornkamm, 'Sünde, Gesetz und Tod' (1950), in: *Das Ende des Gesetzes*, Gesammelte Aufsätze I (1961³), pp. 51–69; J. Kürzinger, 'Der Schlüssel zum Verständnis von Römer 7', *BZ* NF 7 (1963), pp. 270–74.

[2] C. Maurer, συνείδησις, *TWNT* VII 897–918; M. Dibelius in HNT on I Tim. 1.5; M. Pohlenz, 'Paulus und die Stoa', *ZNW* 42 (1949), pp. 77f. (new impression, 1964, pp. 15f.); G. Bornkamm, 'Gesetz und Natur' (1959), in: *Studien zu Antike und Urchristentum*, Gesammelte Aufsätze II (1963²), pp. 111f.; J. Stelzenberger, *Syneidesis im NT* (1961); K. Stendahl, 'The Apostle Paul and the Introspective Conscience of the West', *HThR* 56 (1963), pp. 199–216.

ment. It was developed relatively late in Greek.[1] The New Testament meaning must be distinguished from that of modern idealism: συνείδησις is not the slogan of a 'religion of conscience' and does not describe the freedom of the subject who makes his decision autonomously. Nor does it describe the divine voice within or the bourgeois 'good' conscience as the pillow of the righteous. The expression 'good conscience' does not occur in the genuine Pauline epistles at all. Just as νοῦς describes the judgment and the 'desire', so συνείδησις describes the pure judgment. To understand the meaning we must start from the verb: σύνοιδα and σύνοιδα ἐμαυτῷ is sharing knowledge with one another and with myself, the possibility of contemplating my own conduct critically, the past as well as what is planned, the future. Conscience is given with humanity as such, not first with the enlightenment of the believer. Man can distinguish between good and evil. But he does not set his own norms. The content is determined by God's commandment, through revelation and not through an autonomous moral law. The conscience is not a source of revelation, but a matter of understanding the concrete demand of God. This applies explicitly even for the Gentiles (Rom. 2.15). Rom. 13.5 points to the reference to an objective norm outside myself.

> The civil authority is appointed by God. Therefore I have to subject myself οὐ μόνον διὰ τὴν ὀργὴν ἀλλὰ καὶ διὰ τὴν συνείδησιν, i.e. in acknowledgment of the will of God.[2]

The difference between συνείδησις and the modern understanding of conscience lies in its link with a revealed norm. Dibelius[3] feels it so strongly that he thinks that συνείδησις in Paul means not merely 'conscience', but the conviction that one has of good and evil.[4] But this is to restrict the Pauline meaning too closely.

Conscience is always my conscience; it cannot be replaced by any other authority. At the same time, it is my judge (II Cor. 1.12). It is,

---

[1] The substantives τὸ συνειδός and ἡ συνείδησις occur only sporadically before the first century BC; see Maurer.

[2] E. Käsemann, 'Principles of the Interpretation of Romans 13', *New Testament Questions of Today* (1969), pp. 196–216, against H. Lietzmann in HNT *ad loc*: 'from conviction'.

[3] M. Dibelius, 'Rom und die Christen im ersten Jahrhundert' (SAH 1942), *Botschaft und Geschichte* II, p. 183, n. 16.

[4] According to Pohlenz, *op. cit.*, this interpretation holds for Rom. 13.5, but not for Rom. 2.15. But it is also doubtful for Rom. 13.5; see also Maurer, *op. cit.*, p. 914, lines 22f.

further, a judgment which I share with other men. In II Corinthians, Paul does not only appeal to his own conscience in support of his ministry. He also appeals to that of the reader: if they judge him 'according to conscience', they must recognize his blamelessness (II Cor. 4.2; 5.11). He thus has a good conscience. But he draws the line: conscience cannot pronounce him righteous. It is not a competent authority for that (I Cor. 4.4).

The conscience can err. The conscience of some people in Corinth is weak (I Cor. 8.7).

On I Cor. 8–10: may one eat meat sacrificed to idols? One group gives a positive answer, because 'we' have the knowledge that there are no idols and are made free through this knowledge. The others answer in the negative because for them the flesh is 'unclean'. Hans von Soden observes:[1] modern Christianity might ask whether I have inner freedom from idols, for eating, whether my conscience agrees. The norm in that case would be my conviction. But this would avoid the real ethical question. For Paul there is no question whether we are free or not. To this extent he understands freedom radically, and not in broken terms (as in modern subjectivism). Therefore he does not reduce it to an inner freedom, through which one can do away what is in fact practised. Certainly, freedom has a limit, but it is one which is set in itself: πάντα μοι ἔξεστιν, ἀλλ'οὐκ ἐγὼ ἐξουσιασθήσομαι ὑπό τινος (I Cor. 6.12).

πάντα ἔξεστιν itself presents the possibility for the 'strong' to refrain. I Cor. 10.27f.: if you are invited by a Gentile, then eat. You need not make inquiries whether it is meat that has been offered to idols: your conscience is not involved, you are free. But if a man explicitly says to you, 'That is meat which has been offered to idols', then do not eat. The reason why you must not is for the sake of the one who points it out to you and διὰ τὴν συνείδησιν. But why should that be so, if we are free and know that there is no material, cultic impurity and that flesh is simply flesh? Paul: I do not mean your conscience, but that of the other man. It is not a question of whether you have inner freedom, but of how your behaviour must be understood in this instance: whether it appears as a confession to the idols and would in that case be an act of unfreedom, of fear about the idols, of religious convention. The free man can renounce freedom. He cannot compel the 'weak' to freedom. The same theme is discussed in Rom. 14f. There, however, Paul uses πίστις instead of συνείδησις. The freedom of conscience is thus the freedom of faith. The norm of freedom is given in faith.

4. The use of καρδία has hardly any special peculiarities. The word belongs to Jewish anthropology: the heart is the organ for understanding and willing, the conscious activity of the I (cf. Mark 7.21; Luke 2.35, etc.). Paul uses καρδία to describe man in so far as he desires. The heart is the centre of thought, will, feeling (I Cor. 4.5; II Cor.

[1] H. von Soden, 'Sakrament und Ethik bei Paulus' (1931), in: *Das Paulusbild der neueren deutschen Forschung* (1964), pp. 338–79.

9.7). The heart is hidden; the opposite to ἐν καρδίᾳ can therefore be ἐν προσώπῳ (II Cor. 5.12). God looks into the inner man: he is ὁ δοκιμάζων τὰς καρδίας (I Thess. 2.4; cf. Rom. 8.27). In respect of God and his will, the heart is uncomprehending, stubborn, obscured (Rom. 1.21, 24; 2.5). This happens although it can understand God's will; for his law has been written on the heart (Rom. 2.15). On the other hand, it is enlightened (II Cor. 4.6); the spirit has been poured into men's hearts (II Cor. 1.22; Gal. 4.6).

22 · HOPE

R. Bultmann, ἐλπίς, *TWNT* II 527ff.; W. Grundmann, 'Überlieferung und Eigenaussage im eschatologischen Denken des Apostels Paulus', *NTS* 8 (1961/2), pp. 12–26; H. Schwantes, *Schöpfung der Endzeit* (1963); D. E. H. Whiteley, *The Theology of St Paul* (1964), pp. 233ff.

Two distinctions are necessary: (*a*) over against the thesis that Paul is an apocalyptist, i.e. over against the understanding of his eschatology in the light of his picture of the future. In that case, eschatology would be a description of what was expected. But the question is what the expectation itself is. The apocalyptic interpretation gives no information about that from the texts, but only from the psychological construction of the 'attitude' of Paul; (*b*) over against mysticism. The future element is doubtless there and cannot be eliminated. It forms virtually the chief point in the discussions with unhistorical pneumatism and sacramentalism (I Cor. 15; Rom. 6). But what is the relationship between what is expected and the expectation? To answer this question it is necessary to put a deeper one which underlies it: what is the relationship between past, present and future? A definition of the formal structure of time does not lead to an answer. The determinative feature is the concrete understanding of faith. Faith is self-understanding on hearing the gospel: that is, the possibility of περιπατεῖν κατὰ πνεῦμα in the face of the future disclosed through the word, and thus in the face of my past, sin, and the present, the 'newness of life'. Faith discloses to me whence I come (Rom. 7), where I am, namely in the spirit, in freedom, and whither I am called. To understand time means to understand oneself in time; time is the perspective in which I can understand myself through the message of faith.

This threefold definition cannot be described through the triad 'faith – love – hope'. Hope is certainly an attitude towards the future, love the determining of the present, the content of faith the salvation which has taken place in Christ. But Paul himself resists schematization by declaring love to be the greatest of the three; it embraces the other two determinations. In what sense? Not by degrading faith – on the contrary, this is what he wants to bring out. It is faith that makes love possible. But Paul must show that faith is not only a theoretical consideration; it actually leads to the new life, to freedom, to love. It is πίστις δι' ἀγάπης ἐνεργουμένη (Gal. 5.5f.). The association of faith and hope also appears in the same passage. We should also note the paraphrases and expositions of the triad faith – hope – love (or faith – love – hope) in the following places: I Thess. 1.3; 5.8; in the context of I Cor. 13.13; Rom. 5.1ff.; cf. further the non-Pauline passages: Col. 1.4f.; I Peter 1.21f.; Heb. 10.22ff. Reitzenstein[1] wanted to derive the triad from a fourfold gnostic formula. In polemic against the Corinthian gnostics, Paul left out the fourth term: γνῶσις. The fact that the formula is older than the polemic in I Corinthians does, however, tell against this. It was not developed with polemical intent. Perhaps it has been combined from the two conjunctions πίστις / ἐλπίς and πίστις / ἀγάπη (cf. Gal. 5.5f.). The gnostic expansion to a fourfold formula (see Ev. Phil. 115) is secondary.

In Paul's understanding, eschatology is neither an apocalyptic *locus de novissimis* as the last prospect towards the beyond after the abyss of death or the end of the world, nor is it the postulate of a 'principle of hope' as the sketch of a picture of the world and of man. Hope, too, is simply an exposition of faith. That is its positive and critical principle, its basis and its limitation; it prevents a dissolution into subjective-psychological or objective-apocalyptic fantasy. Paul does not interpret his hope through pictures of what is hoped for. The essential point is the bracketing of the future with the present, the indication that the future can be experienced now.[2] Of course, apocalyptic imagery is there: Paul expects the parousia and expects it soon (I Thess. 4.13ff.; Phil. 4.5; I Cor. 7.29; Rom. 13.11), and on the basis of this expectation he gives instructions for conduct in the present.

Prospect: instructions which are based on the expectation of the end of the

[1] R. Reitzenstein, *Historia Monachorum*, FRLANT NF 7, 1916, pp. 100ff., 242ff.; NGG 1916, pp. 367–416; 1917, pp. 131–51; 1922, p. 256; *Die Hellenistischen Mysterienreligionen* (1927³), pp. 383ff.

[2] To be experienced, not in a subjective way, but as an experience of faith, through hearing the message, in the spirit.

world (I Cor. 7) are to be distinguished from those with general validity. One may note in I Cor. 7 the transition from an eschatological attitude to the world to a general definition of a freedom towards the world which does not depend on the assignment of a particular date to the parousia.

It is significant both that the picture of the parousia does not become an independent theme and that the ideas about the parousia in Paul are not a unity.

In I Thess. 4.13ff. and I Cor. 15, Paul expects the general resurrection of the dead at the end of the world. On the other hand, Phil. 1.21–23 sounds as though Paul expects to be with the Lord immediately after his death. There is a similar juxtaposition in the synoptic gospels (Luke), and even in Jewish apocalyptic. Albert Schweitzer and Ernst Lohmeyer[1] interpret the passage in Philippians to mean that Paul expected special treatment for himself as a martyr. But this interpretation does not fit the context. On the basis of II Cor. 5.1ff., it is sometimes inferred that Paul expected an intermediate stage. But at this point Paul is concerned only with the contrast between earthly and heavenly existence. He does not reflect at all on the time when he will be 'clothed'. The climax of the idea is that we shall all be called before God, independently of our physical condition; here again we find the significant εἴτε—εἴτε.

The most important of the objectifications is the idea of the resurrection of the dead. Paul gives a short sketch in I Thess. 4.13ff.: (a) restoration to life of the faithful departed; (b) transformation of those believers who are alive at the parousia; (c) universal assumption into the air. He says nothing about the fate of unbelievers. One can only conclude from hints that the judgment of wrath goes forth upon them (I Thess. 1.10) and that they will be judged according to their works (Rom. 2.5). The saints will judge the world with the angels (I Cor. 6.2f.). The theme is discussed broadly in I Cor. 15 and also in II Cor. 5.1–10.[2] These two passages seem to contradict the earlier statement that the concept σῶμα designates the I and not the form, as in Greek. For at the clearest point at which our future after death is the theme, in II Cor. 5, a dualistic anthropology appears. The body is simply the outer husk. Only when it is stripped off are we unburdened and free. In I Cor. 15, the body also seems to be the form of a material (vv. 35ff.). We must therefore enquire whether what has been said about the concept of σῶμα must be revised.

[1] A. Schweitzer, *The Mysticism of the Apostle Paul* (1931), p. 137; E. Lohmeyer, *ad loc.* (Meyer Kommentar).

[2] I. Hermann, *Kyrios und Pneuma*, StANT 2 (1961), pp. 114ff.; M. E. Dahl, *The Resurrection of the Body*, SBT 36 (1962); H. Schwantes, *op. cit.*

Bultmann (*Theology of the New Testament*, I, pp. 201f.) explains that on grounds of method it is impermissible to begin from II Cor. 5, because the other 'monistic' expressions about the σῶμα cannot be explained from here. But we can understand from them that at times Paul can also speak in dualistic terms. He is led to do this by polemic against the Corinthian dualists. This explanation is correct. But that still does not explain the evidence of I Cor. 15. Is that also a special case? Yes.

In both passages we can see a conflict, not only between Paul and his Corinthian opponents but also in deeper terms: of Paul with himself, namely between what is meant and the means for describing it, between future and hope on the one side and anthropological ideas on the other. Paul must describe the future being on the one hand as beyond the world and time, and yet on the other hand, still as being. This can only be done in inappropriate terms, and the discrepancy appears in his account.

I CORINTHIANS 15

The starting point of the account is the creed (vv. 3–5). It serves for more than an external foundation: Paul understands that faith itself determines the future. So in two arguments he can infer from the creed: (1) *the fact that* the dead rise; (2) *the way in which* resurrection is possible (vv. 35ff.). The beginning made with the creed is maintained, in that Paul asks only about the future of the believers. In a first argument he discusses thematically the connection of faith and hope (vv. 12–19). If the resurrection of the dead is disputed, then the resurrection of Christ is disputed and faith is in vain. This is no sentimental explanation, but an invitation to understand faith and its self-evident nature. Further arguments follow, first in support of the theme that the dead rise (the correspondence between Adam and Christ), then the course of the eschatological events and then the 'baptism for the dead'. This multiple approach is a sign that Paul himself feels that the individual idea only makes a limited contribution. The correspondence between Adam and Christ is hinted at only sketchily in I Cor. 15; the commentary on it is provided by Rom. 5.[1] Adam embraces mankind representatively in himself; his death is the death of everyman: we all die 'in Adam'. In the same way, Christ's fate embraces our own in itself. He is the second Adam.[2] But at the decisive point the analogy does not work: left to itself, it does not take

[1] E. Brandenburger, *Adam und Christus*, WMANT 7 (1962).
[2] The analogy is expressed by ὥσπερ—οὕτως.

faith into account. Salvation does not follow naturally from Christ (as does death from Adam), but is received by faith.

In Rom. 5, therefore, Paul must break the analogy: ἀλλ 'οὐχ ὡς τὸ παράπτωμα οὕτως τὸ χάρισμα (v. 15). And in I Cor. 15, in a later passage, he contrasts Adam and Christ: the first Adam became εἰς ψυχὴν ζῶσαν, the second and last(!) Adam εἰς πνεῦμα ζωοποιοῦν. Thus the analogy is transcended – fortunately! The myth is not adequate to depict what is meant. It can express the fact that life is grounded objectively, outside us, and comes from outside to us. But it wrongly leads us to interpret death and life as a natural process. Paul therefore breaks off where he turns his attention from death to life. As Rom. 5 shows, for Paul, even death of course is not essentially a natural process, but an indication that the relationship to God is broken, i.e. as a factor of historical existence. This historical intent can already be seen in I Cor. 15.22, in the change of tenses: ἀποθνήσκουσιν-ζωοποιηθήσονται.

Paul continually maintains the futurity of the resurrection. His anti-enthusiastic thrust is clear. The word πάντες changes its meaning: first it describes all men, then all who are in Christ. Being in Christ has a different quality from being in Adam. Paul heightens the idea by saying not that we shall escape death, but rather that death itself will be destroyed. Therefore it no longer has power today against the new life in the spirit.

Paul's remark is not to be reduced to the statement that death is harmless. Then, as ever, it remains the last enemy. It becomes harmless 'in Christ'. We still do not live, as the Corinthians imagine, in the blessedness of the beyond. We experience the overcoming of death in the paradox that we are exposed to it (Rom. 8.35ff.; II Cor. 4.7ff.).

In v. 24, there follows a reference to the sequence of the eschatological events which have begun with the resurrection of Christ: ἀπαρχὴ Χριστός. Attached to this is the argument about representative baptism for the dead (v. 29). The reference of the passage to vicarious baptism is not to be disputed.

A new train of thought begins with v. 35: ἀλλὰ ἐρεῖ τις· πῶς ἐγείρονται οἱ νεκροί; ποίῳ δὲ σώματι ἔρχονται; First Paul works with the comparison of the seed (vv. 36–38). Is it convincing? It does not fit at all. But Paul is not thinking in biological-organic terms. He does not consider the seed in the light of its potentiality as a kernel, for development. He stresses that the seed is not seen as it will be: it is 'naked'. Its future being is a wonder. Paul does not stress the continuity, but the act of creation. He interprets the resurrection as new creation.

It is impossible to press the comparison to further detail. According to Paul, the seed at first has no σῶμα; but God can give it one. Man has one and will lose it. The fact that the seed dies does not fit with the 'naked' corn. Paul's intention is clear: when we die we are nothing, naked, like the seed, and we will be created anew. Karl Barth[1] explains the passage as follows: here Paul presents a pure synthesis. For the two different phenomena of seed and plant he substitutes the same subject: a new creation takes place in the invisible in-between stage.

σῶμα here is evidently the form which can exist in different modes of being, σάρξ or δόξα. It would therefore seem natural to interpret σῶμα as the form and σάρξ or δόξα as the substance. Certainly σάρξ and δόξα are conceived in material terms. But Paul cannot imagine the σῶμα in abstract terms as form. There is no σῶμα -being in itself, but only a σῶμα, which appears each time in a particular substantiality. This is clear from the rest of the argument; there is more than one kind of σάρξ, a fact from which Paul argues to the difference of σώματα, i.e. modes of corporeality; and there are different kinds of δόξα. It therefore follows (v. 42): οὕτως καὶ ἡ ἀνάστασις τῶν νεκρῶν. σπείρεται ἐν φθορᾷ, ἐγείρεται ἐν ἀφθαρσίᾳ . . . σπείρεται σῶμα ψυχικόν, ἐγείρεται σῶμα πνευματικόν.

In these antitheses, Paul's real meaning breaks through his laborious expedients: the hope of the resurrection cannot be reached from an analysis of the nature of man, because the resurrection is a new creation, never grounded and never seen otherwise than 'in Christ'. The division between what is meant and the means of presenting it is an expression of the theological truth that the future life is certain, not *although* it is inconceivable, but *because* it is inconceivable, a miracle which can be perceived in the miracle of the spirit.

Schwantes: Paul does not know of a general resurrection, but only of the creation of the end-time, which he associates with faith in God, the creator (and does not vindicate in apocalyptic terms). This reduction is contradicted by the fact that Paul knows of a general judgment. Cf., of course, E. Schweizer, *TWNT* VII 1060: despite Rom. 5.2f., Paul does not speak of a resurrection to death or to damnation, but only of a judgment which praises or censures the works of the one who has been raised to life.[2]

Terminology: the variation between resurrection of 'the body' and 'the flesh' is simply a matter of linguistic usage. With his σάρξ terminology, Paul cannot speak of a resurrection 'of the flesh'. For flesh is what is to hand, in that it has no future. Flesh and blood will not inherit the kingdom of God. The terminology in John is different: ὁ λόγος σὰρξ ἐγένετο, and so is Luke 24.39. Bultmann (*Theology of the New Testament* I, pp. 198f.): what remains, and constitutes the continuity between my

---

[1] Karl Barth, *The Resurrection of the Dead* (1933).
[2] Cf. E. Jüngel, *Paulus und Jesus* (1962), pp. 66–70.

earthly self and my future self is the σῶμα. But that is precisely not the case: I shall receive a new, pneumatic σῶμα. The stress lies throughout on the newness, the miracle. I shall have a σῶμα in the beyond, for Paul cannot imagine being without a σῶμα. But it is a new body. What, then, remains? This cannot be described directly, in anthropological terms, with either σῶμα or ψυχή. Certainly the πνεῦμα is an ἀρραβών, and the future life is 'spiritual' life. But the spirit is not a perceptible, anthropological factor. The continuity strictly corresponds with the character of the saving event as word: the promise is spoken to me, the spirit is given to me; so I can hope for myself as one who has already been reached by the spirit. Paul refuses to make the continuity clear in II Cor. 5, by stressing that we walk in faith and not in sight (v. 7). It makes little difference to the state of affairs if we understand εἶδος here as εἰκών.[1] Even the experiences of the spirit do not take us beyond the stage of faith. In I Cor. 12–14, Paul stresses that the gifts of the spirit keep the transitoriness of our present existence before our eyes. The spirit is a pledge. It sets us moving, here in the world, but not towards heaven. For we still live ἐν σαρκί and ἐν σώματι, though free and no longer κατὰ σάρκα. Our existence is determined through the cross (Rom. 5.1ff.; II Cor. 4). Precisely through this, we experience ourselves as those who hope.

II CORINTHIANS 5.1–10[2]

Here, in his controversy with the Corinthian proto-gnostics, Paul writes in dualistic terms. Evidently his opponents will have nothing of a bodily resurrection (in the style of I Cor. 15). Their ideal is incorporeal existence in the untrammelled light-world. When this 'tabernacle' is taken away, the soul ascends naked and free.

Paul takes over their mode of expression, but says the opposite: we shall not be naked, our heavenly body awaits us (cf. Phil. 3.21). Unlike the Corinthians, Paul cannot imagine existence without a body. Man does not have life simply by casting off the body; it is not the body that is alien and evil, but sin. For Paul, the contrast is not between matter and spirit (or soul), but between the world and death on the one hand, and new creation on the other. Paul is once again uninterested in anthropological and metaphysical conceptions. The discussion, which sounds so dualistic, leads beyond v. 7, which has already been mentioned, to one of Paul's characteristic εἴτε—εἴτε sentences (v. 9). Paul is thus saying that men's anthropological condition is irrelevant as far as salvation is concerned. The only significant

[1] J. Jervell, *Imago Dei*, FRLANT 76 (1960), p. 270.

[2] W. Mundle, 'Das Problem des Zwischenzustandes in dem Abschnitt 2 Kor 5, 1–10', *Festgabe für A. Jülicher* (1927), pp. 93–109; R. Bultmann, 'Exegetische Probleme des Zweiten Korintherbriefes', SyBU 9 (1947) (new impression, 1963, pp. 3–12); E. E. Ellis, 'II Corinthians V. 1–10 in Pauline Eschatology', *NTS* 6 (1959/60), pp. 211–24; P. Hoffmann, *Die Toten in Christus*, NTA 2, Folge 2 (1966), pp. 253ff.

thing is whether or not we please God; the decisive factor is thus his verdict upon us in judgment, in which we are uncovered. In working with the apocalyptic, dualistic conceptions of his time (body and other-worldly body), Paul leads to a point at which he points beyond the content of the conceptions he uses to the theological substance of the invisible hope that we experience in the word. Like the nature of faith, the goal of hope cannot be perceived.

No picture of the future is painted, in order to stimulate faith. Quite the reverse is true: hope is won only through the faith which accepts the promise where it perceives no worldly prospect of its being realized (Rom. 4.18). It is of the nature of hope that neither the way to the goal nor the goal itself can be seen (Rom. 8.24f.). The very fact that we cannot see hope is the comforting thing. For in this way hope can be the power which determines the present. This is shown in Rom. 5.1ff., in the form of an exegesis of the credal statement Rom. 4.25: δικαιωθέντες οὖν ἐκ πίστεως εἰρήνην ἔχομεν. But where is this peace tangible? It is nowhere to be seen. Afterwards, as before, the world is dominated by sin and death. It would be an admission of defeat in his theological defence of hope were Paul now to argue: salvation is there although it cannot be seen (say, within the redeemed). Paul continues: salvation is here – not *although* it is not to be seen, but precisely *because* it is not to be seen. It is here as the possibility of boasting of hope in tribulation. Hope therefore does not represent the ignoring of the powers of being, a longing look towards better times ahead, a remnant of optimism in wearisome situations of life, but existing in face of the powers, boasting against them.

The usual Christian exhortation concludes with the thought that as long as men have not given up all hope, they have power to endure. And this hope appears on the horizon of our being. So hope leads to our proving. In Paul, the sequence is quite the reverse. The proving creates hope. θλῖψις shatters our human assurance and casts us exclusively on hope. And at this point it emerges that this is the real possibility of existence, the hopeful feature of human life: 'hope will not be put to shame'. In interpreting this sentence it is important to note that Paul alludes to the Bible (Ps. 22.5 LXX; cf. 25.20 LXX). The interpretation is not based on human experience, it is not a rule which has been won from the observation of the course of human life. The sentence is grounded on the fact that God's love has been poured out; and I experience that in being told that it is so. Here Paul is not preaching the philosophical idea of ἀταραξία. The Stoic trains himself in ὑπομονή and δοκιμή. He achieves his attitude by enduring fate, by renouncing the future and hope. He withdraws inside, where he cannot be touched by fate. The believer *is* touched. He stands open in experience and suffering, and learns in faith the freedom by which he can transcend fate.

23 · MAN IN THE WORLD

Paul gives no analysis – moral or psychological – of empirical man.
Is this through a lack of ability to be abstract? It is possible that there
is such a lack and that Paul is not schooled in philosophical methods
of thinking. In place of a philosophical analysis which sets out to gain
a general picture of man, he offers another kind of account. There is a
theological reason for the fact that he gives no empirical analysis:
true, faith has empirical effects, but its nature cannot be grasped
empirically. What can be grasped are the forms of faith, but not faith
which only exists as faith in . . . In an analogous way there are
visible effects of sin (immorality and death); but sin itself is no
empirical state of affairs (Rom. 1.18). The verdict that man is a
sinner affects his relationship to God. This verdict is only to be understood in faith.

This means something more than that man is morally bad. Paul affirms that his
own past before his conversion was morally blameless, and that in his life as a
Christian he knows nothing against himself. But this does not justify him. As a
sinner, I do not see through myself by self-analysis, but by understanding the
message of faith. By the promise of God's righteousness, I experience myself as one
who is directed towards grace, who had fallen into sin and now perceives himself as
one who has been saved.

Now I am righteous, without qualification; but this righteousness
is not in me, but in the word, in hearing. I never come to the point at
which I can make God's judgment my own. I cannot observe my
state of grace, but only accept God's word of grace. The man of grace
is not a theme of theology.

Of course, faith leads to experiences. But the way between my conversion, the
acceptance of the gospel and the present moment is not the object of my observation. I always have my conversion immediately behind me (Phil. 3.13). Luther sets
out to grasp the circumstances of Christian life with his formula *simul iustus et
peccator*. In this way, he gives expression to contemporaneity, whereas Paul contrasts
the once and the now. Nevertheless, there is in fact the same understanding of
existence in each case, since according to Paul my past is immediately there, so that
at no moment can I boast of myself.[1]

---

[1] Bultmann, *Essays* (1955), pp. 49ff., in controversy with P. Althaus, *Paulus und
Luther über den Menschen* (1958[3]).

The categories with which Paul describes the 'natural' man form a double series: (1) the world is creation and as such is limited and transitory; (2) the world is fallen from God. Similarly, man is (1) weak, as a creature; (2) guilty. Are the two approaches simply left in unresolved juxtaposition? The juxtaposition is understandable: Paul takes up two aspects under which the world and man are judged in the Old Testament and in Judaism. The intention of the two aspects is already the same in Judaism: the praise of God. The correspondence is even closer. 'Creation' means that the world has been created good. Man does justice to this by acknowledging the creator. At the same time, 'creation' means that it is limited. For man, that means that he has to confess himself as a creature before God. Even the doctrine that the world is fallen presupposes that it was originally good. And not only was it once good; it is still good, even now. God has not surrendered it. Sin is a mishandling of the good world, making an idol of it. Creatureliness and sinfulness are visible as a unity, as soon as one sees that it is a relationship with God which is expressed in the creed. The twofold situation is disclosed in my confrontation with the word of address: I am a sinful creature when I speak with God on the basis of the word of God, and say to him 'My God'. That I am a creature is again no empirical experience. I cannot see myself as a creature.

'Creatureliness' means that man does not appear isolated, as a being in himself, but is involved in already existing relationships. To put it in an exaggerated way: I am my relationship to God. But that means that I am not in fact what I am: I am in revolt against my nature, in sin, which is alienation from myself. By confusing God and the world, I allow the world to become a power which dominates me, which in fact it is not.

The revolt is not just partial. I am myself the one who carries it on actively: and I can do so because God does not let me go as his creature.

The fact that I have lost myself can be depicted in mythological terms as the surrender of man to demonic powers, the devil and his agents. The meaning is that I am surrendered to the power of the world.

The devil is the god of this age (II Cor. 4.4). The meaning of the idea that demonic powers dominate the world is that they are the world – and at the same time they are not the world, in so far as they are the falsification of the world. They are – deceit. Luther aptly describes the devil as God's ape. The demons have no power of their own, but only in so far as man has fallen victim to them. Through Christ, they are annihilated, not objectively and empirically, but existentially.

Anyone who is 'in Christ' lives in the world, but no longer under the powers – he is, rather, over against them. Demonology is the means of description: it represents the state of the *servum arbitrium*. This has nothing to do with a deterministic theory about the world. It is rather an element in the structure of faith. In the confrontation with God, I know that I cannot swing myself up to faith and promise myself my life. At the same time, I know in this confrontation that my being delivered to the powers is guilt.

Demonology is not a positive object of teaching for Paul. This is clear from the fact that he does not explain sin by demonology. When he describes man as the one who is handed over, he does not make use of demonological ideas, but concepts of existence, or he puts the two together in such a way that the significance is clear: Rom. 8.38f.

The two most important concepts of existence are σάρξ and ἁμαρτία. The two explain each other. The concept of sin derives from Judaism. But in Paul it no longer describes the individual failure against the individual commandment, but a trans-subjective power. Paul therefore uses the word predominantly in the singular. The plural is used only when he borrows from the tradition. This is a deliberate new conception. The continuation of this line can be seen in John. The same is true of the σάρξ: it is a sphere, an all-embracing power. The fact that Paul describes man as a sinner does not mean that he is refusing him *iustitia civilis*. In the civil realm he can easily distinguish between good and evil (Rom. 13.1ff.). 'Sin' means rather that I stand in a context from which I can no more break out than I can from the state of being given over to death (Rom. 5). Death and sin are closely connected: the wages of sin is death. The biological and natural side of this context is quite indispensable.

The problem now arises: if sin is alien to me, then it can dominate me, but cannot really get me in its clutches entirely. It cannot compel me to assent to it. Only in that case would I be fallen. Paul must therefore show how sin comes into being, how it can begin with me and enter into me and how it thus transcends me and alienates me from myself. Paul uses the concept σάρξ to show this.

We have already asserted that σάρξ is on the one hand neutral and on the other qualified. I am σάρξ in so far as I am – and am fallen in the world. The σάρξ is not evil in itself, as a 'substance'. The idea of creation is maintained. There is always the decisive question whether life ἐν σαρκί is my sphere of life or my norm of life. The dominance of the σάρξ is particularized in immorality, in the visible indications of its παθήματα, ἐπιθυμία, in its works (Gal. 5.19ff.). But immorality is only one form of the particularizing of the σάρξ. It can also express itself in other ways, as moral tension, if a man means to use it to win salvation (Phil. 3.3ff.).

The typical attitude of the flesh is ἐπιθυμεῖν, καυχᾶσθαι (=πεποιθέναι)[1] and μεριμνᾶν.[2] Here Paul speaks of the σάρξ in personifying phrases. He speaks of ἁμαρτία: it comes into the world (Rom. 5.12), acquires rule (5.21). Man is enslaved under it (6.6, 17ff.), sold (7.14), pays it wages (6.23). Once it was dead. Then it came alive. It used the law and now dwells in man (7.7ff.).[3] Paul often demonstrates that sin is a universal power and that all men without exception have fallen victim to it: 1. Rom. 1-3, from the relationship between Jew and Greek. The latter replace the worship of God with that of creation as a picture of God. The former transgress the law and make it the means of boasting. Elsewhere Paul contents himself with establishing the situation. He does not derive sin from a cause lying behind it (as the rabbis derived it from the evil desire). Sin comes from sinning. A causal explanation would only be a pseudo-explanation on the basis of an objectification of man and sin. 2. The same thing is true in respect of the demonstration of the universality of sin in Rom. 5.[4] Here sin is derived from the primal sin, Adam's fall, the mythical fall of the primal man who representatively embraces all men in himself. It is the Pauline version of the doctrine of original sin. One question arises: if sin is inherited, how then can it be guilt and not rather a fatal doom, like the fate of death?

Romans 5 offers an illustration of how the myth itself is no explanation, but only an expedient. This is already true for Paul. Otherwise he would not have to introduce a third argument for fallenness into sin at a later stage, namely that from the individual (Rom. 7.7f.). There the existentialist sense of the myth becomes clearer. Romans 5 and 7 go back to the myth of the primal state, paradise – Rom. 5 to explain the situation of humanity, Rom. 7 to explain the situation of man, i.e. how sin entered (a) into the world, (b) into me. The aim of this is not a historical or psychological account of the fall, but an analysis of the present situation, the perversion of creatureliness, self-alienation. How far, then, does the myth hold? Paul can use it to make clear that the nature of sin is not fully grasped if it is explained as the

---

[1] σάρξ as subject of ἐπιθυμεῖν: Gal. 5.16f., 24; Rom. 13.14. Here we have personifying expressions rather than real personification (as demons); πεποιθέναι Phil. 3.4.

[2] I Cor. 7.32ff. These characteristics signalize loss of freedom and thus the condition of anxiety. Rom. 8.15: οὐ γὰρ ἐλάβετε πνεῦμα δουλείας πάλιν εἰς φόβον, ἀλλὰ ἐλάβετε πνεῦμα υἱοθεσίας.

[3] All are sinners: Rom. 3.22f.; Gal. 3.22.

[4] R. Bultmann, Theology of the New Testament I, pp. 249ff.; id., 'Adam und Christus nach Röm. 5', ZNW 50 (1959), pp. 145–65 (=Der alte und der neue Mensch in der Theologie des Paulus (1964), pp. 41ff.); E. Brandenburger, Adam und Christus, WMANT 7 (1962); E. Jüngel, 'Das Gesetz zwischen Adam und Christus', ZThK 60 (1963), pp. 42–74; G. Schunack, Das hermeneutische Problem des Todes (1967).

act of a man who is regarded as being free. Through the act itself there arises a condition which embraces me, a sphere which gains power over me, from which I can no longer break out. This is the significance of the association of ἁμαρτία and σάρξ. Paul makes this clear by means of the phenomenon of death, from which I cannot escape.

With the myth of the primal man, Paul can show that if I encounter myself, sin is always already there. I can always recognize it only as the power which is there before me. I discover myself in my world as one who is always already determined through sin. Paul is clear about the boundaries within which myth is capable of a contribution. He outlines no picture of paradise and primal man. That is not the content of the doctrine.

Nor does he paint a picture of mankind's ideal primal state as an educative model. This primal state is impossible for me to reach, as it is quite unimaginable, and not empirical. It cannot therefore be historically verified. Karl Heim might be quoted by way of comparison: 'At the beginning of the development of mankind, access to God was in fact open. The invisible power was seen.'[1] Such a speculative assertion is open to historical investigation, e.g. to see whether there was death in the world before man appeared. Ernst Haenchen is troubled by this 'problem'.[2]

The mythical primal state is only hinted at as a foil to fallenness in sin. Adam's form remains intangible. Only a single point of his existence appears; that through him sin came into the world.

Of course, for Paul, Adam is a historical person and paradise a historical state. But the way in which Paul works with it can be seen from the difference between what is presented and what is meant. What is meant is that sin cannot be verified historically, in an objectifying presentation. It is not creation, it is a truth of faith. The non-verifiability becomes clear in Rom. 5 itself, and then in the juxtaposition of Rom. 5 and Rom. 7.7ff. Empirically, the world never lived without sin, just as it never lived without law. That Paul knows. Now he must laboriously grasp it and reconcile it with the thought forms at his disposal.

Paul no longer derives the sin of primal man from a mythical cause, the devil. For the mythical causal explanation see Wisdom 2.24: death was caused by the devil; Qumran: by the two spirits; the rabbis: by the evil inclination (mythical psychology); gnosticism: by seduction by matter which played man's image back to him.

According to Paul, sin comes from sinning.[3] But it may be objected that this fact can only be pointed out in the realm of the individual – so why the myth about humanity? It is there because Paul means to

---

[1] K. Heim, *Glaube und Denken* (1934³), p. 217.
[2] E. Haenchen, *Gott und Mensch* (1965), p. 27.
[3] R. Bultmann, *Theology of the New Testament* I, pp. 250ff.

show that the sphere of power arises through action, and that it is through *action, per hominem unum*. This is basically no longer a causal, mythical explanation, but an analysis of existence. The unmythical tendency can be seen clearly in a comparison with Judaism. There the connection of the individual with Adam is set out by means of the idea of representation: the tribal ancestor includes posterity in himself. Paul begins from this idea of representation but brings it to an entirely new conclusion: ἐφ' ᾧ πάντες ἥμαρτον. We are not 'in Adam' substantially, but in so far as we take over his act in our own. The mythical idea of representation is thus limited to the truth that I can no longer break out of sin through decision and action. I always already have the fall behind me.

Now Paul comes into conflict with his own picture of history. On the one hand, there is the principle: no sin without law (Rom. 4.15); on the other, according to the Old Testament picture of history, the law only came later, under Moses. Thus there was no sin between Adam (who nevertheless transgressed against a direct commandment of God) and Moses. That would be the consequence of the mythical account of history. The consequence is, of course, impossible for Paul. In Rom. 5 he resorts to a thesis which is set out *ad hoc* (v. 13), and is no way out: from Adam to Moses, sin was in the world; but it was not imputed. It was thus at work on the one hand, as men died, but not effective on the other.

Brandenburger and Jüngel explain that the emphasis at this point is on the universality of sin, that it was already there before the law. But this does not fit the general pattern of the text. In Rom. 1–3 Paul has given a completely different basis to the universality of sin without recourse to the events of Old Testament history. In Rom. 5, he is evidently in difficulty because the salvation history does not fit his theme. He can only give a real solution to the problem of sin, man and the law in Rom. 7, where he no longer pays any attention to the Old Testament history. The theological significance of Rom. 5.13 also becomes clear there: it is not the law that brings forth sin; sin, already present, is made active by the law. The whole of the lack of coherence in Rom. 5 stems from the conception of time employed there.

A further limitation of the mythical elements present in Rom. 5 can be found in the fact that the main theme is not inherited sin but inherited death.[1] This is indeed an experienced fact, a visible indication of sin. The explanation of death from Adam's fall is, of course, mythological. But Paul does not begin from death as a phenomenon, and then give a theological explanation of a physical process through

[1] *ibid.*, p. 251.

myth. His entry is the experience of justification, i.e. the peace that is received (5.1ff.), freedom in the sight of sin and death, life which is already here as freedom. This life is not future, mythical, apocalyptic. Freedom from death is not understood in natural terms (as myth understands it). Thus the Adam myth becomes a symbol for the structure of being towards death. Death is not exhausted in the physical process of dying. It is the manifestation of loss of the self, of sin.

Paul enlarges the mythical idea in juristic terminology: death is the wages of sin – not in terms of cause and effect but in that I am lost in sin. The doctrine of inherited sin is simply the consistent representation of the truth that my sin is there before me and that my lostness is inescapable.

B. The Saving Event

24 · GOD'S SAVING ACTION 'IN CHRIST'[1]

I   The Foundations ('Objective Christology')

Our starting point is the creed, its christological titles and the aspects of the individual titles stressed there. From a negative point of view, it must be pointed out that the titles 'Son of Man'[2] and 'Servant' do not appear in Paul.

There is a widespread view that the rest of the titles are used indifferently by Paul, especially as in his writings Christ has become a part of the name 'Jesus Christ'. The position is, however, more complicated. The original aspects still come through.[3]

(a) κύριος is an aspect of Christ's presence. It does not mean the personal presence of the Lord in the cult. He is, rather, represented by the spirit.

(b) Χριστός: Paul does not use this word as a title, 'the Messiah'.[4] The word Χριστός is only applied a priori to Jesus, even where it appears with the definite article.[5] Nevertheless, the link with the language of the creed is still clear: Χριστός characterizes Jesus as agent of the saving work. The word is grammatically the subject in Rom. 8.34; 14.9; I Cor. 15.3ff. Romans 14 is of special interest, as here the title Kyrios plays a part, too: the aspect of Χριστός, 'faith', is the basis of the relationship to the Kyrios.

---

[1] Or, 'Revelation'. In Paul's terminology, it should be noted that he does not say 'revelation in Christ'; this occurs first in the Pastorals; I Peter; I John; Ignatius, Eph. 19.2f.; and Magn. 8.2; see D. Lührmann, Das Offenbarungsverständnis bei Paulus und in paulinischen Gemeinden, WMANT 16 (1965), pp. 17–20.

[2] 'Son of Man' is occasionally thought to lie behind ἄνθρωπος; but see A. Vögtle, 'Die Adam-Christus-Typologie und "der Menschensohn"', TThZ 60 (1951), pp. 309ff.

[3] W. Kramer, Christ, Lord, Son of God, SBT 50 (1966).

[4] N. A. Dahl, 'Die Messianität Jesu bei Paulus', in Studia Paulina (Festschrift J. de Zwaan) (1953), pp. 83–95. It is therefore by no means the case that Paul uses the term 'Messiah' generally and then applies it to Jesus; thus the scene of Peter's confession (Mark 8.29) and Luke (Acts 17.3).

[5] With Dahl and Kramer, pp. 206ff.: the use of the article is only for formal reasons (II Cor. 13.3: δοκιμή . . . τοῦ ἐν ἐμοὶ λαλοῦντος Χριστοῦ) or is arbitrary (II Cor. 11.2 with the article, v. 3 without).

(c) υἱός: mission, pre-existence (Rom. 8.3; Gal. 4.4). Particular christological schemata are associated with the titles: (a) κύριος: resurrection and parousia; (b) Χριστός: death and resurrection: (c) υἱός: pre-existence and incarnation.

> Bultmann, *Theology of the New Testament* I, p. 304: 'To the extent that the statements about Christ's pre-existence and incarnation are of mythological nature, they neither have the nature of direct challenge nor are they expressions of the faith that is a surrender of "boasting". Yet in context within the proclamation they express a decisive fact: the origin and significance of Jesus' person and his fate are not within earthly occurrence, but God was acting in them and this action of his took place "when the fulness of time was come" (Gal. 4.4). That is, that it is the eschatological deed of God – a deed, furthermore, for the salvation of men, for whose sake he delivered Christ up (Rom. 8.32).' *Ibid.*: 'As to the assertion that Christ's incarnation is also his own deed of obedience and love (Phil. 2.8; Gal. 2.20; Rom. 8.35, 39), it must first be admitted that the "obedience" and "love" of the pre-existent Son are not visible data and cannot be experienced as directly aimed at the man who is challenged to believe. However, they are indirectly experienced in the fact that Christ is present in the "ministry" of the proclaimer.' *Ibid.*, p. 305: 'Therefore, the incarnation of the pre-existent Son also has "cosmic" dimension – i.e. in reality, historic dimension. The incarnation is present and active in the Christian proclamation. Differently formulated: There exists a divinely authorized proclamation of the prevenient grace and love of God; this is the fact that finds mythological expression in what is said of the pre-existence of Christ. What the hearer affirms when he believes the pre-existence of Christ is that what has encountered him is the word of God.'

Thus the idea of pre-existence embraces the horizon of faith: it comes from outside and towers above the world. Redemption is not a situation in the world, but a determination of the being of the world itself. It becomes concrete in the proclamation, which has power to break the resistance of the world by putting the believer under the direction of the cross and passion.

II   Christ as the Saving Act of God

Romans 1.16f.: the gospel is δύναμις θεοῦ εἰς σωτηρίαν παντὶ τῷ πιστεύοντι, Ἰουδαίῳ τε πρῶτον καὶ Ἕλληνι. δικαιοσύνη γὰρ θεοῦ ἐν αὐτῷ ἀποκαλύπτεται ἐκ πίστεως εἰς πίστιν, καθὼς γέγραπται· ὁ δὲ δίκαιος ἐκ πίστεως ζήσεται.

All Paul's theology is concentrated in a nutshell here:

1. The material basis: the act of God (ἀποκαλύπτεται).

2. Revelation is not a formal statement ('God is righteous'), but is positively gospel – εἰς σωτηρίαν.

3. The objective possibility of σωτηρία: the δικαιοσύνη θεοῦ.

4. The condition of faith.[1] This, too, is not formal knowledge but a positive possibility for every man. It can only be so if it is the only condition: ἐκ πίστεως εἰς πίστιν.

Galatians 4.3–5: Paul describes 'former' existence without faith as the status of the sinner, one without freedom, who is under supervision: ὅτε ἦμεν νήπιοι, ὑπὸ τὰ στοιχεῖα τοῦ κόσμου ἤμεθα δεδουλωμένοι· ὅτε δὲ ἦλθεν τὸ πλήρωμα τοῦ χρόνου, ἐξαπέστειλεν ὁ θεὸς τὸν υἱὸν αὐτοῦ, γενόμενον ἐκ γυναικός, γενόμενον ὑπὸ νόμον, ἵνα τοὺς ὑπὸ νόμον ἐξαγοράσῃ, ἵνα τὴν υἱοθεσίαν ἀπολάβωμεν.

The themes are:

1. The saving event as mission, as the act of God.

2. Pre-existence (hinted at in the title 'Son'; cf. Rom. 8.3, 23).

3. The nature of revelation is defined in two parallel participial clauses: (a) incarnation; (b) subordination to the law.

4. The significance of salvation is described in two parallel final clauses (in chiastic relation to themes 2 and 3): (a) freedom from the law; (b) our appointment to sonship. Here Paul hints at the theme 'the Son and the sons', 'the Son and his brothers'; cf. Rom. 8.14–17.[2]

The historical character of revelation is given through the stress on the reality of the incarnation and the assertion that it happened at a particular time: ὅτε ἦλθεν τὸ πλήρωμα τοῦ χρόνου (Gal. 4.4).[3]

The meaning of the mythical idea of pre-existence is difficult to grasp. Paul certainly shares this idea, but (unlike John) does not develop it theologically. He develops, rather, the significance of the cross. Nevertheless, there are pointers towards its interpretation. That Jesus is not of worldly origin, but nevertheless is 'born of a woman', means that salvation does not develop out of the world, say as the meaning and goal of world history. It is not a possibility immanent in the world, but breaks in from outside and thus remains God's salvation. Pre-existence thus means that salvation is founded on God's miraculous act; the word means the actualization of the prevenient salvation event and this describes the objective priority of God's act to my faith.

---

[1] Paul observes the salvation-historical sequence 'Jew-Gentile', but makes it relative by the addition of παντὶ τῷ πιστεύοντι.

[2] See E. Käsemann, *Das Wandernde Gottesvolk*, FRLANT 55 (1961⁴), pp. 58ff.

[3] Cf. Mark 1.15: πεπλήρωται ὁ καιρός. The meaning is not that Jesus appeared when the time was favourable, say because the world was filled with a longing for redemption. Luther recognized the meaning rightly: the 'fulfilment' was determined by the sending of Jesus, and not *vice versa*.

Father and Son: if we measure the christology of Paul by later dogma, it appears to be subordinationist. The Son is one who is sent, he is raised and exalted by God in his present status as Lord. The subordination does not, however, derive from metaphysical speculation, but serves to determine the nature of revelation. Paul works out the two elements, that God really appears in revelation and that he is only comprehensible in it. This position is described in the objectivization of christology as follows: the Son is utterly obedient and subordinate to the Father. Precisely in this way, the action of the Father and the Son forms a complete unity. It can be said that the Son is the action of the Father. To this extent, co-ordination predominates.

Cf. the parallelism in I Cor. 8.6: Christ is the mediator of creation. This idea is derived from Jewish wisdom speculation. The christological title εἰκὼν τοῦ θεοῦ (II Cor. 4.4; cf. Col. 1.15ff.) has the same significance. The intention is to assert the unity of creation and redemption. The place of revelation and thus of faith is the world. The incarnation affirms the same thing. This idea is actualized in the controversy over the gnostic division of the world and hence of the sphere of God's rule. The unity of the two represents in practice the possibility of existing in the world, in the sense of Rom. 5.1ff.

We thus find a dialectic dominant: (a) revelation is the *act of God*. The Son is passively the one who is sent; (b) revelation is the *act of Christ*.

This duality is already present before Paul, cf. Phil. 2.6ff.: the first part of the pre-Pauline Christ-hymn describes the action of Christ: the pre-existent one humbles himself by becoming man and fulfilling obedience, by dying. The second part describes the act of God: therefore God has also exalted him. Paul marks the beginning of his interpretation by adding the words, 'even the death of the cross', to the original 'obedient to death'. He thus begins, not with the metaphysical framework, but with a fixed historical point.

Examples: (a) act of God: II Cor. 5.21: τὸν μὴ γνόντα ἁμαρτίαν ὑπὲρ ἡμῶν ἁμαρτίαν ἐποίησεν, ἵνα ἡμεῖς γενώμεθα δικαιοσύνη θεοῦ ἐν αὐτῷ.

(b) act of Christ: II Cor. 8.9: Christ δι' ὑμᾶς ἐπτώχευσεν πλούσιος ὤν, ἵνα ὑμεῖς τῇ ἐκείνου πτωχείᾳ πλουτήσετε.

The two aspects are particularly closely interrelated when the saving act is described as an act of love. Here the material unity is clear. Cf. Rom. 8.31–39: God has given his Son. Christ has died and is risen. What shall separate us from the love of God? Nothing can separate us from the love of God – ἀπὸ τῆς ἀγάπης τοῦ θεοῦ τῆς ἐν Χριστῷ Ἰησοῦ τῷ κυρίῳ ἡμῶν. Romans 5.5ff.: the love of God has been poured out. Christ has died for us. God shows his love in that Christ died for us while we were still sinners (cf. John 3.16).

These passages show that the juxtaposition of the two sets of expressions, the 'theological' and the 'christological', has been thought out very clearly by Paul. It serves to interpret the historical process of revelation and thus opens up the perspective of faith. This is also the one intention of the various christological patterns:

(a) death and resurrection: for Paul, the cross forms the climax;

(b) resurrection and parousia: in the centre stands the proclamation of the death of the Lord until he comes;

(c) pre-existence and incarnation: if we begin with the idea of pre-existence, then the saving event is not the death of Christ, but his incarnation (cf. John 1.14). But even in the pre-Pauline hymn Phil. 2.6ff., the incarnation is enlarged by the insertion of Christ's death as the goal of the incarnation. Paul can attach his thought to that.

A similar dialectic of subordination and co-ordination can be seen in the use of the title Kyrios. In Paul, it serves to distinguish Christ from God, cf. I Cor. 8.6: εἷς θεὸς . . . καὶ εἷς κύριος Ἰησοῦς Χριστός.

On the other hand, Paul has the parallel: God is the creator, and the Lord is the pre-existent mediator of creation, the Lord of the world. The balance of ideas is expressed as follows: God has transferred his status as creator of the world to Jesus for a certain time and for a certain purpose, to complete the saving work (I Cor. 15.23–28). Now, after his exaltation, is the time when he rules, in that he is confessed and proclaimed. Once again, revelation and the world as the place of revelation are firmly linked together.

Paul reaches the limits of speculation when he says that after the ending of the work of salvation the Son will restore the rule to his Father, that 'God may be all in all'. This remark has nothing to do with pantheism. It is simply a boundary saying. Paul says nothing further about being in eternity itself. He rather surrounds the horizon of revelation once again by a definition of the relationship between God and Kyrios: this is the act of God. One can only speak of this act in relationship to the world. Revelation is, in fact, God's relationship to the world understood as act, which actualizes itself in the world and thus reaches its goal. With the speculative-sounding statements in I Cor. 15.24ff., any ascent into the realm of metaphysics is virtually cut off. Revelation is not an eternal progress. God does not call us into the void, into an infinite sphere, but speaks into the world and reaches it.

The most important scheme, and most characteristic for Paul, is that of the cross and resurrection.[1] Paul can sum up the whole content of his preaching as 'the word of the cross' (I Cor. 1.18; cf. 2.2). This formulation does not, of course, ignore the resurrection, but

[1] See the remarks on I Cor. 15.3ff. and Rom. 4.25 on pp. 65ff., 71 above.

interprets it. It should be noted that Paul begins from the creed at the point of Christ's death and resurrection. The direction of his thought is clear from this starting point.

It becomes clear in his controversy with various trends in Corinth;[1] there christology and piety are developed from the resurrection, as an orientation to the Exalted One. Faith is participation in heavenly existence. On the other hand, Paul advances the thesis that we have the Exalted One only as the Crucified One.

The resurrection is thus presupposed. But it must be interpreted. Understood in radical terms, it is simply the interpretation of the cross by God himself. The relationship between death and resurrection is not such that the resurrection would be an annulment of the death;[2] the latter is maintained. It can thus be proclaimed as the saving event. So the element of the stumbling block is retained in the preaching, not to be removed by a more profound examination, but as a constituent part of salvation.

The question whether the resurrection of Christ is a 'historical event' is theologically inapposite. Of course it is a historical event for Paul, in so far as he cannot know the modern theoretical distinction between historical and supra-historical (in effect: unhistorical). We for our part cannot retreat behind this reflection. But for faith, the particular stage of consciousness reached by thought is quite unimportant. Faith at any stage is – faith. Its object cannot be experienced. Only the cross can be perceived. In this sense Paul can stress the reality of the resurrection in I Cor. 15 by enumerating witnesses who saw – not the resurrection, but – the Risen One. But he is not interested in the historical aspect further than this. He knows neither the idea of the empty tomb nor the division of the process of exaltation into stages (resurrection, appearances, ascent). The real theological proof of the resurrection is the 'proof of the spirit and power'; that Jesus shows himself today to be the Exalted One, in that reconciliation happens today in the preaching which is a stumbling block and foolishness. Cross and resurrection are understood as 'reality', to the extent that the character of the saving event as word is understood, to the extent that faith knows itself to be founded on the cross and therefore to remain under the determination of the cross; to the extent that preaching understands itself to be an interpretation of the cross, i.e. allows itself to be pointed to the powerlessness, and there comes to be certain of the power, of the crucified Lord. The cross comes about as the destruction of καύχησις, and this is the basis for the certainty of salvation – in faith, not in sight, not even in historical retrospect. The question of the historicity of the resurrection must be excluded from theology as being a misleading one. We have other concerns, 'that the cross shall not be made void of meaning'. One cannot speak of the resurrection without speaking of God's meeting place with man – today.

---

[1] U. Wilckens, *Weisheit und Torheit*, BHTh 26 (1959).
[2] This is the view of the Corinthians. They do not see that in this way the resurrection also falls back into the past.

III   The Saving Act as an Act 'For Me'

The mere fact that the saving event is defined as an act of the love of God and of Christ shows that it is no self-sufficient metaphysical arrangement, but is directed towards man, or rather, represents God's relationship to man. But how does it affect me? To what extent is the appropriation of salvation given in the saving event itself? The saving event is indeed primarily described as an event outside myself, which is played out in the cosmos in a partly mythical, partly historical sphere, e.g. as the course of a mythical being through cosmic spheres. How should, how can that be my salvation? If God loves me, why does he show his love towards me in this way?

Of course, the text can provide an answer only in terms of its particular forms of thought, say with the help of ideas from sacrifice or sacramental participation. At the time they were understandable without further interpretation and could therefore really explain the way in which the saving event was related to man. This is clear from the multiplicity of nuances alone. Christ's death is a covenant sacrifice (eucharistic tradition; Rom. 3.25); an offering for sin (Rom. 3.25; I Cor. 15.3ff.); a passover sacrifice (I Cor. 5.7); a representative sacrifice (II Cor. 5.14). Each of these nuances provides its contribution towards interpretation, but each also has its limitation. Thus the idea of expiation can explain Christ's death, but not the particular death of the cross, the accursed death. Here the idea of representation offers further help (II Cor. 5.21; Gal. 3.13; Rom. 8.3). But even that is not sufficient. So Paul takes up further motives from the tradition: ransom (Gal. 3.13; I Cor. 6.20; 7.23). The climax is, of course, the freedom received through the death of Christ. In II Cor. 5.21 (cf. Rom. 6), we have an echo of the sacramental idea that we have died with Christ in his death. The soteriological interpretation of the title 'Son' takes us further (Gal. 4.4ff.); the aim of the mission of the Son is to free us from the curse of the law, and positively to appoint us sons. How does that happen? It happens by God giving the spirit of the Son in our hearts, and with it the possibility of our calling upon God as Father. The idea is developed further in Rom. 8. The conceptuality of the Son and the sons, or brothers, in turn has a mythical background. But Paul does not now interpret our relationship to Christ in terms of its mythical, natural side, but rather leaves the mythical idea in the air by (a) applying juristic categories to its interpretation: the appointment to sonship by inheritance, in other words, valid recognition by the pronouncement of the Father; and (b) by making the spirit a factor of sonship – in the sense of his historical understanding of the spirit as the possibility of access to God, prayer, freedom from the law and, analogous to this, from the elements of the cosmos.

The interweaving and mutual interpretation of the categories is clear from Rom. 8: (a) vv. 3f., God sent his Son to fulfil the δικαίωμα of the law; (b) in vv. 5ff., Paul explains being in the spirit (v. 14: those who are led by the spirit are the sons of God): for you did not receive the spirit of slavery which again leads to fear, but you received the spirit of sonship, in which we cry, ἀββὰ ὁ πατήρ. The spirit itself bears witness to our spirit that we are children of God: εἰ δὲ τέκνα, καὶ κληρονόμοι· κληρονόμοι μὲν θεοῦ, συγκληρονόμοι δὲ Χριστοῦ, εἴπερ συμπάσχομεν, ἵνα καὶ συνδοξασθῶμεν (v. 17).

Our relationship to God is analogous to Christ's relationship to God, in so far as we have been given freedom and can address God immediately. But here the analogy also has its limitation. For we have this freedom through the mediation of Christ. We never go beyond it, into a relationship of God to Christ. We can overcome the powers of the world – διὰ τοῦ ἀγαπήσαντος ὑμᾶς. There can be no thought of an immediate relationship to God, because Christ is our access to him. We are in freedom in so far as we are in Christ. And we have it as those who are on the way. The eschatological reservation which is hinted at in the concept of 'inheritance' remains. In Rom. 8, it is emphatically developed under the heading of hope (vv. 24–26). The substance of hope cannot be seen. The imagery of 'the Son' and 'the sons' shows freedom from the powers, from the law, sin and death, to be a present reality. But Paul does not follow the course of the myth, for which freedom is habitual; he defines it eschatologically as the proleptic influence of the future, which already manifests itself in the power of the spirit.

Paul can also use the mythical ideas to illustrate a further notion: the dimension in which the saving event is played out is the cosmos, the sphere which embraces and determines me. The saving event does not leave the world so to speak untouched, as in gnosticism, so that only the individual is changed in it by the influx of supernatural power. Rather, the world itself is the scene of the saving event. The individual and his sphere of being are not to be separated. Therefore the world itself must be affected by the saving work. Christologically speaking, this means the actualization of faith in God the creator for the understanding of the saving event in Christ. But the nature of the world is ambiguous, as it is creation and at the same time fallen creation. Similarly, man is a creature and, in the σάρξ, a fallen creature. Paul links the two aspects (Rom. 8.3): Christ becomes man ἐν ὁμοιώματι σαρκὸς ἁμαρτίας. He seeks the σάρξ in its sphere (or the σάρξ as a sphere). The spirit takes the place of the σάρξ as the determining sphere. Empirically, σάρξ, sin and death remain. But freedom is opened up for faith because for faith the powers are made helpless. This freedom presupposes that not only does something change in me, but the world itself is newly determined. This understanding of salvation and the world is particularized in man's attitude to the world in practice, in the eschatological freedom of 'having as though one did not'.

Paul can describe the change in the world-situation by means of ideas from 'salvation history': Christ is the end of the law (Rom. 10.4); or in cosmic-eschatological ideas: the old aeon is done away with. A warning must, however, be given about the use of the slogan 'the turn of the ages'. This dialectic of present and future prevails in respect of the world as well as in respect of the individual: I have died with Christ and will rise with him. Similarly, the old age of the world has passed away. But the new aeon is still to come.

It is significant that Paul does not use the expression 'new' or 'coming' aeon, though he does talk about 'this' aeon (or cosmos). He speaks rather of the new creation and describes it: τὰ ἀρχαῖα παρῆλθεν, ἰδοὺ γέγονεν καινά (II Cor. 5.17). The unspeculative, anthropological meaning of the statement is: εἴ τις ἐν Χριστῷ, καινὴ κτίσις.

A further means of description which shows both the objective universality of the work of Christ and its reference to each individual man is the interpretation of Christ as the second Adam. It is outlined in I Cor. 15, in order to provide a basis for the truth of the resurrection; it is then worked out in broad detail in Rom. 5, to depict the nature and extent of redemption. In this confrontation with Christ, Adam is not simply the Adam of the biblical creation narrative, but the primal man and representative of humanity. As we noted above, there are some discrepancies between the myth and the Pauline statement of it, because the myth presents the fall and with it the redemption in natural terms, whereas Paul shatters the logic of mythical thinking: (a) death does not come simply as a natural force; for sin does not spread in a natural way. Rather, it is actively encountered by each individual man – ἐφ' ᾧ πάντες ἥμαρτον (5.12); (b) the new life does not come naturally through man, but it remains future and is effective in the present as something that is to come. It is achieved only through faith, as 'we are justified through faith'. The myth of the primal man has an automatic tendency to be applied to the individual, though of course only in intention. Its limitation is that as a myth it necessarily remains an idea. As a myth it cannot be proclaimed, but only interpreted in existentialist terms. It therefore needs not only correction (which Paul, in fact, makes), but also expansion: Paul must be able to draw the line from the saving event to the preaching. Here preaching cannot simply remain the narration of an event. Otherwise this would remain alien, an object of contemplation. The direction of the movement would be from man to the knowledge that brings salvation. Rather, preaching must be the present communication of salvation which has taken place objectively. Paul must be asked how the communication of salvation is possible through the word. He must therefore not only give information about the nature of the word, but also show how the saving event itself has the character of word. This is in fact the presupposition for its being comprehensible in the word. He must also show the place where the communication becomes real: the church. The paradigm for this complex is II Cor. 5.18–21: (a) God reconciled the world to himself. God is not the one who is reconciled, but the reconciler. Reconciliation is an act of God; cf. Rom. 5.10. It happens exclusively through grace, without any presupposition on man's part. Reconciliation is an eschatological verdict of God. Paul again uses juristic terminology: God does not impute sin. This cannot be felt inwardly, but only heard as a message; (b) God reconciled 'the world' to himself. The world here means humanity; cf. Rom. 5, where Paul speaks only of man, and the immediate context: τοῦ θεοῦ τοῦ καταλλάξαντος ἡμᾶς: and: θεὸς ἦν ἐν Χριστῷ κόσμον καταλλάσσων ἑαυτῷ, μὴ λογιζόμενος αὐτοῖς τὰ παραπτώματα αὐτῶν. Paul is not speaking of a universal reconciliation here. He is not engaged in cosmic speculation, but stresses the character of the saving event as word: by reconciliation through Christ, God founded the διακονία τῆς καταλλαγῆς, the office of preaching. He founds τὸν λόγον τῆς καταλλαγῆς among us.

IV The Formula ἐν Χριστῷ

A. Deissmann, *Die nt. Formel 'in Christo Jesu'* (1892); on the difference from σύν: E. Lohmeyer, *Σὺν Χριστῷ, Deissmann Festschrift* (1927), pp. 218–57; E. Käsemann, *Leib und Leib Christi*, BHTh 9 (1933); W. Schmauch, *In Christus*, NT Forschungen 9 (1935); E. Percy, *Der Leib Christi*, LUA NF 38 (1942); F. Büchsel, '"In Christus" bei Paulus', *ZNW* 42 (1949), pp. 141–58; F. Neugebauer, 'Das Paulinische "In Christo"', *NTS* 4 (1957/58), pp. 124–38; id., *In Christus* (1961); M. Bouttier, *En Christ* (1962); W. Kramer, *Christ, Lord, Son of God*, SBT 50 (1966), pp. 139–44.

We were concerned earlier with the relationship between the objective saving event and its appropriation by man. We were given an indication in II Cor. 5.17ff. by the critical statement that in Christ God had reconciled the world to himself. This phrase leads to the question what the expression 'in Christ' means. According to a long-standing view, Paul gave two answers to the question of the saving event and its appropriation, (a) a juridical one: we obtain justification through faith; this is imputed to us; and (b) a mystical one: we are in salvation in that we are in Christ. One fact which tells against this mystical interpretation is that the phrase ἐν Χριστῷ appears in the very passages where 'reconciliation' is spoken of in juridical, objective terms, as in the passage cited above; moreover, πίστις and ἐν Χριστῷ are also connected.

Cf. the whole development of thought in Gal. 2 and 3. Gal. 2.16: ἐπιστεύσαμεν, ἵνα δικαιωθῶμεν ἐκ πίστεως Χριστοῦ; for this we have in v. 17: δικαιωθῆναι ἐν Χριστῷ. Gal. 5.5f.: ἡμεῖς γὰρ πνεύματι ἐκ πίστεως ἐλπίδα δικαιοσύνης ἀπεκδεχόμεθα. ἐν γὰρ Χριστῷ Ἰησοῦ οὔτε περιτομή τι ἰσχύει οὔτε ἀκροβυστία, ἀλλὰ πίστις δι' ἀγάπης ἐνεργουμένη.

Albert Schweitzer, for whom 'faith' and 'being in Christ' do not fit together, sometimes quotes only half the passage and then has to seek a laborious explanation. The very expression 'being in Christ' suggests a meaning which the phrase itself does not contain. The stressed 'being' is stronger than the simple copula.

Certainly, the phrase 'in Christ' at first seems to have a mystic ring – 'In him we live and move and have our being' – especially as the reverse can also be said: 'Christ is in me' (Gal. 2.20). This recalls the statements about the spirit: we are in the spirit and the spirit is in us (Rom. 8.9). Here in fact we find ourselves in the linguistic milieu of 'enthusiasm': man knows himself filled with God and at the same time surrounded by him. This is expressed by the reciprocal formula: I in you and you in me. A survey of all the passages, however, shows that the phrase 'in Christ' or 'in the Lord' by no means always has the same weight. It often simply replaces the adjective 'Christian', which has not yet been formed.[1]

Romans 16: Paul's fellow-workers have laboured 'in the Lord', i.e. in the church. Tertius has written this letter 'in the Lord'. Those who receive it are to accept Phoebe 'in the Lord', i.e. as a sister, as a member of the church. Paul immediately explains: ἀξίως τῶν ἁγίων. Romans 14.14: πέπεισμαι ἐν κυρίῳ Ἰησοῦ, where Paul of course does not mean a conviction won on mystical grounds, but one which he has as a Christian. I Cor. 9.1f.: the Corinthians are his work in the Lord. II Cor. 2.14: the mission work makes progress in Christ.

The passages which express a particular theological position can be seen when one recognizes that the Christ or Kyrios of the formula is the Christ of the kerygma and the exalted Kyrios of the confession. The material question is then in what sense we can be 'in him'.

[1] R. Bultmann, Theology of the New Testament I, p. 329.

Deissmann tried to begin from the spatial significance of the preposition ἐν: we are physically in Christ, i.e. the pneumatic Christ. Evidence for this is given in II Cor. 3.17: ὁ δὲ κύριος τὸ πνεῦμά ἐστιν, a passage which is also a *dictum probans* for the mystical interpretation of Paul. But are Kyrios and *pneuma* really identified here? One argument runs as follows: the sentence is a harmless exegetical marginal note. Paul has earlier quoted a sentence from the Old Testament in which the word Kyrios occurs. Now he adds as an explanation: the Kyrios of this quotation means the spirit. But this explanation is too simple. If Paul can interpret this Old Testament sentence in such a way, then he must see a close connection between Kyrios and *pneuma*. The only question is whether it is a mystical one. The continuation shows that the identification is not a simple one: the presence of the spirit in the community is not identical with the presence of the Lord in terms of a local existence. The spirit is – according to its historical derivation – imagined as a sort of fluid; the Lord is a person at a particular place, in heaven. One can call on the Lord, but not on the pneuma. It is rather the pneuma itself which calls, as we cannot pray. The spirit is the work of the Lord in us. This is also the explanation of the observation on which Deissmann relies: in the sayings about the bearing of the saving event on us, the two phrases are to some extent interchangeable: we possess our righteousness in Christ (II Cor. 5.21; Phil. 3.9) and in the spirit (Rom. 14.17). That we are justified in Christ (Gal. 2.17, see above) can also be expressed in this way (I Cor. 6.11): ἐδικαιώθητε ἐν τῷ ὀνόματι τοῦ κυρίου Ἰησοῦ Χριστοῦ καὶ ἐν τῷ πνεύματι τοῦ θεοῦ ἡμῶν. This parallelism is not to be explained in terms of the idea of the pneuma (otherwise it would be incomprehensible how we are justified in the spirit), but in terms of christology and justification: the spirit represents the real transference of the word of salvation. Käsemann seeks to avoid the weakness of the mystical interpretation by resorting to the concept of the body of Christ. 'In Christ' means 'in the body of Christ', i.e. in the church, understood as the body of Christ.[1]

The evidence of the text points us to the objective saving work. In some passages, the ἐν goes over to an instrumental usage and approximates to the significance of διά. We are justified through the ἀπολύτρωσις in Christ (Rom. 3.24). χάρις is given in Christ (I Cor. 1.4). In him we are justified (Gal. 2.17). In him, God has reconciled the world (II Cor. 5.19; cf. v. 21). Here the unity of objective act and transference is particularly clear: Christ was made to be sin by God, ἵνα ἡμεῖς γενώμεθα δικαιοσύνη θεοῦ ἐν αὐτῷ. 'In Christ' thus means that here, in him and not in me, salvation has taken place: therefore it is true for me. Christ is the instrument of God: in him God has shown us his love (Rom. 8.39); in him he has called us (Phil. 3.14); in him is the yes (II Cor. 1.19f.); in him we have freedom (Gal. 2.4), in him we are sanctified (I Cor. 1.2).

[1] E. Percy assumes the reverse, that the idea of the body of Christ was developed from the ἐν Χριστῷ formula. W. Schmauch explains the latter as having been formed in contrast to ἐν νόμῳ.

The instrumental sense is stressed particularly by Büchsel and Bouttier. The two explain that the expression ἐν Χριστῷ or ἐν κυρίῳ is not a formula, as the sense varies. Its meaning is to be derived, not from the phrase itself but from its particular application, from the context. But while it cannot be disputed that the significance of the formula varies, depending on the context, there is still a firm nucleus of meaning at its base.

The phrase expresses the objective foundation and the inner-worldly intangibility of Christian existence. This is the explanation of the apparently mystical passages. Because the saving event is complete, we can glory in it (Rom. 15.17; I Cor. 15.31). Labour in it is not in vain (I Cor. 15.58). I Cor. 4.15: ἐν . . . Χριστῷ Ἰησοῦ διὰ τοῦ εὐαγγελίου ἐγὼ ὑμᾶς ἐγέννησα. That simply means that Paul has preached the word of the cross to them.

In accordance with his understanding of his office, Paul can also say that Christ speaks in him (II Cor. 13.3). That means that he does not preach himself, but the crucified Lord: 'in him' we are weak; but we will live from the power of God 'with him' (not 'in him').

The difference between ἐν and σύν is that life 'in him' is (dialectically) present; life 'with him' is future. The phrase 'in Christ' expresses the same transitoriness of our existence as the concept of faith. It is no coincidence that the concept of faith appears where Paul reverses the phrase so that it becomes 'Christ in me': Gal. 2.19f.: (a) Χριστῷ συνεσταύρωμαι.

(b) ζῶ δὲ οὐκέτι ἐγώ, ζῇ δὲ ἐν ἐμοὶ Χριστός.

(c) meaning: ὃ δὲ νῦν ζῶ ἐν σαρκί, ἐν πίστει ζῶ τῇ τοῦ υἱοῦ τοῦ θεοῦ τοῦ ἀγαπήσαντός με καὶ παραδόντος ἑαυτὸν ὑπὲρ ἐμοῦ.

The juxtaposition of 'I in him' and 'he in me' never makes the two participants mystically equal. I am never there for Christ in the same way as is Christ for me. He is there for me as the one who intercedes for me. I am there for him as the believer who is directed to him. Rom. 8.10f. (earlier: you in the spirit – the spirit in you): εἰ δὲ Χριστὸς ἐν ὑμῖν, τὸ μὲν σῶμα νεκρὸν διὰ ἁμαρτίαν, τὸ δὲ πνεῦμα ζωὴ διὰ δικαιοσύνην; then parallel to 'Christ in you': εἰ δὲ τὸ πνεῦμα τοῦ ἐγείραντος τὸν Ἰησοῦν ἐκ νεκρῶν οἰκεῖ ἐν ὑμῖν, ὁ ἐγείρας ἐκ νεκρῶν Χριστὸν Ἰησοῦν ζωοποιήσει καὶ τὰ θνητὰ σώματα ὑμῶν διὰ τοῦ ἐνοικοῦντος αὐτοῦ πνεύματος ἐν ὑμῖν.

Summary: the spirit is the actual and proleptic conveyance of salvation. So we have in II Cor. 5.17: εἴ τις ἐν Χριστῷ, καινὴ κτίσις. A special question is whether one can also note a different use of the titles of Christ in the phrases with ἐν.[1] As in the title, so too in the formulae, one cannot differentiate sharply, but clear tendencies are to be noted. Christ is Jesus as the one who has accomplished the saving work. Accordingly ἐν Χριστῷ (with or without 'Jesus') appears in a soteriological context. In him we are justified; in him God has

---

[1] This is dealt with by Neugebauer, Bouttier and Kramer.

reconciled the world. Jesus is called Kyrios as the one who reigns now: in the Lord our labour is not in vain.

Neugebauer asserts: 'in Christ' expresses the indicative of the saving event; 'in the Lord' the imperative that results from it. This does not fit the meaning. The 'Lord' is not only the one who makes demands but also the one who protects, on whom man may call. In any case, the significance of the title overlaps, and Neugebauer cannot dispute this. His refutation of the mystical interpretation is apt.

C. THE RIGHTEOUSNESS OF FAITH

25 · ΧΑΡΙΣ, ΔΙΚΑΙΟΣΥΝΗ

Here, too, Rom. 1.16f. offers the best approach. Bultmann appropriately remarks on this passage: 'For this does not mean that the preached gospel expounds some teaching about righteousness, but that through it righteousness becomes a possibility (which in faith becomes reality) for the hearer of the gospel.'[1] If all salvation is summed up in the expression 'revelation of the righteousness of God', we must discuss: (a) the presupposition: χάρις; (b) the concept of righteousness; (c) the condition: πίστις – now no longer understood formally, but materially: in other words, the relationship of faith to the law.

I χάρις

G. P. Wetter, *Charis* (1913); J. Moffatt, *Grace in the NT* (1931); W. T. Whitley, *The Doctrine of Grace* (1932); J. Wobbe, *Der Charisgedanke bei Paulus* (1932); R. Bultmann, *Theology of the New Testament* I, pp. 288ff.; W. Grundmann, 'Die Übermacht der Gnade', *NovTest* 2 (1958), pp. 50–72. Further literature in Bauer (-Arndt-Gingrich), s.v. χάρις.

The Old Testament equivalent is the root חן. In Greek, χάρις means what is delightful, attractive, pleasing – both what is experienced and what is demonstrated, thanks. In Hellenism, there is often praise for the χάριτες of the rulers, and in Philo for the χάριτες of God.

Paul speaks of χάρις in the singular. He does not, therefore, orientate himself by individual illustrations, but by the saving act, which is characterized as pure gift through the concept of χάρις.

Bultmann divides his description of man under πίστις into the following sections: (1) δικαιοσύνη θεοῦ; (2) χάρις; (3) πίστις; (4) ἐλευθερία. δικαιοσύνη is the character of the revelation, χάρις its realization in practice. Under this heading, Bultmann discusses christology, the significance of the death and resurrection of Jesus, the church. πίστις is the appropriation of salvation, ἐλευθερία the characteristic of life in faith. It becomes clear from this arrangement that χάρις does not denote a disposition of God but his action, as shown in Christ (hence the title of section 32: χάρις as event). It is rightly asserted that Paul describes neither God as gracious nor man as given grace. He simply speaks of the act of grace. χάρις is no more an affect or a property than is ὀργή.

---

[1] R. Bultmann, *Theology of the New Testament* I, pp. 274f.

χάρις thus designates the historical manifestation of salvation (Rom. 5.20f.) and its consequence: the new situation into which we are transposed, the state of grace (Rom. 5.2). The state of the believer does not, however, become a *habitus*, as he constantly remains determined by grace. This does not confer any indelible character: if you want to be justified by the law, you have fallen from grace (Gal. 5.4).

Paul also speaks of a state of grace in a special sense, in respect of his office (Rom. 15.15f.).

Grace is not tolerant forbearance. Paul does not say that God kindly supplies what good works are still lacking in us. This is the idea in Judaism: if we strive, God rejoices at our efforts and completely supplies our deficiencies. Paul, on the other hand, declares that God takes no delight in our efforts, for this is concern for our own righteousness. Only if we surrender them do we experience his grace. Furthermore, God overlooks nothing: the time of patience is past. Now he blots out guilt. He does not turn graciously to the one who is already as righteous as possible; he gives grace to the sinner (Rom. 4.5; 5.20; 11.32; Gal. 3.19, 22). The grace that is displayed and that comes to me in the word destroys καύχησις; it leaves me no contribution of my own which I could bring to God. It thus brings judgment with it, under the sign of salvation, the destruction of damnation.

Paul can also use the word ἔλεος in a similar sense, but only in Rom. 9–11, where he speaks of his personal experience of mercy. Does he avoid this word elsewhere because it could be misunderstood – in the sense of 'indulgence'? Paul also uses ἀγάπη like χάρις. Even love is not an affect, but a demonstration (Rom. 5.8; 8.39). On the basis of these passages, we can establish the rule that the object of theology is not the dear, the gracious God, but the love and grace of God in Christ.

II δικαιοσύνη θεοῦ

A. Schlatter, *Gottes Gerechtigkeit* (1935); A. Oepke, '*ΔΙΚΑΙΟΣΥΝΗ ΘΕΟΥ* bei Paulus in neuer Beleuchtung', *ThLZ* 78 (1953), cols. 257–64; E. Käsemann, 'The Righteousness of God in Paul', *New Testament Questions of Today* (1969), pp. 168–82; E. Jüngel, *Paulus und Jesus* (1962), pp. 17ff., 263ff.; C. Müller, *Gottes Gerechtigkeit und Gottes Volk*, FRLANT 86 (1964); P. Stuhlmacher, *Gerechtigkeit Gottes bei Paulus*, FRLANT 87 (1965); against Käsemann: R. Bultmann, *ΔΙΚΑΙΟΣΥΝΗ ΘΕΟΥ, JBL* 83 (1964), pp. 12–16. Further literature in G. Schrenk, *TWNT* II 194; Bauer (-Arndt-Gingrich), s.v. δικαιοσύνη; Bultmann, *Theology of the New Testament* I, p. 271. There are surveys of the state of present scholarship in the books by Müller and Stuhlmacher.

This concept stands at the focal point of present controversy. Paul can sum up the whole content of revelation in it. But what is the meaning of (a) δικαιοσύνη; (b) the genitive θεοῦ?

Possibilities: 1. subjective genitive: righteousness as a property which God has and exercises: 'God is righteous', i.e. *qua iustus est in se*. 2. *Genitivus auctoris*: the righteousness which God provides. 3. Genitive of relation: the righteousness which holds before God: man's righteousness before God; thus Luther, cf. Augustine (*PL* 35, 1607): *iustitia Dei . . . non qua iustus est Deus, sed quam dat homini Deus, ut iustus sit homo per Deum*.

Augustine understands this righteousness as a property granted to man by God; Luther in the sense of the *fides ex auditu*. Schlatter[1] agrees with Luther that God's righteousness is the central theme of Paul, but charges him with having misunderstood the meaning of Paul in his translation, 'righteousness, which stands before God'. Luther does not ask about God's righteousness, but about my possibility of being righteous: 'How do I find a gracious God?' Paul's approach is theological, that of Luther anthropological. Schlatter, p. 38: 'The exegete (sc. Luther) began from his own person, Paul from God; the prerequisite of the exegete was his own need, that of Paul was Christ's commission.' Luther has constricted Paul's statement so that it becomes theory. For Paul, the gospel is God's action which effects faith; for Luther it is a lesson about justification. Here Luther is grossly misrepresented. He is made to stand father to the orthodox Protestant view of justification.[2] Schlatter disregards the historical context and the pattern of thought in Luther. The monk Luther begins from the scholastic idea of God; the righteousness of God is God's property, the proof of his majesty. The question then indeed becomes, 'How do I find a gracious God?' But that is merely Luther's historical starting point. He takes the question to the point where it breaks down as a question – by the discovery of the Pauline significance of righteousness. *Et hic iterum iustitia Dei non ea debet accipi, qua ipse iustus est in se ipso, sed qua nos ex ipso iustificamur, quod fit per fidem evangelii*. God is righteous *in sermonibus suis*. And we declare God righteous when we accept his verdict on us as righteous (Schol. Rom. 1.17 and 3.4: WA 56, pp. 172, 226f.).

Luther did not make Schlatter's philological error: the genitive θεοῦ with δικαιοσύνη must be the same as with εὐαγγέλιον, δύναμις and ὀργή, i.e. a subjective genitive. For we read: God's righteousness is revealed ἐν αὐτῷ (i.e. in the gospel). Schlatter, p. 36: 'Righteousness is proper to God just as much as power and wrath. That is assured by the ἐν αὐτῷ, i.e. ἐν τῷ εὐαγγελίῳ. For the message is τὸ εὐαγγέλιον τοῦ θεοῦ.' However, Schlatter refuses to designate righteousness as the property of God. Of course, he rescues his thesis by defining property as 'the property of a static substance'. In this way he sets out to draw a distinction between

---

[1] For Luther, see above all Schlatter; Stuhlmacher, pp. 19ff.; W. Grundmann, *Der Römerbrief des Apostels Paulus und seine Auslegung durch M. Luther* (1964).

[2] Schlatter misinterprets a considerable number of Luther's statements; cf. Stuhlmacher (who nevertheless follows Schlatter's interpretation of δικαιοσύνη θεοῦ). Schlatter does not notice the terminology, *iustificatio Dei, iustitia Dei activa* and *passiva*.

this and a Greek concept of God, but he does not get down to the exegetical evidence. In criticism of Schlatter, it may be said that Paul does not remark that the gospel of God is 'revealed'. 'Gospel' is not parallel to 'righteousness'. The two concepts are not interchangeable: this is clear from the phrase ἐν αὐτῷ. Moreover, the expression δύναμις θεοῦ cannot be isolated from the defining phrases εἰς σωτηρίαν and παντὶ τῷ πιστεύοντι. The apparent parallelism of Rom. 1.17 and 18 proves nothing for Schlatter, as it is broken at the decisive point: righteousness is revealed in the word: wrath is revealed 'from heaven'. This revelation does not take place by means of words; nor is wrath an affect of God, but the judgment which he brings about (note that Paul does not use verbs to describe God's wrath or anger).

The History of the Concept

The Greek meaning of the word δικαιοσύνη as one of the cardinal virtues or a combination of the virtues has no significance for Paul.

Old Testament[1] (primarily without the genitive θεοῦ): Klaus Koch stresses that צדק צדקה is not a forensic concept (cf. von Rad, *Old Testament Theology* I, p. 373). The group of words does not designate God's formal judging (i.e. that he acquits or condemns in each case according to the norm of the law), but refers positively to his saving action. von Rad (*ibid.*, p. 377) declares: 'There is no evidence for the concept of a retributive צְדָקָה; it would be a contradiction in terms'.

Righteousness is a relationship in community (*a*) among men; (*b*) between God and man. Anyone who accords with this relationship of community, i.e. the covenant, is righteous. Righteousness is a sphere in which the action immediately creates the result. God is righteous by carrying through his promise.[2]

It is true that the group of words does not designate a formal distributive justice, and that righteousness is orientated to the covenant. Nevertheless, its significance must be described as forensic; for the decision is made by God's word.[3] The covenant, too, is a legal entity: it has its prescriptions, for the keeping of which God is concerned. Hence the Old Testament also knows of God's retributive righteousness: Dan. 9.13–18. This passage, of course, falls under von Rad's judgment on apocalyptic: in Daniel the commandments are detached from their reference to the saving history. Stuhlmacher also includes the idea of the legal dispute in this set of ideas: it is a matter of the demonstration of the righteousness of Yahweh which penetrates the world in salvation. In respect of the genitive, he stresses that the connection of the genitive as in צדקה יהוה occurs only in Deut. 33.21. The Septuagint translates: δικαιοσύνην κύριος ἐποίησεν. Stuhlmacher rightly concludes that the Septuagint cannot be regarded as a possible model for the phrase δικαιοσύνη θεοῦ, as

---

[1] K. Koch, Sdq *im AT*, Diss. Heidelberg 1953; G. von Rad, *Old Testament Theology* I (1962), pp. 370–83; F. Horst, *Gottes Recht*, ThB 12 (1961), pp. 286ff.; id, 'Gerechtigkeit im AT', *RGG*³ II 1403–06; Stuhlmacher, pp. 113ff.

[2] Cf. the grouping of concepts in Ps. 89.15: righteousness and right, grace and faithfulness. In human terms: Yahweh is my righteousness (Isa. 33.16).

[3] von Rad, I, p. 379: 'Yahweh alone determines what righteousness is, and who is righteous, and man lives in the light of this recognition.'

it does not know this expression. Only occasionally, and not as a special terminology, do we find δικαιοσύνη κυρίου (I Sam. 12.7; Ps. 7.18; 30.2), in the meaning of
God's own legal action, but not righteousness before God or from God.

Judaism retains the forensic sense, but modifies it by transferring
the judgment to the beyond (apocalyptic). A second feature is
connected with this: the position of the individual comes into view.
In fact, a twofold development is to be noted: (a) elaboration of the
formal, juristic sense (Psalms of Solomon, Jubilees); (b) on the other
hand, the 'positive' components are also developed: righteousness
acquires the sense of faithfulness to the covenant, mercy. Cf. IV Ezra
8.36: 'For in this, O Lord, shall thy righteousness and goodness be
declared, if thou wilt compassionate them that have no wealth of
good works'. This significance is also to be found in the Qumran texts:[1]
1 QH IV 30: 'Righteousness, I know, is not of man'; 1 QS XI 12: 'If
I stagger because of the sin of flesh, my justification (מִשְׁפָּטִי) shall be
by the righteousness (בְּצִדְקַת־אֵל) of God which endures for ever'.

Paul and Judaism

Paul shares the following views with Judaism: (a) righteousness is
the precondition of salvation (Rom. 1.17; 4.13; 5.17, 21; 8.10; Gal.
3.6ff.). (b) It is decided upon by the eschatological verdict of the
judge. The Jewish understanding is, however, modified by Paul to the
extent that the verdict has already been given 'in Christ', and that
righteousness without works, from grace alone, is promised to faith.
Christ is the end of the law (the Jewish passages quoted above do not
annul the law, but confirm it). God's righteousness, like his grace, is
not kind indulgence, but a positive establishment of salvation.

Christian Müller would find a closer connection with Judaism: Paul begins
from the meaning 'faithfulness to the covenant', but replaces the covenant with the
creation and so arrives at the meaning 'faithfulness to the creation'. In effect, this
ends up once again as an understanding along the lines of a subjective genitive.
But the case of Paul is precisely the reverse. The creation is understood in the light
of the saving event in Christ. Müller further thinks that Paul goes back to the idea
of God's legal dispute. But this Old Testament theme had vanished in contemporary Judaism. It appears in Paul only once, in a quotation from the Psalms. Stuhlmacher follows Müller: God's righteousness is the carrying through of God's
justice. In apocalyptic, especially in Qumran, the 'righteousness of God' is a
technical term, 'the law of God which reveals itself as faithfulness to the covenant,

---

[1] H. Braun, Radikalismus I, pp. 45–47, 136 n. 7; J. Becker, Das Heil Gottes,
Studien zur Umwelt des NT 3 (1964); Stuhlmacher, pp. 148ff.

demanding service, related to judgment and carrying itself through in eschatological struggle' (p. 166). Müller and Stuhlmacher want to take Schlatter's interpretation of the genitive further and set it on a better foundation: as δικαιοσύνη θεοῦ
is a Jewish technical term, it must also be recognized as such in Paul. The starting
point must therefore be, not the meaning of δικαιοσύνη, but the stereotyped, total
expression δικαιοσύνη θεοῦ. This must have the same sense everywhere, and that can
only be subjective. This remarkable 'philological' principle anticipates what is to be
proved. It should be pointed out: 1. That in not a single Jewish passage is the
expression a technical term; 2. That the evidence in Paul should be assessed on the
basis of his own usage.

On the basis of the evidence, Lietzmann comes to the conclusion that both subjective genitive and *genitivus auctoris* occur in Paul. The thesis is modified by A.
Oepke. A distinction is to be made, depending on whether or not the article is used:
the expression ἡ δικαιοσύνη τοῦ θεοῦ denotes God's conduct. On the other hand,
δικαιοσύνη θεοῦ is a general concept which is neutral in itself, and can only be given
its meaning by the context; it designates the predicate given to man. The Pauline
characteristic is not to be found in the concept δικαιοσύνη θεοῦ, but in its definition,
that it is promised, ἐκ πίστεως. It is a *genitivus auctoris*, which is similar to an objective
genitive or a genitive of relationship.

Criticism: Stuhlmacher (pp. 182f.) shows that Oepke's evidence (Targums on
Deut. 33.21) cannot be used, as these always have the plural. It should also be
pointed out that the use of the article is no criterion. Oepke himself has to use the
expedient of arguing that exceptions prove the rule.

The Evidence in Paul

In some passages, righteousness is in fact the property of God, in
the sense of a subjective genitive: Rom. 3.3–5. The theme of the legal
dispute is echoed, but only in a quotation. It is not taken up and
developed as an independent statement. The subjective sense of the
genitive is clear from the anthropological context: ἡ ἀδικία ἡμῶν. But
this theme is only outlined, to be immediately rejected as inappropriate: κατὰ ἄνθρωπον λέγω. The same thing happens in Rom. 9.14:
μὴ ἀδικία παρὰ τῷ θεῷ; these two passages are not an appropriate
beginning for taking up Paul's overall understanding.

Of course, for Paul, too, God is righteous. But it is not his intention to define
God's nature in an objectifying way. Rather, in both the passages we have mentioned, Paul makes it clear that this is no way of imagining God. It is no excuse that
my unrighteousness manifests God's righteousness; this is the very way in which I
am shown to be guilty. Paul interprets grace as an event: I can accept it only as
grace, i.e. by acknowledging that I am guilty. I cannot exploit it against God for
myself. Outside the confession of my unrighteousness I know nothing of God's
righteousness. I cannot say anything true about God if I am not in the truth.

The 'positive' passages: Rom. 1.17.[1] Paul's theme is not 'God's

---

[1] The fact that the word ἀποκαλύπτειν occurs here does not prove that Paul's

righteousness', but the gospel as the δύναμις θεοῦ, because in it God's righteousness is revealed for faith. 'God's righteousness' is thus given *a priori* the definition 'of the gospel'. It cannot, even hypothetically, be separated from ἐκ πίστεως. The direction of the thought culminates in the quotation ὁ δὲ δίκαιος ἐκ πίστεως ζήσεται, which speaks of the righteous man: the climax is thus anthropological.

The subjective interpretation takes no account of the fact that Paul uses (*a*) righteousness in the absolute; (*b*) God's righteousness; (*c*) righteousness from God; (*d*) righteousness by faith – and the antithesis, not from works of the law, all with the same meaning. The subjective interpretation is in fact suppressed by Paul when he speaks of the revelation of righteousness 'from heaven'. 'In the word', then, applies only as a secondary definition: the word becomes the formal proclamation of power; cf. Käsemann: righteousness is 'personified as power'. The gift has the character of power; power and gift are indissolubly connected; the power enters into us. Divine power is also the strength, love, peace, wrath of God. The Gospel is the manifestation of God, 'in which he himself enters the lists in his sovereignty and prevailing power' (*New Testament Questions*, p. 173 n. 4). What does this explain? Here 'power' has become etiquette which can be adopted here or there at will.

Rom. 3.21ff.: the association is not through a technical term, but through a quotation. The concept of God's righteousness is attached to the passive of the verb, i.e. not to the question of God's righteousness, but to the justification of man, his salvation. Later, in 3.25f., the genitive is in fact subjective. But, first, it is a pre-Pauline formula quoted by Paul, and secondly, the genitive is already interpreted in a different way by the passage from vv. 20–21. Here, too, the theme is not God's righteousness but the righteousness of faith: δικαιοσύνη δὲ θεοῦ διὰ πίστεως Ἰησοῦ Χριστοῦ. Paul then continues:[1] δικαιούμενοι δωρεὰν τῇ αὐτοῦ χάριτι. The apparently subjective phrase εἰς τὸ εἶναι αὐτὸν δίκαιον is interpreted by Paul: καὶ δικαιοῦντα τὸν ἐκ πίστεως Ἰησοῦ. The anthropological application follows: faith leads into individualization; this is the condition of the universality of salvation.

The same anthropological beginning is to be found in Gal. 2.16ff. Again, Paul does not stress the concept of God, but the element of the verdict of faith (εἰδότες) and the appropriation of righteousness by faith. There follows in Galatians and Romans the formula that faith is 'reckoned' as righteousness (Gal. 3.6; Rom. 4.3). The theme is thus

---

thought is determined by apocalyptic; cf. Ps. 98.2 LXX: ἐναντίον τῶν ἐθνῶν ἀπεκάλυψεν τὴν δικαιοσύνην αὐτοῦ. Paul's formulations are in the tradition of the psalms, later prophecy and wisdom.

[1] Stuhlmacher excludes the verb δικαιοῦν from his survey.

again appropriated righteousness, the righteousness of faith. This accords with the association of ideas in Rom. 5.1: δικαιωθέντες οὖν ἐκ πίστεως. The same theme dominates the section Rom. 9.30–10.4: Paul confronts the righteousness of God and man's own righteousness and defines the righteousness of God: εἰς δικαιοσύνην παντὶ τῷ πιστεύοντι (v. 4); ἡ ἐκ πίστεως δικαιοσύνη (v. 6). Philippians 3.9 offers the key for the definition of the concept.

For the use of the genitive see II Cor. 5.21 (cf. 1.12), and I Cor. 1.30 in comparison with 6.11. Here, too, the mention is of our righteousness.

Result: Paul's theme is not 'God's righteousness' (that is the Jewish version of the problem), but God's righteousness as the righteousness of faith. It remains God's 'alien' righteousness, to be experienced in the word, by being spoken. In hearing, we recognize ourselves as really being made righteous, and are freed for 'newness of life'.

Righteousness is not the goal of our movement, but its presupposition. Hence there is no possibility that we can credit ourselves with any achievements. Righteousness is given; cf. the kinship of the statements about righteousness and grace in Rom. 5.17.

The dialectic of present and future is expressed in a variation of linguistic usage: on the one hand, righteousness appears as a condition of salvation; on the other, as the benefit of salvation itself (Rom. 10.10, parallel to σωτηρία). On the one hand, it appears as a present gift (we are made righteous), on the other as a future gift (Gal. 5.5; Rom. 5.19). This variation is possible because the present character is not understood in habitual terms, nor the future apocalyptically.

χάρις and πίστις have in common a contrast with the law and human works (Gal. 5.4; cf. 2.21; Rom. 6.14; 9.32; 11.6). So we must now discuss the law.

26 · THE LAW

R. Bultmann, *Theology of the New Testament* I, pp. 259ff; C. Maurer, *Die Gesetzeslehre des Paulus* (1941); W. Gutbrod, νόμος *TWNT* IV 1061ff.; G. Ebeling, 'Reflexions on the Doctrine of the Law', *Word and Faith* (1963), pp. 247–81. Cf. the literature above on πίστις (section 20) and δικαιοσύνη (25 II).

I General Problems

So far this theme has occupied our attention primarily in its negative aspect; righteousness is acquired by faith, without the works of the law. The law cannot justify (Rom. 1.18–3.20, 21–31). Then what is the purpose of the law? What does it do? If it does not bring salvation, it would seem to point in a misleading direction. In that case, is it not the ordinance of God at all? Or is it the work of a misleading God, the God of the world?[1] Or does Paul think in terms of salvation history; that the law once had a positive function, but has now been superseded? And if the law is finished, why does Paul concern himself with it at such great length? A psychological or a historical explanation is not enough. Many things cannot be derived from the historical situation: the Pauline conception of justification and the law; the positive understanding of freedom; the connection between spirit and freedom on the one hand, and flesh and law on the other. The range of the theme of the law not only extends to the Jewish understanding of salvation, but also puts in question any possible way of salvation, by the preaching of the gospel. The doctrine of the law must be understood in specifically theological terms, as a contribution to the explanation of the gospel, which is not only a doctrine, but an event for man, a transformation of his situation.

Terminology: νόμος denotes[2] 'the Old Testament law or the whole Old Testament conceived as law'.[3]

Paul does not work with the Greek understanding of law, say the contrast between the written law and the unwritten law, between φύσις and νόμος, the idea of natural law. This is true in spite of Rom. 2, where there is an echo of these Greek terms.[4] Paul argues that the Gentile has the law written on his heart; he follows it by nature. Bornkamm aptly remarks: we should not dispute that there is an echo of Greek ideas here. But the terms are only used in an *ad hoc* way. The main point is not a doctrine of natural law, but a confirmation of the universality of the divine norm of judgment on the grounds that even the Gentiles do what is required by the law. Pohlenz stresses that Paul knows of no independent nature alongside God. The Greek ideas are completely transformed. For the Greeks, nature is the highest

---

[1] Marcion! In that case, redemption would be liberation from the world, the constitution of which was the law.

[2] Apart from some passages in which νόμος means quite generally 'norm'.

[3] R. Bultmann, *Theology of the New Testament* I, p. 259.

[4] On this, cf. M. Pohlenz, 'Paulus und die Stoa', *ZNW* 43 (1949), pp. 75ff. (=new impression (1964), pp. 12ff.) and G. Bornkamm, 'Gesetz und Natur', in: *Studien zu Antike und Urchristentum*, Gesammelte Aufsätze II (1963²), pp. 93–118.

authority, for Paul it is the law. In his use of the formula 'written on their hearts', Paul is not influenced by the idea of ἄγραφα νόμιμα, but by the written law; 'it is occasioned by the contrast between this law and the law recorded on the tablets and in the books of Moses', to 'warn the Jews not to rely on the mere possession of this written tradition' (p. 76, cf. p. 13).

Paul outlines no picture of the world and of men within the framework of which the nature of the law is defined. He simply presupposes that God's will holds everywhere, even among the Gentiles, and that he is known everywhere.

The question of the way in which the Gentiles recognize God's will is not made an independent theme. Paul contents himself with a few hints. Man has his conscience as an authority to control him. By and large, he simply supposes that man has a moral awareness; he can also draw the attention of Christians to such a general kind of knowledge (Phil. 4.8).

EXCURSUS: ON THE THEOLOGY OF ORDINANCES AND ROMANS 13

Paul does not use 'ordinance' as an abstract concept, and is not acquainted with any subject-matter which corresponds to such a concept. Paradoxically, this is shown by his remarks about authorities in Rom. 13.1–7.[1] No doctrine of ordinances of creation and preservation is developed in this section; there is not even a doctrine of the state. Paul simply gives a paraenesis which is directed, not towards the state but – in view of the political power – to Christians. The ἐξουσία is no part of the ordinance of salvation.[2] It is not a factor of the new world, but a datum of this world, the place in which believers find themselves. The world remains creation; Christians do not live in another world, but 'manifest by their doings that the earth, and all that therein is, belongs to the Lord (and) is not abandoned by him'.[3] The reality of the world 'is not concealed in favour of an ideology'.[4] 'So here we have the particularity of the demand, which is never complete and can never be described beforehand, whereas in a theology of ordinances everything can be calculated systematically

---

[1] A. Strobel, 'Zum Verständnis von Röm. 13', ZNW 47 (1956), pp. 67–93; E. Käsemann, 'Römer 13, 1–7 in unserer Generation', ZThK 56 (1959), pp. 316–76; id., 'Principles of the Interpretation of Romans 13', New Testament Questions of Today, pp. 196–216; G. Delling, Röm. 13, 1–7 innerhalb der Briefe des NT (1962).

[2] E. Käsemann, 'Römer 13, 1–7 in unserer Generation', p. 351.

[3] E. Käsemann, 'Principles of the Interpretation of Romans 13', pp. 199f.

[4] E. Käsemann, 'Römer 13.1–7 in unserer Generation', p. 376.

beforehand and each concrete demand can be cogently referred back to an abstract construction'.[1] Paul does not go into the question of the limits of obedience in Rom. 13, because he has no immediate occasion for doing so.

Unlike Jesus and the Hellenists of Jerusalem, Paul does not play the moral law off against the cultic law. The whole of the law is from God, and with Christ it is all at an end. In practice, of course, things are different. When Paul speaks of the law in positive terms, as the will of God, he is in fact thinking of the moral commandments. This is shown by the examples which he cites in Rom. 2: you shall not steal, shall not commit adultery. He sums up the whole of the demand of the law in Rom. 7.7 as 'You shall not covet', and, following Jesus, describes the commandment to love as the sum of the law (Gal. 5.14; Rom. 13.8–10).

But if the law is the will of God, how then can it be at an end, and in what sense can this be so? Paul gives a twofold answer to this question: (1) by defining its function in salvation history; (2) by a positive account of freedom as the freedom of faith.

II   Law and Salvation History (Gal. 3f.; Rom. 5)

In Gal. 3f., Paul distinguishes the two eras of history before and after the giving of the law, i.e. from Abraham to Moses and from Moses to Christ. Abraham did not receive the law, but the promise. Temporally, and thus also materially, the promise precedes the law. The law 'came in between'. The fact that it was mediated by angels shows that its value is comparatively less. So it cannot make the promise of no effect (Gal. 3.17). It was given only for an intermediate period, and has an end, just as it had a beginning; the end is Christ (Rom. 10.4; cf. Gal. 4.4). But what is its significance?

1. W. Elert: there remains only the *usus elenchticus*: the law convicts. For criticism, see W. Trillhaas, *Ethik* (1965[2]), pp. 41f.

2. A. Schweitzer (*The Mysticism of Paul the Apostle*, pp. 177ff.). The end of the law has begun. The law belongs to the natural world and the rule of angels. There is no place for it in the messianic kingdom. This world has already received its death blow, but is still maintaining itself for the present. 'Where the supernatural world is already a reality, angel dominion and the law have no more validity', and that is the case 'within the sphere of the corporeity of those who are in Christ, filled as it is with the death- and resurrection-producing forces' (p. 188). Against

---

[1] *ibid.*, p. 335.

Schweitzer, however, it must be said that the end of the law is not a cosmic process in Paul. The end is rather presented in the freedom of faith promised in the word.

3. H.-J. Schoeps (pp. 168ff.): Paul always keeps to the limits of what is possible within Judaism, as Judaism, too, presupposes the ending of the law in the messianic kingdom. For Paul, this kingdom had already dawned. But Schoeps' assertion that Judaism, too, expected the end of the law is not a correct one.

4. U. Wilckens: Paul replaces the law with Christ. This thesis remains an objectifying presentation.

It is relevant to the understanding of Rom. 10.4 to note that with Christ a new situation, a new epoch of salvation history has in fact begun. But this is not verified historically. The new element cannot be perceived in the world. It is visible there only as the presence of the word, the proclamation of the end of the law. This thesis cannot be used as a principle for a Christian interpretation of history; it can only be understood as a disclosure of the nature of faith.

E. Fuchs, *Gesammelte Aufsätze* III, p. 20: The end of the law 'has only been reached for those who believe that Christ is or was the end of the law that brings death to the sinner'. But what is the relationship between the 'is' and the 'was'? Fuchs, pp. 383f.: it is a matter of the constancy and unity of the word of God. The law denied man righteousness. But this can only be recognized in faith. 'The theology of Paul shows that faith understands God in the gospel when man learns to understand himself in the law.'

Because the end of the law is not a worldly state of affairs but a situation 'in Christ', it also becomes clear that on the one hand it has come to an end as a way of salvation, as its requirements have been fulfilled by Christ and we have therefore been ransomed from it (or, in a completely different category, we have died to it: Rom. 7.6), whereas on the other hand it remains in force as a moral demand. The law is certainly not false! Indeed, it was given for life (Gal. 3.12; Rom. 7.10). Fulfilling it would create life – but it would of course have to be complete fulfilment, because the demand is indivisible (Gal. 3.20). That, however, is an achievement of which no man is capable (Gal. 3.11; Rom. 3.19f.).[1] Hence the problem arises: the law has been given for salvation, but its demands have been set so high that no one is adequate for it. Is the law, then, a serious demand?[2]

---

[1] Paul does not think in casuistic terms, and does not intend to demonstrate the failure to obey individual injunctions case by case (although on one occasion, in Rom. 2, his interpretation can take this direction). He means, rather, that the whole of the demand is not obeyed. That happens where man *strives* to fulfil it, for in his concern he is not whole, but divided.

[2] The same question is posed by the ethics of Jesus.

Christ is the end of the law, but it is still valid. We are free, but confronted with a demand; justified by faith, but judged according to works. It is clear that the conception of salvation history alone will not lead us to a proper understanding. An indication of this can be seen even in Paul himself: his outline of salvation history remains fragmentary. In Gal. 3f., history from Adam to Abraham is simply missing altogether, in order to enable Paul to demonstrate his thesis of the pre-eminence of the promise. In Rom. 5, there is a sweep from Adam to Moses, but here Paul pays no attention to Abraham. Here, too, the tendency is to portray the law as an intermediate factor, but under a different aspect. Whereas Gal. 3f. deals with the relationship between law and promise, Rom. 5 is concerned with the relationship between law and sin. Paul can let this lack of balance go by, because he is not concerned with the idea as such. Similarly, it is not *expressis verbis*, but only in occasional hints that he distinguishes between the two aspects of the law:[1] (a) as the will of God, it has absolute validity for all the world; (b) as an ordinance of Moses it has only relative validity, for an intermediate period and only in one part of the world. Of course, it is always the world in which *I* find myself. The difference can be seen more clearly when Paul works with timeless categories, as with 'letter' and 'spirit' in II Cor. 3.

If we attempt to reconcile all the salvation-historical conceptions, we find ourselves in a dilemma. How did men live from Adam to Moses? Really without the law? But in that case they would also have lived without sin, if the principle in Rom. 4.15 holds: where there is no law, there is no transgression. Of course, Paul cannot assert that simply because of the fact that death was in the world. So he resorts to an expedient: men indeed sinned (though not like Adam against an explicit command), but their sins were not reckoned to them; nevertheless, they still had to die (Rom. 5.13f.). Again, these theses cannot be verified in historical terms. Their intention, however, is clear enough: the objectifying presentation in terms of salvation history is meant to provide grounds for the supremacy of grace (a) over the demand of the law, (b) over sin. Paul's account is comprehensible as an attempt to describe the horizon of faith: I experience my freedom through the gospel that communicates to me the saving act that has taken place earlier and opens my eyes to what I have been freed from, what my world is, how it is made and how it determines

---

[1] For the distinction, see Bultmann, *Theology of the New Testament* I, pp. 268f.

me. I have freedom in Christ. The new age is promised. The end of
the law is not 'tangible', either in the world or in me. It is there in
Christ, i.e. in the presence of the preaching which brings about freedom.

The question posed above still, however, remains. What is the
relationship between the alleged aim of the law, that it has been given
for life, and its alleged effect, that it creates sin and death?

III   The Aim of the Law

A distinction must be made between the aim which God pursued
in the dispensation of the law and the use of the law by men. The law
reveals the will of God. But it cannot itself bring about fulfilment – it
is 'weak' (Rom. 8.3).

This makes all the more pressing the question whether in that case Paul is not
outlining a senseless theory. Even the further assertion, that the law was hampered
by the σάρξ (Rom. 8.3), is not a satisfactory answer. What kind of a God is it
who makes known his will and cannot carry it out? Once again, we must go
beyond objectification and examine the structure of faith.

Paul explains that sin is present before the law. That is, sin is the
condition of the world in which I find myself, and the law is the factor
which discloses this condition. It brings about a division between myself and my world; it leads to a confrontation as a condition for my
being able to penetrate to this situation. Thus the law is not meant to
attain fulfilment. In objectifying terms: its ineffectiveness is not
conditioned by God's weakness, but is in accordance with his plan.
Paul does not feel that the way of the law does not lead to its goal
because the demands have been screwed up too high and therefore
cannot be fulfilled. Were that the case, the way would not be wrong;
it would be man who was not up to it. In fact, however, the whole
direction is wrong. If I try to bring about my salvation by fulfilling
the law, my wish is not for what befits God and his law; what I seek
is my own righteousness. And in doing this I find myself in conflict
with the law. As I make my way towards my own righteousness, the
law itself crosses my path and in so doing fulfils its purpose of bringing
about a knowledge of sin (Rom. 3.20). There is a comment on this
passage in Rom. 7.7ff. It is not Paul's view that one can read what sin
is out of individual commandments and can measure oneself by them
as though with a self-examination manual. Coming to know sin
happens in a different way. Man is driven into sinning by the law,

and learns to assess sin in practising it. Romans 7.7 does not mean that I now know theoretically what covetousness is, but that I have experienced it, tried it.[1] Gal. 3.19: the law is given τῶν παραβάσεων χάριν; that does not mean, to obviate transgressions and keep the world – at least to some extent – in order, but to provoke transgressions and thus to make quite clear where man stands, that is, in conflict with God (Rom. 7.7ff.) and thus in conflict with himself. The statement must be interpreted precisely. Paul does not say that the law begets sin; in that case, God would be the author of sin. His position is that sin came into the world through sinning. This presupposes that sin was present before the law; the law first sets it going. In this way, sin takes itself *ad absurdum* (Rom. 5.20). Thus man is portrayed as he is: he has nothing to show before God, he remains directed towards grace.[2] Galatians 3.24 has the same sense: the law was our παιδαγωγὸς εἰς Χριστόν, ἵνα ἐκ πίστεως δικαιωθῶμεν. No pedagogy along the lines of salvation history ('education of the human race') is postulated here. The 'pedagogue' is not the educator, but the task-master, who keeps men at God's demand until the coming of Christ. εἰς Χριστόν does not mean 'up to Christ';[3] its sense is objective, 'until his coming'. The law is an educator only in the above mentioned sense, that man is led into sin and thus shown the way to faith. Confronted by the gospel he can understand the either/or: either works of the law, or faith. Here, too, it is clear that the doctrine of the law serves to expound faith in the proclamation of the gospel.

The law does not lead to subjective despair about one's own wickedness, but into an objectively desperate situation, which one understands on hearing the gospel.

Paul does not describe faith as an escape from the pangs of conscience. Where he speaks of his situation before conversion (Phil. 3.4ff.), he points out that he was blameless by the standards of the law. And where he describes the actual conflict within man (Rom. 7), he does not speak of conscience and inner torments.

The question why God did not simply see that his will was carried out, and why he 'allowed' sin, is senseless from Paul's starting point. God does not 'allow' sin, but leads men into sinning by the law, in order to take them to the point at which sin is disclosed. The Pauline doctrine of sin leads to absurdities if it is objectivized so that it becomes either a metaphysical theory about the course of

---

[1] Cf. the significance of 'knowledge' in II Cor. 5.21; there it is said of Christ: τὸν μὴ γνόντα ἁμαρτίαν.

[2] Bultmann, *Theology of the New Testament* I, pp. 267f.: the law leads to death, to show God as the God who 'raises the dead'.

[3] Thus the 'Barthians'; similarly Rom. 10.4: Christ, the end of the law.

history as a process fixed by God or a psychological theory about the course of the inner history of the individual. The theological significance of this doctrine is that it interprets the cross of Christ as God's way of carrying out salvation and that it shows that salvation is God's act and the gospel, in pointing to what is not gospel. The whole doctrine of the law is therefore simply a theological interpretation. It becomes comprehensible when it is exemplified in the case of the individual man, as a disclosure of where he stands and whence he comes. The arguments are complicated, but it must be asked whether their complexity is not appropriate. The gospel is not complicated, but my position is; it is therefore difficult to describe it in abstract terms. Paul sets out to show not only *that* man's situation is hidden from him, but also *how* this is so: that he believes that he can do God service on the basis of the fulfilling of the law. Now the web is untangled. As soon as a man sees that the point of the law is to uncover the human situation, he can recognize a consistent, comprehensible state of affairs. At the moment that my situation is disclosed through the gospel, I know that I am – and always have been – dominated by the law, and recognize that this is not the position that God intends. In my alienation, my sin, I am in a situation where I do not 'originally' belong. I discover that I am put in action by the law and thus actively bring about this alienation myself; in other words, I miss the direction in which I am intended to go. I understand this when hearing the word brings me to myself. Now I see that God has been guiding me even in my active failure, to the point at which I now stand, to the moment of the communication of grace. In this way, it also becomes clear what freedom is. It does not mean that I am released from God's demand, but rather that the possibility of disobedience, of καυχᾶσθαι, of using the law, is elevated to an end in itself. From the beginning, this 'end' was the aim of the law – i.e. faith. God does not utter two kinds of word; commandment and promise are both the word of the same God. God wants one thing: me. That he makes demands on me through the law means that he does not let me go. That is the significance of the law: salvation encounters me in such a way as to guide me once again in the right direction. That means, that the law shows the continuity between the new man and the old. Under faith, I am the same man as I was before. Faith is not a *habitus*, but the experience that I, a sinner, am justified.

27 · *DE SERVO ARBITRIO* (ROMANS 7)

W. G. Kümmel, *Römer 7 und die Bekehrung des Paulus*, UNT 17 (1929); R. Bultmann, 'Römer 7 und die Anthropologie des Paulus', in *Imago Dei* (Krüger Festschrift) (1932), pp. 53–62 (=*Der alte und der neue Mensch* (1964), pp. 28ff.); P. Althaus, *Paulus und Luther über den Menschen* (1958³); E. Fuchs, *Die Freiheit des Glaubens* (1949); id., 'Existentiale Interpretation von Römer 7, 7–12 und 21–23', *ZThK* 59 (1962), pp. 285–315 (=Gesammelte Aufsätze III, pp. 364–401); G. Bornkamm, 'Sünde, Gesetz und Tod' (1950), in *Das Ende des Gesetzes*, Gesammelte Aufsätze I

(1961³), pp. 51–69; E. Ellwein, 'Das Rätsel von Röm. 7', *KuD* 1 (1955), pp. 247–68; W. Joest, 'Paulus und das Luthersche *simul iustus et peccator*', *ibid.*, pp. 269–320; H. Braun, 'Römer 7, 7–25 und das Selbstverständnis des Qumran-Frommen', *ZThK* 56 (1959), pp. 1–18 (=*Gesammelte Studien zum NT*, pp. 100–19); H. Hommel, 'Das 7. Kapitel des Römerbriefes im Licht antiker Überlieferung', *ThViat* 8 (1961/2), pp. 90–116; H. Jonas, 'Philosophische Meditation über Paulus, Römerbrief, Kapitel 7', in *Zeit und Geschichte* (Bultmann Festschrift), pp. 557–70.

We still have to discuss the encounter between the law and the individual man. In this connection, it will be necessary to give an answer to the following objection: the assertion that the law sets sin in motion shows that the law itself is a factor in sinning. In that case, it is no longer God's word. That means that if Paul's thought is consistently followed through it leads to antinomianism.[1] Paul goes into this objection in Rom. 7.7: τί οὖν ἐροῦμεν; ὁ νόμος ἁμαρτία; He rejects it: μὴ γένοιτο. But in that case, how is the law not sin? Can Paul really show that this consequence need not be foisted on him? His explanation is that the 'fault' of my sinning lies not with the law, but with sin. But this fault can only be seen for what it is through the law. That presupposes that it is 'holy', and the commandment is holy and just and good (v. 12).

The context: Romans 6 dealt with freedom from sin on the basis of baptism (we have died with Christ, and in him are dead to sin). In this way, freedom is particularized. It does not have the formal meaning that a man can do what he wants, but is freedom from sin. We no longer stand under the law, but under grace. That means that it is impossible to sin (Rom. 6.16–18). Freedom is therefore service of a new kind. But if that is so, how is it still freedom? Because sin is the alienating power which tears me away into death. The new possibility is one of serving where I am at home.

Romans 7.1–6 grounds the reality of freedom in a juristic argument and once again presents the results in the 'once – now' pattern, in vv. 5f. Verses 7–25 then comment on v. 5, and ch. 8 comments on v. 6. Thus the theme of ch. 7 is the unredeemed man, that of ch. 8 the redeemed man.

Of course, a different exposition of ch. 7 has been advocated, right down to the

---

[1] Marcion drew this consequence. In the case of Paul, it should be noted that sin was already in the world before the law, and therefore was not first created by the law. In the salvation-historical account of Rom. 5, however, this is not clear enough; in the salvation-historical objectivation of this chapter, the law first came into the world through Moses, but there was already a commandment for Adam.

present day:[1] the man in revolt is in fact the man of faith (thus the Reformers). Certain specific statements seem to support this interpretation: I will the good, but fail to do it. Only of the man under faith can it be said that he wills the good. At the end of the chapter, Paul gives thanks for the redemption he has experienced. Nevertheless, it must be maintained that the 'I' of Rom. 7.7–24 is the man outside faith.

Paul – or the ἐγώ – makes statements about himself which the justified man cannot make: ἐγὼ δὲ σάρκινός εἰμι, πεπραμένος ὑπὸ τὴν ἁμαρτίαν (v. 14). οὐκ οἰκεῖ ἐν ἐμοί, τοῦτ' ἔστιν ἐν τῇ σαρκί μου, ἀγαθόν (v. 18). Paul says of the man of faith that he lives ἐν σαρκί, but no longer κατὰ σάρκα. He lives, rather, in the spirit (or the spirit dwells in him) and in freedom; he is therefore no longer sold under sin. Furthermore, it is precisely the lot of the unredeemed man that he wills the good but fails to do it. Rom. 8.12–14 describes the redeemed man. The redeemed man no longer cries for redemption from the body of death (Paul is no dualist). Faith knows that εἰ δὲ Χριστὸς ἐν ὑμῖν, τὸ μὲν σῶμα νεκρὸν διὰ ἁμαρτίαν, τὸ δὲ πνεῦμα ζωὴ διὰ δικαιοσύνην (Rom. 8.10).

Romans 8 is decisive for an assessment of the 'I' in Rom. 7. Here we have a description of the redeemed man, of life in the spirit.[2] Nevertheless, Paul does not describe his subjective experience before his conversion.[3] He does not speak personally about himself; he uses 'I' in a general sense. Paul describes in general terms the objective situation of the man outside faith – where 'objective' means the perspective which faith has on unbelief.[4]

Now there are apparently some contradictions here: 1. This 'I', in other words every man, is said to will the good. He does not do this only on occasion; it is meant to be the general determination of his being. But it is also said in equally general terms that no good dwells in him. The conflict is resolved if we do not regard the 'I' as the abstract subject, the good as what is morally good and the will as a deliberate plan. Paul does not speak of the good will, but of willing as intending the good, which is synonymous with 'life'.

For the 'necessary character' of the statements and the phenomenological

---

1 Scheme for the possibilities of interpretation: the 'I' can be: 1. (a) individual; (b) general; 2. (a) before faith; (b) in faith. This gives four possibilities.

2 Thus the pietistic interpretation; it understood Rom. 7 as a description of inner redemption, of the consciousness of being saved: the unconverted man lives in inner conflict, and conversion leads to peace of soul.

3 According to Phil. 3.2ff., blameless. W. G. Kümmel, op. cit., shows that Rom. 7 is not an account of Paul's inner experience and his conversion.

4 Unbelief is quite unaware of itself; cf. v. 15: ὃ γὰρ κατεργάζομαι, οὐ γινώσκω.

analysis of the I and of willing, see H. Jonas, *op. cit.*, p. 561: 'Understood in these terms, the will is not some kind of individual psychological act among others . . . something like an explicit resolve or the like; it is nothing that can appear and then vanish again . . . : *a priori*, it is always there, lies behind all individual acts and thus makes something like "willing", as a special phenomenon of the psyche, and its opposite, lack of will, possible'. Jonas works out the 'act-phenomenon of the reflection of the will' in phenomenological, and not exegetical terms: the will does not in the first place will something, but 'itself, and on each occasion has always chosen itself'. In itself it is hardened. Jonas believes that he can demonstrate this hardening as the universal structure of existence. Paul means the fallenness of sinful man, which is visible only to faith.

2. The second apparent contradiction is: if the unbeliever does not realize his own situation, how can he lament it? Furthermore, faith does not lament, because it has put lamentation in the past. Does Paul, then, describe the conflict within the believer as the one who is tempted? There is only a contradiction here if the lamentation is understood as a psychological act. For Paul, however, it is the means of depicting a trans-psychological condition.

What is meant can be clarified from the gnostic lament of the soul. The gnostic I is in the world in a state of stupefaction. It is roused by the cry from heaven (Eph. 5.14), and perceives with horror that it has been thrown into the alien world. So it breaks out into a lament,[1] and this lament is already an act of knowledge, the beginning of the ascent into light.

The moment of lamentation cannot be verified in biographical or experiential terms; at the moment of awakening it is already a retrospect on the period of lostness, which is now left immediately behind. Once again, the account can be understood as a disclosure of the structure of faith. Faith comes to understanding in comprehending whence we have been called and what sin is, i.e. in seeing its past clearly. In putting these words in the mouth of the Jewish Paul, the Christian Paul is asserting the identity of the believer with the unbeliever, the ontological continuity between the two: faith is not an ontological transformation; it is not a *habitus*. Unlike the gnostic I, the believer is not a heavenly man, but one who is called, who knows that he has been freed from the wretchedness of his past.[2]

The Qumran texts provide a further model. I QS XI 9ff.: 'As for me, I belong to wicked mankind, to the company of ungodly flesh. My iniquities, rebellions and

---

[1] See the 'Naassene Hymn' (Hippolytus, *Ref.* V 10.2) in W. Völker, *Quellen zur christlichen Gnosis* (1932), pp. 26f.; H. Leisegang, *Die Gnosis* (no date), pp. 137f.

[2] H. Jonas, *Augustin und das paulinische Freiheitsproblem*, FRLANT NF 27 (1965²), pp. 63f.

sins, together with the perversity of my heart, belong to the company of worms, and to those who walk in darkness. For mankind has no way, and man is unable to establish his steps since justification is with God and perfection of way is out of his hand . . . As for me, if I stumble, the mercies of God shall be my eternal salvation. If I stagger because of the sin of flesh, my justification shall be by the righteousness of God which endures for ever.' Here a deep consciousness of sin is predominant. Therefore sin is recognized not only in respect of the past, but as a power that is constantly present. Sin is not only the individual act, but a general condition (cf. the singular in 1 QH I 27). Here, too, there are two ways in which the lostness can be described: (a) as sinfulness; (b) as creaturely nothingness. Because man is flesh and is weak, he falls victim to sin. He cannot free himself, but can only confess his sinfulness before God. He is at the same time a sinner and justified. How, then, is this 'at the same time' understood? As a divided relationship to the law. The way to salvation is indeed the way of radical fulfilment of the law. Man is always stumbling, and must find his way back to obedience. In Paul, on the other hand, grace is liberation from the law (for all this, see H. Braun).

The argument of Romans 7.7–25

Verses 7 and 8 show how 'I' came to know sin: it was through the commandment that I learnt sinning.[1] 'Apart from the law, sin lies dead.' That does not mean that it is not there, but that it is ineffectual. Paul presupposes that if it only becomes active on the appearance of the law, it is already present in man, but – to put it metaphorically – sleeping. Paul does not consider whence it comes and how it has come about. At any rate, it was already there before the law. That is, I am already corrupt before my encounter with the law. And it is I who pervert the commandment, by using it as a means of self-assertion. I always encounter it as one who covets, and thus as one who has been deceived, who has fallen short.

The action of sin is described in personifying terms: sin seizes the opportunity, deceives me, dwells in me. It is reminiscent of the serpent in the paradise story.

On the word ἐπιθυμία: the Jewish paradise haggadah has a story that Eve was corrupted sexually by the serpent. Lyonnet[2] refers to Shab. 145b–146a: 'Why do the goyyim covet? Because they were not on Sinai. When the serpent approached Eve, it implanted covetousness in her.' The connection between paradise and Sinai means that man's sinful condition was removed by the law.

Of course, this style does not represent a real personification of sin,

---

[1] The commandment is summed up in the words: οὐκ ἐπιθυμήσεις.

[2] S. Lyonnet, '"Tu ne convoiteras pas" (Rom. VII 7)', SupplNov Test 6 (Cullmann Festschrift) (1962), pp. 157–65, esp. 162; id., 'L'histoire du salut selon le chapitre VII de l'épître aux Romains', Biblica 43 (1962), pp. 117–51, esp. 146.

so that it becomes a mythical demon of sin. Paul also speaks of the law in similar personifying terms. Even vv. 7f. cannot be understood as a description of the individual's personal experience of sin. He does not experience its coming consciously. When he comprehends it, it has already been there for a long time, and has already been finished. Verse 9 shows quite definitely that Paul is not thinking of empirical experiences: ἐγὼ δε ἔζων χωρὶς νόμου ποτέ. When, where, how? Certainly not empirically, biographically or psychologically!

Attempts at interpretation: 1. the psychological interpretation. Paul means the time of childlike innocence and growing out of it, into law and sin. Certainly, the commandments only become binding on the Jewish child at a particular age. But for Paul, childhood is not a period without law, especially as the law is a historical entity. Once it is there, it is always there. If v. 9a is interpreted in terms of childhood, then the next clause can only be understood in a weakened sense: 'but when the commandment came, sin revived and I died'. If that is understood in psychological terms, the dying is weakened so that it becomes a spiritual death. But Paul means ἔζων and ἀπέθανον theologically: I possessed life, sin has destroyed me and my body has become the body of death. 2. The mythological interpretation: the I represents Adam (following Rom. 5). Cf. also the similarity between sin and the serpent. There are, however, discrepancies: (a) according to Rom. 5, sin comes through Adam. According to Rom. 7 it is already there; (b) Lyonnet:[1] according to Codex Neofiti, Adam was put in the garden of Eden to guard the law. Nevertheless, Paul can say that he lived without the law, in so far as this was no alien power for him. Once again, we find that the myth is echoed, but that Paul does not keep to it consistently. Paul is thinking of Adam, but (following Rom. 5) we may not objectify or verify his thought in terms of salvation history. Paul does not equate the I with Adam directly, but recasts the idea of Adam and paradise in accordance with his wisdom style. He replaces Adam with himself, the Adamitic man, and thus draws time together into one point.[2] As long as we do not objectify, there is no difficulty in the fact that sin was there from the beginning (in mythological terms, the serpent in paradise). The recollection of Adam is in fact simply a means of representation, in order to describe the horizon of the I, the moment of encounter. Hence the I-style.[3] The I-style is appropriate, because law, sin and death cannot be defined as phenomena in themselves, isolated from my reality. Only in the horizon of the I are they demonstrable as trans-subjective powers, without thereby being mythicized.

Verses 8–12 depict on the one hand the attitude of the I, its reaction

---

[1] *Biblica* 43 (1962), pp. 137f.

[2] Syr. Apoc. Baruch, 54.19ff.: 'Adam is therefore not the cause, save only of his own soul, but each of us has been the Adam of his own soul.'

[3] Bornkamm, *op. cit.*, p. 59; the Adam of Rom. 5.12ff. finds expression in the ἐγώ of Rom. 7.7ff. Cf. E. Brandenburger, *Adam und Christus*, WMANT 7 (1962), pp. 214ff.

to the commandment, and on the other hand the attitude of sin. The fate of the I results from this interplay: it finds itself in death and illusion, it is 'deceived'. Sin could only succeed in the deception with the help of the law. Only with the law could it conjure up life before me (it is presupposed that the law is there to give life). Sin appropriates the call to life which belongs to the law. Thus it does not use immorality, but moral striving. This consequence, my covetousness that is occasioned through sin by means of the law, does not affect the law, but me: v. 12. It is not that the good has become evil for me (v. 13), but rather that through this misuse it can seem to be good. In the same process of understanding, sin is also visible for what it is. And thus at the same time I am myself disclosed: the contradiction in which I am involved with the law speaks for the law and tells against me (v. 14). The contradiction expresses itself in the fact that I do not do what I want, the good, and therefore come in conflict with myself. This conflict is objective, in that my actions conflict with myself and my striving. This is underlined by the repetition in vv. 15b, 18b, 19. This conflict between me and my action is not to be psychologized, so that it becomes an ethical conflict in the ego. Paul does not say that I sometimes fail despite my good will,[1] nor even that I fail completely; even that would still be too little. Such pessimism still thinks in quantitative terms.[2] On the contrary, Paul states as a principle that I am constantly and necessarily concerned for the good, and equally necessarily fail, because of my very striving. The will itself gets in my way. To show this, Paul uses the concepts νοῦς and ἔσω ἄνθρωπος, synonymously (cf. v. 22 with v. 23). They describe the I in so far as it wills the good, in contrast to what it does.

A warning should be given against reading idealistic anthropology into the passage, e.g. the νοῦς is the spiritual subject which is good, and is thus a good nucleus which has not been reached by sin. In that case there would be a conflict with Rom. 1.28: παρέδωκεν αὐτοὺς ὁ θεὸς εἰς ἀδόκιμον νοῦν. In fact, this conflict does not exist.

Paul does not say that part of me has not been affected by sin and stands up against it, but that sin possesses me wholly and utterly (vv. 17f.). He does not distinguish between a good and a bad part in man,

[1] Which is a common topic of wisdom, from which Paul doubtless borrows the formulation. Instances in Lietzmann, HNT ad loc., and Hommel, op. cit.; one example is Ovid, Metamorphoses VII 20: video meliora proboque, deteriora sequor.
[2] Nor does he say that there is a worm, i.e. a remnant of egoism, in every good deed.

but asserts the total conflict in the I which appears in the abyss between willing and doing. The 'good will' is not a positive entity, a point of contact which can still reach the good. 'Willing the good' itself exists only in a conflict; it is the indication of my situation, that I have fallen victim to a strange power, an indication that I never understand as such as long as I do not get out of this situation: ὃ γὰρ κατεργάζομαι οὐ γινώσκω[1] (v. 15a). Compare the argument in vv. 17f.: my acts are alien to me; I am not I.

The I is not an anthropological datum like consciousness or understanding, nor even the identical centre of acting in the sense of idealism. It is not an empirical entity. It only becomes concrete as I when it has already been split. Now I am, in being against myself. In Pauline terms, sin dwells in me. This statement is not intended to be mythical or psychological (like the in-dwelling of a demon). It shows that I am not relieved of responsibility for myself through the *servitudo* of my *arbitrium*. I may be subjected to an alien power and incapable of freeing myself, but the seat of my actions is still myself. It is I who bring about the compulsion of sin. I am, so to speak, nothing more than its housing.

Paul can express the situation in a different terminology by distinguishing two kinds of νόμος. One is ὁ νόμος τοῦ νοός μου.

This expression means that I know God's will and assent to it, as I will the same thing, namely, to live. Against this, however, stands the ἕτερος νόμος ἐν τοῖς μέλεσίν μου, ὁ νόμος τῆς ἁμαρτίας. Here, of course, νόμος is used improperly.

There is no positive tabulation of sin, as it were a codex of immorality. Paul does not mean false moral views, but the 'law' that I fail to achieve.

The account ends in a lament (v. 24), followed immediately by thanksgiving (v. 25a; cf. 8.1ff.). The result is that the doctrine of the end of the law in Christ is not antinomian. Indeed, it presupposes the validity and holiness of the law. In faith, what the law intends comes into effect (Rom. 3.28–30).

---

[1] Cf. οἴδαμεν in v. 14 and οἶδα in v. 18. This is always *retro*spective knowledge.

D. REVELATION IN THE PRESENT

28 · THE WORD AS THE CRISIS OF SELF-ASSERTION

R. Bultmann, 'Church and Teaching in the New Testament' (1929), *Faith and Understanding* (1969), pp. 184–219; E. Molland, *Das paulinische Euangelion* (1934); R. Asting, *Die Verkündigung des Wortes im Urchristentum* (1939).

The historical saving event is actualized in the word: cf. the inner outline of the understanding of revelation in Rom. 1.16f. (see 24 II above). Paul speaks about the nature of the word in more detail in I Cor. 2.1f. In connection with the theme of 1.18ff., the λόγος τοῦ σταυροῦ, which is a σκάνδαλον to the Jews, and folly to the Greeks, he says: κἀγὼ ἐλθὼν πρὸς ὑμᾶς, ἀδελφοί, ἦλθον οὐ καθ' ὑπερβολὴν λόγου ἢ σοφίας καταγγέλλων ὑμῖν τὸ μαρτύριον τοῦ θεοῦ. οὐ γὰρ ἔκρινά τι εἰδέναι ἐν ὑμῖν εἰ μὴ Ἰησοῦν Χριστὸν καὶ τοῦτον ἐσταυρωμένον.

So this is the only content! Of course, Paul is not thinking of the portrayal of the historical passion, the picture of the man of grief, but of preaching the exalted Lord, who can only be 'had' through faith in the Crucified. Preaching necessarily brings the stumbling block with it. This is shown in three respects: (*a*) by the proclamation: it has to renounce any demonstration outside itself, λόγος and σοφία; (*b*) by the effect which this scandalous preaching has: it gives offence to both Jews and Greeks. Precisely in this scandalous form it shows itself to be θεοῦ δύναμις and θεοῦ σοφία (1.24; for the word δύναμις cf. Rom. 1.16); (*c*) by the appearance of the apostle: this corresponds to the nature of the word (2.3–5). Thus the preaching does not set out to make the nature of God comprehensible to the hearers. This is disclosed to no human power of comprehension, whatever its fashion. For the δύναμις of God is not his property, but his demonstration, which is particularized only in the word itself (1.18; cf. v. 24).

Paul does not therefore invite his hearers to see the rule of God in nature and history. His power appears in the fact that the preacher refuses his hearers such a demonstration and by pointing to the cross delivers an immediate verdict that directs him eschatologically one way or the other, to salvation or damnation. Furthermore, God's power can never become a secret force possessed by the pious man or by the preacher. The course of the preacher is simply the constant delivery of the word of the cross. Therefore the form of the community also corresponds to the form of the preaching: 1.26ff.

It is clear that the destruction of καύχησις is neither the work of a numinous power nor the schematic overturning of wordly relationships and values.[1] It is simply a representation of the freedom of the choice of grace.

The crisis brought about by the gospel *eo ipso* is developed in two directions: towards Judaism, as the end of righteousness by works, with the help of the law (Romans); towards Greece as the end of wisdom (I Corinthians).

Paul is aware that the destruction of the Jewish and Greek ways of self-assertion are simply two sides of the effect of the cross. He therefore discusses the basic theme in the sections at the beginning of I Corinthians and Romans in such a way that the two forms of the crisis can be seen. And he takes criticism of Judaism and of Greek thought to the same point. The statement in I Cor. 1.29 (ὅπως μὴ καυχήσηται πᾶσα σὰρξ (!) ἐνώπιον τοῦ θεοῦ), which in the context is primarily directed towards wisdom, is matched in Rom. 3.27, which is directed against man's own righteousness. At the same time, the two groups, Jews and Greeks, are each treated from a twofold point of view. First they are considered collectively. Paul points to the crisis in the way of salvation which is believed in each case, the crisis of the law and of wisdom. This is not a matter of moral or spiritual deficiency, but of the supreme achievements of humanity. At the same time, the crisis of the individual is also disclosed. He emerges from his collectivity and is immediately confronted with the message of the cross. The crisis of the individual is the theme of Romans 7, where it is not the Jew or Greek who speaks, but I.

It is a consequence of the presupposition of this destruction that Jews and Greeks can be taken together under a loftier perspective. This presupposition does not stem from a formal dialectic of existence, an anthropology of the perpetual crisis, but from the sole content of preaching, the cross. It is not a crisis in itself, but the end of the human possibility of gaining salvation by one's own efforts, the end *coram Deo*, from grace. The primary element is not destruction, but the gospel.

The fact that the two groups, i.e. all humanity, as far as Paul is

---

[1] This overturning is a widespread theme; it occurs in the Old Testament, Judaism (apocalyptic), and throughout antiquity. One example in the New Testament (following the Old), is Luke 1.52. This theme is the historical background to Paul. But he alters it in accordance with the *theologia crucis* and the association of the saving event with the word, the gospel.

concerned, are put on the same level before the word presupposes that the 'law' is not in fact limited to the Jewish law. Certainly, Paul's historical starting point is the Jewish law, revealed in the Old Testament. But he does not take it as a sum of precepts. He understands it as a whole view of man's existence in the world: man is addressed by God, confronted with a demand, and kept and held in his course. For the law makes human life together possible. Romans 13.1–7 shows how far Paul extends the scope. Here the political constitution of the world is represented as an indispensable factor of social life (and not as a factor of salvation!). It is thus a form of the manifestation of the law.

With his view of two groups determined by God's ordinance, Paul can show how while there are collective (in terms of salvation history) and psychological distinctions between their respective situations in face of the proclamation, in eschatological terms their relationship to salvation and condemnation is the same. Therefore Rom. 1 and Rom. 2 stand side by side (with the demonstration that the Gentiles, too, not only have, but keep, the law).[1]

In I Cor. 1.21ff., Paul describes the way in which the crisis is particularized for each of the two collectivities: ἐπειδὴ γὰρ ἐν τῇ σοφίᾳ τοῦ θεοῦ οὐκ ἔγνω ὁ κόσμος διὰ τῆς σοφίας τὸν θεόν, εὐδόκησεν ὁ θεὸς διὰ τῆς μωρίας τοῦ κηρύγματος σῶσαι τοὺς πιστεύοντας. ἐπειδὴ καὶ Ἰουδαῖοι σημεῖα αἰτοῦσιν καὶ Ἕλληνες σοφίαν ζητοῦσιν, ἡμεῖς δὲ κηρύσσομεν Χριστὸν ἐσταυρωμένον, Ἰουδαίοις μὲν σκάνδαλον, ἔθνεσιν δὲ μωρίαν . . .

[1] This analysis of existence has a topical significance in that the juxtaposition of the two groups repeats itself *mutatis mutandis* in the period of the church: Christianity in turn constantly returns to being a law and the church to being a legally constituted institution. In this way, both Christians and non-Christians find themselves in the same situation, to the extent that each is called from their law into the freedom of the gospel. All this also makes the spiritual *Weltanschauung*, the psychological condition, the intellectual situation, the difference between the man of a former time and (allegedly) modern man, of quite secondary theological importance. Preaching is not oriented to ancient or modern man, but to man as he is determined through the saving event; as the sinner who first experiences his condition through the disclosure of the word of grace.

29 · THE WRATH OF GOD

F. Büchsel, θυμός *TWNT* III 167f.; G. Stählin, ὀργή *TWNT* V 422ff.; H. Conzel-mann, 'Zorn Gottes. Im Judentum und NT', *RGG*³ VI 1931f.; G. Bornkamm, 'Die Offenbarung des Zornes Gottes' (1935), in: *Das Ende des Gesetzes*, Gesammelte Aufsätze I (1961³), pp. 9–33; G. H. C. MacGregor, 'The Concept of the Wrath of God in the NT', *NTS* 7 (1960/1), pp. 101–9.

In I Cor. 1, Paul makes a distinction which is primarily one of popular psychology: the word of the cross is a stumbling block to the Jews and folly to the Greeks. This distinction acquires theological relevance, as Paul shows that it points to two different manifestations of a common, indeed universal, attitude towards God, namely καύχησις, trusting in the flesh. Man subjects God's pronouncement to human judgment. He thus makes God an object of knowledge and expects him to stand still to be grasped. This is an illusionary attitude, as it does not realize that it is doomed to failure before it even begins. The theme of the first part of the epistle to the Romans arises from this reaction of man to the word of God.

Its three themes are: 1. chs. 1–4: God's righteousness as the righteousness of faith. 2. chs. 5–8: existence under the determination of faith. These four chapters are marked out by their conceptuality: instead of righteousness and faith, the relevant concepts here are spirit and life, dying with Christ and living in newness. 3. chs. 9–11: the election of Israel in the light of the past, present and future. What have these three themes to do with each other? Is there a juxtaposition of three different theories of a doctrine of redemption here, one juristic, one physical and one in terms of salvation history? If so, the middle one would represent Paul's own view; the juristic one would be a rabbinic expedient for the controversy with Judaism; and the one in terms of salvation history would also be an expedient, to be explained in psychological terms: the Jew Paul must justify his apostasy before himself and Judaism. For this interpretation, one might cite the threefold beginning in Paul's own person, in chs. 9, 10, 11. The discrepancy between the three parts of the letter, which is often said to exist, is in fact there only if we presume that Paul has a restricted concept of justification.[1] The three parts are simply a threefold interpretation of justification by faith. True, the key word πίστις does not occur in 5.2–9.30. But the link between 4.25 and 5.1 shows faith to be the basis of all the

---

[1] Only if this is narrowed down to a theoretical verdict of God upon man does justification need to be supplemented by 'sanctification'.

statements: δικαιωθέντες οὖν ἐκ πίστεως εἰρήνην ἔχομεν. It is similarly clear that ch. 10 is the basis of chs. 9–11. Moreover, the unity of the theme is clear in the constant reference to law and Christ, righteousness and sin, election. The theme of Rom. 1.16f. extends through the whole letter: the revelation of the righteousness of God in the gospel, for all believers. First the background of this revelation, the wrath of God, is disclosed (Rom. 1.18–3.20); it is then shown that righteousness has already been realized, and how this is so (3.21–31, with a scriptural proof in ch. 4.) The thesis is then particularized in an analysis of 'existence in faith', which is defined in the light of the fact that the substance of salvation is still not visible, and that the dreadful powers of sin and death still prevail as before. What is the relationship between the righteousness and the wrath of God?

Paul does not say that God is wrathful because he is righteous. Rather, righteousness and anger are opposed to each other; cf. the connection of Rom. 1.17f. with 3.20f. It should be noted that the demonstration of the wrath is not the starting point. Paul's argument is not that reference to the wrath of God should terrify men and thus drive them to the gospel. Rather, the theme of 'wrath' is subordinate to the theme of the 'revelation of righteousness in the gospel'.

Even to speak of a tension between judgment and grace is not an apt description of the situation portrayed by Paul. Paul does not mean a timeless juxtaposition of ὀργή and δικαιοσύνη. Examples of this interpretation: Bernhard Weiss ad loc. (Meyer Kommentar): the revelation of wrath is an element of God's rule of the world. It emerges within historical development. 'The wrath of God is the necessary correlate of the love of the holy God towards all good.' T. Zahn ad loc.: 'a . . . disclosing of a wrath of God again and again in this age'.

The timeless interpretation does not do justice to the text, which expressly contains an element of time: νυνὶ δὲ . . . (3.21). So Lietzmann explains that the revelation of wrath and righteousness are two stages in salvation history. The first has now come to an end. On the other hand, however, the parallelism of the two presents ἀποκαλύπτεται in vv. 17f. speaks against this. In ch. 2, the time before the coming of Christ does not appear as the time of wrath but as the time of God's patience. We are thus confronted with a dilemma: wrath is on the one hand limited to a period of time, but on the other hand it is general and encounters all man's injustice. We shall find a solution if we once again free ourselves from an objectifying consideration of God and his relationship to the world and recognize the place at which Paul finds these statements: righteousness and wrath are not properties of God and not generally discernible modes of action. God's righteousness is his salvific act, and similarly, his wrath is his judgment. Both are 'revealed'. With Christ, a new situation is given (νυνί):

that of revealed righteousness, which is constituted by the preaching of the gospel. Anger was always poured out and will continue to be. The new element since Christ is that now, through the proclamation of the gospel, man can recognize what God's judgment on sin always was. The historicity of this νυνί is the historicity of revelation, which is a historical act and is constantly actualized anew in preaching. Salvation is present deliverance from the wrath to which I had fallen victim. I can understand that now: I understand from what I am saved. Thus, wrath is made visible to me by the preaching of the gospel.

Verses 17 and 18 are parallel in construction. But the parallelism is broken. Righteousness is revealed 'in the gospel' and wrath 'from heaven'. Wrath is not an ingredient of the gospel. Its content is not that God is gracious, but also angry. It does not say anything about what God is in himself. In that case, nothing real would be said about me. It says what he does to me. Only in this way can we understand what wrath is. Conclusion: the church does not have to preach judgment and grace. It cannot use the wrath of God as a pedagogical means of forcing men to faith through fright. The wrath of God is not to be played with, even pastorally. Preaching has to offer unconditional salvation, which is there in the cross. The fear that grace will then be too cheap is unfounded. It only arises if grace is not defined exactly as grace, if it is debased and made the indulgence of the dear God.

30 · THE WORD AS FOLLY (THE CRISIS OF WISDOM)

U. Wilckens, *Weisheit und Torheit*, BHTh 26 (1959).

The thesis is stated in I Cor. 1.18. But what is the meaning of the word 'folly'? It does not mean that the word is incomprehensible, like a mystery formula or an initiation into the numinous, the irrational. Nor does it require a *sacrificium intellectus*. That would again be a way of passing judgment on God, faith by resolve, salvation through one's own achievement. The folly lies exclusively in the content of the preaching, in the cross, which is preached as God's saving act. Folly means that this preaching not only requires decision, but brings decision with it.

Therefore I can never measure it by criteria introduced from elsewhere. I am already qualified at the moment of hearing. It is illusory to want to act as a neutral assessor at this moment.

Does Paul, then, require blind faith? No, for precisely in coming to me, revelation remains what it is; disclosure through the strange word on the basis of which I can see into my situation. By its very character as folly, the word leads to understanding, to wisdom of a new kind: I Cor. 1.23f.

Verse 18 (cf. vv. 23f.) is not just concerned with the subjective judgment of the hearer (μωρία, δύναμις θεοῦ), but also with his objective determination by the word (ἀπολλύμενοι, σῳζόμενοι).[1] The connection with the concepts of judging should be noted. Schlier[2] understands wisdom in this way: dogma discloses mystic knowledge, a knowledge in the sense of the original wisdom of creation, 'a comprehending awareness of God through the bright illumination of the entity from being itself' (p. 210). The alternatives are (p. 225): 'Is it (sc. wisdom) such . . . that the believer always simply believes and says, "Christ is wisdom", that he is therefore only wise as a believer at each particular moment of faith? Or is it also that the kerygma and faith release the believer into the movement of their wisdom, that Christ is wisdom in disclosing to the believer, through the kerygma, a new wisdom and a new way of being wise and uttering wisdom?'

The necessary conclusion is that the preacher must produce and prove himself as a wise man, and that the foolish preaching is obstructed by psychological and cosmological assertions about the world and man.

For Paul, the structure of folly is permanent. Wisdom is no new glory, but the comprehension of the end of καύχησις, of the permanent strangeness of the word, as Christ is the wisdom of God.[3] The folly of the word means the destruction of man's own salvific action and thus the realization of the cross as saving event. Man has the experience that when he boasts that he is choosing God, i.e. the truth, he has already become a fool. The original possibility for me to act freely in the world as a creature has been lost as a result of my perverted autonomy, by καυχᾶσθαι.

The word-group καυχ—[4] designates far more than an exaggerated self-awareness, namely the basic attitude of emancipated man, including his unconscious action.

---

[1] Ulrich Wilckens, op. cit., pp. 21f.

[2] H. Schlier, 'Kerygma und Sophia', EvTh 10 (1950/51), pp. 481–507 (= Die Zeit der Kirche (1956), pp. 206–32); cf. also U. Wilckens, 'Kreuz und Weisheit', KuD 3 (1957), pp. 77–108.

[3] It is to be asserted, against Wilckens, that 'wisdom' is not a hypostasis (mythical person), but a concept; cf. the formulation in I Cor. 1.30: Christ became for us σοφία ἀπὸ θεοῦ, δικαιοσύνη, ἁγιασμός, ἀπολύτρωσις.

[4] R. Bultmann, καυχάομαι etc., TWNT III 646–54.

In practice, it makes no difference whether the emancipation is secular or religious, the attitude of the Greek or the Jew who relies on his own works and perverts obedience so that it became an achievement. In I Corinthians and Romans, Paul takes Jews and Gentiles together under the characteristic term καυχᾶσθαι.[1]

Faith as unconditional obedience goes beyond καύχησις. It knows only boasting in the Lord (I Cor. 1.31; II Cor. 10.17).

This boasting in the Lord is not, however, a new possibility inherent in being a Christian. It does not mean that the *homo christianus* can boast of his new wisdom. The emphasis lies one-sidedly on the ἐν κυρίῳ, on the 'not in me' (cf. I Cor. 4.7). Boasting in the Lord means boasting in the cross (Gal. 6.14). Paul particularizes this new way of boasting in his 'foolish' self-glorification (II Cor. 11f.). What he can point to is his weakness (II Cor. 11.30), and that is enough (12.9). It is boasting ἐπ'ἐλπίδι, in the face of θλίψεις (Rom. 5.2f.).

The destruction of καύχησις is not psychological self-contrition; it is a theological process, i.e. the refusal of the possibility of demonstrating revelation and faith, and thus in a positive sense it is the possibility of the certainty of salvation.

After Paul has destroyed wisdom, in I Cor. 1.18ff., a new possibility of wisdom appears in I Cor. 2.6ff.: Paul declares that he also knows a wisdom apart from folly, but that he has not yet communicated it, because the Corinthians are not yet ready for it. Does Paul, then, know two stages of insight, two stages of believing? Does the religious man now become the theme? After he has shown that faith always presents a stumbling block, Paul now seems to show that the pneumatic can fly over this and gain insight into the cosmic background of revelation.

On the basis of this section, Reitzenstein interprets Paul psychologically, as a gnostic. Schlier supports his conception of the initiation into the new wisdom on it. Bultmann sees in these remarks a slip which Paul has made in the eagerness of his polemic. But the section has no polemical concern. It evidently reflects Paul's lessons. It is thoroughly permeated with features of a pneumatic enthusiasm similar to that prevailing at Corinth. But critical elements can also be detected within it, when Paul describes τὰ χαρισθέντα ἡμῖν as the object of the wisdom discourse. The direction of the line of thought is clear when we consider Paul's historical starting point, i.e. the Jewish theme of hidden wisdom. It is taken up by Paul and its direction is heightened: wisdom is not a possibility which is proper to man as such. In this section, too, he achieves the destruction of autonomy and καύχησις. He works out: (a) the positive possibility of understanding revelation; (b) the nature of revelation as gift. Even here, Paul does not base the authority of his account on his pneumatic experiences and visions, which he does not make the subject of doctrine at all.

---

[1] The expression πεποιθέναι ἐν σαρκί (Phil. 3.3) is also related: for the Jew, the law is a means of self-assertion.

The old line also appears clearly again in ch. 3: here the perfect are no longer pneumatics in the habitual sense; perfection has to show itself in a man's way of life, i.e., it demonstrates itself in such a way that no boasting is possible (v. 3). The criterion is the community. Similarly, the apostolic office is defined as service (vv. 5–9), and the community as the temple of God (vv. 16f.)

EXCURSUS: THE POSSIBILITY OF 'NATURAL' KNOWLEDGE OF GOD?[1]

The most important passages are I Cor. 1.18ff. and Rom. 1.18ff. In neither passage does Paul investigate the abstract possibility of man's knowing God; he starts from his actual situation. Indeed, he does not know man in himself, apart from his reality, sin. Systematic theology could certainly outline such a picture, to measure reality by the true nature of man and obtain a generally valid criterion with which it could also comprehend man outside faith. The question is, however, whether it does not inevitably do that at the expense of the word.

Paul does not begin with a definition of the sphere of the activity of human reason, its capability of knowledge, but with the assertion that God shows himself. Knowledge of God is the constant reality of the world. Paul does not say that God showed himself in a primal time, but that he shows himself now: τὸ γνωστὸν τοῦ θεοῦ φανερόν ἐστιν ἐν αὐτοῖς, and: καθορᾶται (Rom. 1.19f.). The world is God's creation: God continually makes himself known in it. Paul does not, of course, demonstrate this either by the structure of the world or by reason. It is rather the case that ὁ θεὸς γὰρ αὐτοῖς ἐφανέρωσεν. Doubtless Paul takes up ancient popular philosophical ideas, though not in their original Stoic form, but as they have been transformed in Hellenistic Judaism.

The Stoic *theologia naturalis* occurs in a systematic context (cf. Bornkamm): God is the life principle of the cosmos, man is a microcosm. The universe is pervaded by the Logos. By this, man recognizes the world, God, and together with them, himself.

Paul's immediate presupposition is provided by Hellenistic Judaism (Wisdom): here we find a relapse into the abomination of

---

[1] M. Pohlenz, 'Paulus und die Stoa', *ZNW* 42 (1949), pp. 69–104 (= new impression, 1964); G. Bornkamm, 'Die Offenbarung des Zornes Gottes' (see literature on section 29); S. Schulz, 'Die Anklage in Röm 1.18–32', *ThZ* 14 (1958), pp. 161–73; H. P. Owen, 'The Scope of Natural Revelation in Rom. I and Acts XVII', *NTS* 5 (1959), pp. 133–43; J. Jervell, *Imago Dei*, FRLANT 76 (1960), pp. 289f., 312ff.

Gentile worship, which brings with it moral corruption. The way to overcome it is instruction about the true nature of God, a summons to insight and repentance. This pedagogic aim is lacking in Paul, 'because it is not the purpose of the apostle to disclose God's being from the world, but to disclose the nature of the world from God's revelation. Nor does Paul expose God's revelation to the world's judgment; he discloses God's judgment on the world that is manifest in the law.'[1]

Now Paul does not simply say that God is manifest, but τὸ γνωστὸν τοῦ θεοῦ. What is that? This γνωστόν is not to be defined in quantitative terms. What is meant is simply that man does not see God, but God himself makes his rule comprehensible. Cf. v. 20: man can know τὰ ἀόρατα αὐτοῦ; ἡ ἀΐδιος αὐτοῦ δύναμις καὶ θειότης is understandable. Knowledge of God has a critical content: man can understand that God is not to be imagined as world, as an entity in the world; object-ive knowledge cannot grasp him. Man can only know him as the invisible one, indirectly, by realizing his position as a creature and acting accordingly. God therefore makes it clear that he is not world. The climax of Paul's remarks is the assertion that men did not realize this possibility through which they would really have remained men. This is not a verdict which Paul derives from salvation history or the myth of the primal fall;[2] he gains it directly from his concept of revelation.[3] Accordingly, he modifies the ideas of Jewish-Hellenistic polemic against a paganism which he already finds in existence: to know God means to acknowledge him and honour him as God. Paul chooses religion itself as an object of demonstration: men offer wor-ship, but not to God – they worship an image of God, and reverence the numinous in nature and history, the divine in a tangible form. In this way God has become a possessible object, a worldly being, albeit the 'supreme being'. The consequence is that a falseness not only finds its way into human existence, but even embraces the whole of man: 'they became fools'.

Paul does not assert the reality of the knowledge of God with the aim of leading men out of ἀγνωσία. His assertion contains no positive

[1] Bornkamm, op. cit., p. 26.

[2] In Rom. 1 he does not allude to the Fall at all. Romans 7, where the 'Fall' is no more than the projection of the I, shows how freely he treats traditional concep-tions.

[3] His understanding of the ὀργὴ θεοῦ is taken directly from his understanding of the gospel and the righteousness of God. In I Cor. 1.18ff., the μωρία form of the revelation seems to be God's reaction to man's conduct.

element on which a man could rely. It is simply the foil for the
assertion of man's guilt, indeed the claim that guilt is his permanent
condition. The perversion does not lie in a false religiosity, but in
religion itself. The consequence is that the world, instead of being an
object of reverence, becomes a dominating deity: man has fallen
victim to himself through confusing God and the world. παρέδωκεν
αὐτοὺς ὁ θεός – not to a natural fate, seizing a man from outside and
dragging him with it, but to a fate which a man experiences as his own
action: ἐπιθυμίαι, πάθη, ἀδόκιμος νοῦς. The second indication (after the
practice of religion) is the corruption of morality. Immorality is not
directly designated sin here; it is said to be punishment for the one
primal sin of perverting the worship of God. This punishment, too,
man carries through in free assent (Rom. 1.32). Paul chooses the most
objectionable of all pagan abominations in Jewish eyes, homo-
sexuality, as a model of immorality; in addition, he appends a long
catalogue of vices as a pattern of pagan conduct, following the style of
Jewish apologetic.

At this point Paul seems to ignore completely the fact that honest
seeking, deep sensitivity and fine spirituality are to be found in
humanity, and precisely in religion. Does he give early testimony to
the barbarian revolt against classical culture from the East, which is
expressed most vividly in gnosticism and ultimately leads to the
barbarizing of antiquity? Is this at the same time a document of the
failure of Judaism to comprehend the quality and depth of mysticism,
the beauty of the gods, the content of myth, the loftiness of the picture
of man which is formed in religion? Is it also a primitive misunderstanding of the imagery of the gods? All apologetic considerations
must be disregarded in giving an answer. Paul is in fact untouched by
the Greek education of his time and works with the vivid means of
Jewish polemic. But we must try to think through to what he is
setting out to present. Paul sings no hymn of praise to Christians by
making derogatory remarks about Jews and Gentiles. He is asserting
the end of all man's own righteousness, including Christian righteousness, if a man claims it as his own. He is not concerned with a historical,
cultural, philosophical, psychological verdict on religion, with its
analysis as a realm of the human spirit. His sole question is whether it
brings me into a right relationship with God. What applies to the rest
of man's conduct applies also to religion. If man clearly understood it
as a question about God and involved himself in the question, he
would know that he was not the questioner, but the one who was

being questioned. That Rom. 1 is neither a psychological portrayal nor a moral assessment is also clear from the fact that this section does not contain all Paul's remarks about the Gentiles. A completely different aspect is to be found in ch. 2. How the two aspects are related must be discussed in the following section.

31 · THE WORD AS A STUMBLING BLOCK

I The Crisis of Man's own Righteousness

L. Mattern, *Das Verständnis des Gerichts bei Paulus*, AThANT 47 (1966).

In his remarks in I Cor. 1.18ff., Paul expressly draws a parallel between Gentiles and Jews: (a) Greeks – wisdom – folly; (b) Jews – sign – stumbling block. The superior concepts are folly and wisdom. Now Paul cannot, of course, simply argue along the lines of a formal parallelism. For when he turns to the Jews, a historical factor comes into play which does not apply in the case of the Gentiles: the law and the historical election of Israel. Paul begins from what the two have in common: in either case the cross is the destruction of self-glorification. For the Jews, that means the transcending of righteousness on the basis of the works of the law. In that case, of course, Paul has to show that it is not the law that is sinful, but only its use for man's achieving of his own righteousness. In addition, he has to give a positive account of the significance of the law. Even in Romans, Paul begins by showing the fundamental equality of the Jewish and Gentile situations. Romans 1 contains the destruction of Gentile religion as a way to salvation. The Jew could evade this argument on the grounds that he had the right morality and the right knowledge of God. Paul demolishes this excuse in ch. 2: in fact the Jew has the law, but he does not do it and therefore falls under the divine judgment. For God will judge each man according to his works (Rom. 2.6–10.13), and will do so solely on the basis of works. Thus the two groups find themselves in the same position before God. Paul goes one step further: even the Gentiles are not without a law; they are a law to themselves, as the works of the law are written on their hearts. That is shown by their conscience.

The thesis of judgment according to works stands very close to the thesis that no man is justified by works of the law, but through faith without works of the law (3.28). Is there a contradiction here? Does not an undigested remnant of Jewish thinking appear in Rom. 2? Nevertheless, this chapter stands between the two theses of 1.16f. and 3.21ff. and agrees with 3.20, at least in the negative point that in fact no man is righteous before God.

Lietzmann: in Rom. 2, Paul is speaking only theoretically. He does not really take seriously the possibility that someone might reach blessedness through his works. For the sake of argument, he puts himself quite theoretically for a moment in the Jewish position: given the fall, that the law could in fact save and that judgment was made on the basis of an assessment of man's works – how would you then stand? You have not fulfilled the law. Against this interpretation, however, must be set the fact that the idea of judgment in Paul is not just conceived in polemical, hypothetical terms. It also occurs in passages where Paul is outlining a straightforward argument. The argument in Rom. 2 is convincing in itself because it rests on the true state of affairs about judgment. The juxtaposition can be understood, if we do not restrict the concept of justification to the mere imputation of an 'as if' (or to the negative element of the abolition of sin) and if we do not make the fact that God institutes reconciliation into an abstract doctrine of the attributes of God. That God is gracious does not mean that he is kind by nature, but that he attributes righteousness to me in an act. I can only meaningfully say that God is good to make this action comprehensible. The assertion of God's grace does not do away with any talk of judgment; it presupposes it. If God judges, then it is according to works; indeed, it is important not to blunt the point: he *only* judges according to works. Paul sharpens the point where the Jew bends it. The latter also says 'according to works', but he knows that these will not completely secure his righteousness. Therefore he continues, but God is also merciful. Or he says that in the judgment man will stand by works *and* faith. Paul deprives him of this possibility by stressing the 'alone'. So man has no other possibility than grace, righteousness from faith alone, which is the end of man's own righteousness. Here grace is no longer a compensation for what righteousness man still lacks, but the complete provision of righteousness by God. I can receive it only by renouncing my own righteousness. Thus works and faith are each given their own place.

II   Israel ('Salvation History')

J. Munck, *Christus und Israel*, *Acta Jutlandia* 28 (3), 1956; C. Müller, *Gottes Gerechtigkeit und Gottes Volk*, FRLANT 86 (1964).

Why is the theme of 'salvation history' to be discussed under the main heading of 'the crisis of Israel'? The answer is based on the following considerations: Paul does not outline a positive picture of history, either of world history or of the history of Israel. Paul's understanding of salvation history stems rather from his understanding of word and saving event.

His conception of history cannot be attached directly to what Old Testament scholarship has shown to be the constant process of Israel's interpretation of itself. Besides, the outline of a picture of history would mean that real or supposed historical facts, issues and connections would be interpreted in metaphysical or mythical categories, i.e. would be subjected to a particular view. The theologian would become the interpreter of the oracles of history.

In what sense, then, is Israel still the subject of theology? On the basis of the historicity of the revelation and its character as word. The starting point of the account is the theme of Rom. 1–3: the revelation of God's righteousness for every believer implies the crisis of Israel (in so far as Israel wants to exist by its own achievements), the crisis of the pre-eminence which it thought that it had. Paul does not dispute, but confirms that Israel enjoys a historical pre-eminence, as the promise was entrusted to it. But this pre-eminence is historical and relative, not eschatological and absolute. The Jew is equal to the Gentile in the judgment, because God judges by works alone and even the Jew receives righteousness only by faith. In Rom. 9–11, this systematic beginning leads to a particular way of dealing with the Old Testament history. It is not depicted as a continuum. Paul simply extracts individual events, and only those by means of which he can demonstrate the essential factors of Israel's existence: the free election of Israel and its direction towards faith. Jacob and Esau, Moses and Pharaoh are introduced for this purpose alone. In addition, at the end there comes a prospect of the future, of Israel's entry into salvation. Romans 9–11 does not offer a picture of history but a doctrine of election and grace. Certainly there is a continuity, but it is an intangible continuity, the continuity of the freedom of God's election.

On the connection of the subject matter in Romans: 9.1 looks like an abrupt new beginning, but it is prepared for by the conclusion of ch. 8. The connection of thought in fact points even further back: chs. 9–11 are a commentary on 3.1: what is Israel's advantage? 9.4f. gives the answer. The advantage is historical and collective. It does not mean preferential treatment of the individual Jew in the judgment. The Jew does, however, stand nearer to the preaching of the gospel in historical terms (cf. 1.16 πρῶτον). At first glance, the start of the account at the beginning of Rom. 9 seems to be subjective; this is repeated in chs. 10 and 11. But it is not enough to find a personal apologia from Paul there simply for that reason. The actual theme appears in the argument: Paul is a missionary to the Gentiles not although, but because he is a Jew.

Israel has been chosen – that still remains true. But in that case, how can we explain the fact that it refuses to believe and thus forfeits the promise? An answer can only be given by a fundamental account of the nature of election, not in the sense of an objectivized theory of election, but by showing the proclamation of the gospel to Jews and Gentiles as its horizon. It is not enough to assert that it is the one-sided, free and irrevocable act of God, which happens without any human activity, which man cannot count on or prepare for in advance. True as that is, these statements only become theological when they explain the present event of proclamation, the encounter of proclamation and the world.

The election of Israel as God's free act immediately leads to a dialectical determination of Israel: Israel as the object of election is to be distinguished from the empirical Israel (Rom. 9.6-9). Paul shows this by the examples which he introduces (vv. 10-12). In this way he arrives at the principle: ἄρα οὖν οὐ τοῦ θέλοντος οὐδὲ τοῦ τρέχοντος, ἀλλὰ τοῦ ἐλεῶντος θεοῦ (v. 16). Free election has as its correlate free rejection (v. 18). Now Paul can show the relationship between election, understood in radical terms, and the actual hardening of Israel. This hardening is not a general attitude (godlessness, irreligion), but concrete behaviour in the face of the preaching that offers salvation without conditions and in this way realizes the freedom of election. This is where the decision is made about Israel's election.[1] Thus Israel is kept in view in so far as the nature of the preaching is made clear by it (salvation through the stumbling block of the cross). The connection between election and preaching also shows in what sense one can speak of an elected collective, Israel. Only an individual can be freely elected. If a collective were chosen, it would be a tie on God. The solution to this dilemma is that the collective is chosen in the sense that a promise has been given to it. Revelation appears in a historical situation and has its human representatives.

This is rather different from saying that each representative, each member of the group will be blessed. In this sense, then, a distinction must be made between empirical Israel and true Israel. Müller: this distinction is a result of the different ideas of God. No, it stems, rather, from the theology of the cross.

As election is realized in encounter with the message of faith, it can happen that the Gentiles occupy the place which should be held by the Jews (Rom. 9.30-32).

Paul does not have completely clear motives in distinguishing between the two

---

[1] Bultmann, *Essays* (1955), p. 177.

Israels. On the one hand, he says that Israel forfeits its privileges to the Gentiles, and thus distinguishes the Gentiles, as the true Israel, from the empirical Israel. On the other hand, he maintains a continuity with the help of the idea of the 'remnant', and thus makes a distinction within Israel. On the one hand he declares that Israel forfeits its privileges, and on the other that these were only of a provisional nature and were intended to be replaced by the fulfilment: the law, the testament (Gal. 4.1); the cult (Gal. 4.8f.); the δόξα (II Cor. 3.7ff.). That means that in Paul's thought the conceptions of the church as the new people of God and the true people of God stand side by side. It is the new people of God where the conception of the dismissal of Israel from salvation history is the dominant factor; it is the true people of God in so far as what had always held true in Israel is made manifest in the church. This juxtaposition of opposition and continuity has a definite function in terms of the content of Paul's thought: it explains his understanding of law and gospel, or rather, of the relationship of the gospel to the law.

Paul does not disparage the religious behaviour of the Jews. Rather, he bears out their zeal for the law (Rom. 10.2). But he asserts that this zeal is in vain. For their works serve to establish their own righteousness, and it is this that is the false direction. Nevertheless, revelation remains related to the empirical Israel; this remains the historical starting point. Indeed, it is precisely because of his distinction between the empirical Israel and the elect remnant of Israel that Paul can avoid disruption. So he undertakes a positive move of reconciliation, again precisely in the light of the present saving event – his mission to the Gentiles. This has, of course, the immediate purpose of exercising the ministry of reconciliation among the Gentiles, but in addition it is indirectly aimed at making Israel zealous for the salvation of the Gentiles, so that it is converted. In this way Paul finds a unity between his work as apostle to the Gentiles and his nature as a Jew.

On the basis of this theory, that the Jews will become zealous for the salvation of the Gentiles, Paul develops the historical forecast that at the end of history the Jews will be converted. But this becoming zealous cannot be imagined as a historical process. The Jews can only be zealous if they see that faith brings salvation and that the Gentiles have it, whereas they themselves do not. But if they can see that, then they themselves already believe and also have salvation. Finally, Paul sets out in fact to show that faith cannot be derivative, that it only arises from preaching. He makes his forecast on the basis of the demonstration that just as man cannot create his own salvation, so, too, he cannot destroy it against God's will. This forecast is a conclusion from the doctrine of predestination, that God has mercy on whom he will and that he hardens whom he will. We must realize that this is not a statement of a deterministic view of the world. For Paul, salvation and condemnation are not contrasted on the same level. He makes his statement as a promise of the gospel itself and in this way shows that God's salvation is free grace. However, Paul uses the statement, that God's promise remains itself, in a speculative way, because he wants to make it historically comprehensible and to derive future events directly from it. Of course, the speculative element is smaller than it seems to us, in that Paul believed that there would only be a short interval before the end, i.e. in that he imagined that the conversion of his people would be the result of his own work. His original intention breaks through when once again at the end of the passage the incomprehensibility of God's will to save is celebrated in a glowing hymn: ὅτι ἐξ αὐτοῦ καὶ δι' αὐτοῦ καὶ εἰς αὐτὸν τὰ πάντα (11.36).

These remarks will perhaps become clearer if we illustrate them from our own position in the church. It is analogous to Paul's position in Israel to the extent that the church is our past, the present bearer of the proclamation. We already find ourselves in a historical relationship to it. In it we hear the preaching and learn that we are not saved as Christians, but as believers. We inherit our membership of the church, but not faith. So the concept of the church, if the church is understood in the light of the proclamation, contains the constant distinction between the true church and the empirical church. The two cannot be separated, as in the idea of a purely spiritual community. The empirical church is promised that it is the true church, 'in Christ', against all appearances.

III Predestination and Theodicy

G. Nygren, *Das Prädestinationsproblem in der Theologie Augustins* (1956); E. Dinkler, 'Prädestination bei Paulus', *Festschrift für Günther Dehn* (1957), pp. 81–102; C. Müller (see literature on II above), pp. 75–89; U. Luz, *Der Geschichtsverständnis des Paulus* (1968), pp. 227–64.

Here, too, the main question is whether and to what extent the structure of faith is disclosed.

The fully developed theory of predestination put forward by orthodox Calvinism (eternal predestination of the individual to salvation or damnation) is a hindrance to understanding. Behind it lies a concept of God which is connected with the transformation of the first beginnings in the Reformation into a theory about God and the world: the statement that God brings about everything is no longer related strictly to revelation and understanding, but has itself become the *credendum*. This immediately raises the question, in terms of a view of the world: what, then, is the relationship between divine determination and human freedom, God's omnipotence and the responsibility of man? Can I know to what I am predestined? These are pseudo-questions, which are to be seen as such from the original conception of predestination. Originally, predestination represented liberation from concern for myself on the basis of the word that tells me that my salvation is already taken care of. I do not receive an answer to the question of my care, but the care itself is superseded. God does not reveal a doctrine of predestination, but his grace. In this way I learn my determination. I do not find that I am elected through self-observation, but through hearing. So originally predestination does not amount to a theory about God's rule at all; it is an explanation of what I am when I hear the gospel. I am elect in hearing it. In this situation of hearing, the statement that God does everything is strictly related to his revelation. And what does the question of human freedom look like from here? The theological explanation is not that my action is generally determined by alien factors, but that I can do nothing to achieve my own salvation. The *servum arbitrium* is the condition of the *libertas christiana*.

Historical presuppositions: Paul goes back to the Old Testament (Rom. 9.13: Mal. 3.2f.). The idea of predetermination is developed in apocalyptic: 'And thou didst set apart Jacob for thyself, but Esau thou didst hate' (IV Ezra 3.16). It is heightened in the Qumran texts (1 QS III 15ff.; cf. 1 QS XI 10ff.).

Paul discusses predestination thematically only in Rom. 9–11. There he introduces it into a context in which he analyses the course of the proclamation. Predestination is a constitutive element of the event of preaching, i.e. it has no independent function as a positive doctrine. It serves, rather, to draw out the character of revelation as grace – in so far as it is contained in all Paul's writings. It guarantees the 'through grace alone' and hence the 'from faith alone', by preventing man from reserving a particular share in salvation for himself.

The conceptuality appears in a compressed form in Rom. 8.28f.

Here the election terminology is permeated with the mystical conception of the Son and the brothers (see above). This in fact means that when Paul speaks of God's counsel, he is from the beginning setting it in a twofold relationship: (a) to the saving event in Christ; (b) to the man who is encountered by this saving event. What he says does not apply to man in general, but only to those who are in Christ. To this corresponds the continuation with the catena on v. 30. It is wrong method to systematize the individual concepts as a series of different metaphysical acts or different stages of inner experience. The sequence is simply meant to point to the whole extent of salvation as God's act.

The relationship between pre-historical counsel ($\pi\rho oo\rho i\zeta\epsilon\iota\nu$) and historical vocation ($\kappa\alpha\lambda\epsilon\hat{\iota}\nu$) is a constitutive element here. The starting point for the two is the call given through the preaching. The $\pi\rho oo\rho i\zeta\epsilon\iota\nu$ (or the $\pi\rho\acute{o}\theta\epsilon\sigma\iota\varsigma$) designates the horizon within which it is understood, or rather, within which I see myself. Otherwise the usage of individual words is not strict; in Rom. 9.11f, καλεῖν is hardly different from πρόθεσις. The aim of the doctrine of predestination is not to explain from outside what election and damnation are, and not even to explain who is elect and who is damned. Election and damnation are not theologically on the same plane. Damnation is only mentioned as the shadow which is cast by election from grace. It ensures the purity of the gospel message.

Election implies the destruction of καύχησις; it alone guarantees man's salvation. In this context, there can be no question of man under grace or under condemnation as a theological theme.

The question whether election applies primarily to the individual or to a collective is an irrelevant one. The church is entrusted with the message; it calls the individual and grants him election.

On the basis of his starting point, Paul can simply reject the problem of theodicy: what is moulded has no right to question the moulder. This answer seems unsatisfactory. The question seems to be cut off at the point where man's being becomes obscure to him. In fact, Paul gives no answer if God is objectivized as the omnipotent, the embodiment of the absolute, of being. But if it is understood as a reference to the God who has shown his grace in Christ, then Paul's answer is the only possible one. In that case, the question as such is superseded. It is then clear that just as no claim can be made upon God for salvation, so, too, no protest is possible.

32 · THE CHURCH

Literature in Bultmann, *Theology of the New Testament* I, pp. 364f.; W. G. Kümmel, 'Das Urchristentum', *ThR* NF 22 (1954), pp. 138f.; R. Schnackenburg, *New Testament Theology Today* (1963), pp. 119f.; N. A. Dahl, *Das Volk Gottes* (1941); L. Cerfaux, *La Théologie de l'Église suivant saint Paul* (1948²); A. Oepke, 'Leib Christi oder Volk Gottes bei Paulus?', *ThLZ* 79 (1954), cols. 363–68; R. Schnackenburg, *Die Kirche im Neuen Testament* (1961), pp. 146–56; E. Schweizer, *Church Order in the New Testament*, SBT 32 (1961), pp. 89–104.

I Foundations

Paul takes over the eschatological conceptuality of salvation history:

ἐκκλησία, ἅγιοι, ἐκλεκτοί.[1] The church is the Israel of God (Gal. 6.16), the new covenant (II Cor. 3.6ff.; cf. the eucharistic tradition). These concepts contain the following connotations: 1. it is the last time; 2. the church is set apart from the world; 3. it is a visible assembly, primarily for worship. For the latter, the constitutive element is calling upon the Lord, the acclamation of the Kyrios. In this way it is made clear that the church is not a this-worldly entity. That the Lord rules and that the church makes his rule known to the world is visible only in the confession itself and – as a consequence – in the suffering of the confessor. The word ἐκκλησία can denote the individual community, e.g. when it occurs in the plural (Rom. 16.4; I Cor. 16.1, 19). But the idea of the church does not begin with the individual community. The church is primarily the whole church, which is particularized in the individual community (cf. the use of the singular: ἡ ἐκκλησία τοῦ θεοῦ Gal. 1.13). For Paul there is no all-embracing church organization.

Karl Holl assumed that the well-known collection which Paul made for the Jerusalem community was a church tax. It presupposed the acknowledgment of the group of apostles as a church authority. But the collection is simply the demonstration of the unity of the church through an act of love.[2]

What is true of the relationship of the church to the communities, that the one church is primary and makes possible the existence of the individual community, is true *mutatis mutandis* of the relationship of the community to the individual: the community is the prior entity, even though from an empirical point of view it of course comes into being by people believing and thus assembling together. But they know that the nature of their community is not determined by its meeting together (on the basis of their resolve), but by the summons from a church which already exists.

In relation to the world, the church is 'holy', i.e. marked off from the world (in what sense, see below). It is exclusive:[3] one God – one Lord; a man cannot sit at the Lord's table and at the demons' table. This distinguishes the church from the mystery groups. The practical problems caused by this exclusiveness are shown in I Cor. 8–10. Historically, the exclusiveness is an inheritance from Judaism. In

---

[1] Cf. the heading in I Cor. 1.1f.
[2] Cf. D. Georgi, *Die Geschichte der Kollekte des Paulus für Jerusalem*, ThF 38 (1965).
[3] See Bultmann, *Theology of the New Testament* I, pp. 100ff.

practice, it expresses the fact that the new life in the spirit is historical life in the community. The church exists not only in worship, as a cultic assembly, but in a permanent form. This is shown, for instance, in its concern for welfare.

Otherwise, everything is still free. One can hardly speak of an organization. There are still no definite administrative officials.[1] The office of the elder is unknown to Paul. The separation of the world is not organized; the Christians do not separate themselves externally from the world (as does, say, the Qumran sect). The Christians do not generally break off relationships to their environment. They remain in the world, not only because a break in relationships would be impossible, but also because of the fearlessness and freedom of faith (I Cor. 5.9ff.; 8ff.; Rom. 14f.). Faith in God as the creator is put into practice. The earth is the Lord's. The church practises the attitude of those who have already been freed from the world and therefore do not first have to organize their separation in order to achieve salvation.

Departure from civic ordinances would require the appointing of new, 'Christian' ordinances, which would then be taken to be holy. This would mean the organization of a sacral sphere. This is the very idea that the church negates. The dialectic of its relationship with the world is depicted in I Cor. 7.17ff.: Paul appeals to each person to remain in his own κλῆσις. Here, too, freedom is practised simply: no worldly status can hinder faith and none can further it. Eschatological, critical neutrality to the world prevails.

These ideas are at least approached even before Paul. Paul's specific contribution is that he thinks through their theological significance. This is shown by means of four examples: 1. the eschatological understanding of the church; 2. worship; 3. the position of the individual in the church; 4. the concept of the 'body of Christ'.

II   Church and Eschaton

The church does not yet live in the new age, but in the last time of the world. Paul imagines that this will be extremely short (I Cor. 7.29; Rom. 13.11; Phil. 4.5). He hopes that he himself will be alive to experience the end (I Thess. 4.17). What conclusions does he draw from this? He does not give an apocalyptic interpretation of the world situation, or calculate apocalyptic signs and periods – that is

---

[1] Phil. 1.1: ἐπίσκοποι and διάκονοι; I Thess. 5.12: κοπιῶντες and προϊστάμενοι; among the charismata in I Cor. 12.28: ἀντιλήμψεις and κυβερνήσεις. For the whole, see H. von Campenhausen, *Kirchliches Amt und geistliche Vollmacht*, BHTh 14 (1953).

what he rejects (I Thess. 5.1ff.). But, 'Let us then cast off the works of darkness' (Rom. 13.12).

Eschatology is not detached from Paul's conception of time. But there is no speculation about time. It is only considered as the time of the church, which is regarded as an intermediate period: the church is a foundation for the period from the resurrection to the parousia. The space of time is not understood as a new epoch or world history – Paul is not aware of any Christian interpretation of history; it is exclusively defined as the time in which the church proclaims the death of the Lord. As a result, it constantly qualifies the world as a transitory one, by measuring it against the eschaton: the sufferings of the present time are not ἄξια to be compared with the future glory (Rom. 8.18). This is the time in which the Lord rules through the word that proclaims his Lordship and leads faith into suffering.

From a historical point of view, this definition of the church is a reinterpretation of the apocalyptic idea of the messianic intermediate kingdom. The difference lies in the fact that for Paul it is already present, in the church. Of course, Paul does not call this βασιλεία Χριστοῦ. For him, 'the rule of Christ' means the exercising of Christ's Lordship during this time, the carrying out of the work of salvation, the subjection of the powers.

How can a community which understands itself eschatologically, that is, as a visible community which is not of this world, exist in practice? Is not every organization a piece of worldliness? On the other hand, how is historical existence possible without organization? The leading criterion is the question, how is the church to be shaped in the light of its foundation, the saving act, and the task presented with it, that of preaching? What role is played by the spirit? The following points relate to the question of organization; community life receives its ordering from the fact that Christ has died for the brethren. Over against the world, Paul steers a critical middle course between rejection of the world and a programme of Christian shaping of the world, by showing that the church is holy and that it possesses its holiness 'in Christ'.

III   Worship

If holiness is defined as a strange holiness in Christ, which is experienced through the word, then there is a cult only in the sense of hearing. There is no question of it having a particular influence on God. The one-sided movement from above downwards may not be reversed again in the cult, say, by the offering of a sacrifice through priests.

Again, Paul begins from the primitive Christian beginnings and thinks further ahead. The first Christians could still participate in the Jewish cult. But in fact they had deprived it of value, because they expected salvation from their faith. Preaching, confession, hymns, prayer and the two sacraments make up the Christian assemblies. The question is, how this worship is now understood; is it a new method of influencing God, like a sacrifice or the offering of gifts to gain his good pleasure, or an action to bring about holiness? The acquiring of such effects will soon once again be bound up with correct ritual performance, with consecrated people, rooms, times, utensils (altar). What role does the spirit play? Will the movement from above downwards be preserved in thought here, as well, or will the spirit be understood as the power of ascent to God?

Paul defines the cultic in terms of the *theologia crucis*, as he does the nature of the spirit and its effects;[1] the cult is not man's action towards God. Even prayer is not man's own possibility of influencing God, but the activity of the spirit (Rom. 8.26), made possible by the fact that the Lord intercedes to God for us (I Cor. 5.2; 8.34). Confession of the Lord is acknowledgment of his rule and its proclamation, not a spiritual ascent to him. Liturgy, places, rites, have no role at all. When the Galatians revere cosmic elements, they are told that they have lapsed into servitude, into the law. The presence of God or the Lord in the church is not associated with any mystical conception. When Paul says that God is ἐν ὑμῖν (I Cor. 14.25), he simply means the same thing as Matt. 18.20: 'Where two or three are gathered in my name, there am I in the midst of them'. Experience as such has no value of its own. Of course, worship is an experience which is even expressed with ecstatic phenomena (I Cor. 12.14). But these have no value in themselves; they must be subordinated to a higher purpose, the 'edification' of the community. The οἰκοδομή is not understood in cultic terms, but as an ordering of the everyday common life of Christians. The spirit is manifested in individual details: 'For as πίστις is individualized in various concrete ways of acting, so divine χάρις is also individualized in various concrete gifts of grace.'[2] Here, of course, there is a temptation to develop an individual spiritualism. Paul counters this by arguing that the spirit has been primarily given to the community. Therefore the pneumatic is bound to it precisely as a result of his gift. The way in which the different standpoints and

---

[1] I Corinthians, esp. chs. 10–14.
[2] Rom. 12.6: see Bultmann, *Theology of the New Testament* I, p. 325.

expressions of the pneumatics divide the community at Corinth is impossible in the light of the spirit itself, for it is a spirit of peace. Paul must therefore at the same time correct the understanding of the spirit by the understanding of the church.

IV   Charismata

Bultmann, *Theology of the New Testament* I, pp. 153ff.; E. Schweizer, πνεῦμα, *TWNT* VI 413ff. *passim*, esp. 420; J. Brosch, *Charismen und Ämter in der Urkirche* (1951); G. Friedrich, 'Geist und Amt', *WuD* NF 3 (1952), pp. 73ff.; E. Kohlmeyer, 'Charisma oder Recht? Vom Wesen der ältesten Kirchenrechte', *ZSavRG* 69, Kanon. Abt. 38 (1952), pp. 2ff.; E. Käsemann, 'Sentences of Holy Law in the New Testament', *New Testament Questions of Today* (1969), pp. 66–81; H. Greeven, 'Die Geistesgaben bei Paulus', *WuD* NF 6 (1959), pp. 111–20; I. Herrmann, *Kyrios und Pneuma*, StANT 2 (1961), pp. 69ff.; W. Schrage, *Die konkreten Einzelgebote in der paulinischen Paränese* (1961), pp. 141–46.

For Paul it goes without saying that the spirit manifests itself in visible workings: ecstasy, glossolalia, visions, wonders. But these phenomena are not themselves the criteria of Christian existence. They in turn need assessing. In itself, ecstasy is ambiguous. It can also be pagan and demonic (I Cor. 12.2). The criterion which Paul sets up is an objective one, confession of the Lord (I Cor. 12.3). That means that the manifestations are to be judged according to the extent that they edify the church of the Lord (I Cor. 14.26; and ch. 14).[1] There is therefore an order of value: comprehensible prophecy – contrary to the judgment of the Corinthians – has precedence over incomprehensible glossolalia. Paul sets the church over these phenomena by regulating the appearance of the pneumatics (I Cor. 14.39f.). How is that possible, if the spirit blows where it wills? The spirit is free, but not arbitrary. It appears where the Lord is made known. So the spirit itself becomes the principle of church order.

The doctrine of the gifts of the spirit has still another side. So far we have been talking about the spirit in so far as it is expressed in individual phenomena, in particular persons and moments. This understanding is universal in primitive Christianity. It was particularly cherished in Corinth, but tied by Paul to the confession and the church. It is not the pneumatic who becomes the subject of theology, but the spirit, as a factor in the edification of the church.

[1] P. Vielhauer, *Oikodome* (1939), pp. 9off.; G. Bornkamm, 'Zum Verständnis des Gottesdienstes bei Paulus', in *Das Ende des Gesetzes*, Gesammelte Aufsätze I (1961³), pp. 113ff.

Alongside this, Paul presupposes that the spirit is the gift which constantly fills all Christians. That, too, is a view which was common in Christianity before Paul.[1] Paul also actualizes this conception by destroying Corinthian enthusiasm: the work of the spirit is not only ecstasy, but any service to the community (I Cor. 12.8–11). Pneumatics are no longer prominent individuals. All Christians are pneumatics to the degree that they serve the community. And indeed each has his own gift (I Cor. 12.4–7; cf. Rom. 12.3ff.). Thus the understanding of the spirit has become a theological one. Faith understands itself in its connection with the community. In this way, too, even the offices of ἐπίσκοποι, διάκονοι etc. can be understood theologically, without a hierarchical concept of office.

The workings of the spirit are not a manifestation of the 'eternal in the today' (this is the view in Corinth). 'The eternal' appears on the cross, in the preaching of the cross. The workings of the spirit disclose the very transitoriness in which we now possess the new life. They will pass away with this world. Paul thus stresses the eschatological qualification. In their place, he points to what remains: faith, hope, love.

The sequence of the three concepts is variable. Cf. the structure of I Cor. 12–14: ch. 13 interrupts the remarks about the charismata. It has so little connection with the context which precedes and follows that it is at least possible that it may have been introduced into its present position by later redaction. On the other hand, there are direct connections between chs. 12 and 14. The most obvious assumption is that the basic material in ch. 13 arose independently, and was then put in context by Paul in such a way as to make love the criterion of the charismata. Exegetes dispute whether love is itself a charisma (Bornkamm, *Aufsätze* I, p. 100, n. 18, says that it is not). But the dispute is a useless one. In summing up the triad in I Cor. 12.31, as 'higher gifts', Paul is in any case designating them as the criteria: through their permanence it can be seen that the charismata are limited to the period of the church in the world.

V The Unity of the Church (σῶμα Χριστοῦ)

H. Schlier, *Christus und die Kirche im Epheserbrief*, BHTh 6 (1930); E. Käsemann, *Leib und Leib Christi*, BHTh 9 (1933); id., 'The Pauline Doctrine of the Lord's Supper', *Essays on New Testament Themes*, SBT 41 (1964), pp. 108–35; E. Percy, *Der Leib Christi*, LUA NF 38 (1942); G. Bornkamm, 'Zum Verständnis des Gottesdienstes bei Paulus' (1952), in *Das Ende des Gesetzes*, Gesammelte Aufsätze I (1961³), pp. 113ff.; J. A. T. Robinson, *The Body*, SBT 5 (1952); E. Schweizer, 'Die Kirche als Leib Christi in den paulinischen Homologumena', *ThLZ* 86 (1961), cols. 161–74

---

[1] R. Bultmann, *Theology of the New Testament* I, pp. 153ff.

(=*Neotestamentica* (1963), pp. 272–92); id., σῶμα, *TWNT* VII 1064ff.; E. Brandenburger, *Adam und Christus*, WMANT 7 (1962), pp. 151ff.

In paraenesis, Paul can work with the image of the body as an organism with members (I Cor. 12). Therefore Paul's idea of the church largely takes the pattern of an organism, and the life of the church is seen as growth and development in the world. But in Paul, this picture of the body is in no way a beginning or basis or even a direct representation of the idea of the church itself. It is an *ad hoc* means of description, and one that is widespread in antiquity.[1] Paul uses it only to make one point: that the individual is a member of the church and has his separate existence only as such.

The literal use of σῶμα is to be distinguished from the metaphorical usage. Here the church is not only *like* a body (an organism); it *is the* body. As a result, being a member is also defined in a different way: the body is regarded as a sphere which includes its members within itself. At the root of this understanding lies a mythological, and not a realistic, conception of the body.

This distinction between the metaphorical and the literal use of the word is not beyond dispute.[2] In fact, the evidence is complicated. In I Cor. 12.12ff., Paul first of all depicts the body as an organism in broad terms. Then follows the formulation 12.27: ὑμεῖς δέ ἐστε σῶμα Χριστοῦ. This also illuminates the expression in v. 12: . . . οὕτως καὶ ὁ Χριστός. If we interpret it precisely, then Christ is the body that we form. But it can also be explained as an abbreviated form of expression: 'thus it is with Christ and us'. But the next sentence (v. 13) does not fit into the picture of an organism. There the point is the difference, the individual contribution of each member; here, it is their equality. It is not the members that constitute the body, but the body that constitutes the members.[3] The same unity appears in the formulation in Gal. 3.26–28: you are one, the one man.

Physical and social distinctions are done away with in the body of Christ. This sublimation is to be distinguished from the idea of a universal equality: it has its place 'in Christ'. This idea is not understandable in the light of the organism; it only makes sense in terms of the body as the comprehensive sphere.

The same idea appears in connection with the eucharistic tradition in I Cor. 10.16f.: the sacramentally acquired share in the body of Christ makes us the body of Christ.

---

[1] The fable of Menenius Agrippa, e.g. in Livy, II 32.

[2] But see F. Mussner, *Christus, das All und die Kirche*, TThS 5 (1955); against him, E. Käsemann, *ThLZ* 81 (1956), cols. 585–90. Cf. P. Neuenzeit, *Das Herrenmahl*, StANT 1 (1960), pp. 201–19.

[3] R. Bultmann, *Theology of the New Testament* I, p. 310.

The origin of the expression 'body of Christ' probably lies here, in the eucharistic tradition. There is no other model either in the history of religion or in the history of the concept. Besides, Paul only uses the expression once outside the eucharistic tradition: I Cor. 12.27. Elsewhere, the formulation he uses is 'one body (in Christ)'. This origin of the expression does not, of course, explain how it is understood by Paul, and with what conceptions he associates it.

H. Schlier, in particular, has clarified the historical origin of the conceptions contained in this concept.[1] He derives it from the mythical conception of the primal man which is attested in gnosticism. This man is both in heaven and in the world, and gathers his own to himself and ascends again (as the redeemed redeemer). The investigations were taken further by E. Käsemann. He pursues the understanding of the body in Hellenism: there 'I' have a body; man consists of soul and body; their relationship is defined in terms of the relationship between form and matter. In gnosticism, on the other hand, the body has me; it is a sphere. According to Käsemann, the starting point is the cosmological aeon-myth (aeon= world-god; the world=his body), which has been transformed in the anthropological myth of the primal man.[2]

H. Hegermann[3] points to Jewish speculations; in Alexandria, the aeon–conception was modified by speculations about Sophia and the Logos. C. Colpe[4] also draws attention to Philonic speculations: the world is 'the greatest body, which embraces the fullness of other bodies as its own parts' (Plant. 7).

All these attempts at derivation have right elements in them, but they are still not satisfactory. The cosmological derivation is not sufficient. A transformation of the cosmological myth into an anthropological one cannot be demonstrated. What has happened, rather, is that a cosmological and an anthropological element have been combined. The anthropological element is still detectable in Jewish speculation about Adam as the primal man of cosmic dimensions.[5] E. Schweizer again stresses the Greek components: σῶμα is a periphrasis for the unity of a totality consisting of different members. In addition, the conception of the tribal ancestor who includes his descendants in himself (corporate personality) appears in Paul, as does the idea of the body of the Crucified One, who now lives and determines the being of the baptized.

Now what is the significance of this concept? Käsemann writes: 'For the conception of the church as the body of Christ is the adequate expression for a community which carries on a worldwide mission in the name of Christ. In this respect it far surpasses the other concep-

---

[1] Schlier, op. cit., though he only accepts the proper meaning of σῶμα for Colossians and Ephesians. He interprets the passages in I Corinthians and Romans in terms of the idea of an organism.

[2] Naassene sermon; Mithras liturgy.

[3] H. Hegermann, Die Vorstellung vom Schöpfungsmittler im hellenistischen Judentum und Urchristentum, TU 82 (1961), p. 148.

[4] C. Colpe, 'Zur Leib-Christi-Vorstellung im Epheserbrief', BZNW 26 (Jeremias Festschrift) (1960), pp. 172–87.

[5] Cf. Schweizer, op. cit.; Brandenburger, op. cit.; J. Jervell, Imago Dei, FRLANT 76 (1960).

tions of the people of God and the family of God.'[1] But is the conception really adequate? In any case, Paul must not have noticed that,
although he himself created the conception. How does he make use
of it? Only sporadically! It does not become a theme in itself. It is
echoed only a couple of times, and then hardly in soteriology, or in
respect of the world mission (for this, see rather Rom. 9–11), but in
paraenesis (Rom. 12.5). One certainly cannot say that it is 'adequate',
simply because it is primarily a mythical conception concerned with
space and collectivity. Moreover, it is dangerous, as it encourages
speculative constructions. It would then no longer serve merely as an
interpretation, but the meaning of the conception would become
completely self-contained; it would become an object of meditation.
The σῶμα Χριστοῦ would be understood as the mystical body of Christ.
In that case, redemption would be achieved by the vision of the
world-embracing Christ, who is identical with the church. There is
thus the danger that the direction of movement might become
reversed, that the 'body of Christ' would no longer mean our acceptance into the saving event but our possibility of ascent. Käsemann
himself points out that christology and ecclesiology are not interchangeable. That is true, but it is precisely this fact that Paul has to
make clear by other remarks, because the expression 'body of Christ'
is insufficient. What positive contribution can the conception make?
It indicates the 'dimension' of the church, its temporal priority: the
church is not formed by the assembly of believers; it is there before
them and first makes this assembly possible.

Aspects of priority

(a) The place of salvation lies above the world. In this way, both
its objectivity and the direction of its movement are established: from
above to me. This statement still remains in the realm of ideas, but it
became comprehensible as a determination of existence. That the
saving event transcends its visible sphere, the world, in fact means
that preaching is capable of putting the world in its power. We therefore have a quite unmythical situation, the very making possible of
preaching. The believers for their part exist in the world, but not
from the world. Of course, such a remark sounds commonplace, and
it must be made more precise. In what sense is it to be understood?
Existence is not given any mystery-type connotations. The church is

[1] E. Käsemann, 'Paul and Early Catholicism', *New Testament Questions of Today*
(1969), pp. 236–51.

neither a copy of the heavenly world nor its cult a copy of the heavenly cult. Such a notion would lead to a fantasy existence. Were that the case, Christ would indeed be constituted by the church, and not *vice versa*.

(b) All worldly distinctions are done away with in the body of Christ (I Cor. 12.13; Gal. 3.27f.; cf. Col. 3.11). The physical, social and other distinctions among men are not disputed; it is taken for granted that they should exist in the world, but in the church they are robbed of all force. This transcendence of distinctions cannot be made into a Christian programme for changing the world. If it were, the distinctions would be reactivated, though now under a Christian title. For example, in I Cor. 11.2ff., Paul protests against the emancipation of women, through which the woman elevates her status as the copy of man so that it becomes the content of her own confession. Against this, Paul argues that the woman is called as a woman, that she can remain what she is in the world, and precisely for that reason may not imitate man. The removal of distinctions immediately becomes comprehensible if it is understood as a rule for the life of the church: what does a community look like from this perspective? This removal of distinctions makes true worldliness possible. The ordinances of the world are there, but they are neutral in relation to salvation. In this way, the world is opened up as a sphere of movement.

(c) One further aspect is the unity given in the σῶμα Χριστοῦ, which forms the basis of the appeal to be of one heart. Once again, the unity is not made by the conduct of the members; they simply portray it.[1]

Summary

Paul modifies the essentially timeless, mythical, spatial conception by conceiving of it in historical terms: he understands the body as the sphere in which the baptized live together, experience newness of life and put it into practice. In other words, here is the sphere of Christ's rule. It is the sphere of faith, defined as the sphere of freedom, as the possibility of confronting the world. How is this translation into a historical understanding possible? The possibility is shown in I Cor. 10.16f., where the ecclesiological significance of σῶμα is associated with the sacramental significance, with the saving event, the dead body of Christ.[2] We enter the body of Christ by obtaining a share in the death of Christ. Thus we stand in the community in which the

[1] Rom. 12.5 and I Cor. 12.13; developed in Eph. 4.4–6.
[2] In Rom. 7.4, the body of Christ is his dead body.

Crucified One is proclaimed as the universal Lord. In this way we are given brothers, and thus life together has its historical character. It is no longer played out in cultic terms reminiscent of the mysteries, but in concrete everyday giving and receiving.

σῶμα Χριστοῦ and ἐν Χριστῷ

The mythical interpretation of σῶμα brings with it a tendency to explain the formula ἐν Χριστῷ as 'in the body of Christ', following the analogy of 'in Adam' (I Cor. 15.22).[1] Scholars widely recognize that the ἐν formula has been developed from the conception of Christ as the universal personality.[2] Now it is beyond dispute that the areas of σῶμα and ἐν overlap: Gal. 3.26–28. But they do not coincide. The derivation from 'in Adam' is itself questionable. This phrase is an *ad hoc* construction, which has been made from the formula 'in Christ', which is already presupposed.[3] Statistics show that the ἐν formula reaches much wider, especially in soteriology. Even the formal meaning of ἐν cannot be inferred from a spatial conception. The preposition has the significance of a 'general definition of circumstances'.[4] A personal, spatial conception is associated with the formula ἐν Χριστῷ only on the periphery of its appearances (in the Galatians passage, mentioned above). σῶμα primarily means what embraces us; ἐν Χριστῷ defines the place of the saving event as lying outside us. 'In Christ' can be interchanged with 'Christ in us' and 'in the spirit'. 'In Christ' is the characteristic of the intermediate period. The very phrase 'one body in Christ' (Rom. 12.5) shows that the two areas do not coincide.

33 · THE SAVING EVENT IN THE PROCLAMATION: THE OFFICE OF PREACHING

R. Asting, *Die Verkündigung des Wortes im Urchristentum* (1939); J. Brosch, *Charismen und Ämter in der Urkirche* (1951); H. Greeven, 'Propheten, Lehrer, Vorsteher bei

---

[1] R. Bultmann, *Theology of the New Testament* I, p. 311.
[2] W. G. Kümmel, in H. Lietzmann, *An die Korinther* I, II, HNT 9 (1949[4]); A. Oepke, *TWNT* II 538.
[3] M. Bouttier, *En Christ* (1962), p. 120.
[4] F. Neugebauer (see literature on section 24 IV); cf. the contrast: in the law, in Christ.

Paulus', *ZNW* 44 (1952/3), pp. 1–43; H. von Campenhausen and E. Schweizer, see on section 7 I; E. Käsemann, 'Ministry and Community in the New Testament', *Essays on New Testament Themes*, SBT 41 (1964), pp. 63–94.

Paul's understanding of ministry cannot be explained from his thoughts about his own position. Such an explanation would be a circular one. Certainly his understanding of ministry is determined by the experience of his call: Paul received his commission directly from the risen Lord. Therefore he is an apostle, with a precisely circumscribed task: to preach the gospel to the Gentiles. Theologically, this means that he has not only to make known the *sola fide*, but also to practise it. In speaking of his ministry, he does not describe his inner experience, but his external determination by the cross (II Cor. 4.7ff.). He can describe his commission as χάρις. He understands it as grace, in realizing that he does not have the capability of carrying it out from his own resources (II Cor. 3.5). Paul even derives his understanding of ministry from the character of the saving event as word.[1] He defines preaching as 'the word of the cross'. In this way, Paul rejects any understanding of salvation along the lines of the mysteries. Positive points are: this content corresponds to (*a*) the form of the preaching; (*b*) the appearance of the preacher; (*c*) the form of the community (I Cor. 1.18ff.). For the world, the preaching is folly. Just as the preaching cannot be translated into immediately comprehensible wisdom, so, too, there is no authority in the preacher which points beyond folly and weakness.

This is the main theme of II Corinthians. In Corinth, the authority of Paul is disputed: he does not have a convincing appearance, he does not possess the power of convincing speech. Against this, Paul argues that his authority does not rest on his personality, but on the character of his preaching. This demands that the preacher shall not make himself the subject of his proclamation: οὐ γὰρ ἑαυτοὺς κηρύσσομεν ἀλλὰ Χριστὸν Ἰησοῦν κύριον, ἑαυτοὺς δὲ δούλους ὑμῶν διὰ Ἰησοῦν (II Cor. 4.5). Paul deliberately refrains from demonstrating his strength as a pneumatic and visionary. The only legitimate form of the strength of the preacher is one that accords with the cross. Paul understands his fate, his weakness in the light of the cross: in it appears the working of the cross. The remarks about the sorry form of his appearance are not a personal outcry, but an interpretation of the event of proclamation (they are therefore not a 'mysticism of suffering').[2]

---

[1] The establishment of the λόγος τῆς καταλλαγῆς and the διακονία τῆς καταλλαγῆς is part of the establishment of the καταλλαγή. In this way, both the content of the preaching and the authority of the preacher are defined positively and controlled critically.

[2] E. Güttgemanns, *Der leidende Apostel und sein Herr*, FRLANT 90 (1966).

By subjecting himself to the criterion of the cross, Paul possesses real authority, because he does not claim it for himself. It is the authority of service.[1] In the sense of this authority, he refuses to 'commend' himself to the Corinthians (II Cor. 3.1ff.); he shows his παρρησία and πεποίθησις on the basis of his higher legitimation. Thus we have the paradox: he is no more than a servant – but he claims superhuman authority. He will be judged by no man – and subjects himself to the judgment of the Corinthians' conscience (II Cor. 4.2; 5.11). They think him presumptuous. He disputes that, because he raises his claim as the claim of what he represents, at the same time renouncing human honour. He refrains from boasting: but he boasts (II Cor. 11f.), with the qualification that he speaks as a fool, with the aim of taking the Corinthians' boasting to extremes. His renunciation of self-glorification is the condition on which he can describe the positive effect of his ministry: II Cor. 2.15f. The originally apocalyptic conception of judgment and separation is used here to interpret encounter with his preaching.

Paul can also describe the nature of his preaching in conceptions drawn from salvation history: service in the new covenant (II Cor. 3.4–18); and also in cosmological conceptions: as a new creation which takes place through preaching (II Cor. 4.4–6; cf. 5.17).

Paul's personal relationship to his office is also determined theologically. He must give an account of his ministry at the judgment. There he will produce his community as the evidence for his work (II Cor. 1.14; I Thess. 2.19; Phil. 2.16). Here he seems to touch on the idea of merit. But he does not lapse into this line of thinking: ἐὰν γὰρ εὐαγγελίζωμαι, οὐκ ἔστιν μοι καύχημα · ἀνάγκη γάρ μοι ἐπίκειται · οὐαὶ γάρ μοί ἐστιν ἐὰν μὴ εὐαγγελίσωμαι. εἰ γὰρ ἑκὼν τοῦτο πράσσω, μισθὸν ἔχω· εἰ δὲ ἄκων, οἰκονομίαν πεπίστευμαι (I Cor. 9.16f.). Because of this account that he must give, he is concerned that the community shall not split up and the Pauline communities break off from the rest of the church. Therefore the making of the collection for the Jerusalem community is a theological necessity for him, as a visible demonstration of the unity of the church.

There is no organization of the whole church, but only minimal beginnings of organization in the individual communities. But no form of organization is capable as such of bringing salvation; there is no holy form of community life; only one which is appropriate to its

[1] The self-designations δοῦλος and διάκονος are not an expression of personal humility, but designations of office; see the prescript of Romans.

end. There is no hierarchy of ministries, no priestly state with a position of mediating salvation, no separation of clergy and laity, no firm regulating of the cult, but only the occasional instruction when the 'management' threatens to get out of control (I Cor. 14). Even here, however, no definite liturgy is introduced – cultic enthusiasm is guarded against, but that is all. The Corinthians are not initiated into fixed forms of cult, but called to οἰκοδομή.

The relation between spirit and ministry is much disputed.[1] Rudolf Sohm set the two in opposition: in the original church there was only charismatic authority and not ministerial authority, and therefore no church law. The charismatic received his instruction directly. No other authority, no legal regulation could get in his way. Against Sohm, Harnack argued that there had been a legal organization in the church right from the beginning. Holl introduced a synthesis, by claiming to find a twofold concept of the church: that of the primitive community (understood in legal terms) and that of Paul (charismatic). Bultmann[2] tries to get beyond this way of putting the question by investigating the legitimacy of each of the understandings of the church, and seeking criteria for evaluation.

In fact, the rule of the spirit cannot be regulated. But this spirit itself creates tradition, and therefore law. The content of the preaching of the charismatics is not simply given by inspiration, but is bound up with the kerygma.[3] The constitutive element is the making present of the saving event. The spirit does not lead beyond the cross. It is understood as the spirit of the Exalted One, whom we can grasp in preaching and sacrament as the Crucified One.

34 · INCORPORATION IN THE CHURCH THROUGH THE SACRAMENTS

Baptism: W. Heitmüller, O. Cullmann, G. Delling, G. R. Beasley-Murray, G. Braumann and J. Ysebaert (see section 7 III); K. Barth, *The Teaching of the Church*

---

[1] Cf. section 7 I. Literature is also mentioned there.
[2] R. Bultmann, *Theology of the New Testament* II, pp. 95ff.
[3] Bultmann, *ibid.*, p. 103; E. Käsemann, 'Sentences of Holy Law in the New Testament', *New Testament Questions of Today* (1969), pp. 66–81.

regarding Baptism (1948); against him, H. Schlier, 'Zur kirchlichen Lehre von der Taufe', *ThLZ* 72 (1947), cols. 321–36 (=*Die Zeit der Kirche* (1956), pp. 107–29); E. Fuchs, *Die Freiheit des Glaubens* (1949), pp. 27ff.; id., *Das Sakrament im Licht der neueren Exegese* (1954); R. Schnackenburg, *Baptism in the Thought of St Paul* (1964); G. Bornkamm, 'Taufe und neues Leben' (1952), in: *Das Ende des Gesetzes*, Gesammelte Aufsätze I (1961³), pp. 34–50; O. Kuss, 'Zur Frage einer vorpaulinischen Todestaufe', *MThZ* 4 (1953), pp. 1–17; G. Wagner, *Das religionsgeschichtliche Problem von Römer 6, 1–11*, AThANT 39 (1962); E. Lohse, 'Taufe und Rechtfertigung bei Paulus', *KuD* 11 (1965), pp. 308–24; N. Gäumann, *Taufe und Ethik*, BEvTh 47 (1967).

Eucharist: H. Lietzmann, E. Käsemann, G. Bornkamm, P. Neuenzeit, J. Betz on section 7 IV; H. von Soden, 'Sakrament und Ethik bei Paulus' (1931), in: *Das Paulusbild in der neueren deutschen Forschung* (1964), pp. 338–79; E. Rietschel, 'Der Sinn des Abendmahles nach Paulus', *EvTh* 18 (1958), pp. 269–84.

I Prospect and Problems

There is a dispute as to whether the word 'sacraments' can be used at all to describe the significance of baptism and the eucharist in Paul. Is not an alien element introduced simply by the use of the concept? It certainly does not appear in Paul.

To use a common nomenclature which takes in both baptism and eucharist means that the two are no longer seen independently, each for itself; instead, a pre-existing, all-embracing conception of the effect of rites (and perhaps substances) or a general definition of the relationship between 'sacrament' and 'word' is superimposed upon them.[1] Now the concept of sacrament can encourage erroneous suppositions. On the other hand, Paul hints at the beginnings of a comprehensive understanding which takes in both baptism and eucharist (I Cor. 10.1ff.).[2]

Karl Barth defines the effect of baptism as 'significative'. Wilhelm Heitmüller for long represented the opposite position: baptism works *ex opere operato*.[3] The relationship between baptism and justification poses a further problem: Albert Schweitzer claimed that the two stand side by side without connection. Where Paul deals with justification – in the first part of Romans – he omits baptism; where he deals with baptism, he says nothing about justification.

II Method

The starting point must be the understanding of the sacrament that Paul already finds in the community.[4] He finds there the baptismal

---

[1] See W. Trillhaas, *Dogmatik* (1962), pp. 354ff.
[2] Thus, rightly, E. Lohse.
[3] Cf. H. Schlier, *op. cit.*, p. 113.
[4] See G. Braumann.

confession, baptism in the name of Jesus, the idea of the transference of the saving event. The effect of baptism consists in the forgiveness of sins, being placed under the protection of the Lord, and the bestowal of the spirit. Paul's link with pre-Pauline tradition is clear at I Cor. 1.30; 6.11; II Cor. 1.21f. There is a dispute as to whether baptism was interpreted as the establishment of a community of fate with the death of Christ even before Paul. That is to be assumed, but the details cannot be followed up here. In the tradition and in Paul himself, it is taken for granted that the rite of baptism has a real effect (I Cor. 5.5; 15.29). Purely symbolic actions, in the modern sense, are unknown at the time. However, we can ask whether a remnant of magical thought has been left, which Paul has not worked over. The criterion will be whether the reality of the effect of baptism is to be seen only in terms of the mystery religions, or whether it can be understood theologically.

An analysis of the relationship of Paul to tradition shows a uniform direction in the Pauline interpretation of the sacraments. It leads to the notions of justification, of being in the church, of re-presentation and particularization in the περιπατεῖν (in the sense of an overall understanding of indicative and imperative).[1] This direction of interpretation works out in practice in a demarcation from an unhistorical understanding along the lines of the mystery religions (I Cor. 10).

III Sacrament and Ethics

The sacrament brings about salvation by transferring the saving event to the person being baptized.[2] But this transference is not a transformation of a mystery type, which alters man's *habitus*. A person can fall from salvation again; we do not possess salvation in ourselves, but in Christ. Baptism leads to the new way of life, to the community. Does Paul, then, ethicize the cultic, magical element? We can describe the evidence in this way when we realize that ethics is not an autonomous sphere, that it is not a man's way of life that makes the sacrament efficacious, but that this way of life is an effect of the

---

[1] E.g. at the end of Rom. 6: the key word is χάρισμα. Cf. E. Dinkler, 'Die Taufterminologie in 2 Kor. 1.21f.', SupplNovTest 6 (Cullmann Festschrift) (1962), pp. 173–91, esp. p. 190.

[2] E. Dinkler (see previous note) remarks that baptism is preceded by faith, to which salvation is given. But for Paul, baptism and faith do not form alternatives. Faith demands baptism.

sacrament itself. Precisely for that reason, when I refuse obedience, I annul the effect.

IV Baptism

A firm connection between faith and baptism is presupposed; on this rests the fact of the baptismal confession. Now as Paul interprets faith by the doctrine of justification, there is a close connection between baptism and justification in his writing. Both are particularly closely associated with the idea of the church (Gal. 3.26ff.; Rom. 6). The assertion made by Albert Schweitzer and others, that in Romans the two themes of justification and baptism are treated separately, is therefore erroneous. The overall evidence in the epistle must be considered:[1] (a) in Rom. 6 itself the basis of interpretation is the creed, i.e. faith; (b) the connection between baptism and the doctrine of justification is provided by the link between Rom. 4.25 and 5.1ff. Chapter 6 is directly attached to ch. 5. The theme is not baptism as such, but the peace which is brought about by justification: peace as freedom 1. from death (ch. 5); 2. from sin (ch. 6), the wages of which is death.

What is the effect of baptism? On the negative side it must be stated that it is not a symbolic content of the rite, in which the immersion symbolizes dying with Christ and the reappearance the rising with him. The positive effect can be illustrated by means of the controversy between Fuchs and Delling. Paul writes: We are baptized εἰς τὸν θάνατον αὐτοῦ, συνετάφημεν αὐτῷ, σύμφυτοι γεγόναμεν τῷ ὁμοιώματι τοῦ θανάτου αὐτοῦ (Rom. 6).

According to Fuchs, that does not mean that Christ's death is repeated in the rite of baptism and transferred to us (because the symbolism of the action does not play any part, see above), but that our death is anticipated in Christ's death, and that we are therefore made contemporaneous with his death.[2] So our salvation does not take place in baptism: it has happened with Christ. It is actualized in such a way that we are received into this salvation (in the body of Christ).[3]

[1] Thus, rightly, E. Lohse.

[2] Cf. G. Bornkamm, *Aufsätze* I, p. 37, 'We are immersed in his death'; p. 38: 'assignment to Christ'.

[3] G. Bornkamm, *op. cit.*, p. 41: 'The death died by the baptized person and Christ is only one, i.e. the death of Christ, and this becomes the death of believers through baptism.'

But an objection may be made. Does not the phrase σύμφυτοι
γεγόναμεν τῷ ὁμοιώματι τοῦ θανάτου αὐτοῦ mean that we have grown
together into the likeness of his death, i.e. with baptism? In that case,
this would be the saving event.

Lietzmann explains this phrase as an abbreviated expression: 'grown together
with him through the likeness'. In that case, baptism would be the transference.
Bornkamm shows that ὁμοίωμα τοῦ θανάτου αὐτοῦ does not designate baptism. Otherwise the continuation would be incomprehensible. But in that case, what does καὶ τῆς
ἀναστάσεως ἐσόμεθα mean? What is the significance of the future? The answer does
not cause any difficulty if we interpret the future 'logically'. In that case, it corresponds in practice to the present. But if it is meant temporally, the statement
becomes incomprehensible. The word ὁμοίωμα then requires another interpretation.

Concretely, ὁμοίωμα means the form of the Crucified One (cf. Rom.
7.4: ἐθανατώθητε . . . διὰ τοῦ σώματος τοῦ Χριστοῦ). On the one hand,
Paul has to say that we have really died with Christ. On the other, he
cannot say that we are σύμφυτοι τῷ θανάτῳ αὐτοῦ. That would be an
identification in terms of the mysteries, which is impossible for Paul.[1]

Delling's solution of the difficulties is that Paul does not mean
immersion in the body of Christ, but the transference of the work of
salvation to the person baptized. To baptize εἰς Χριστόν 'designates
the action of God in the person being baptized in respect of the saving
event, which is associated with the name of Christ'.[2]

Both Delling and Fuchs have correct insights. Both conceptions, of
contemporaneity and of the transference of the work of salvation,
occur in Paul. Both are already there before him, and are now
developed by him in a particular direction: (a) the transference of the
work of salvation, the significance of the name, the association with
the cross and the crucified body of Christ are already given by Paul's
reference back to the creed (Rom. 7.4; I Cor. 1.13); (b) the contemporaneity of baptism and the death of Christ arises from the association of baptism with the idea of the body of Christ and the interpretation of baptism by the σὺν Χριστῷ formula.[3] Paul makes the ὑπέρ
tradition (transference) present by his doctrine of justification; Rom.

[1] For ὁμοίωμα see Rom. 8.3: God sent his son ἐν ὁμοιώματι σαρκὸς ἁμαρτίας.
[2] G. Delling, op. cit., p. 80. Discussion with E. Fuchs, ibid., p. 73, n. 248.
[3] Delling does not do justice to this second group of ideas. Cf. the obscurity on
p. 79: 'He (sc. Paul) says in v. 6 that our old man has died with Christ on the cross,
cf. v. 8, and not "has died in baptism".' True, Delling aptly remarks that there is
no thought in Rom. 6 of being immersed in the body of Christ = the church; there
is simply a reference to the body of the cross in Rom. 7.4. But there is a connection
between baptism and the ecclesiological body of Christ in Gal. 3.26ff.

3; 4; 5; I Cor. 1. The 'mystery' tradition (contemporaneity) is interpreted by means of the σὺν Χριστῷ formula: Rom. 6.

σὺν Χριστῷ or σὺν κυρίῳ: this formula is not identical with ἐν Χριστῷ. It designates, rather, on the one hand the final communion with the Lord (I Thess. 4.17: πάντοτε σὺν κυρίῳ ἐσόμεθα; cf. 5.10), and on the other sacramental fellowship with him. This cannot be experienced inwardly, but can only be shown objectively and then taught.[1]

The specifically Pauline element (and here, too, the doctrine of justification exerts its influence) lies in his understanding of the temporal sequence: justification has already taken place; the resurrection is still to come. There is still a temptation to change the creed in the style of the mystery religions: Christ has died and risen, and so we have died and risen with Christ. But Paul turns it in the opposite direction: we *have* died with Christ, we *shall* rise again with him.

The futures are meant temporally. The interpretation of them as 'logical' futures refers to Colossians and Ephesians. But it misunderstands the specific difference between Paul and the Deutero-Paulines (see below). It comes to grief: (*a*) on the phrase πιστεύομεν ὅτι καὶ συξήσομεν αὐτῷ (Rom. 6.8); (*b*) on the consistency with which the futures are maintained. The evidence in I Cor. 15 should also be noted here. This interpretation of the tenses also corresponds to Paul's further interpretation of baptism, where he understands the result of baptism concretely as a way of life, in the relationship of the indicative to the imperative. From his sacramental starting point, it might have been expected that he would designate freedom from death as the fruits of baptism, particularly after ch. 5. But following the recasting of the idea in 6.4, Paul interprets freedom here as freedom for the new life. What must still be said about the Pauline doctrine of baptism therefore belongs in the section on 'freedom'.

V The Eucharist

The starting point is given in the analysis of the eucharistic texts in Part One (section 7 IV). It is significant that Paul develops his understanding in antithesis to the Corinthian enthusiasm and sacramentalism. Through baptism, the Corinthians find themselves in possession of salvation and constantly taste it afresh by receiving the substance

[1] See J. Dupont, ΣΥΝ ΧΡΙΣΤΩ (1952); T. F. Glasson, 'Dying and Rising with Christ', *London Quarterly and Holborn Review*, 186 (1961), pp. 286–91; R. C. Tannehill, *Dying and Rising with Christ* (1967).

of the sacrament. That means that each eats it for himself (ἴδιον δεῖπνον; I Cor. 11.21). The community is split into groups by pneumatics. What has Paul to set against them? First, a reference to the cultic formula contained in the tradition (11.23ff.). For this asserts the historical character of the foundation: 'The Lord Jesus, on the night that he was betrayed . . .' Paul stresses the eschatological prospect towards the parousia ('until he comes'). The eucharist is not already the heavenly meal, but a foundation for the intermediate period, the time of the church, the time of the proclamation of the death of the Lord. This death is the saving act; it is passed on to us through the proclamation, but precisely because it is 'gospel', it puts us under the cross, by which the intermediate period is determined. This is the time of faith and hope.[1]

Paul's drawing of the line from the sacramental body of Christ to the body of Christ as the church has exactly the same significance: 'this is my body' is interpreted in I Cor. 10.16f., by means of the idea of the church, the idea of community (Käsemann, Bornkamm).

There is a dispute as to whether the eucharist confers a share in the Crucified One or in the Risen One. The point made by Paul is that the Exalted One is not to be separated from the Crucified One. We have a share in the one who is proclaimed as the Crucified One. The crucified body (Rom. 7.4) and the 'body of Christ' are the same.

Eating and drinking do not bring about a magical, substantial assurance of salvation through the consumption of a fortifying substance, any more than baptism has a similar effect. Paul has added a preliminary qualification: I Cor. 10.1–13. What happened to the people of Israel took place πρὸς νουθεσίαν ἡμῶν, εἰς οὓς τὰ τέλη τῶν αἰώνων κατήντηκεν. ὥστε ὁ δοκῶν ἑστάναι βλεπέτω μὴ πέσῃ. The eating and drinking leads to the body of Christ understood in historical terms, to responsible life together. Because the eating and drinking is efficacious, it is impossible to celebrate the meal unworthily, because in that way one would destroy 'the body' (I Cor. 11.27–29).[2] The sacrament offers a choice of proclaiming the death of the Lord or coming to grief in the Lord (Käsemann).

---

[1] The same thing holds in chs. 12–14 for the χαρίσματα: the spirit as ἀρραβών denotes both the gift and the limitation. Only in v. 15 is hope related to the future.

[2] The demand for 'worthiness' does not relate to an inner condition as a requirement for receiving the sacrament; it refers to a man's attitude to the sacrament itself.

35 · DE LIBERTATE CHRISTIANA

R. Völkl and R. Schnackenburg, see on section 11 III; W. Schrage, *Die konkreten Einzelgebote in der paulinischen Paränese* (1961); J. N. Sevenster, *Paul and Seneca*, SupplNovTest 4 (1961); H. Braun, 'Die Indifferenz gegenüber der Welt bei Paulus und bei Epiktet', *Gesammelte Studien zum NT* (1962), pp. 159–67; C. Spicq, *Théologie morale du NT* (2 vols., 1965); C. F. D. Moule, 'Obligation in the Ethic of Paul', in: W. R. Farmer, C. F. D. Moule, R. R. Niebuhr, *Christian History and Interpretation* (Knox Festschrift (1967)), pp. 389–406. Further literature in Bultmann, *Theology of the New Testament* I, pp. 365f.

I Freedom

Paul cannot simply define freedom in purely formal terms as the possibility of doing what one wants, on the basis of his concept of faith and his anthropology. Nor can he define it along idealistic lines as the freedom of the subject, because he has no idea of the free subject. Man is always seen in his relationships.[1] As Paul does not consider freedom in itself, but only the freedom of faith (and lack of freedom, as fallenness into sin and the flesh), he does not find himself confronted with either the psychological problem of the freedom of the will or the cosmological problem of determinism or indeterminism as part of a world-view. Paul's theme is not the formal structures but the concrete factors of sin and the flesh and my freedom from these powers, which is not my own simply as a man, but is given to me through justification. Freedom must therefore be described by a contrast of the 'once' and the 'now', by a description of the transition or transportation from servitude to freedom, the process of grace and justification, the act of liberation. Freedom is 'strange freedom' in Christ.

Paul can describe the process in legal terminology, as liberation from the claim of the law (Rom. 8.2ff.; Gal. 4.2ff.). Rom. 7.1–6 states in what way we are freed from the law: we have died to the law διὰ τοῦ σώματος τοῦ Χριστοῦ. In this way it has lost its jurisdiction over us. Paul describes this process appropriately by the use of the 'once-now' pattern: Rom. 7.5f. The freedom from the law is particularized in two directions: (*a*) over against legalism (1) of the Judaizers (Galatians), (2) of the Jews (Romans); (*b*) over against the libertinism

[1] Romans 7: see section 27 above.

of the Corinthian enthusiasts. The polemic against the two over-laps (I Cor. 1.18ff.), but does not coincide. In the delimitation over against legalism, the position of the Jews in salvation history and the role of the law are to be noted. Therefore the controversy with legalism within the church has a different intensity from that with libertinism.

Not only Paul's personal life-work, but the whole nature of salva-tion and the church depend on the assertion that the law is finished as a way of salvation. He is called to be apostle to the Gentiles. His warning, 'If you fall back into the law, then you will destroy my life-work' is no sentimental appeal: 'Do not leave me in the lurch!' His commission to be missionary to the Gentiles depicts the very nature of salvation. It is given – from grace alone. Nor is he concerned with the tactical side of the mission. His argument is not that the Gentiles can-not be burdened with the mass of Jewish precepts. He asserts, rather, that the gospel and the law are fundamentally exclusive (Gal. 1.6–9). If – as the Judaizers teach – one can only come to faith by means of circumcision and the law, then a human contribution would be necessary apart from and before faith.

The opposite possibility is antinomianism, the complete abolition of the law, even for Jewish Christians. But that again would be a contribution, i.e. negative righteousness by works. It is rather that the Jews are to continue to practise the custom that has been en-trusted them, and in freedom, as they are no longer to be made blessed by means of it. Everyone can believe in his position (I Cor. 7.17–24). Here Jews and Gentiles are put on the same level. In this way, the concrete understanding of freedom becomes visible: we are not free and equal in that we are equal as men, but because each man is free in his own position.

For this reason, the idea of freedom cannot be translated into a political, social programme. The direct derivation of right from making righteous is impossible. Freedom does not have to be created – it is given.

The measure of faith that the Lord gives to each man differs according to the individual (Rom. 12.3). The charismata with which the individual is endowed also differ. Their unity is related to the community and its constitution. Paul's requirement that each man shall remain in his κλῆσις (I Cor. 7.20) is a dialectical demand. It is not raised because my 'calling' has human (moral, social, etc.) value as such or is a divine ordering of creation and is therefore sacred, but precisely because that is not the case. By the saving event, it is neutralized so that it becomes simply a human, worldly condition, which can neither further me nor hinder me in faith. Therefore I am to remain where I am, so that I do not succumb to the illusion that I can achieve blessedness for myself by a transformation of my human status. It is for this reason that Paul declares the lapse of the Galatians into the law as impossible, because by so doing they destroy the absoluteness of grace (Gal. 2.21). I have all freedom, e.g. to eat and to drink, and even to refrain from this privilege for the sake of the brethren. But I cannot surrender this freedom myself. For the Galatians, this means that they may not lapse into the position that they formerly occupied (Gal. 4.3). They cannot return to bondage, because otherwise freedom cancels itself out. In metaphorical terms: if they are accepted into sonship, they can no longer behave as slaves (Gal. 4.3ff.).

But for the very reason that law and grace are exclusive, I am not excused from God's demand because I am free. Now I am really taken up into it. I am not set down in an empty room, but transported into sonship: therefore I can only behave as a son. Gal. 5.1 shows how the imperative is attached to the assertion of freedom: τῇ ἐλευθερίᾳ ἡμᾶς Χριστὸς ἠλευθέρωσεν · στήκετε οὖν καὶ μὴ πάλιν ζυγῷ δουλείας ἐνέχεσθε. An urgent question then arises. If the law, though not its demand, is said to be at an end, with what right can this condition be called 'freedom' at all? The answer can be given by a demonstration of *how* we are freed: by the objective act of salvation. This also provides the explanation *from what* and *for what* we are freed: from the flesh, for the spirit. Because of this, it is no longer possible to act according to the flesh, to allow oneself to be dominated by an alien power (Rom. 8.12). We have no freedom to sin. That would be a contradiction in itself (Gal. 5.13).

Flesh and spirit are both active powers. I stand under the one or the other; but the standing here or there is on different levels, and not on the same formal, ontological plane. Under the σάρξ I am alienated from myself; in the πνεῦμα I fulfil what I am. Both powers are transsubjective. But the πνεῦμα is not alien to me in the sense that it falsifies and annihilates my being. Here I am in the truth in myself (Rom. 8.13). In the spirit I am not only driven, but I can lead my life freely, actively in the face of the σάρξ (Gal. 5.16–18).

If I now ask what I am to do, the 'works' of the flesh are enumerated in a catalogue of vices and the 'fruits' of the spirit in a catalogue of virtues (Gal. 5.19–21, 22f.). The unity of freedom and demand (and the possibility of fulfilment) is understandable above all in the remark which is also made in the context of Gal. 5.13ff.: the commandment stands. But the demand is no longer understood in the light of the individual injunction, and the law is not the sum of its precepts. It has its summation, rather, in the commandment to love (Gal. 5.14; Rom. 13.8–10).

Romans 13.8–10 is one of the few places where the Pauline paraenesis corresponds with the synoptic paraenesis almost word for word. The commandment to love as the fulfilment of the law is – as a tradition from the Lord – the basic ingredient of early paraenesis. There is an awareness that this is not a new commandment, but one that has already been revealed in the Old Testament. It is quoted in its Old Testament wording.

In the gospel of John, on the other hand, the commandment to love is emphatically called the 'new' commandment. Of course, John does not consider whether Jesus formulated it anew: 'newness' is an eschatological category and designates the quality of this commandment in relationship to the world. I John is rather different. It takes over the expression used in the gospel of John, but in the light of its idea of tradition sets out at the same time to show that this commandment has already been there in the church for a long time. In fact, it has been there from the beginning, as a commandment given by Jesus. There is therefore a word play in I John with the two expressions 'old' and 'new'. It is new in so far as it has been given anew by Jesus; it is old in so far as it has held in the church for a long time. There is no reflection on the Old Testament and its law in either the gospel of John or in I John.[1]

Love is not a moral principle, to be applied in each individual case. It is impossible to establish first what love is here and now in a given case and then realize it. Establishing what love is and doing it, rather, coincide.

If love were an ethical principle, there would be no answer to the question how love can be commanded: 'You *shall* love'. This commandment is possible, first, under the presupposition of the gospel – in so far as this is not just doctrine, but the gift of salvation; secondly, as an absolute commandment. The conjunction of the commandment to love and the saving event finds its clearest expression in the New Testament in the Johannine farewell discourses (15.9ff.).

---

[1] H. Conzelmann, 'Was von Anfang war', BZNW 21 (Bultmann Festschrift) (1954), pp. 194–201.

Nor is love an ideal to be striven for. It is to be realized on each several occasion; it is and can be practised wholly and completely, not only by way of an approximation, as if it were an ideal. At the moment of help, I do not bring partial love, but *love*. The modern psychological question whether there is not a remnant of egoism in my love is remote from Paul and the rest of the New Testament. For them, man can acknowledge the good deed without qualification, precisely because he is aware that we do not achieve salvation through works.

What love is and how it is possible is clear from its underlying basis: the deliverance that has already been achieved. This gives me the possibility of taking up and doing what is now commanded, in freedom from care, learning to see the person who encounters me as a person, acting freely, without having to ask about my success. Love can afford not to seek its own. This 'you can afford it' must be heard in addition to the 'you shall'. In that case, the unity of the demand and my free assent becomes evident. The cleavage between the two arises from my concern for myself. In other words, love is the particularization of an eschatological relationship to the world, made possible by the faith which works through love (Gal. 5.6). In this way it creates freedom over against all human conventions. I can afford to decide whether I have to act for or against the letter of a precept (even a biblical precept) for the sake of its meaning, i.e. for the sake of love. No authority can deprive me of this decision, not even the Bible, taken as a resource document.

Does this not lead to subjective arbitrariness, to libertinism? This is prevented by the fact that this freedom has its place in the body of Christ, in which each has to bear the others' burdens. Paul exemplified such freedom in his own life's work (I Cor. 9). He asserts his power as an apostle, and renounces his privileges.

The alternative is not: to serve sin – to do what one wants (under some circumstances, nothing at all); but: to serve sin – to serve the Lord (or righteousness). This is expressed sharply in Rom. 6.16. Therefore liberation means: νυνὶ δὲ κατηργήθημεν ἀπὸ τοῦ νόμου, ἀποθανόντες ἐν ᾧ κατειχόμεθα, ὥστε δουλεύειν ἡμᾶς ἐν καινότητι πνεύματος καὶ οὐ παλαιότητι γράμματος (Rom. 7.6). The truth is that: οὐδεὶς γὰρ ἡμῶν ἑαυτῷ ζῇ, καὶ οὐδεὶς ἑαυτῷ ἀποθνήσκει · ἐάν τε γὰρ ζῶμεν, τῷ κυρίῳ ζῶμεν. ἐάν τε ἀποθνήσκωμεν, τῷ κυρίῳ ἀποθνήσκομεν. ἐάν τε οὖν ζῶμεν, ἐάν τε ἀποθνήσκωμεν, τοῦ κυρίου ἐσμέν. εἰς τοῦτο γὰρ Χριστὸς ἀπέθανεν καὶ ἔζησεν, ἵνα καὶ νεκρῶν καὶ ζώντων κυριεύσῃ (Rom. 14.7–9). Paul develops what has been said over against the *law*. His controversy with the Corinthian enthusiasts for freedom leads in the end to the same point as the controversy with the Galatian nomists. The issue is the same in each case; the only difference is the context of the discussion. The Galatians preach 'faith and the law'. Paul retorts, 'through faith alone'. This makes freedom, and the possibility of its fulfilment in obedience, understandable. The Corinthians argue, 'All is permissible' (I Cor. 6.12; 10.23). Against this, Paul cannot say 'no, no freedom'. He says, 'Yes, freedom, but freedom of faith or freedom in the body of Christ, freedom from the powers for the edification of the church'. From here stem the regulations about eating and abstinence, about attitudes towards flesh offered to idols and to the demons. In each case, freedom is the eschatological form of existence. This finds its sharpest expression in the ὡς μή of I Cor. 7, in which the critical mean between acceptance of the world and renunciation of the world is drawn. It is clear why there can be no acceptance of the world: the world is passing away. I Cor. 10.26 shows why there can be no renunciation of the world: τοῦ κυρίου γὰρ ἡ γῆ καὶ τὸ πλήρωμα αὐτῆς; cf. Rom. 14.14, 20. What is in question is not purity or impurity as a quality of things, but use or misuse (I Cor. 7.29–31). I Corinthians 3.21ff. shows that Paul is not speaking here only with the prospect of an apocalyptic catastrophe engulfing the world; behind his remarks there is an understanding of the world as a whole in the light of God's being in Christ: πάντα γὰρ ὑμῶν ἐστιν, εἴτε Παῦλος εἴτε ᾿Απολλῶς εἴτε Κηφᾶς, εἴτε κόσμος εἴτε ζωὴ εἴτε θάνατος εἴτε ἐνεστῶτα εἴτε μέλλοντα, πάντα ὑμῶν, ὑμεῖς δὲ Χριστοῦ, Χριστὸς δὲ θεοῦ.

The theological starting point helps us to understand that the most comprehensive standard which Paul produces for the assessment of our actions is not formulated in negative, critical delimitations, nor thetically, as an ethical principle or as the statement of a supreme value. It has its eminently positive significance precisely in this critical presentation: 'Whatever does not proceed from faith is sin' (Rom. 14.23).

II Freedom from Death

Literature: see Bultmann, *Theology of the New Testament* I, p. 366.

This follows from our liberation from sin, as death is the wages of sin. Without sin there is no death – by which, of course, is meant no eternal death. Once again, two sets of statements stand side by side: topical statements, in which the impotence of death is shown by means of us, the believers; and objective statements, which demonstrate the cosmic context: (a) Death is settled for us, because we have died with Christ. So physical death cannot destroy our fellowship with him. We have the certainty of the resurrection. (*b*) Death itself has been annihilated. Significantly, there is no distinction here between bodily dying and eternal death. Here death itself appears as a power (in personifying imagery), as the last enemy. Its annihilation is the last act of the work of salvation (I Cor. 15.25f.).

That means that Paul declares that dying is not a process which takes place in the foreground of our human existence. Death affects *us*. Just as we are wholly sinners, so too we wholly die. Death is not the passage of the soul through a dark door. It annihilates us, but those who have died with Christ will be raised to eternal life. Hope for life is exclusively founded on the saving act, not on a doctrine of the soul or the rhythm of perishing and coming to be in nature. We have our certainty in the fact that life not only lies in the future, but is also already with us abundantly in the spirit, as freedom – in the form of hope in face of θλῖψις, if not yet in the form of resurrection δόξα (Gal. 2.19f.). The this-worldly reality of the future life is experienced in practice in the paradoxical manner of suffering in which our daily dying comes about (II Cor. 6.9; Rom. 8.36; II Cor. 4.10–12). This suffering is a proof of the truth of hope (Rom. 5.2ff.).

Paul does not ask the theoretical question why there is suffering in the world. He does not even explain it with the help of the devil. He develops no theodicy, no theory of how God 'allows' suffering or even brings it about. The question how one can still believe in a righteous God in spite of suffering is impossible in the light of Pauline theology. Faith holds, not despite suffering, but in it. So the question of a theodicy only emerges on the periphery, to be immediately rejected as a question: this is not the way to talk about God; talk like this indicates a failure to understand him. Besides, this (rejected) question is not raised in the context of a discussion of the problem of suffering, but in connection with the doctrine of election. One cannot speak at all of a 'problem' of suffering in Paul, as it is not discussed as a universal phenomenon and found a place in the totality of life and thus 'explained'. It is only one's own suffering that is ever mentioned. Thus there are no general statements about the 'meaning' of suffering. Paul does not give any comfort and encouragement, but passes on the positive knowledge (in the sense of his *theologia crucis*) that the grace of the Lord is made strong in weakness. Suffering is thus itself an indication of grace (II Cor. 12.7–10).

Reconciliation to suffering is an eschatological, christological manner of interpretation: suffering is a fact in the aeon that is passing away, whose end is constituted by the cross and resurrection of Christ (II Cor. 4.16–18). If the present and future world is contrasted, it is recognized that οὐκ ἄξια τὰ παθήματα τοῦ νῦν καιροῦ πρὸς τὴν μέλλουσαν δόξαν ἀποκαλυφθῆναι εἰς ἡμᾶς (Rom. 8.18). It might be objected that such a vision of the better world beyond is doubtful comfort at the moment of suffering, because for the sufferer himself this moment stretches out to infinity. But Paul does not intend this eschatological reference to be a silver lining gleaming on the horizon of the world: he does not put his readers off with hopes of a fairer future. By suffering, God shatters the props of my self-assertion, leaving me nothing but grace (II Cor. 4.7; 1.9). In these passages we find a pedagogic interpretation of suffering. But the sense is not to be restricted to a psychologizing or moralizing one, say that suffering damps excessive pride. These are not subjective moods; Paul is referring to the basic, universal human attitude of καύχησις. The effect of suffering is an objective one: it can have this effect on us only because it actualizes what has happened beforehand in Christ. The saving act, the dying of Christ in us, is accomplished through suffering. Christ's own suffering takes place in our suffering: Gal. 6.17;[1] Phil. 3.9ff.; II Cor. 4.10–12.

This idea is usually called Paul's passion mysticism. But it is intended as unmystically as dying with Christ in baptism. Here, too, fellowship with Christ is understood along the lines of the concept of faith, and not as a mystical union. The apostle does not suffer the same suffering as Christ suffered. He does not bring about this fellowship through an imitation of the suffering of Christ, still less does he appropriate Christ's suffering by being immersed in his passion. Rather, he understands his everyday experience as the form of life to which faith and the commission of proclamation lead: salvation is not of a worldly nature, but presents itself as the overcoming of the world.

In experiencing the dying of Christ, the apostle communicates the life of Christ to the community. From this, too, it is clear that we do not have a mystical exchange here; Paul is simply describing the effect of the preaching on the preacher and on the community.

During earthly life, then, being delivered over to death and freedom from death coincide. Their unity by no means realizes itself only in occasional experiences; rather, it is everyday reality: Phil. 4.11–13.

III   The New Life

Freedom is the consequence of justification. But the relationship between the two is not simply like that of cause and effect: first justification – I do that for you; then sanctification – now you do your part for me. If the relationship is understood in these terms, then justifica-

[1] The στίγματα τοῦ Ἰησοῦ which Paul bears on his body have nothing to do with 'stigmatization'.

tion is formalized, and the possibility left open for the pious man to desire to establish himself again – by the activation of his piety. But justification remains the constant condition of freedom.

The fact that Paul divides his letters into first a 'dogmatic' part and then an attached 'ethical' part shows that ethics cannot be treated as an independent theme. It is no coincidence that ethics is not dealt with in the same self-contained way as the themes of faith, righteousness and the law. The looseness of the account is a material indication: ethics must remain open as an indication of the open field of the freedom of the children of God.

On the form and content: what could earlier be asserted about primitive Christian paraenesis still applies here. The individual ethical demands are not specifically Christian; for the field of action is the world, and in this men know what is moral. Thus the content of ancient, Jewish and Hellenistic morality is taken over. This can be bourgeois, because the basis for it is eschatological (Phil. 4.8). Specifically Christian instructions appear, where the concern is for the ordering of the life of the community. Paul does not strive for completeness. For example, he has no interest in the state as such, in culture, in the social order, as the world and its concerns have become eschatologically indifferent. It is a characteristic mark of style that unexpectedly eschatological references keep emerging in paraenesis (Rom. 13.11f.; I Cor. 7.31; Phil. 4.5). However, the indifference does not lead to a retreat from the world – because of apocalyptic or gnostic motives – through which the wise man saves himself. The knowledge of being at the end of the world in fact brings about a disclosure of man's relationship to the world: the opening up of freedom from the world is liberation from concern about myself and my salvation, because this is already taken care of. It is liberation from the compulsion of works, and thus freedom to turn to the brother with whom I am in solidarity as a sinner, because Christ has also died for him. In practice, the eschatological attitude to the world is love. In this way, it is clear that ethics does not describe the pious man, but the life and rule of love. Certainly, the imperative follows from the indicative. But it is wrongly defined unless it is clear that it is God himself who creates the willing and the accomplishing (Phil. 2.13). In that case, what is the imperative for? It is appointed because God does not work as a natural force, but through faith, by making men children, and by the spirit which is the spirit of freedom (II Cor. 3.17). By this token it can be seen how we are set in motion and what we have to do: to consecrate ourselves (I Thess. 4.3). Sanctification is not an undertaking to produce sanctity. That it is already there is a pre-supposition of our activity. Ethics is not a guide to blessedness, but an instruction for the saints, i.e. those who are taken out of the world, for life *in the world*. The imperative 'Thou shalt' does not apply *in spite of* the indicative of the promise of salvation; it springs from it and is its particularization. How can that be? It is because we are endowed with the spirit, but have experienced no habitual change as a result of it. We are not yet in the heavenly state. The spirit is ἀπαρχή (Rom. 8.23), ἀρραβών (II Cor. 1.22; 5.5); it thus remains an other-worldly force. It is part of the concept of the spirit that it does not allow us to by-pass the this-worldly. It holds us fast in the world, in faith. It is the freedom of the new way of life (II Cor. 3.17).[1] I am no longer in the grip of sin, but can move forward. But because this is not my own possibility, but a given, strange possibility, there arises the apparently paradoxical rule: εἰ ζῶμεν πνεύματι, πνεύματι καὶ στοιχῶμεν (Gal. 5.25; cf. Rom. 8.14). In these verses, the material relationship between what we are and what we should be is precisely the same as that between present and future. For Paul, these are not periods of time, which alternate. The future is the mode which is opened up for man only through the gospel, the possibility of standing in his time and place in the world, that is, at the end of the world. As a result, this is not pessimistically devalued, but eschatologically disclosed, because salvation is now at work in and with us.

This material significance of presence and future is clearly shown in the fact that Paul does not sketch a free outline, even in working out the connection between indicative and imperative. Here, too, he is an interpreter, who brings to consciousness what is implicitly contained in the tradition of the community and sets it in a systematic context. He shows the understanding of salvation as being on the way, and the foundation of paraenesis on the evangelical significance of the message. From the beginning, the community knows that the saving event leads to a new way of life, and that this does not represent a way of acquiring salvation, but the consequences of the salvation that has been given; that it is possible on the basis of the forgiveness of sins, in gratitude for it. In this way, the parable of the unmerciful servant is the basis of the demand that we for our part should practise forgiveness of sins. Therefore the community delivers paraenesis at baptism. All this occurs in Paul, and points clearly back to fixed tradition. Now, however, he raises these beginnings to the level of reflection. To this belongs the fundamental determination of the relationship between demand and freedom: the foundation of the commandment in faith, which in fact already exists before Paul, must be

---

[1] Earlier exegesis was fond of talking about an ethicizing of the understanding of the spirit (Bousset). But the pattern of thought is the opposite: the spirit means that the possibility of moving freely in the world is a miracle (Bultmann).

made understandable with the help of a clarified concept of faith (in which its connection with its content must always be remembered). Put in other words: the demand must be presented on the basis of the doctrine of justification.

An account of Pauline ethics cannot, then, begin from individual ethical demands. It is a mistake, say, to collect the catalogues of virtues and vices together in order to make a description of Pauline ethics out of them. The Christian element does not lie in the catalogues; these are essentially traditional and for that very reason show where the special characteristic of Christian ethics does *not* lie, that is, in the individual moral demands.[1] Of course, specifically Christian virtues appear in these catalogues, for example, love. Nevertheless, the theological element does not lie in the individual content as such. By and large, this is remarkably bourgeois (Phil. 4.8). The important thing is the point at which the bourgeois character is heightened: in the community, at the end of the world (cf. the context of Phil. 4.4-8).

The systematic structure of ethics appears particularly clearly in the connection between Rom. 7 and 8. Romans 7 ends with the cry for redemption and the thanksgiving of the redeemed. Thus the situation of the redeemed can be described in its radical newness: what am I now in the world? In any case, I am free from the law: Rom. 7.6 is taken up at the beginning of ch. 8. Now the freedom which has been given must be presented in concrete terms. Romans 8.1 provides the basis: οὐδὲν ἄρα νῦν κατάκριμα τοῖς ἐν Χριστῷ Ἰησοῦ.[2]

Will Paul now begin to exult in loftier tones: once my fleshly I, now my spiritual I with its properties and actions? The consequence would be the cultivation of a holy life in the circle of enthusiasts, in direct withdrawal from the world by ascesis or in intensive mutual edification – and in the constant anxiety of spiritual legalism about being stained by the world. It would be the cultivation of sanctity by renouncing freedom, openness to the world and thus eschatological existence, in favour of enthusiasm.

The tone which Paul strikes in Rom. 8 is very lofty, and it continues to rise right to the end of the chapter. Simply on the basis of ch. 7, however, where he does not depict his own experience, but a disclosure which encounters 'me' from outside, we may assume that he is not celebrating the pious subject. It is no chance that in ch. 8 he leaves the I style. The train of thought hangs closely together with the three preceding chapters. Chapter 5 (on freedom from death)

---

[1] Luther, *On Good Works* (Clemen I 231): From faith and from no other work do we have the name that we are called believers in Christ, as from the chief work. For Gentiles, Jews, Turks, sinners can also do all the other works. But to trust firmly that he is well pleasing to God is possible only to a Christian enlightened and strengthened by grace.

[2] R. Bultmann, 'Glossen im Römerbrief', *ThLZ* 72 (1947), col. 199, explains the verse as a gloss; G. Bornkamm, *Aufsätze* I, p. 67, n. 33, argues against this.

ended: οὗ δὲ ἐπλεόνασεν ἡ ἁμαρτία, ὑπερεπερίσσευσεν ἡ χάρις, ἵνα ὥσπερ ἐβασίλευσεν ἡ ἁμαρτία ἐν τῷ θανάτῳ, οὕτως καὶ ἡ χάρις βασιλεύσῃ διὰ δικαιοσύνης εἰς ζωὴν αἰώνιον διὰ ᾽Ιησοῦ Χριστοῦ τοῦ κυρίου ἡμῶν.

Paul makes the transition to ch. 6 (on freedom from sin) by raising an imaginary objection to this statement made by the Jews, the representatives of the law.

If the rule is, the greater the sin, the greater the grace, then grace can be increased by sinning (6.1). This imaginary logic, on the part of opponents who want to charge Paul with libertinism, is absurd. This can only be the argument of a man who does not know what sin is, because he does not know what grace is. From the liberation that I have experienced, I know how great grace must be; thus I also understand that sin drove me to faith through the law, though not of course in a rectilinear development, as though faith were the direct aim of sin. Sin achieved this success (faith) against its will, as its own overthrow, in the paradoxical way that is described in Rom. 7.13. Only in the hand of God is sin preparation for the gospel. I can only understand it as such when I am freed from it. Then I lose the delight of playing with it, and using it for a tactical contact. Sin is a way by which God led me to himself, not a way that I can take in order to find God.

After ch. 7, ch. 8 takes up the theme of chs. 5 and 6 once again. After the demonstration in the person of the I, it can now be highlighted even more sharply. The end of ch. 8 (about the love of God in Christ as the preservation of faith in the face of the powers) leads back to the beginning of ch. 5 in almost a circular way.

PART FOUR

THE DEVELOPMENT AFTER PAUL

36 · PROBLEMS

R. Sohm, *Kirchenrecht* I (1892); A. Harnack, *Entstehung und Entwicklung der Kirchen-verfassung und des Kirchenrechtes* (1910); K. Holl, H. von Campenhausen and E. Schweizer, see section 7 I; M. Goguel, *The Primitive Church* (1964); H. Lietzmann, *The Beginnings of the Christian Church* (1937); L. Goppelt, *Die apostolische und nach-apostolische Zeit*; Die Kirche in ihrer Geschichte, Band 1 (A); P. S. Minear, *Images of the Church in the NT* (1961).

If we begin from Paul, we shall have to measure post-Pauline theology by Paul's doctrine of justification.[1] Here the danger of an unhistorical assessment is not easily avoided. It must be kept in mind that the doctrine of justification is itself a *historical* criterion. It cannot be applied simply as a theoretical standard for distinguishing between good and bad theology, between proper belief and heresy. The 'application' of this standard is itself a theological procedure. The important thing is not whether Paul's statements are repeated, but whether others know how to carry out the matter itself theologically in the existence of the church – in continually new situations. One external reason alone shows why formal repetition would not preserve the matter: Paul formulates his doctrine in actual controversy with Judaism and Judaizing Christianity. In the later period, the actual controversy with Judaism retreats into the background. In essentials, the mission is limited to the Gentiles. The orientation of the church's thought matches this trend.[2]

The retreat of Pauline formulas does not by itself represent the transition to 'early catholicism'. We have to investigate the material

[1] R. Bultmann, *Theology of the New Testament* II, pp. 95ff., deals with the theme of 'The Development towards the Ancient Church' *after* his account of Johannine theology. This order conceals a value judgment: the heights of Pauline and Johannine theology are not maintained. This assessment corresponds to Protestant tradition: after the purity of the primitive period follows a decline and the way to catholicism (R. Sohm). It leaves its mark today in an uncritical use of the phrase 'early catholicism'.

[2] The fact that there is a strong influence of the Diaspora synagogue does not conflict with this. For the intensive intellectual controversy with Judaism is no longer directed towards the actual winning of the Jews for faith; it serves more to prompt reflection on the nature of Christian belief. See, for example: Acts 7 and the rest of Luke's work; Hebrews and the Epistle of Barnabas; cf. A. Oepke, *Das neue Gottesvolk* (1950).

understanding of salvation, its communication and its appropriation.

If we investigate the transition to early catholicism, we may notice considerable uncertainty as to method, which is stronger today than it used to be. R. Sohm still had a firm criterion with which he could mark the transition accurately. The uncertainty is, by and large, greater on the Catholic side than on the Protestant. Understandably enough, the Catholic interpretation of history is governed by a tendency to depict the unbroken continuity in the development of church and doctrine, the form of which was there in germ from the very beginning. History is seen in analogy to the growth of a plant.[1] The Reformation challenged the legitimacy of setting the church above the understanding of the message of faith. It saw the way in which tradition covered over the original faith, and reached back behind this to scripture.[2] If the development of the church is thus assessed critically, there will also be an attempt to brand it as a false development in historical terms. In fact, we cannot renounce historical criteria and judgments. But the criteria must themselves be historical. We shall attempt to define the phenomenon of early catholicism where it is fully developed. In crude terms: we do not have early catholicism simply where there is the notion of tradition. This notion is part of theology itself. The decisive turning point occurs where the tradition is assured institutionally, by being bound to a ministry and a succession in this ministry. Early catholicism has not appeared simply where we find a fixed ordering of ministry – even though this may already have a monarchical head. It first appears where the ministry has the quality of communicating salvation, where the working of the spirit and the sacrament are bound up with the ministry. As Bultmann puts it: the decisive process is the transformation of the regulative significance of church law into a constitutive one.[3]

The difficulty of understanding this period historically can already be seen in the customary designation of it as the 'post-apostolic age'. This gives a false emphasis to the historical situation. It suggests that an 'apostolic' age is already past. But in fact there never was an 'apostolic age'. The apostolic age is an idea, the product of a picture of history, even if this picture was first drawn at an early stage. Of course, there were followers of Jesus who formed the nucleus of the

[1] R. Schnackenburg, *New Testament Theology Today* (1963), pp. 18f.: 'New Testament theology is still a new field, and is still fairly shapeless and incomplete, but its roots are strong, and the source from which it springs is fruitful.' Hence, 'it is not possible for dogmatic theology and New Testament theology to be opposed to one another, either in their content or in their outcome – they simply probe into, and light up, the same revelation from two different viewpoints; what is more, they are the complement of each other.' This thesis is only possible on the presupposition that revelation has been entrusted to the institution of the church for its administration.

[2] Scripture is not regarded as an abstract norm; it is related to the *viva vox evangelii* which precedes it.

[3] R. Bultmann, *Theology of the New Testament* II, pp. 97f.

primitive community after his death. The founding of the primitive community is identical with the constituting of the circle of the twelve (I Cor. 15.3ff.). But the twelve are not the 'twelve apostles'. This idea is only developed in the post-apostolic period, and this gives rise to the 'apostolic time'. The twelve have no concrete influence on the theology of the Hellenistic church nor on the form of the church. They are influential only as an idea.[1]

The historical question is therefore one of the significance of the construction of this picture of the church and its history. What does this construction of the idea of tradition, which presupposes a certain distance from the first beginnings, mean? When, where, how, through what did an *awareness* of the difference develop? The phenomenon is made up not only of the actual distance from the first beginnings, the fact that the church existed for a long period in the world contrary to expectation, but also of the awareness and interpretation of this distance. This consciousness can be detected where people begin to define their own standpoint historically, by understanding themselves as the *third* Christian *generation*.

This is where the idea of the twelve apostles is developed (cf. e.g. Luke). It should be noted that no one defines themselves as the second generation. There is a retrospect to a completely closed epoch, a vanished generation. As a result, the new generation already puts intermediate figures between itself and the first generation, so that between the apostles and its own time there is the generation of the apostles' disciples. This consciousness can be detected round about the turn of the century and far beyond:

(a) Luke already places Paul in the intermediate period. The 'apostles' vanish from the account where his activity begins. Luke expressly announces his own standpoint along the lines of the conception held by the third generation, in the introduction to his work (Luke 1.1–4).

(b) The Pastoral epistles are directed to the pupils of 'the' apostle. Attempts are continually made to define the position of Timothy and Titus in terms of church law (as a kind of archbishop). But this is unsuccessful, because they do not function as ecclesiastical figures, but symbolize the communication of the tradition from the apostle to the present.

(c) A similar situation may be established for the first epistle of John. The idea of the third generation is presupposed in Jude and II Peter, and outside the New Testament in I Clement, the letters of Ignatius, the letter of Polycarp, and Papias. It continues until Irenaeus and is finally given classical formulation by Eusebius in his Church History, III 32, 7f., allegedly according to Hegesippus: until the death

---

[1] It is significant that not even the names of all the members of this group have been preserved clearly. Only in the case of Peter can we trace any activity; with John it is hardly possible, and quite impossible with the rest. The relationship between the 'twelve' and James the brother of the Lord is also unexplained.

of Jesus' nephews, the church remained a pure virgin. But when the holy choir of apostles vanished and the generation of those who were honoured to receive the divine wisdom personally from them, there began the godless heresy that is falsely called gnosis (cf. I Tim. 6.20).

We can use this self-awareness of the third generation as a key to the understanding of the theology of this period.

It is a misunderstanding to speak of it as a 'development'. There is no logical consistency or causal regularity. On the other hand, there is more than pure chance. For the historical course of the church is determined by the fact that a binding doctrine is handed on, which has to be taken over and passed down as an authority. In this way, continuity is given. At the same time, this doctrine must be appropriated and worked out in the tradition.

All the theological themes of this period can be brought under one general heading: a new stage of *reflection* has been reached. There is tradition from the beginning. But now the nature of tradition is considered, in that men define their own position in it. Now a picture of the apostles, or the apostle (Luke, II Timothy, I Clement, the redaction of II Corinthians) belongs to the tradition. In this way the historicity of the church, its relationship to its origin, is maintained. In this way, too, criteria are gained: for the distinction of true and false doctrine; for the overcoming of the problem of eschatology; for the form of the church (teaching, discipline, organization).

The idea of the apostolic period has a still wider effect: the creed becomes the *regula fidei*. The apostolic character is not only asserted, but laid down as a standard. With complete consistency, the apostolic canon is added to the rule of faith. True, its delimitation is only detectable at a later stage; but its presupposition is the idea of tradition held by the third generation.

The idea of the canon suggests the conception of a 'New Testament' period, which is itself an idea. It has the effect, among other things, of putting the canonical writings in a different perspective from the contemporaneous non-canonical writings. In reality, however, both canonical and non-canonical writings belong immediately together in time.

On the basis of the source material, one's first inclination is to assess the period under consideration by the question: how strong is, or remains, the influence of Paul? If we look beyond the canon, the impression is that it is astonishingly or depressingly small. Nevertheless, there is sometimes evidence of a knowledge of Paul: I Clement, Ignatius, Polycarp (who quotes him incessantly).

Christianity is reduced to a to some extent primitive nucleus of general religious conviction which is expressed (among other things) in a change in the significance and style of the basic concepts (πίστις, ἐλπίς, χάρις, δικαιοσύνη, ἁμαρτία, etc.). In places the influence of the Hellenistic synagogue is very strong, especially in I Clement and Hermas. It appears not only in the use of the Old Testament (I Clement) and the methods of interpreting it (Barnabas), but also in liturgical forms and content (I Clement, Didache).

Faith is essentially fear of God and trust in God, and in addition, accepting as true the basic statements of doctrine. Conversion can be characterized as knowledge of God (I Clem. 59.2; II Clem. 17.1). The summary in Hermas, Mand. I is significant: πρῶτον πάντων πίστευσον, ὅτι εἷς ἐστιν ὁ θεός, ὁ τὰ πάντα κτίσας καὶ καταρτίσας, καὶ ποιήσας ἐκ τοῦ μὴ ὄντος εἰς τὸ εἶναι τὰ πάντα, καὶ πάντα χωρῶν, μόνος δὲ ἀχώρητος ὤν. πίστευσον οὖν αὐτῷ καὶ φοβήθητι αὐτόν. God is the creator (I Clem. 20); he is omnipotent, righteous and merciful (I Clem. 27.1; 50.2).

Cosmological eschatology is handed on further (I Clem. 21.3; Barn. 21.3; two aeons: II Clem. 6.3). The dominant feature, however, is the expectation of the resurrection of the individual (cf. the significance of the word ἀνάστασις).

Soteriology and paraenesis correspond to this doctrinal situation. The essential features of salvation are – on the basis of knowledge of God, resurrection and judgment – repentance and the forgiveness of sins through the saving work of Christ, worship and obedience to the 'new' commandment.

The saving work: Christ is the High Priest (I Clem. 36.1; 61.3; 64; cf. the Epistle to the Hebrews), who brought salvation through his death (II Clem. 1; Ign., Philad. 8.2). He was pre-existent and became incarnate (Ignatius; II Clem. 9.5). The result of the incarnation and the passion is redemption (I Clem. 12.7), forgiveness of sins (Barn. 5.1), purification and sanctification (Barn. 8.1), renewal (Barn. 6.11), etc. Of course, the condition is repentance (I Clem. 7f.; 57.1; Ign., Philad. 8.1). The matter of salvation is the resurrection and 'life': ζωῆς ἐλπὶς ἀρχὴ καὶ τέλος πίστεως ἡμῶν (Barn. 1.6). πίστις and ἐλπίς are almost synonymous (I Clem. 12.7). Sin and sinlessness are understood in essentially moral terms (the plural of ἁμαρτία predominates!). The life of the converted is determined through the commandments of God, or Christ (I Clem. 1.3; 3.4; 13). Christ is the bringer of the 'new law' (Barn. 2.6), the example of a humble way of life (I Clem. 16.17). He is himself the law (Hermas, Similitudes VIII 3.2).

Salvation is a future as well as a present possession. The relationship between present and future is defined in different ways, but it is quite clear that the consummation still lies in the future. In this, the 'Apostolic Fathers' differ completely from gnosticism.

Even Ignatius, who has taken up ideas which are more strongly gnostic, or near to gnosticism, than any others in this group, is no gnostic in this respect, even though his reference to the futurity of the consummation (Ign., Eph. 17.1) has only the function of a corrective, and not even the most important one at that. In marking the boundary against the heretics and repelling docetism, a stress on the reality of the incarnation and the passion is the dominating factor. But even if the present character of salvation is stressed extremely strongly, the distance between Christ and the redeemed is still preserved: Christ is our life. Thus he does not function merely as an exponent of our 'I'. This is clear in the understanding of existence that is brought about by sharing both death and life with him.[1]

If death, resurrection and the judgment still stand between the present and eternal life, the powers of salvation are already at work in the present. They are communicated in worship, and especially in the sacraments, that is, in the church. The idea of the church must be considered in defining the relationship between present and future. One of its essential elements is the guaranteeing of tradition by succession (I Clem. 42; 44). The church is organized as a saving institution: the liturgy has salvific power (Did. 16.2). The hierarchical distinction of the clergy is a constitutive element (Ignatius: bishops, presbyters, deacons; cf. e.g. Trall. 2f.). The sacrament becomes the means of salvation in a new sense (Ign., Eph. 20.2: φάρμακον ἀθανασίας). In the face of this, tradition about the actions of Jesus fades completely into the background, and tradition about his teaching almost to the same extent; it is limited to isolated sayings.[2]

Bousset sums up the general impression in somewhat exaggerated terms: 'Christianity is a diaspora Judaism which has become universal and has been freed from its limitations, but although it has been freed from its limitations it is still diaspora Judaism'.[3]

The Sources

The canonization of part of the writing from the period under discussion suggests not only the conception of a 'New Testament period', but also that of a vacuum between a 'New Testament period' and a 'post-New Testament period'. In this interval, the tradition about Jesus and Paul seems as it were to have seeped away – only to re-appear again in a miraculous way towards the middle of the second century with Marcion and the beginnings of the formation of the

[1] R. Bultmann, *Theology of the New Testament* II, pp. 191ff.
[2] As before, they are handed down orally: see H. Köster, *Synoptische Überlieferung bei den Apostolischen Vätern*, TU 65 (1957).
[3] W. Bousset, *Kyrios Christos*, p. 291.

canon, where 'Lord' and 'Apostle' are united. The impression of a vacuum is partly caused by the lack of sources, and also by the impossibility of putting the sources we have in an exact chronological order. But this impression can be partially removed if we disregard the boundary between canonical and non-canonical writings. There are, in fact, quite a number of sources which belong in the post-Pauline period: all the New Testament writings apart from the genuine Pauline epistles, and the writings of the Apostolic Fathers.[1] Within this material, some guidelines can be recognized, above all the continual transmission and development of the creed from the early formulas up to the Roman Creed.[2] Paulinism represents a particular tradition,[3] to which the collecting and editing of the Pauline corpus also belongs.[4] The Pastoral epistles and Luke's history work give evidence of a conscious reflection on the (Pauline) tradition and their own stage within it.[5] I Peter and, to a lesser degree, the epistle to the Hebrews also lie within the sphere of deutero-Paulinism. On its periphery lie the epistle of James (in so far as it repeats the theme of faith and works) and I Clement. All the rest stand outside: Jude and II Peter (the latter knows the letters of Paul, but is not essentially influenced by them), Mark and Matthew, Barnabas and what is known as II Clement, the Didache and Hermas. The Johannine writings are also uninfluenced by Paul (Revelation absolutely).

It would be an unhistorical judgment simply to evaluate this period by Paul (having taken into account the special position of the synoptic gospels and the gospel of John (together with the epistles)). His letters are one factor of the tradition; doubtless they form a strong,

[1] Didache, I Clement, II Clement, the Epistle of Barnabas, the seven letters of Ignatius, the letter (or two letters) of Polycarp to Philippi, the Shepherd of Hermas; in addition, a number of fragments: Papias, the remnants of apocryphal gospels, etc. The texts are accessible in editions of 'The Apostolic Fathers' and in E. Hennecke – W. Schneemelcher – R. McL. Wilson, *New Testament Apocrypha* I (1963); II (1966).

[2] Literature: A. Hahn, *Bibliothek der Symbole und Glaubensregeln der alten Kirche* (1897³). Further literature in section 9.

[3] There is, however, the qualification that questions of authenticity within the Pauline canon are vigorously disputed. Therefore reconstruction remains hypothetical. Nevertheless, one can attempt to relate literary criticism and (hypothetical) historical reconstruction.

[4] The details are not known; cf. the histories of the canon.

[5] Even if the theology of Luke has not been shaped by that of Paul, he finds himself a place in the apostolic chain of tradition, which for him reaches from the apostles, through Paul, to the present.

influential force. But alongside Paul and the tradition of his school there flows a stream of doctrinal material, in both oral and written tradition, whose own particular importance must be recognized.

All in all, then, there is an extremely varied picture: the creed is handed on and developed further by the extension of the two articles about God and Christ. The Old Testament is quoted and interpreted. It becomes a factor in the development of Christian thought and also a medium for the extension of christology. Doctrinal development is further influenced by Hellenistic ideas which find expression in the terminology: particular religious concepts like σωτήρ, ἐπιφάνεια, good conscience (see the Pastorals) and Greek concepts of virtue (II Peter 1.5–7) appear. It should also be noted that gnosticism becomes influential to an increasing extent. The whole picture would be still more colourful had not a great complex of sources been destroyed by the later exclusion of 'heresy' from the church.

Thus the all-important question is not raised: is there a material theological criterion for the distinction between orthodoxy and heresy, or must we content ourselves with the assertion that 'orthodoxy' was simply what managed to find acceptance in the church?

37 · THE *REGULA FIDEI*

E. von Dobschütz, J. N. D. Kelly and V. H. Neufeld, see on section 9; for further literature, see Bultmann, *Theology of the New Testament* II, p. 257.

The creed is the starting point of theology and at the same time its regulator – not only from outside, but also from within, because theology understands itself to be the interpretation of the creed. Now we must investigate the functioning of this rule. This also raises the question of the significance of the extension of the creed: what is happening in the church if the rule: (*a*) is extended at all; (*b*) is extended in the way that we can see? How does the church understand its message and thus itself here? How does this self-understanding influence the form that the church takes?

Sacred formulae[1] are a universal feature of the phenomenon of religion:

---

[1] G. van der Leeuw, *Religion in Essence and Manifestation* (1964), sections 58ff.

prayers, hymns, blessings and curses, oaths. One of these formulas is the 'symbol'. The Islamic symbol, 'There is no God but Allah, and Mohammed is his prophet', is well known. For primitive Christianity, the Jewish symbol εἶς θεός exercises a decisive influence.[1] This had its original setting in the cult. It represents the acknowledgment that Yahweh's claim to lordship over Israel is exclusive. This significance is modified in the Jewish diaspora. It becomes a programme for monotheism and Israel's 'symbol' against paganism and polytheism. This is the sense it has in Mark 12.29, in Jesus' answer to the question of the greatest commandment.[2] The Christian symbol, too, is related to the cult. Indeed, it is constitutive of it: the confession κύριος 'Ιησοῦς is an act of lordship on the part of the Lord.

The relationship between faith and the historical revelation is brought about in the confession as such. Where this relationship is lost, say because there is dispute over the humanity of the revealer, i.e. in gnosticism, the form of the community also changes immediately.[3] This historical character of the creed is also preserved in the 'third generation', but it is modified in a characteristic way. We do not have a rectilinear development; there is continuity and at the same time change along the lines of the reflection that has been outlined.

1. *Continuity*. The content remains. Where the formula is extended in form, it is not a matter of more or less random new content. Now, rather, there is an explicit statement of what belonged implicitly to the conviction of faith from the very beginning, e.g. one God, God is the creator, the Father of Jesus Christ.

2. *Development*. Faith is understood more and more as timeless doctrine, and thus becomes the *fides quae creditur*. As such, it corresponds to the conviction of the truth of this doctrine, the *fides qua creditur*.[4] The original object of faith is the revelation itself, the God who reveals himself. Now the accent shifts in the direction of doctrine about the revelation. The epistle to the Hebrews[5] and the epistle of Jude,[6] etc., offer instances of this.

Now this hardening of the *viva vox* so that it becomes a fixed element of tradition is still not the heart of the matter. The really important

[1] V. H. Neufeld, *op. cit.*, pp. 34ff.; E. Peterson, *ΕΙΣ ΘΕΟΣ*, FRLANT NF 24 (1926).

[2] G. Bornkamm, 'Das Doppelgebot der Liebe', BZNW 21 (Bultmann Festschrift) (1954), pp. 85–93.

[3] Bultmann, *Theology of the New Testament* II, pp. 123ff.

[4] *ibid.*, pp. 135f.

[5] E. Grässer, *Der Glaube im Hebräerbrief*, Marburger Theologische Studien 2 (1965).

[6] Jude 3 issues a summons to fight for τῇ ἅπαξ παραδοθείσῃ τοῖς ἁγίοις πίστει.

development lies in the element of reflection, which now takes its place in the understanding of tradition. By virtue of this very fact, the statements of the 'faith' alter their meaning during the course of tradition. They are not timeless, logical formulas, which can simply be taught directly; they are historical statements, a historical interpretation of the revelation. These statements are originally developed as an illuminating communication which is meant to be understood as such and can also be understood as such. Here understanding and acceptance are one. But they change their character when they are handed down at second hand as ready-made truth. Originally the word brings immediate conviction. With the course of time, however, express attention must be paid to its truth. A guarantee of truth is added to the statement of truth. How is this possible? In terms of the idea of tradition itself, it is by showing where the tradition originates, by demonstrating its apostolic origin.[1] For an assertion of apostolic origin there must, of course, be proof that the tradition was not altered later, as this would represent a falsification. A chain of tradition must therefore be produced.

Examples:

1. Heb. 2.3: the σωτηρία, ἥτις ἀρχὴν λαβοῦσα λαλεῖσθαι διὰ τοῦ κυρίου, ὑπὸ τῶν ἀκουσάντων εἰς ἡμᾶς ἐβεβαιώθη. This εἰς ἡμᾶς can speak to each following generation from now on. The creed is moulded into a permanent form.

2. The prologue of the gospel of Luke:[2] Luke derives his account from eye-witnesses and points to the intermediaries, the 'many', who put down the tradition in writing. It is he himself who sums them up and brings them to a final form. The chain of witnesses proves the reliability: ἵνα ἐπιγνῷς περὶ ὧν κατηχήθης λόγων τὴν ἀσφάλειαν.[3] In this way, its validity for the future is ensured. Now all that matters is to preserve faithfully what has been handed down – within the church against false teaching, and externally, in mission and in persecution. This position cannot, however, be called 'early catholic', as Luke does

[1] Jude 17; cf. II Peter 3.2; Ignatius, Philad., 5.1; Polycarp 6.3. 'Apostolic' writings are composed: Deutero-Paulines, Catholic epistles; 'The teaching of the twelve apostles' is collected and summed up in the Apostles' Creed. The first stage on the way to the apostolic rule of faith and the apostolic canon of faith is being disclosed.

[2] G. Klein, 'Lukas 1, 1-4 als theologisches Programm', Zeit und Geschichte (Bultmann Festschrift) (1964), pp. 193-216.

[3] This element of the reliability of tradition is to be seen alongside two others, the idea of the 'twelve apostles' and the role of Paul as the mediator.

not regulate the process of tradition by the teaching ministry of the church, but secures it by a reliable record.

3. The Pastoral epistles, on the other hand, associate the preservation of tradition with the church's ministry. They give regulations for bishops, presbyters and deacons. Nevertheless, even they are not 'early catholic'. For purity of doctrine is not constituted through the ministry, but rather the reverse: the ministry is constituted by the preservation of the doctrine.[1] This does not happen through succession in the ministry, but by fixing the wording, by quotation in a stereotyped summary, which is derived from Paul (I Tim. 2.5–7; II Tim. 2.8).

One further element serves to guarantee the tradition: a picture of the apostle is handed down alongside the doctrine (II Timothy).

The faith, lucidly summed up in this way, makes possible a convenient measure for distinguishing between true and false doctrine. This holds not only for individual points of doctrine, but for the whole understanding of revelation and redemption. For the confession of faith retains its historical character and thus provides criteria against the dehistoricizing of faith in gnosticism. But this confession, once it has become a rule of faith, not only has a critical influence against false doctrine, but in fact works primarily in a positive way. Even the acknowledged writings need to be interpreted properly, and this in turn calls for a criterion.

The writings are claimed by different groups. Spiritualists, who deny works altogether, also appeal to Paul. The opponents in the Pastoral epistles, who assert that the resurrection has already taken place, may have understood themselves as thoroughgoing followers of Paul. So, too, may the advocates of an enthusiastic expectation of the end, against which there is polemic in II Thessalonians. One symptomatic feature is the warning contained in II Peter 3.16 against the misuse by heretics of the letters of the beloved brother Paul, which are in part hard to understand.

38 · ORTHODOXY AND HERESY

W. Bauer, *Rechtgläubigkeit und Ketzerei im ältesten Christentum*, BHTh 10 (1934; 1964²); M. Goguel, *The Birth of Christianity* (1953), pp. 406f.; H. Köster, 'Häretiker

---

[1] Doctrine is 'sound doctrine' (I Tim. 1.10, etc.), παραθήκη (I Tim. 6.20).

im Urchristentum', *RGG*³ III 17–21; id., 'Häretiker im Urchristentum als theologisches Problem', *Zeit und Geschichte* (Bultmann Festschrift) (1964), pp. 61–76; L. Goppelt (see on section 36), pp. 112ff.

Here, too, the element of reflection provides the key. Even Paul uses the confession as a critical authority (I Cor. 12.3). It is the objective criterion for assessing the gifts of the spirit. But the division is brought about in an immediate action, and not as yet by means of theoretical reflection on the confession as such. A new style arises with the formalizing of the authority of the apostolic rule of faith which begins after Paul. Paul makes his decision by bringing the Lord himself to bear in the confession. Now it is the confession that it is brought to bear by a reference back to the authority of the apostle. In the former case the confession is made and with it the decision; in the latter, there is the additional question what confessing and the confession are. Originally, the confession brought with it the overcoming of the world by faith; now the new situation is seen in a different way. Hebrews, for example, pictures it thus: the people of God – with its confession – has been on the move through the world for a long time and has grown weary. What now? Are they to keep singing the confession? Yes, but that is no longer enough, for the people know it by heart. Now the confession itself must be reactivated, so that new impulses may be gained from it. But how is that to come about? By pointing to the 'inheritance' that is given in it, the ἐπαγγελία, the goal of the wandering: the rest, the heavenly city. This new understanding is reflected in the use of the word πίστις: faith 'is evidently no longer understood as the entry of salvation into existence itself (*fides justificans et salvificans*), but as its presupposition (πίστις as an attitude)'.[1] Here the confession is applied to a theme which arises out of the existence of the church itself, its long stay in the world.

A further area of the application of the confession is opened up with the emergence of false doctrine. This phenomenon is in itself a symptom of the altered form of the church. Not that the doctrine was completely uniform right from the beginning: it is not a timeless factor. One need only think of Paul's controversies with the Judaizers and enthusiasts. Nevertheless, a new element now appears: with the establishment of doctrine, the controversy becomes theoretical in a new sense.

We have here a process, the wide extension of which was first recognized by

---

[1] E. Grässer, *Der Glaube im Hebräerbrief* (1965), p. 197.

Walter Bauer. The old picture of church history (see above, Eusebius) still keeps influencing our conception: the first period of the untainted church was followed by the invasion of heresy – from outside – and this coincided with the cooling off of the first love. But there was still a possibility of overcoming heresy, because the powers of salvation and faith remained as effective as ever. The church, in the true faith, kept out heresy by a heroic battle. Bauer, however, shows that this picture of history is that of the victorious trend.

In fact, it was by no means easy to tell true teaching from false, right from the beginning. What was later excluded as heresy first had a life in the church as a way of understanding the faith.

There is a common tendency to regard gnostic ideas as an alien body, which forced a way into the church from outside. But they were there from the beginning (Paul). 'Christianity' is a particular construction in its environment, a syncretistic religion. The gnostics formed themselves into groups because they believed that they understood the nature of the faith more profoundly, indeed, that they were the only ones who understood it. They, too, refer to the apostolic tradition,[1] which thus becomes ambiguous.

A question will indicate the new element in the situation. Why does gnosticism now become intolerable? What boundary was over-stepped? How was this boundary defined? How was the category of heresy arrived at in the first place? Its introduction means that a change has also taken place on the other side. In the view of 'orthodoxy' that it alone represents the original, unaltered faith, we can in reality recognize a new structure, a new relationship to the object of faith. It is clear from the style of the polemic against heresy and the doctrine that is expressed in it.

First of all, the polemic is primitive: it is claimed that the heretics are morally corrupt. The background to this is a view which is already to be found in Jewish polemic against the Gentiles, that false doctrine about God and false morality are causally connected. The criticism of the morality of the false teacher is not a realistic account, but a dogmatic assertion. The teaching of the opposite side is not first described and then refuted; it is simply attacked in a formal way (Pastoral epistles). In the long run, however, this procedure is not enough. The church has to be clear about the basis of its own teaching, and has to submit the relationship between πίστις and γνῶσις to a thorough examination. Nevertheless, the Pastorals make a start in this direction: they contrast with the 'myths and genealogies' of gnosticism the παραθήκη which hands on the historical revelation, and

[1] E.g., Ptolemy to Flora, 6.6 (ed. G. Quispel, Sources chrétiennes 24, 1949).

particularize this by confronting the gnostic negation of the world with the existence of believers in the world. The doctrinal basis for this is the confession of God as the creator. In this way they maintain that the world is not excluded from the realm of God, the saving event, and prevent world and salvation from being torn asunder.

I John – on the basis of Johannine theology – takes the process of reflection further. The solidarity of faith and knowledge is fundamental to the theology of the gospel of John: faith is meant to be understood, and it can be understood, because that is its concern. I John takes this thought to the level of reflection: he not only fights against the heretics, but also considers the nature of heresy by defining the nature of faith as orthodox faith. The gospel of John declares that the truth can be understood on hearing the message of the gospel. I John asks, how can faith recognize that it is true, that it is the right faith? It gives the answer by a new use of the confession as a principle of knowledge. Originally, the confession led to a decision for or against faith; now it leads to a decision for or against particular groups in the church. In the gospel of John, the disclosure of the world through revelation, the separation between church and world, truth and lies, is brought about through believing and knowing. In I John, on the other hand, different Christian groups confront each other, each claiming the truth for itself. Now it is necessary to explain which truth is the 'right' one. This process of reflection gives birth to a significant expression: John 6.69 runs: 'And we have believed, and have come to know, that you are the Holy One of God'. I John 2.3, on the other hand, says: 'And by this we may be sure that we know him . . .'; how? '. . . if we keep his commandments.' The controversy is complicated by the fact that the opposition, too, appeals to the confession 'Jesus is the Son of God'. So this formula is no longer sufficient distinction. As a result, there is a need not only for the confession, but also for its proper interpretation: (a) ἐν τούτῳ γινώσκετε τὸ πνεῦμα τοῦ θεοῦ· (b)πᾶν πνεῦμα ὃ ὁμολογεῖ ᾿Ιησοῦν Χριστὸν ἐν σαρκὶ ἐληλυθότα ἐκ τοῦ θεοῦ ἐστιν (I John 4.2).

The author does not understand ἐν σαρκί as a new doctrine, as an addition to the doctrine, but as its correct interpretation. Anyone who disputes this statement not only rejects a part of the faith, but rejects *the* faith, because it is indivisible. We see here the first beginnings of the extension of dogma by the positive development of the confession of faith and a critical defence against false doctrine.

39 · THE CHURCH AS AN INSTITUTION

H. von Campenhausen and E. Schweizer, see on section 7 I; J. Brosch, see on section 33; further literature in R. Bultmann, *Theology of the New Testament* II, pp. 255f.

Paul knows no fixed organization. True, there are particular activities and positions (Phil. 1.1; I Cor. 12.28), but there is no hierarchy. There is a church order, but it does not in itself represent the nature of the church. The order is not sacred; it is there to serve a purpose.

H. von Campenhausen points out that there are no elders in Paul, because even this office was evidently too institutional for him. The controversy between Sohm and Harnack[1] may serve to illuminate the problems. Bultmann[2] rightly says that this controversy is still not concluded. Sohm: legal ordering contradicts the nature of the church; there can only be charismatic authority in it. Harnack: there was legal ordering right from the beginning; it does not contradict the nature of the church. The primitive church had a double organization, (*a*) that of the individual community; (*b*) that of the whole church. The ministers of the individual community had an administrative function, whereas the church as a whole was directed by charismatics. If, for example, the treasurer of the community at Philippi moved to Thessalonica, he did not automatically get another office there. On the other hand, a charismatic, a prophet travelling from community to community, was a prophet everywhere and possessed authority everywhere.

Criticism: (*a*) H. Greeven[3] and H. von Campenhausen (pp. 65f.) point out that the place of apostles, teachers and prophets was, according to I Cor. 12.28, precisely in the individual community. This objection does not, however, touch Harnack's case. The prophets, etc. could indeed travel and still remain what they were. (*b*) Bultmann takes the argument further, first in the question of the double organization. He remarks that one should not talk in these terms, 'for the work of the apostles, prophets and teachers cannot be termed an organization. But it is correct to say that the activity of the elders and episkopoi is restricted to their specific congregation, while by the person and the work of the apostles, prophets and teachers, the ἐκκλησία is represented as the *one* church. But this oneness is at first not an organizational but a charismatic unity wrought by the spirit' (pp. 103f.).

Bultmann above all makes the delineation of the problems involved more

---

[1] Cf. above, sections 7 and 36, and the literature there.

[2] Bultmann, *Theology of the New Testament* II, p. 96.

[3] H. Greeven, 'Propheten, Lehrer, Vorsteher bei Paulus', *ZNW* 44 (1952/3), pp. 1–43.

precise. Harnack began from the empirical form of the church as a legally constituted institution, Sohm from its nature. Bultmann sets out to go beyond the
alternatives: it is necessary 'to make clear to ourselves the difference between the
Ekklesia as an historical phenomenon and the Ekklesia as the eschatological
congregation guided by the spirit's sway' (p. 96). It is not legal ordering as such
that contradicts the nature of the church. For the spirit itself creates law, tradition.[1]
The contradiction first arises when the law 'ceases to be regulative and becomes
constitutive' (p. 98), that is, when it no longer serves the ordering of the church.
Then the church as such becomes a legal institution and measures itself by the legal
ordering. This happens when e.g. the judgment whether the church is properly
ordered is made dependent on a particular kind of organization and its hierarchical
constitution, when the office becomes the criterion of the spirit and the spirit is in
turn tied to the office; when the doctrine of ministerial succession and the efficacy
of the sacraments is associated with ordinations and ministries; when church
discipline is no longer pneumatic, but regulated by a ministry, in such a way that
following or failing to follow church law can lead to salvation or damnation.

External developments lead to a coalescence of the two types of
constitution, those of Paul and the elders.[2] We find elders in the
Pastoral epistles and in Luke (cf. I Clement). This is the basic form
for the ordering of the ministry, which is determinative for the future.
The synthesis achieved by the time of Ignatius then has the following
appearance: at the head stands the monarchical bishop, and under
him are presbyters and deacons. Above this is raised the office of the
apostle, as an ideal head in whom the unity of the church is represented. This is, of course, already a conclusion. In the New
Testament and the writings surrounding it, things are still on the
move. The designations of office are not yet strictly defined. For
example, the ἐπίσκοποι (Acts 20.28; in the plural) cannot be distinguished from the presbyters (20.17). The Pastoral epistles always
speak of the ἐπίσκοπος in the singular, but of presbyters in the plural.
Is there already a monarchical episcopate here? Hardly, for the
instructions which each of the two receives overlap, so that we get
the impression that there are here two designations for the same
position. The division into singular and plural may derive from the
use of stereotyped formulas (Dibelius). Hebrews, Barnabas and the
Didache still maintain the community as a free fellowship. In Didache
15, the bishops have the same functions as the charismatics.[3]

The cult falls within the competence of officials. Here an analogous

[1] E. Käsemann, 'Sentences of Holy Law in the New Testament', *New Testament
Questions of Today* (1969), pp. 66–81.
[2] H. von Campenhausen, *op. cit.*, pp. 82ff.
[3] *ibid.*, p. 76.

change can be detected. In Paul, worship is defined as λογικὴ λατρεία. This contains a critical element, the crisis of the idea that God can be influenced by the bringing of offerings. There is only the verbal form of offering, the prayer. The understanding of worship stems from the saving act. But it is not long before worship again becomes a cult with the connotation that it has a direct influence: (a) by the offering of Christian sacrifice as being well-pleasing to God (first hints in the Didache and with Ignatius and I Clement; developed in Justin); (b) in the celebration of the Christian mystery, through which the powers of the world beyond stream into the initiates (Ignatius). Of course, this is understood as an effect of the saving act of God. In Ignatius, the realism of the understanding of the sacrament is immediately linked with christology, and the stress on the reality of the incarnation (in the battle against the docetic heresy). Nevertheless, in practice the understanding of the working of the cult is no longer derived only from the saving event. This emerges from the fact that the sacrament must now be performed by the persons appointed for it, the priests. The church becomes an institution of salvation. The first stage on the way to the catholic institutionalization of the church has been reached. Supervision of doctrine (vigorously exercised by Ignatius) is added to the administration of the cult. Of course, the extension of the supervision of doctrine is favoured by the emergence of the heretics.

Reminder of section 38: it is not immediately clear what heresy is. First the standards have to be constructed. The formation of the ministry has a constitutive significance in this process.

The building up of an organization and of dogmatic criteria affect one other. In addition, practical norms have to be worked out for life together; this in turn has the result of making necessary a permanent authority to administer these norms.[1] Of course, one has to beware of schematization, both in respect of the course of the development and in respect of passing judgment upon it. The search for fixed rules and orders is at first simply a matter of what circumstances demand and is thus no 'lapse', no fundamental transformation of the church. The original free regulation of each individual case in the light of the spirit was not something that could be retained permanently, simply because it was now necessary to deal with collective phenomena of a new kind (heresy). Here only rules and measures were of any help.

[1] Bultmann, Theology of the New Testament II, pp. 223ff.

The question is, however, once again whether the regulation as such is constitutive of salvation. The development of penance to the fully-fledged catholic institution of penance is a paradigm. Here the problem of the so-called second repentance can serve as a guide-line. For Paul, this cannot possibly be: the church is holy and must be kept holy by the spirit itself (I Cor. 5.1ff.; cf. Acts 5.1ff.). But if a permanent form of regulation is found, the question is, how is this related to the nature of the church?

The problem emerges first in Hebrews 6.4–6: the possibility of a second repentance and forgiveness is roundly rejected. However, the apparent rigorism of this statement is weakened by its limitation of the refusal of second repentance only to major sins: apostasy, unchastity, adultery (12.16f.; 13.4), or to 'deliberate' sins (10.26). There are the beginnings of a distinction between deadly sins and venial sins. But what is to be our judgment on the refusal of second repentance? E. Grässer[1] refers to Luther's judgment that Hebrews has a 'hard knot' in chs. 6 and 10 and that '. . . it is hard to see how it could be undone'. Grässer sees that there is a theological reason for the refusal to allow second repentance, i.e. in the once-for-allness of Christ's sacrifice, but he does not feel that it is logically necessary: 'Historically, it (sc. the refusal to allow a second repentance) is to be seen against the background of the eschatological development which ultimately leads to the surrender of the dialectic of existence in faith'. It is connected with the 'corruption of the primitive Christian understanding of faith', and is in no way an expression of the primitive Christian certainty 'that faith will reach its goal'.[2]

Here a line of development has been correctly noted. Fuchs' generalizing explanation does not elucidate the exegetical evidence sufficiently. Nevertheless, Grässer's theological judgment has been made too quickly. For the understanding of sin in the epistle to the Hebrews is determined by the conception of the people of God on the move, and is therefore oriented towards a collective: sin is a matter of remaining behind the wandering people, or, without the metaphor, is apostasy, surrender of the confession and of faith, and thus of salvation. Moreover, one important element in the refusal of the possibility of second repentance is the fact that forgiveness is contingent. Man cannot count in advance on God being generous and

---

[1] E. Grässer, *Der Glaube im Hebräerbrief* (1965), pp. 192–98. The quotations which follow are on pp. 197f.

[2] Against E. Fuchs, *Studies of the Historical Jesus*, SBT 42 (1964), p. 52.

forgiving him yet again. Forgiveness can only be asked for in penitence, and thus each time it is asked for the last time. That God's grace is new every morning can only be said as a confession of thanksgiving, and the statement may not be taken as a reason for assuming that it is always possible to count on new forgiveness. Finally, it must not be forgotten that in the epistle to the Hebrews, forgiveness has not yet passed under the administration of an institution. The church can only 'administer' it in the sense of the Word.

The juxtaposition of a fundamental solution and practical regulations which is characteristic of the epistle to the Hebrews also appears in I John,[1] though of course with a different material solution: (a) the practical regulations follow very much as in the epistle to the Hebrews. But the distinction of 'deadly sins' and lesser sins is clearer. The extent of the deadly sins is not defined. In practice, however, we have approximately the same conditions as in Hebrews. (b) the fundamental solution is remote from that of Hebrews. For here the idea appears that we are continually pointed towards new forgiveness, and that it is promised to us. A further development can follow from this point. Of course, it leads to the regulation of the constantly renewed forgiveness by the institution of the church. But this is still not spoken of in I John.

40 · ESCHATOLOGY

M. Goguel, *The Birth of Christianity* (1953), pp. 271ff.; E. Grässer, *Das Problem der Parusieverzögerung in den synoptischen Evangelien und in der Apostelgeschichte*, BZNW 22 (1957); A. Strobel, *Untersuchungen zum eschatologischen Verzögerungsproblem*, SupplNov Test 2 (1961); O. Knoch, 'Die eschatologische Frage, ihre Entwicklung und ihr gegenwärtiger Stand', *BZ* NF 6 (1962), pp. 112–20; O. Cullmann, *Salvation in History* (1967).

Here, too, the divergence of orthodoxy and heresy is to be noted. At the same time, a new aspect will emerge.

Reminders: (a) Luke, who replaces the imminent expectation with

[1] R. Bultmann, in: *In Memoriam E. Lohmeyer* (1951), pp. 192ff., explains I John 5.14–21 as an addition of the 'ecclesiastical redactor'.

a picture of salvation history, belongs in this period. (*b*) The interpretation of eschatology has led to the following positions in scholarship.

1. Thoroughgoing eschatology:[1] the whole development is determined by the failure of the parousia to materialize. As a result, the church was forced to establish itself in the world by reflection and organization.

2. Realized eschatology (C. H. Dodd): futuristic eschatology is a secondary stage.

3. The outlines of a salvation-historical interpretation of the New Testament (O. Cullmann, and others).

It should be noted that in some places (II Thessalonians, II Peter), the failure of the parousia to materialize was felt to be a problem, but did not bring about any fundamental crisis. The question which confronts the historian is not: How did the church deal with the shattering of the foundations of its belief which was brought about by the delay of the parousia?,[2] but: Why did no crisis break out, although the early church was expecting the parousia very soon?[3]

Even with Paul, before there was a consciousness of the delay, and thus before it was necessary to discuss the problem that it raised, ideas were conceived which made the problem of the distance of the parousia in time an obsolete one, even before it appeared. Paul is convinced that 'the Lord is near', but this conviction is no part of his creed. He does not base his hope on any apocalyptic conception, but on the creed, which is independent of dates. He therefore teaches the believers that they need not worry about dates and times, because they are already children of the day, children of the light (I Thess. 5.1ff.). From the beginning, eschatology is not primarily an apocalyptic conception, but an understanding of being in faith. Hope remains prior to waiting. Once that has been understood, the delay of the parousia is not a problem for existence in faith. But is this condition fulfilled in the church?[4]

If we want to understand on the one hand the different attempts to solve the problem of the delay of the parousia, and on the other, the fact that it largely does not appear, we must be aware of the historical character of the relationship to the eschaton. What we

---

[1] M. Werner, *The Formation of Christian Dogma* (1957).
[2] Thus M. Werner.
[3] With O. Cullmann.
[4] Bultmann, *Theology of the New Testament* II, pp. 151ff., 161ff.

have is neither a timeless doctrine about the time of the Lord's appearance, nor the psychological element that people felt oppressed by the delay. The real problem lies rather in the eschatological expectation itself. The assertion that in fact it was superseded in faith from the very beginning does not contradict this. It *is* superseded in fact, even though the expectation is primarily portrayed in apocalyptic conceptions. But this insight must now be worked out in thought. There are two possibilities: either one begins from the apocalyptic conceptions; in this case it is only possible to find a solution if the understanding of existence contained in the imagery can be demonstrated. Alternatively, one begins with the understanding of faith. Both ways have been tried, and in each case there are again different types of attempts at a solution.

1. Attempts at a solution beginning from the eschatological conceptions:

(*a*) the Revelation of John: a construction of the drama of the end time from apocalyptic material;

(*b*) Luke: an interpretation of the time before the parousia as the period of the church.

2. Attempts at a solution beginning from the understanding of faith: Colossians, Ephesians, Hebrews, the gospel of John.

From today's standpoint, the first way seems the simpler and more obvious one. On the other hand, it is understandable that within the sphere of Paul's influence his thought was taken up and used as a starting point for further reflection. There is even an advantage here over against the first attempt at a solution, in that there is no need to keep taking along the difficulties out of which a way must be found. Indeed, the problem arises precisely from the fact that while the hope can be made tangible by the presentation of it in pictures of what is hoped for (the heavenly city, etc.), it is only the pictures that can be handed on: the hope itself, the eschatological attitude, the imminent expectation cannot be handed down. Certainly, the statements that express it can be repeated, but the attitude changes the longer people have to wait.

But the problem must be posed in still sharper terms. The attitude changes not only in the course of time, but 'with' time. It is necessary to distinguish: (*a*) the conception of time which is held; (*b*) the time in which people live. The expectation is determined not only by the conception of time but also by the duration of time which has elapsed. The primary question is not: How did people regard the end of the world and how near did they think it to be? but: What was their attitude to it – in giving shape to the church and thus to their own lives? We have to see not only what stand was taken up towards heaven, but what conclusions were drawn for the present time in the world in the light of heaven, or rather, of the future.

If the passage of time is itself a factor in the development of eschatology, there cannot be a uniform New Testament, or even Christian, eschatology. It is therefore senseless to play off the various eschatological sketches against each other, e.g. Paul against Luke. Their solutions are not arbitrary, but each belongs to its period. They must be understood in their context within the history of the church and of theology, as sketches of the horizon against which the church saw itself at a particular time and which constantly shifted both in time and in history. Here, too, of course, we may not postulate a logical development, but we can detect different attempts at solving the problem. Before it set out on theoretical consideration, the church expressed its practical attitude to continued existence in the world by the development of a church order (see section 39). That means that the church no longer sees itself right at an end-point, but in an epoch of the world. Of course, this epoch is not understood from the per- spective of the world and of world history, but against the course of salvation history. It is seen as the time of the reign of the exalted Christ, i.e. – from the world's point of view – as the time of the church (Luke) or as the time of the wandering of the people of God (Hebrews). It follows from this shift in approach that (a) the kingdom of God (or kingdom of Christ) is no longer seen in primarily temporal terms – as the coming kingdom – but in supra-temporal, spatial terms, as the heavenly kingdom (II Tim. 4.18; Colossians; Hebrews; Luke; Revelation).[1] (b) From the beginning, the cosmological expectation of the general resurrection of the dead and the individual expecta- tion of entering blessedness at the moment of death stand side by side without any attempt at reconciliation. It is understandable that in the course of time the second form of expectation comes more markedly into the foreground. (c) The relationship between eschato- logy and ethics alters, and with it the form and content of ethics. Put in rather crude terms, the place of the eschatological call to repentance and the summons to 'watch' (I Thess. 5.1ff.) is taken by the regulation of the *vita Christiana* – in a bourgeois pattern in the Pastoral epistles, in an ecclesiastical pattern in Hebrews (rules for the wandering), and

[1] R. Schnackenburg, *God's Rule and Kingdom* (1961), pp. 259ff.

differently again in I John. In addition, there is a more and more intensive concern with persecution and martyrdom (I Peter; Revelation). Now, of course, the danger threatens that the regulation of life will become the condition of salvation, that obedience will no longer be the portrayal of the new life (as it is in Paul), but the presupposition for gaining it, i.e. that the ethical commandment will once again be understood as a new law.

Any judgment on this change must again take into account the historicity of the process, and not 'evaluate' it in an abstract, unhistorical way. The shift of the eschatological aspect and thus men's attitude to the world is itself temporally determined in the literal sense. Caution is therefore necessary with negative value judgments. A conservation of the imminent expectation of the parousia would only have been an artificial and, in reality, an impossible solution, because it would have led to enthusiasm. There are still indications that this did in fact happen in individual cases: II Thessalonians is written against people who cultivate an imminent expectation of the end and appeal to Paul for their view. Formally, they are right, but they do not understand the heart of the matter, that is, they do not understand time.

EXAMPLES OF ATTEMPTS AT A SOLUTION USING APOCALYPTIC CONCEPTIONS

II Peter[1] develops its ideas in a struggle against heretics. It defends the original imminent expectation. But a formal appeal to the tradition is no longer sufficient, although it is made with due solemnity. What is the substance of the arguments? The letter works with the old theme that the end will suddenly break in, and with the idea of the relativity of time: for the Lord, a thousand years are like a day (3.8). That means that the author has in reality himself given up any imminent expectation. The argument of 3.8 can also be turned against him. The new element that has come in is the latent 'nevertheless': despite everything, it is necessary to keep to the tradition. The apologetic is in itself already a symptom that the imminent expectation has disappeared. In essentials, the expectation in II Peter is timeless: 'Two worlds confront each other'.[2] Eschatology is

---

[1] E. Käsemann, 'An Apologia for Primitive Christian Eschatology', *Essays on New Testament Themes*, SBT 41 (1964), pp. 169–195; A. Strobel, *op. cit.*, pp. 87–97.

[2] Käsemann, *op. cit.*, p. 180.

detached from christology. It looks forward to a transformation of 'nature'. Christ is seen essentially as judge.

The epistle to the Hebrews goes considerably deeper.[1] Here, too, there is an interweaving of temporal and spatial concepts, prospects forward and above. In effect, the spatial concepts predominate.True, remarks about the imminent expectation are repeated (1.2; 9.26; 10.25, 37), but they do not govern the eschatology; they primarily serve paraenetic purposes (10.36: patience). Under the token of the imminent expectation, the epistle prepares its readers in reality for the long period of striving and suffering. The picture of the people of God on the move shows how the church understands itself, and in what relationship it sees itself to the promised, hoped-for salvation. The temporal and spatial elements are associated here to make up the wandering through time: salvation is future, the goal is the future city (13.14). But this already exists, as the Jerusalem that is above (12.12–25). Grässer rightly asserts that the main point is not the futurity of salvation, but its certainty – despite the length of the way. This conception moulds the individual concepts: faith is remaining in the wandering group; sin is loitering behind it. Endurance is in practice synonymous with faith, particularly in connection with weariness on the wandering. This danger threatens the church, and the epistle fights against it – not through an elaborate description of the heavenly city, but by the summons to hold fast to Jesus Christ, the author and finisher of faith (10.32ff.), by practising the confession, in which the community has the ἐπαγγελία, the promise of the future rest. The guarantor is Christ, the high priest, who achieved the once-for-all and final sacrifice. This christological foundation to hope and christological interpretation of the church make an explanation of the delay of the parousia no longer necessary. The long way is constitutive of the nature of the church.[2] There is no need for the intermediate period either to be explained in salvation-historical terms or passed over by apocalyptic mythology; it is traversed. Hope is not just the prospect of the beyond. On the one hand, the ἐπαγγελία has already been realized; the believers are already citizens of the heavenly city (12.22–25); they are illuminated

---

[1] E. Käsemann, *Das wandernde Gottesvolk*, FRLANT NF 37 (1957²); F. Schierse, *Verheissung und Heilsvollendung*, MThS I 9 (1955), pp. 92ff.; R. Schnackenburg, *New Testament Theology Today* (1963), pp. 108ff. (literature); E. Grässer, *Der Glaube im Hebräerbrief* (1965).

[2] For the whole subject, see E. Grässer, *op. cit.*, pp. 171ff.

through baptism and have tasted the heavenly gift and the powers of the age to come. On the other hand, they are still on the way to the rest, though under the sign of promise and hope. They have faith and the possibility of ascending from its elementary content (6.1f.) to the λόγος τέλειος. Present and future are linked by worship and the confession, in which salvation is not only continually assured in words, but is actually communicated.[1]

Here, however, the limitation of this attempt at a solution has been shown: the promise applies to the people; the individual is considered only as a member of the group.

Persecution makes up one motive for the reshaping of eschatology. It can have the effect of re-intensifying the imminent expectation; this happens in I Peter, and above all in the Revelation of John. Here, too, conceptions of time and space are interwoven. The theme is the end of the world, the portrayal of the eschatological drama. But the heavenly world, which will manifest itself in the future, is already in existence. Remarkable though it may seem, precisely in the Revelation of John one can detect a remarkable elimination of time; it is absorbed by the apocalyptic imagery. This is clear above all in the understanding of the church and its place in the world.[2] The church is the people of the twelve tribes, but there are no reflections on pre-Christian Israel. There is no retrospect on salvation history. In accordance with this, no time-line is drawn from Christ through the apostles to the present, and no idea of tradition is developed. Instead, the immediate vision of the seer, the sight of the heavenly world, of the lamb in heaven, predominates. From the present, time only stretches forward, through lamentation to victory. But the vision of the seer – and, as a result of his communication, of the believer – is already hastening to its fulfilment.[3] That Christ reigns in heaven and that Satan has already been cast out has an influence on the apocalyptic outline and on the understanding of salvation and the end.[4] It is possible, because of the orientation on the saving work of

[1] G. Bornkamm, 'Das Bekenntnis im Hebräerbrief' (1942), in: *Studien zu Antike und Urchristentum*, Gesammelte Aufsätze II, pp. 188–203.

[2] E. Schweizer, *Church Order in the New Testament*, SBT 32 (1961), pp. 115ff.

[3] Bultmann's explanation (*Theology of the New Testament* II, pp. 173ff.) that there is basically the same relationship between future and present in the Revelation of John as in Jewish apocalyptic does not do justice to the facts. See W. G. Kümmel, *Introduction to the New Testament* (1966), p. 332; R. Schnackenburg (see note 1, p. 310), pp. 271ff.; E. Lohse, *Die Offenbarung des Johannes*, NTD 11 (1962²), pp. 3f.

[4] Unlike the book of Daniel and other Jewish apocalypses, the author does not

Christ, to interpret the nature and task of the church in the inter-mediate period: its suffering is part of its nature, and its task is the witness that leads it through suffering to glory.

EXAMPLES OF ATTEMPTS AT A SOLUTION OF A TIMELESS KIND

These are developed in the school of Paul. The most important indication for the change in eschatological understanding is the alteration of the Pauline futures into past tenses in Col. 2 and Eph. 2.[1]

Colossians[2]

There are still indications of a temporal perspective on the parousia: ὅταν ὁ Χριστὸς φανερωθῇ, ἡ ζωὴ ἡμῶν, τότε καὶ ὑμεῖς σὺν αὐτῷ φανερ-ωθήσεσθε ἐν δόξῃ (3.4). But there is nothing to say that this manifesta-tion will take place soon. The stress lies on the present: that Christ is our life (cf. Phil. 1.21). The prospect of the parousia is in fact with-out significance for the theology of the epistle. The spatial aspect, as it is expressed for example in the word σῶμα (Christi), predominates.[3] In the hymn in Col. 1.15ff., which the author found already in existence, σῶμα originally means the world. The author interprets it in terms of the church. But the cosmic background remains: the world is the sphere of the saving event; this is realized in the church, which is extended to cosmic dimensions. It reaches as far as the work of Christ, the subjection of all hostile powers. The non-speculative meaning is that the lordship of Christ may be experienced in the church as freedom. The place of revelation is the empirical world, which is not only summoned, but effectively placed under the lord-ship of Christ by the proclamation of the 'mystery'. The stress thus lies on the fact that salvation is already present. By the crucifixion and

---

reach back into the past; he does not follow a divine plan through stages of the course of the world.

[1] Col. 2.12: συνηγέρθητε – διὰ τῆς πίστεως; Eph. 2.6f.: συνήγειρεν καὶ συνεκάθισεν ἐν τοῖς ἐπουρανίοις—χάριτι. The affinity with, and at the same time the difference from, gnosticism, is clear.

[2] Bultmann, Theology of the New Testament II, pp. 175ff.; G. Bornkamm, 'Die Hoffnung im Kolosserbrief', TU 77 (1961), pp. 56–64; E. Lohse, 'Christusherr-schaft und Kirche im Kolosserbrief', NTS 11 (1964/5), pp. 203–16.

[3] A further development beyond Paul has begun, through a combination of σῶμα and κεφαλή; similarly in Ephesians.

ascension of Christ we have already been transported from the power of darkness into the kingdom of his beloved son, the 'kingdom of light' (1.13f.). The orientation of the saving benefits on the present shows the significance of 'hope': this word designates the hoped-for good preserved in heaven (1.5). The concept of knowledge and wisdom point in the same direction. Wisdom is insight into the mystery (2.2f.), whose revelation is spoken of in the characteristic revelatory pattern (1.26–28).[1]

We must, of course, ask whether the course that has been begun does not lead straight to gnosticism. The letter itself provides the answer. It is a polemic against gnosticism. But has its author really succeeded in drawing the dividing line? He could be infected with gnosticism without being aware of the fact. In fact, however, he rejects gnosticism at a decisive point: he highlights their practice, their relationship to the world, their ritual enactments, their reverence for the elements. These are the expression of an unhistorical doctrine of redemption and an unhistorical christology: for the heretics, Chirst is the embodiment of the cosmos, which is brought to itself by the reverencing of the elements. Over against all this, Colossians insists that the world is indeed the body of Christ, but that its nature must be understood historically. Redemption took place through the historical saving act of the cross. It does not lead to a speculative view of the world, but forms the basis of the common life of the believers in the freedom from guilt and from the powers which is disclosed through faith. The relationship between the Christian and the world is particularized in a positive way in the relationship between the indicative and the imperative (3.1–4). The demand τὰ ἄνω ζητεῖτε is not an invitation to an ascent through meditation and morality; paradoxically, it is a demand to seek the place where we are already, though intangibly and unknown to ourselves, in the way of the mystery.

Ephesians

The time factor is excluded, apart from the irreducible minimum which is necessary in order to be able to describe a phenomenon at all, namely, the church as the realization of the divine οἰκονομία.[2]

---

[1] D. Lührmann, *Das Offenbarungsverständnis bei Paulus und in paulinischen Gemeinden*, WMANT 16 (1965). Cf. section 11 I above.

[2] For the concept, see J. Reumann, *NovTest* 3 (1959), pp. 282–92, and TU 78 (Studia Patristica III) (1961), pp. 370–79.

Ephesians 2.11ff. provides one example: the erstwhile Jews and the erstwhile Gentiles have become one in the church. The past is not traced back in salvation-historical terms, but is merely a foil to the present unity. True, there is still the expression 'the coming age' (1.21), but it is taken together with the present age under the viewpoint that Christ is enthroned at the right hand of God now and in the future. The beginnings to be found in Colossians are developed systematically: the alteration of tenses (2.4ff.); the idea of the church (σῶμα and κεφαλή); the revelation pattern (3.4ff.). Ephesians combines the mythical-cosmic conception of the body of Christ with the mythical-anthropological conception of the 'redeemed redeemer': Christ is the 'perfect man' who gathers his own to himself and leads them up to himself. He is the beginning and the end and the sphere of this movement upwards; the head of the body and at the same time the totality; head and body: head of the cosmos and head of the church. Salvation is realized in the church. Its place is the cosmos, which is open upwards, towards the highest point where God is enthroned and Christ is at his right hand.

Christ and the church are thus identified in a certain way, but this definition cannot be reversed. The identity stems from Christ as the one who discloses the mystery to the church. The church represents Christ in so far as it proclaims the mystery in the world. But it cannot for its part commandeer Christ for itself. That would make Christ a mere cypher for what the church does and represents.

In this way, the boundary over against gnosticism is also drawn for the individual believers: their movement is that of ascent to the head. But it is an ascent 'in Christ', not an independent movement upwards. The believers possess the full reality of salvation; they have already been transported into the ἐπουρανία – in faith, under the imperative: Eph. 2.6–10. The temporal prospect of future salvation is replaced by the understanding of the mystery that has been revealed (3.1ff.).

On closer inspection, what are at first glance highly speculative and meditative formulations of the epistle reveal a surprisingly sober content.[1] The subject of the teaching is not speculation, the mythical cosmology and soteriology as such. Although the formulations largely reveal a gnostic background[2] – the identity of redeemer and redeemed, timelessness, the redeemed is already transported above the

---

[1] Cf. M. Dibelius – H. Greeven, HNT 12 (1953³).
[2] H. Schlier, *Christus und die Kirche im Epheserbrief*, BHTh 6 (1930).

world – all these expressions and themes describe the nature of the church in the world and the nature of the Christians in the church as freedom, as movement in faith, not as a condition in sight. The conception that the church stretches right into the ἐπουράνια means that it is able to treat the world in its preaching, that it cannot be overcome by the world. There is thus a description of the nature and possibility of the preaching and the freedom for the believers, which is particularized in the fact that they can confront the powers. This is matched by the broad elaboration of the paraenesis in chs. 4–6 with the weighty closing accent. In Ephesians, as in Colossians, the paraenesis makes it clear that our nature as heavenly man is not a *habitus*. We are not invited to soar above the world in mystical meditation, but to do what is commanded in the world, in our place, in the church; to live in accordance with what we already are in Christ.[1]

Retrospect and Prospect

From a historical point of view, in the period under consideration there were two possibilities of depicting the other-worldliness of salvation: 1. On the right hand, apocalyptic. This portrays the future in a picture of the future. Time seems to be to a large extent constitutive of this outline, as it transposes salvation into a future. In reality, it is envisaged in timeless terms, as it is oriented on the picture of the future, not on time itself. But the original intention remains – that of depicting the unworldliness of salvation. 2. On the left hand, gnosticism. This, too, has formally eliminated time. The content of its teaching is a direct retreat from the world, the surrender of the world. Between these two limits, the possibilities of the Christian presentation of salvation also move. On the right hand lies the Lucan outline of salvation history with the pattern of the two comings; on the left, continuing Paul's teaching, the elimination of time. But a retreat from the world, as it is to be found in gnosticism, is never reached; at the most we have separation from the world in terms of the freedom of faith. The theology of John, which we must now discuss, lies on the same side.

---

[1] Ignatius also represents the timeless type; see Bultmann, *Theology of the New Testament* II, pp. 191ff.

PART FIVE

JOHN

41 · THE HISTORICAL CONTEXT OF THE JOHANNINE WRITINGS

R. Bultmann, *Theology of the New Testament* II, pp. 3ff.; id., *Das Evangelium des Johannes*, Meyer Kommentar II (1962[17]), cf. the literature in the *Ergänzungsheft* (1957); R. Schnackenburg, *New Testament Theology Today* (1963), pp. 90ff.; id., *The Gospel of St John* I (1968); W. F. Howard, *The Fourth Gospel in Recent Criticism and Interpretation*, revised by C. K. Barrett (1955[4]); E. Haenchen, 'Aus der Literatur zum Johannesevangelium 1929–56', *ThR* NF 23 (1955), pp. 295–335; C. H. Dodd, *The Interpretation of the Fourth Gospel* (1953[2]); S. Schulz, *Die Stunde der Botschaft* (1967), pp. 297ff.; J. L. Martyn, *History and Theology in the Fourth Gospel* (1968).

I Introductory Questions

W. G. Kümmel, *Introduction to the New Testament* (1966), pp. 134–75; R. Schnackenburg, *The Gospel of St John* I, pp. 1ff.

A gospel, three epistles and an apocalypse have been handed down under the name of John (meaning the son of Zebedee). The apocalypse stands very much on its own, as regards both style and content. It is hardly relevant for the investigation of 'Johannine' theology. The author is unknown; it certainly cannot be the son of Zebedee. There is dispute whether the gospel and the epistles (or at least the first epistle) were written by the same author. The evidence seems most probably to indicate that the epistles derive from the school of the evangelist.[1]

The author of the gospel is not an eye-witness of the story of Jesus. He does not give personal reminiscences, but a theological interpretation. He already uses written sources.[2] This raises the question of his relationship: (a) to the synoptic gospels; (b) to the synoptic tradition. The question is not only a purely literary one; it must be seen in a wider framework: can the historical context of this book and this theology be established, or at least set within reasonable limits? Here we must distinguish (a) its place in church history; (b) its place in religious ideas.

[1] John 21 indicates that there was a group of disciples. Cf. E. Haenchen, 'Neuere Literatur zu den Johannesbriefen', *ThR* NF 26 (1960), pp. 1ff., 267ff.

[2] But others assume that he is only working over oral traditions (C. H. Dodd; B. Noack, *Zur johanneischen Tradition* (1954)).

II   The Place of the Gospel in Church History

It is only possible to establish the context of the gospel by delimiting its possible place. Just as the author of the book remains unknown, so, too, there is no exact time, no particular community, in which it can be found a place.

On the basis of two papyrus fragments, the year 100 is usually accepted as the time of its origin. The fragments are: P 52 (Rylands 457) with two passages from John 18, written at the beginning of the second century; and P. Egerton 2 with fragments from an 'unknown gospel'.

We must therefore try to determine the relationship of the gospel to other writings, above all, of course, to the synoptics, and then to Paul.

I. JOHN AND THE SYNOPTIC GOSPELS

Questions:

(*a*) Is John dependent on the synoptic gospels at all?

(*b*) If so, then on which of them?

(*c*) In what way does John regard his relationship to the synoptic gospels?

(*d*) If he is independent of the synoptic gospels, then how is his relationship to the synoptic tradition to be explained?

The differences are quite obvious, right from the prologue. John takes only a minimum from the narrative material of the synoptics. There is only one exception, the passion narrative. This is connected with its special literary character. In addition, there are a few miracles: the feeding of the five thousand; the walking on the water; a variant of the story of the centurion of Capernaum.[1] The story of the baptism of Jesus also has a parallel. There are no exorcisms. No parables at all are taken from the synoptic sayings material. Instead, there are two 'Johannine' parables: the parable of the shepherd and the parable of the vine. Finally, only a few individual logia are common to both.

The style is different: the Johannine Jesus does not speak in sayings and parables. He delivers discourses full of symbols: 'I am . . .'

The themes are different. Jesus does not announce the coming of the kingdom of God,[2] but the present judgment which is being played

[1] Two miracles in John have no synoptic parallel: the wedding at Cana and the raising of Lazarus.

[2] This expression appears only in John 3.1ff., in the Johannine revision of a 'synoptic' logion.

out in belief or unbelief. He does not teach about questions of the law (fasting) and about self-righteousness; he does not dispute with the scribes, but with the 'Jews'. There are no longer any differentiations within Judaism. The church and the synagogue confront each other from fixed positions. The Jews represent the world, which refuses to believe.

The synoptic and Johannine accounts cannot be compared historically. The historical Jesus cannot have preached in this way. John is conscious of this: he shapes the sayings of Jesus quite freely, starting from a few traditional sayings. He even shapes the logia he takes over to suit his theology: cf. John 3.3 with Mark 10.15. If the independence of the Johannine account is thus immediately clear, on the other hand John cannot be completely independent of the synoptic tradition. His passion narrative largely agrees with that of the synoptics. Analysis shows that he is using a source which is closely related to the basic material of the Marcan passion. He then provides this with his own additions by way of comment.

Even the outline of his book is not independent of the type of the literary gospel, probably created by the author of the gospel of Mark, despite all its peculiarities. It is, however, disputed whether John knew and used the present synoptic gospels (or a part of them). It is also possible that he worked over related sources or merely drew on oral tradition, which partly coincided with the traditional material contained in the synoptics. In the latter case (the use of oral tradition) he would not – from the point of view of the history of tradition – be subordinate to the synoptics, but co-ordinate with them.

This is the direction in which conservative scholars[1] look for a solution to the riddle of John. They conclude from this co-ordination that the Johannine account has the same historical value as that of the synoptics.

All possible solutions have been advanced at one time or another:[2]

1. John knows all three synoptic gospels;

2. John knows Mark and Luke;

3. John knows Mark (or a source of Mark);

4. John knows Luke (particularly because of points of contact in the passion narrative);

[1] B. Noack, *Zur johanneischen Tradition* (1954); C. H. Dodd, *Historical Tradition in the Fourth Gospel* (1963). For a criticism, see G. Strecker, *Gnomon* 36 (1964), pp. 773ff.

[2] There is a survey by W. G. Kümmel, *Introduction to the New Testament* (1966), pp. 134ff.

5. John knows none of the synoptic gospels, but only traditions common to both.

No compelling proof has been advanced of literary dependence of John on one of the synoptic gospels. Where the similarity is greatest, in the passion narrative, it can be shown that John is using a source which is not identical with, but only related to the original form of the passion in the synoptic gospels. The same is true of the miracle stories which both have in common. John uses a written source which differs from the synoptic version.[1] He seems to have taken over the logia common to both from oral tradition. This does not mean that John knows nothing of the other gospels. That is to be concluded from the fact that he shapes his book in accordance with the literary pattern of the gospels. But he does not use them as his sources.

Why not? This is an old dispute: does John mean to supplement the synoptic gospels or to replace them? In fact this is not a real alternative. Of course he does not mean to supplement them in the sense that one would first read one of the synoptic gospels and then his own. His account stands by itself: anyone who has read his book, will know what a man needs to believe (20.30f.). But on the other hand, he does not mean to supersede other books. He writes for a special group in the church: for these he created the 'perfect gospel'.[2]

The most characteristic feature of the gospel of John is the series of great discourses which Jesus delivers. Two groups must be distinguished: the public discourses and the farewell discourses before the disciples. On the basis of a subtle stylistic analysis, Bultmann infers a written source for the discourses, the 'revelation discourses', which the author has taken over and commented on with his own expansions. This source is pre-Christian and gnostic.[3] There are, however, the following objections to the hypothesis of a discourse-source: (a) the stylistic analysis is not so clear as to provide a compelling demonstration of the use of a source;[4] (b) if there is an underlying independ-

---

[1] Bultmann: σημεῖα source. An analysis is given by E. Haenchen, 'Johanneische Probleme', *ZThK* 56 (1959), pp. 19–54 (=*Gott und Mensch* (1965), pp. 78–113).

[2] Clement of Alexandria (in Eusebius, H.E. VI 14.7; see K. Aland, *Synopsis*, p. 539): πνευματικὸν εὐαγγέλιον.

[3] This thesis was taken further (with a reconstruction of the source) by H. Becker, *Die Reden des Johannesevangeliums und der Stil der gnostischen Offenbarungsrede*, FRLANT 68 (1956).

[4] For the analogous situation in I John, see E. Haenchen, 'Neuere Literatur zu den Johannesbriefen', *ThR* NF 26 (1960), pp. 25ff. Bultmann's reconstruction (*Festgabe für A. Jülicher* (1927), pp. 138–58; cf. *Die Johannesbriefe*, Meyer, XIV (1967), pp. 10f.) is simply rhythmic prose.

ent gnostic discourse-source, it is hard to explain how individual discourses have been attached to the miracle stories (the discourses about the bread of life); (c) the distinction between public and esoteric discourses is Johannine. It corresponds to the construction of the gospel. An analogous division can hardly be imagined in gnostic sources; (d) from a religious-historical point of view, the hypothesis of a discourse source presupposes that the gnostic revealer also had a history in the world. This is not only without analogy, but altogether quite impossible. It is therefore best to assume that the author of the gospel created the discourses. Quite apart from the problem of the sources, it can be stated that the discourses are the means by which the author discloses the meaning of events to the reader. After he has described the significance of the incarnation as a whole in the prologue, he interprets through the discourses: (1) the meaning of the miracles of Jesus (concentrated in the ἐγώ εἰμι sayings); (2) the meaning of the death of Jesus.

Comparison of John with the synoptic gospels raises a series of problems which must be discussed here. For the miracle stories, John uses a source in which the miraculous element is vividly heightened (the raising of Lazarus). What is the relationship between this and the interpretation of the miracles in the discourses, in which their significance is reduced to a purely symbolic one: 'I am . . .'? The interpretation is so intensive that behind it the question whether the evangelist believes the miracles really happened seems to vanish (Bultmann). Moreover, he himself adds references to the source which point in the same direction. In John 4.48, he inserts, 'Unless you see signs and wonders you will not believe' (cf. 6.26). Ernst Haenchen concludes from this that for John the miracle is only a 'sign', an indication of something higher. The important thing is to seek Jesus himself, and not something through him. This spiritual interpretation is in fact the essential element for the evangelist. But it presupposes miracle in all its crudeness.

There is a similar tension between crude realism and spiritual interpretation in the Easter stories. In John we find the *theologia crucis* at its sharpest. In Paul, the cross is the saving event; it belongs most closely with the exaltation; we know the Exalted One only as the Crucified One. John goes one step further: the crucifixion is itself already the exaltation. A realistic understanding of resurrection and ascension seems irreconcilable with this identification. The idea is evidently broken up in interpretation, in gnosticism. But in no other gospel are the Easter stories so crude as in John. This can be explained from the fact that John found stories of this type in his source. In that case, however, we must ask why he sought out this source in particular. No satisfactory answer has so far been found to this question.

There is the same problem about the sacraments. The sacrament has virtually vanished from John, apart from a few traces. Why? Has it become unimportant to the evangelist in comparison with the understanding of Jesus' 'I am'? Or does John simply presuppose the sacrament as something that is there, about which he need say no more because the practice of it goes without question, so that the evangelist can concentrate on the interpretation? There is the same question, finally, about eschatology. If all the stress is on the fact that the hour of judgment is already here, does John challenge the popular futurist eschatology? Or does he presuppose it, but actualize it and bring it to a deeper understanding?

2. JOHN AND PAUL

Paul does not write a history of Jesus. So the question, Does John know the Pauline epistles? can only be concerned with whether John takes up Paul's ideas to interpret the saving work of Jesus. The two agree in the fact that the cross is the saving event. At any rate, a literary dependence of John on Paul cannot be recognized.

Nor can the relationship between the two be forced into a scheme of development, say, that John represents the further development and completion of Paul's theology. This is in fact true: in John, the intentions of Paul and indeed of all early Christian theology are conceptualized. But this does not indicate any clear dependence or even a deliberate taking over of ideas and development of them in theological work. It is not a rectilinear continuation, but an independent new interpretation of the tradition. Here there is a considerable simplification in the ideas. For instance, Paul's anthropological terminology, which is determined by Hellenistic-Jewish ideas, is missing: συνείδησις, νοῦς, ἔσω ἄνθρωπος, φύσις, ψυχή, ἀρετή.

If we want to assess common elements and differences, we should notice that both Paul and John do not simply make free formulations. Both stand in the community's tradition of thought and language. Both take up the themes of a mythical soteriology. We must therefore suppose that similarities not only rest on literary dependence but are also given by a common milieu in the history of religion. That the christological titles are in essentials identical, follows from the fact that both go back to the creed of the community.

There is affinity not only in the material, but also in the way in which it is worked out, the theological intention. Both work with the concept κόσμος and neither has any cosmological interest. In each instance, κόσμος primarily refers to the world of men. Each uses the word in a qualified sense: 'this' world = the evil world. The evil in the world is not understood in mythical-cosmological terms, but in line with the idea of sin: the world is fallen creation. The identity of creator and revealer is maintained. The revealer, the Son of God, is pre-existent; he has made the world. He is 'sent' by the Father in love; he is obedient, by dying. After completing his saving work, he returns to his heavenly place.

The verdict on the human situation is in principle the same in both cases; man has succumbed to sin. Sin is not the individual transgression, but the whole situation of rebellion against God, of self-assertion against him. John predominantly uses the singular ἁμαρτία,[1] very much in the same way as does Paul. Present and future, indicative and imperative, are so related that the material meaning coincides in each case: the future life is already effective in the present. The believer is endowed with the spirit; this is freedom of movement in the world, the possibility of love. The communication of salvation is the basis for the commandment, which is summed up in the commandment to love: ἐντολὴν καινὴν δίδωμι ὑμῖν, ἵνα ἀγαπᾶτε ἀλλήλους, καθὼς ἠγάπησα ὑμᾶς ἵνα καὶ ὑμεῖς ἀγαπᾶτε ἀλλήλους (13.34). In John, of course, the assertion that eternal life is already present is much more intensive than in Paul. This is where we reach the difference.[2] ὁ τὸν λόγον μου ἀκούων καὶ πιστεύων τῷ πέμψαντί με ἔχει ζωὴν αἰώνιον, καὶ εἰς κρίσιν οὐκ ἔρχεται ἀλλὰ μεταβέβηκεν ἐκ τοῦ θανάτου εἰς τὴν ζωήν (5.24). If we take this sentence by itself, it sounds gnostic. But John keeps a distinction by stressing that this applies to believers. He does not destroy the dialectic that – in Pauline terms – we walk in faith and not in sight. True, John, unlike Paul, speaks a good deal of seeing the glory, and seeing it in the present. But by this he does not mean either a mystic inner vision or a mythical 'knowledge of higher worlds', but the 'seeing' of the Son in understanding by believing and hearing his word.

The essential difference lies in his use of the elements of objectifying conceptions. Paul shows the relevance of eschatology in interpreting the present, but he keeps its cosmological framework: parousia on the

---

[1] μετάνοια and ἄφεσις ἁμαρτιῶν are also absent from John.

[2] D. Mollat, 'Remarques sur le vocabulaire spatial du quatrième évangile', TU 73 (Studia Evangelica I) (1959), pp. 321–28.

clouds, resurrection of the dead at the end of the world. In John, on the other hand, the apocalyptic ideas are stripped away. The only point at issue is whether a minute remnant (a prospect of the last day) is left, which has lost all its imagery, or whether even that is no longer present. In any case, eschatology is concentrated on its significance, the interpretation of the condition of faith in the world.

Just as the prospective dimension of time is missing, so too is its retrospective dimension: there is no extension of salvation history in time, no retrospect to the history of Israel. Indeed, even the temporal distance between Jesus and the church's present plays no part.[1] Similarly, there is no conceptuality of salvation history: the designation of the church as ἐκκλησία (also σῶμα), of Christians as ἅγιοι, ἐκλεκτοί. We can still detect suggestions that these words were known to the writer (ἐκλέγεσθαι: 6.70; 13.18; 15.16, 19; ἅγιος: 17.17, 19), but they are no longer used technically. Just as there is no retrospect of salvation history, so, too, there is no interpretation of the church in this kind of category. In John, the church does not understand itself as the true Israel or as the new Israel, but sets itself up in antithesis to the 'Jews'. Of course, John knows that the church arose out of Judaism. He also says this expressly (he himself was probably a Jewish Christian): the Messiah comes from this people (salvation is of the Jews: 4.22); the scripture testifies to Jesus. But the Jews have refused to believe and have thus become 'the Jews'. Here no positive connection is developed, but a critical antithesis.

Of course, this polemic is not 'anti-semitic'. It serves exclusively to depict the faith which is exposed to the attack of the world. The Jews represent the world in its attitude towards faith. One example is 8.30–59: John goes back to the figures of the Old Testament, Abraham and Moses, for the purpose of critical discussion only.[2]

Salvation can be described throughout the New Testament as 'peace'.[3] The 'mood' of peace is joy: 'Behold, I bring tidings of great joy' (Luke 2.10). Peace and joy describe the eschatological condition – in the world. John, too, works with this conceptuality: 14.27; 17.13. The eschatological significance is clear. The characteristic Johannine

---

[1] Cf. E. Schweizer, 'Der Kirchenbegriff im Evangelium und den Briefen des Johannes', TU 73 (*Studia Evangelica* I) (1959), pp. 363–81 (= *Neotestamentica* (1963), pp. 254–71); O. Cullmann, *Salvation in History* (1967), pp. 268ff., differs.

[2] E. Grässer, 'Die antijüdische Polemik im Johannesevangelium', *NTS* 11 (1964/5), pp. 74–90.

[3] Rom. 5.1; Phil. 4.7: the peace of God; Luke 2.14.

element lies in the christological concentration; 'my peace', 'my joy'. These are the words of the one who departs, who first leaves his own in 'sorrow'. But his departure is the condition for the establishment of peace. Thus this establishing of peace is more closely connected with the church than in other parts of the New Testament; peace is visible as love of the brethren. The community is the group of those who love one another, who are kept together through the world's hate and in precisely this way experience peace, as the spirit rules in the community and leads it into all truth.

The Pauline terminology of justification is also absent from John. True, the verb πιστεύειν plays a central role in John. But the noun πίστις does not occur.[1] The word χάρις appears only in the prologue, in the one passage where the Pauline antithesis of law and grace appears (1.16f.). Here we do in fact have the conceptuality and thought of Paul. But the basis is too narrow to show any literary dependence. The problem of law and justification plays no role in John outside this passage. The concept χάρις is not developed. Significantly, it is expanded, and thus illuminated, by a Johannine concept: καὶ ἡ ἀλήθεια. Similarly, the antithesis of works and faith and the concept of the 'righteousness of God' are also absent.[2] Faith is developed in a different direction from that in Paul, not in antithesis to the law, but in terms of the connection between faith and knowledge.[3]

None of Paul's ethical conceptuality, i.e. the terms which in Paul characterize man's general attitude, καυχᾶσθαι, ἐπιθυμεῖν, μεριμνᾶν, is to be found.

The use, or rather lack of use, of σάρξ and πνεῦμα is particularly interesting. These two concepts could well have fitted into the series of Johannine antitheses: light and darkness, above and below, life and death, truth and lie. True, John knows the contrast between spirit and flesh, as two passages show: 3.5ff.; 6.63. But he does not use it for a comprehensive definition of man.

Whereas the main part of Pauline conceptuality falls into the background in John – almost to vanishing point – instead, an antithetical conceptuality which is only occasionally hinted at in Paul comes into

[1] This is not the case in I John.

[2] δικαιοσύνη occurs only in the farewell discourses (16.8–10). Jesus' righteousness is his victory in the controversy with the world.

[3] The use of the verb predominates throughout: γνῶσις is also absent, as well as πίστις.

the centre: the opposition of light and darkness.[1] This leads us to the question of the historical setting of the gospel of John.

III   The Historical Setting

W. Bauer, *Das Johannesevangelium*, HNT 6 (1933[2]); R. Bultmann, *Das Evangelium des Johannes*; C. H. Dodd, *The Interpretation of the Fourth Gospel*, pp. 10ff. For a derivation from Judaism: F.-M. Braun, *Jean le théologien* (1959), pp. 65ff.; O. Böcher, *Der johanneische Dualismus im Zusammenhang des nachbiblischen Judentums* (1965). For Qumran: G. Baumbach, *Qumran und das Johannes-Evangelium* (1958); K. G. Kuhn, 'Johannes-Evangelium und Qumrantexte', SupplNovTest 6 (Cullmann Festschrift) (1962), pp. 111–22; H. Braun, *Qumran und das NT* I (1966), pp. 96ff.

It has been conjectured that the conceptuality and themes of the gospel of John derive from the following backgrounds: (1) from the Old Testament (traditional); (2) from Judaism in general (Böcher); (3) particularly from wisdom (F. M. Braun); (4) from Qumran (Baumbach); (5) from gnosticism (Bultmann). Each of these theses can appeal to supporting evidence. The only question is the stage of assimilation at which it is in John.

Examples are:

1. The Old Testament: the first sentence of the gospel points back to the Old Testament account of creation. But the Logos as creator can no more be derived from there than the dualism of light and darkness.

2. Judaism: dualistic ideas occur in post-biblical Jewish writings. But their emergence in Judaism is itself a problem; moreover, they have a completely different shape in the gospel of John from elsewhere.

3. 'Wisdom': the Logos is in fact related to Sophia (Wisdom, Philo). But there are themes here which cannot be explained from a development within Judaism. Early gnosticism makes an impact.[2] It is important that the elimination of time is anticipated in the wisdom literature.

4. Qumran: there is dualistic conceptuality here, and – in contrast to gnosticism – there is no thinking in substances. Here the Qumran texts and the gospel of John meet. But in Qumran there is no mythical conception of the descent and ascent of the revealer. Qumran knows

[1] Cf. Paul: children of light (I Thess. 5.1ff.).

[2] John is not dependent on Philo; but a common religious background can be seen in the figure of the Logos.

no redeemer figure, nor the idea of rebirth nor basic Johannine concepts like 'life'.[1]

5. Gnosticism: gnostic writings, both Christian (the Odes of Solomon, Ignatius) and non-Christian (Hermetic and Mandaean writings) provide the best material for comparison. But the gnostic literature has – with significant exceptions – a much stronger mythical stamp than the gospel of John. Mission, descent, call, the gathering together of the scattered fragments of light, and ascent, form independent themes there in a quite different way. There is no mythical background in John: the fall of the primal man and the scattering of the fragments of light, the notion of the consubstantiality of redeemer and redeemed. There is no cosmological apparatus (stages of descent through the spheres, etc.). John portrays no other-worldly scenes of the sending of the revealer by the supreme God, no heavenly conversations. He has concentrated the theme of the heavenly conversation on one point: Jesus declares that he has seen and heard the Father. But he gives no other content to the conversation than his ἐγώ εἰμι, and that the Father bears witness to him and he to the Father. John knows the pre-existence of the Logos, but not the pre-existence of souls. Redemption is not understood in substantial or natural terms, but as a free act of election. John maintains the unity of creation and redemption.

There is a debate as to whether the gnostic myth was already fully developed right at the beginning of gnosticism, as the presupposition for it, and whether John was already familiar with it in this form. In that case, the trend of his thought would be a radical reduction of the myth (Bultmann). Alternatively, we are to presuppose a gnosticism in only a fledgling state: in that case, John toyed with gnostic ideas to a considerably greater degree than any other theologian before him.

IV   The 'Aim' of the Book

There are the following theses: the gospel of John is a missionary writing, (1) for the world; (2) for Jews; (3) (in a modified form) for Diaspora Jews.[2]

---

[1] See H. Braun, op. cit.

[2] On 1.: C. H. Dodd, The Interpretation of the Fourth Gospel; on 2.: K. Bornhäuser, Das Johannesevangelium eine Missionsschrift für Israel (1928); on 3.: J. A. T. Robinson, 'The New Look on the Fourth Gospel', Twelve New Testament Studies, SBT 34 (1962), pp. 94–106; W. C. van Unnik, 'The Purpose of St John's Gospel', TU 73 (Studia Evangelica I) (1959), pp. 382–411.

Against this it must be asserted that the book does not have a missionary character. For the author, Israel and the world are not alternatives. The Jews represent the world (see above). The Johannine idea of the church does not match the idea of mission, but that of 'testimony', the strengthening of faith. This fact is already reflected in the construction of the gospel: the first part depicts the revelation of the glory before the world; the second, its revelation before the community.

42 · CHRISTOLOGY

R. Bultmann, *Theology of the New Testament* II, pp. 33ff.; R. Schnackenburg, *New Testament Theology Today*, pp. 92ff.; E. M. Sidebottom, *The Christ of the Fourth Gospel* (1961); J. Blank, *Krisis* (1964).

It could be said that the whole of Johannine theology is christology, though it could equally well be argued that it is soteriology (or anthropology). The same is true, of course, for Paul and for all primitive Christian thought, though it holds for John in rather a different way. He concentrates christology on the self-disclosure of the revealer: 'It is I'. The cosmological framework is stripped off completely.

For example, on one occasion Paul can designate Christ the εἰκών of God (II Cor. 4.4). This is a christological notion, which is taken over from Jewish wisdom speculation.[1] Personified wisdom is the power of the divine revelation. In Jesus, men's expectations of God and his revelation, and thus of wisdom, were found to be fulfilled. Now the figure of wisdom is related to that of the word. So when John conceives of Jesus as the λόγος he seems to be near to the Pauline christological idea and to draw out at length what is only hinted at in it. But things are not as simple as that. There is no rectilinear development; we have here a new conception. This does not, of course, simply lie in the fact that whereas Paul says εἰκών, John says λόγος. In Paul, the hypostasis of wisdom certainly lies in the background, but the designation of Jesus as εἰκών only serves as a characterization: it has not yet become a title. In using the word 'wisdom' (I Cor. 1.20ff.,

[1] Cf. Col. 1.15ff.: εἰκών is synonymous with σοφία.

30), Paul is not operating with the figure of wisdom. He begins from abstract wisdom. He asserts that the Greeks seek wisdom, and shows that their wisdom is folly in face of the wisdom of God and that God's wisdom became wisdom 'for us'. This is a pointed formulation, an identification in the semitic style, and not a real personification (cf. II Cor. 5.21: in Christ we have become God's righteousness).

In John, on the other hand, the Logos is thought of a priori as a person. John does not say 'the Logos of God', but, in absolute terms, 'the Logos'. The statement, 'Jesus is the Logos', is not a pointed expression or a rhetorical exaggeration: it is meant literally, as a direct description of the nature of Jesus. All other christological titles in John serve in the end merely to interpret this one fundamental title.

Certainly the particular significance which the individual titles possess in the creed still shine through. But the important thing is that John subordinates them to the conception 'Logos' = 'Son' = 'the one who is sent', and shapes them all in this sense. He documents this by putting the title Logos thematically at the beginning of his book, but not working with it after that. So this title is as it were exempt.

To interpret his statement that Christ is the wisdom of God, Paul describes the content of the wisdom that has been revealed: I Cor. 2. John, on the other hand, cannot offer such information about the content. For the Logos is itself the entire and exclusive content. That means that revealer and revelation are in the strict sense identical. The revelation offers no knowable content apart from the fact that the revealer is 'it'.

This provides the themes of Johannine christology:

i The Logos;
ii The development of the traditional christological titles;
iii The description of the revelation in the ἐγώ εἰμι statements.

I The Logos

C. H. Dodd, *The Interpretation of the Fourth Gospel*, pp. 263–85; E. Käsemann, 'The Structure and Purpose of the Prologue to John's Gospel', *New Testament Questions of Today*, pp. 138–67; R. Schnackenburg, 'Logos-Hymnus und johanneischer Prolog', *BZ* NF 1 (1957), pp. 69–109; S. Schulz, 'Die Komposition des Johannesprologs und die Zusammensetzung des 4. Evangeliums', TU 73 (*Studia Evangelica* I) (1959), pp. 351–62; id., *Komposition und Herkunft der johanneischen Reden*, BWANT 5, Folge 1 (1960), pp. 7–61; E. Haenchen, 'Probleme des johanneischen Prologs', *ZThK* 60 (1963), pp. 305–334 (= *Gott und Mensch* (1965), pp. 114–43). Cf. the commentaries on John 1.1ff.

The historical problems of the derivation of this title will be taken for granted here. In them is repeated the question of the historical context of the whole Johannine terminology and thought-world, or rather, it is concentrated here in a nutshell.

Survey of Attempts at Explaining the Derivation

1. This is a definition created by John himself. But in that case, the question is how he arrives at it.

2. The title has been developed from the Old Testament. There the word of God plays a significant role. Above all, God created the world through his word. Indeed, John deliberately follows the first sentence of the Bible with the first sentence of his book:

$$\dot{\epsilon}\nu \ \dot{a}\rho\chi\hat{\eta} \quad \begin{array}{l} (a) \ \hat{\eta}\nu \ \dot{o} \ \lambda\dot{o}\gamma os \\ (b) \ \dot{\epsilon}\pi o\acute{\iota}\eta\sigma\epsilon\nu \ \dot{o} \ \theta\epsilon\dot{o}s \ \tau\dot{o}\nu \ o\dot{\upsilon}\rho\alpha\nu\dot{o}\nu \ \kappa\alpha\grave{\iota} \ \tau\dot{\eta}\nu \ \gamma\hat{\eta}\nu. \end{array}$$

In that case, it means that the Logos is the mediator of creation. But the Johannine significance of the Logos cannot be explained from the Old Testament. True, God speaks in the creation narrative and in so doing creates the world. But his word is word, and not a person. Nor does the key word Logos occur in the creation narrative. The 'word' is never a hypostasis in the Old Testament, but is always the spoken word of God. Nor is the concept used in an absolute, technical way ('the' word).

3. The concept Logos derives from Greek philosophy. Heraclitus is said to have introduced it here, in the prologue to his work: 'Men do not understand this Logos, which is eternal, either before they have heard of it or when they have heard of it. For although everything happens in accordance with this Logos, they are like novices.' This Logos is not a person and not a creator. Later, the Logos is one of the basic cosmological and anthropological concepts of the Stoa. But although the Stoics can occasionally speak in personifying expressions of the Logos, it does not become a person even here. The Logos remains a concept. On the other side, the Johannine Logos has nothing to do with an understanding of the world in terms of reason.

4. Jewish wisdom has already been mentioned above as a counterpart of the Logos. In addition, in Philo, even the Logos is endowed with personal features: it is called δεύτερος θεός, it is mediator of creation and revelation. However, it does not become a real person. Its figure remains fluctuating. Nevertheless, in the background one does notice a figure akin to wisdom. Traces of it occur elsewhere, above all

in gnosticism, e.g. *Corpus Hermeticum* I 6: τὸ φῶς ἐκεῖνο, ἔφη, ἐγὼ Νοῦς ὁ σὸς θεός . . . ὁ δὲ ἐκ Νοὸς φωτεινὸς Λόγος υἱὸς θεοῦ.[1]

John

The nature of the Logos is not defined. It is introduced as a figure which is known to John's community.

This is also demonstrated by a literary-critical analysis of the prologue. Underlying it is a pre-Johannine hymn, on which the evangelist comments. It presents the pre-existent word as the second, revelatory stage of the deity, and the work of this word: the creation of the world, the illumination of men. That means that the word makes men understand the world as creation and at the same time themselves as creatures. John evidently found this hymn already there in his community. There are some problems: 1. the Logos is with God, and he is God. Is there ditheism here? The Jewish wisdom is the first creature and is thus removed from God. The Johannine Logos, on the other hand, is not created. In fact, the idea of two gods breaks through. Bultmann differs: the prologue deliberately presents the paradox that the Logos is on the one hand identified with God, and on the other hand is simultaneously differentiated from him. This paradox is a proper one. It is given with the idea of revelation itself, namely 'that in the revealer God really appears, and that God does not appear directly, but only in the revealer'. Thus in fact John's ultimate intention is achieved. But the idea has not been as completely demythologized as Bultmann thinks. 2. 'And the light shines (present) in the darkness, and the darkness did not comprehend it.' Is this said of the pre-existent Logos or the historical Logos? The answer depends on literary criticism and the historical determination of the source. (*a*) Literary criticism: the evangelist inserted vv. 6–8 into the source (the remarks about John the Baptist). Thus he relates v. 5 to the historical appearance of Jesus. But did the source understand it in this way? (*b*) Bultmann regards the source as a pre-Christian one and characterizes it as a revelation hymn in the style of Jewish gnosticism, that probably derives from circles which revered the Baptist as the revealer. The evangelist has made it into a Christian hymn.[2] In the source, v. 5 referred to the pre-existent rule of the Logos and its rejection during pre-existence. Of course, in that case the present φαίνει does not fit any more, and Bultmann has to postulate that the past tense stood in the source. He supports his interpretation by referring to the construction: up to v. 12, the pre-existent rule of the Logos is described, and from v. 14 onwards its historical rule.[3]

Against Bultmann's interpretation: the sentence ὁ λόγος σὰρξ ἐγένετο (v. 14) belongs to the source.[4] And this statement is not possible either in Judaism or in

---

[1] For further details see Bultmann, *Das Evangelium des Johannes*, and W. Bousset, *Kyrios Christos* (1965⁵), pp. 304ff.

[2] This process is not inconceivable; E. Käsemann assumes the same thing for Col. 1.15ff. (*Essays on New Testament Themes*, pp. 149ff.) The two psalms, Luke 1.46ff. (Magnificat) and 1.68ff. (Benedictus) are probably of Baptist origin.

[3] Verse 13 is redactional.

[4] Against Käsemann, who makes it end with v. 12. But v. 15 breaks the contact between vv. 14 and 16 and is thus redactional. Verses 14 and 16 therefore belong to the source.

gnosticism. It is genuinely Christian. Thus *a priori* the thought is not of a mythical Logos, but of Jesus as the Logos. Therefore v. 5 referred to the historical revelation even in the source.[1]

What is the Logos? What are we meant to understand when Jesus is interpreted with this concept? The significance does not consist in communicable notions about the being of the world and of man. In John, there is no material cosmology and anthropology as a content of the doctrine of salvation. The sense is simply: he himself – as the Incarnate One. The point is that the word is not detached from the person of the revealer so that it can be communicated as free content. It is based exclusively on his existence, and therefore cannot be taught and learnt as knowledge. Anyone who has the person, i.e. who believes in him, has salvation.

But what is 'to believe in him'? What concrete, comprehensible content does faith have? In the commentary offered by the gospel, we learn that the content is 'that it is he'. But this information does not seem to be information at all; it seems to provoke the question of the content of faith all the more. In fact, this 'I am' must now be interpreted and concretized. That also happens: I am the light, the bread, the way, the truth, the resurrection, the life.

II   The Christological Titles

J. Dupont, *Essais sur la Christologie de Saint Jean* (1951); S. Schulz, *Untersuchungen zur Menschensohn-Christologie im Johannesevangelium* (1957); W. Thüsing, *Die Erhöhung und Verherrlichung im Johannesevangelium*, NTA 21(1/2) (1960); E. Haenchen, ' "Der Vater, der mich gesandt hat" ', *NTS* 9 (1962/3), pp. 208–16 (= *Gott und Mensch* (1965), pp. 68–77); J. Blank, *Krisis* (1964); J. L. Martyn (see on section 41), pp. 91ff.

John, too, deliberately takes up the church's tradition, from ch. 1 onwards: (*a*) he inserts the election of the Baptist into the Logos-hymn. In this his own style immediately becomes visible: he does not interpret the Baptist as the apocalyptic figure of the 'forerunner', Elijah redivivus, but interprets him by the category of the witness; (*b*) there is a primarily negative commentary in 1.19ff., on what the Baptist is not: he is not the Messiah or Elijah or the Prophet (titles of the apocalyptic conception), but the witness; (*c*) it is then stated that Jesus is the Messiah. But his nature is defined in completely different terms from those in Jewish and primitive Christian apocalyptic.

[1] Thus, too, Käsemann. The use of the originally mythological figure resulted in discrepancies in the conception, even for the source.

In the very first chapter, John gives a careful survey of the titles which apply to Jesus and describe his nature and work aptly. The first passage, 1.18, one of his additions to the prologue, unfortunately has a doubtful text. There are two different readings: *(ὁ) μονογενὴς θεός* (P. 66, 75 Alex.) and *ὁ μονογενὴς υἱός* (Byz, Θ, latt. syr^cur). The former is to be preferred. The testimony of the Baptist follows in v. 29: Jesus is the 'lamb of God' (cf. v. 36). The Baptist himself explains this title: it is synonymous with 'Son of God' (v. 34). The designation of Jesus as lamb, of course, contains the notion of sacrifice: he takes away the sin of the world. In v. 41, there follows the title 'Messiah',[1] with the insertion of a Greek translation; its significance is explained in the conversation with the Samaritan woman: Jesus discloses himself as the fulfiller of the expectation of the Jews and the Samaritans (4.25). The woman 'knows that the Messiah comes, who is called *χριστός*'. Jesus retorts: *ἐγώ εἰμι*. John's theological interest in the title Messiah becomes evident in 1.45: it is he, *ὃν ἔγραψεν Μωϋσῆς ἐν τῷ νόμῳ καὶ οἱ προφῆται*. The formulated confession of the community is spoken in direct address for the first time in 1.49: *σὺ εἶ ὁ υἱὸς τοῦ θεοῦ, σὺ βασιλεὺς εἶ τοῦ Ἰσραήλ*. The title Son of Man concludes the survey of christological titles (v. 51).

As in the synoptic gospels, this last title is not used in address and in the confessional formula, but only on Jesus' own lips. But the meaning is changed to match the Johannine style. In the synoptics, the Son of Man is the one who comes, the one who suffers and the one who has come. There is no notion of pre-existence. In John, 'Son of Man' designates the constant heavenly nature of the pre-existent, incarnate and exalted one. Odeberg[2] and Bultmann, on the other hand, believe that the Johannine Son of Man is by no means the same figure as the Synoptic Son of Man: he does not derive from Jewish apocalyptic, but represents an analogous derivation from the gnostic primal man. But apart from the fact that there is no evidence at all for this hypothesis, the connection with the primitive Christian Son of Man tradition is evident.

Further passages also demonstrate a deliberate reference back to the community tradition: the Johannine variant of the confession of Peter (6.69); the little catechism in the conversation with Martha (11.27ff.). Here it becomes clear that the appropriate response to the 'I am' of Jesus is the confession of the church. The linking of several titles, above all those of Messiah and Son of God, in this verse is also traditional; cf. the Matthaean version of the confession of Peter (Matt.

[1] The Jewish form is deliberately used, as in 4.25. It is not used elsewhere in the New Testament.
[2] H. Odeberg, *The Fourth Gospel* (1929).

16.16): in John, it also occurs at 20.31. Shortly before and, deliberately, only after the resurrection, John finally introduces the title Kyrios, in Thomas' convinced confession: ὁ κύριός μου καὶ ὁ θεός μου (20.28).

III The Significance of the Differentiation of the Titles

John interprets the meaning of the christological titles (1) by differentiating them expressly from Jewish messianology; (2) by a positive interpretation in his own terminology of sending and witness. In differentiating the title 'Messiah' from Jewish messianology, John does not depict the Jewish expectation of the Messiah in historically faithful terms. He already sees it from the perspective of Christian doctrine. The mere statement that he presupposes a uniform Jewish doctrine of the Messiah is itself inaccurate.

His starting point is that the Old Testament promises not only the Messiah, but Jesus (5.39). But John does not make the controversy with the 'Jews' into an exegetical discussion about who interprets scripture correctly. His technique is that of the misunderstanding: the Jews know the Messiah's genealogy: he must stem from David; he must be born in Bethlehem (7.42). At the same time, they know that neither of these things is true of Jesus: he is the son of Joseph (6.42); he comes from Nazareth, and what good can come out of Nazareth (1.46)? No prophet ever came out of Galilee (7.52). The mistake of the Jews does not lie in the fact that they have been falsely informed about the physical descent of Jesus. They have been rightly informed. But they err, because they think that with this knowledge they can pass judgment on Jesus' real nature.

The whole Johannine understanding of revelation, promise and fulfilment is expressed in the literary technique of misunderstanding. The scripture bears witness to Jesus. The Jews take this remark to mean that a kind of warrant can be read out of the Bible, with which the Messiah can be identified when he comes. But this is a misunderstanding of the nature of the 'witness', for human judgment is not the measure by which the heavenly emissary is to be judged. The scripture points forward to him in such a way that he can be heard when he comes, that his call 'It is I' can be understood, and thus his claim can be understood to be true. Only in this understanding of his message, the understanding of faith, is it evident that the scriptures have been understood. There is no understanding of scripture outside faith. Not to understand it is not to believe it. The failure of Jesus' opponents to

understand is disclosed by their demand that he should perform signs
(6.30). Only a wrong understanding would do this, and that is
identical with unbelief. For the signs are indeed there; they only have
to be seen. Jesus' opponents accuse him of failing to submit to the
sabbath law, of making himself equal with God (5.18). They do not
recognize that this is in fact his nature. The consequence is – and here
we can see the failure of human standards over against the revelation:
if a man appears in his own name and wrongly raises a messianic
claim, they will receive him (5.43).

Jesus must, of course, verify his assertion that he has been sent by
God. How else can its truth be recognized? And in fact he does verify
it. But he can only advance a proof that is commensurate with the
revelation itself. In John's view, miracles that Jesus does are quite
capable of proof; but they disclose themselves as such only to faith.
The appropriate proof at first sight looks like a negative: it consists in
Jesus' utter refusal to authenticate himself before a human authority.
He does not receive glory from men (5.41), indeed he seeks no glory at
all (8.50). This shows that he does not come in his own name. If his
hearers had the love of God in them, they would understand that
(5.42f.; 7.16ff.). It is impossible to judge Jesus without falling in with
the will of God. Once again, the christological circle appears: this will
is learnt – from Jesus.

In that case, is blind faith demanded? No, but rather faith leads
into all truth and thus into understanding and self-understanding.
God's will discloses itself as the truth over the world and over me.
Faith becomes knowledge.

This understanding of revelation is expressed in the definition of
the relationship between the Father and the Son, and in the conceptuality of sending and witness.

43 · THE FATHER AND THE SON

Literature: as on section 42 II; for the 'Son', see section 10 II.

The mythological conception that two divine beings exist side by side
can still be traced in the prologue. The nearest analogy is offered by

the juxtaposition of the God of the beyond and the emissary in gnosticism. Cf. also Philo: the Logos is πρωτόγονος υἱός and δεύτερος θεός; *Corpus Hermeticum* I 6: the Logos is the Son of the Father, the Nous. Among the Mandaeans, the emissary is called Manda d'Haiye, 'the Son of the Great Life'. This juxtaposition poses no problem for gnosticism: the Son is of the same substance as the Father, as the first stage of the emanation. In turn, the redeemed have the same substance as he. At the end, all return into the primal divine unity, the light. Therefore gnosticism can increase the number of emissaries at will. The Jew Philo solves the problem by characterizing the Logos as a creature. He is 'God' only in relation to the world. For John, a solution is much more difficult. In contrast to gnosticism, he does not make the Logos a stage of emanation, and in contrast to Philo he does not make the Logos a creature. If he did this, the idea of revelation would be contradicted: the revelation would be an ingredient of the world. John rejects cosmological speculation, e.g. about a primal state of silence, by his refusal to declare the Logos a creature. Compared with Philo and gnosticism, the Johannine definitions sound vague and imprecise: ἦν πρὸς τὸν θεόν, θεὸς ἦν. Does John deliberately put it this way, so as to seek particularization not in speculation, but in interpretation of the being of the world? It is not coincidence that the prologue of John says nothing about God and the Logos as they are in themselves. Verses 1 and 2 simply mark out the horizon for the interpretation of the revelation: the Logos creates the world (vv. 3ff.). He is God, in so far as God has disclosed himself to the world and can be experienced here, in the Logos. In referring all statements to the revelation, John avoids the danger of ditheism. God and his Son do not become the subject of metaphysical doctrine. Statements about them are only made in the world, as statements of faith, as an interpretation of the situation which comes about in the world from the entry of the word. The statement ἐν ἀρχῇ ἦν ὁ λόγος has the critical significance of rejecting any remark about God outside his word and leading to the point where God can be found in the world. In this way the statement becomes a positive interpretation of revelation: in the Son men see the Father himself. We do not get a doctrine about God, but are confronted by God himself, in the world, and not just at the end of an ascent to him. That the Logos is the creator means that God is accessible in him. With the identification of the revelation of Christ and the revelation of creation, no 'natural theology' can come before the theology of the word. That means that the definition of the relationship of Father and Son explains the possibility of belief. The reference of faith to its object, the Son and his offer, is made comprehensible in the interpretation of the work of the Son as 'sending'. The key-words 'sending', 'the one who is sent' (emissary) mean that God himself is responsible for salvation (3.16; Rom. 8.32, 39 shows the connection with tradition). Because Jesus is the one who is sent, and is otherwise nothing, he is one with the Father. Their unity is the unity of the saving work. In this way, a metaphysical ditheism is no longer a problem: πιστεύετέ μοι, ὅτι ἐγὼ ἐν τῷ πατρὶ καὶ ὁ πατὴρ ἐν ἐμοί (14.11). That means that ὁ ἑωρακὼς ἐμὲ ἑώρακεν τὸν πατέρα (14.9). This seeing is nothing other than faith in the Son.

The next stage by which John describes the process of revelation is characterized by the fact that the relationship of the Son to the Father is matched by the relationship of 'his own' to the revealer (14.20). His relationship to the Father becomes comprehensible for his own through faith in him, and at the same time they learn that no relationship to God is possible except through him. That does not mean that ascent to God would be possible through him, but that his own have an immediate relationship to God in him (17.20–23).[1] This final point in the account is appropriately reached in the farewell discourses. Now Jesus can show that the presupposition of this relationship is his departure, which discloses the immediacy. Now he can issue a summons to faith in God (14.1). In this way, the way is opened (14.8ff.); the believers have become his friends (15.14).

44 · THE SENDING OF THE SON

Literature: as on section 42 II.

I Pre-existence and Incarnation

The parousia does not fit the pre-existence – incarnation pattern, the appropriate conclusion to which is the return to heaven followed by an enthronement. This is the christological conception of Phil. 2.6ff.; Col. 1.15ff.; I Tim. 3.16. Here, of course, there is a danger of mythicizing, of making the incarnation seem a mere

---

[1] W. Grundmann, *Zeugnis und Gestalt des Johannes-Evangeliums* (1961), pp. 65ff.

progress, of orienting faith by the heavenly picture of the Exalted One and then making it a means of ascent for the believers. It may be asked whether in view of the exaltation, the reality of the incarnation is maintained in the idea of the presence of faith in the world. This does not happen simply by asserting that it is a real incarnation (and not just an apparent one, as in docetism).[1] Nor is it enough to assert that Jesus' death was an actual death.[2] The important thing is, rather, whether this death can really be interpreted, i.e. as a form of the existence of the dead one in the world with his own, the believers. The decision depends on whether the unity of death and departure remains a mythical conception, or whether it is understandable as 'word'.

What means of interpretation does John have at his disposal? He extends the incarnation – ascension pattern (in agreement with the usual christology of the community) by associating it with the parousia. Of course, a unity can only be produced when the parousia, too, is taken up into the Johannine shift in the definition of faith. But it is not only the end-point, the parousia, which must cease to be a mythical idea; the historical starting point, the incarnation, and its presupposition, pre-existence, must also be transformed.

In Phil. 2, the time between the incarnation and death of Jesus is to some extent empty; and as empty time it is not really time at all. The life and actions of Jesus are not essential for the fate of the Incarnate One. He does nothing but die. His sole achievement is obedience to death. This is a mythical way of saying that the revelation is not a worldly power or a worldly event. It remains intangible.

John fills the time between the incarnation and death of Jesus with a report on the actions of the one who has appeared and his way through the world. He makes him not only come and go, but also 'dwell among us'. This 'dwelling' is made vivid in narrative form – as an epiphany of the θεῖος ἀνήρ. Thus John supplements the incarnation christology with an epiphany christology. But does this combination remain a merely external one,[3] or can John use the synthesis of the incarnate God and the manifest θεῖος ἀνήρ to show that and how salvation has come about in the world and has reached mankind? Bultmann answers in the affirmative. This cannot, however, be shown from the acts of the θεῖος ἀνήρ, but only from the character of the revelation as word (i.e. from the incarnation). The incarnation represents the character of the revelation as word and as a stumbling

[1] Philippians 2.6ff. can easily be interpreted in a docetic way, as in *Excerpta ex Theodoto* 38: ἐκένωσεν ἑαυτόν means that the revealer has emerged from the *pleroma* and crossed the boundary.

[2] Even gnostics can recognize the reality of the death; cf. the so-called *Evangelium Veritatis* 20.25ff.

[3] The scheme of Phil. 2.6ff., with the content of a 'gospel'.

block. Here the stumbling block is an essential element. It shows that the revelation does not come from the world. The understanding of the actions of the revealer is also determined from here. The miracles are signs, a disclosure of his glory; but as signs they are ambiguous, and are a disclosure only to faith. The dialectic is clear: the revelation reaches the world, but does not enter it in such a way as to become an ingredient of the world, so that the world can have control over it as a means of life.

Bultmann rightly recognizes that the stumbling block is part of the structure of the revelation and is not just its temporary manifestation. But this Johannine stumbling block must be defined in more precise terms. It is not the incarnation as such that is the stumbling block,[1] but the means and mode of the manifestation of Jesus, the way of the incarnate one into death – by renouncing the honour of men. Nor are the miracles a stumbling block, in so far as they are paradoxical phenomena. They provoke indignation at the Incarnate One, in so far as the onlookers regard them as miracles and do not recognize them as signs. The incarnation becomes a stumbling block as a result of the unbelief which wants to see without faith and to subject the revelation to its own criteria.

For the direction of the development of Johannine thought see Blank's criticism of Bultmann: Bultmann puts the accents wrongly in explaining the relationship of the glory and the stumbling block of the cross as, 'the hour of δοξασθῆναι is the hour of the passion'. The statement must be put the other way round: 'the hour of the passion is already the hour of δοξασθῆναι'. But the two formulas are not really alternatives. Blank's formulation is meaningful where the cross is suppressed as something painful and scandalous; Bultmann's formulation has its function over against a *theologia gloriae* which makes the cross vanish behind the glory. He thus does justice to the intention of the evangelist. Blank, on the other hand, does not think in historical terms, but makes his judgment in the light of catholic dogma.

John achieves a unitary conception by not isolating the incarnation from its presupposition, the pre-existence of the Logos, and its continuation, the career and work of the Incarnate One. He can take these conceptions together, under one condition – that he avoids making them detailed myths. There are no pictures either of the pre-existence[2] or the course of the incarnation.[3] Both come under the

[1] Cf. Käsemann (see literature on section 42 I): belief in incarnation was current at the time.

[2] John does not relate any heavenly conversation between the Son and the Father before the incarnation.

[3] There is no virgin birth!

radical reduction made by John. There is only a portrayal of what happens after the incarnation, the appearance of Jesus in the world. Pre-existence and incarnation form the foil to this description: they designate the indescribable origin of Jesus. Within this framework, Jesus appears as a θεῖος ἀνήρ. As such, he proves himself through his wonderful knowledge (in his words) and his wonderful capability (in his wonders). Speaking and acting form a unity. This is possible because of John's reduction to the meaning alone. Thus, for faith, the two together are a unitary account of the revelation as action.

II   The Wonderful Knowledge of the Emissary: the 'Testimony'

The θεῖος ἀνήρ is omniscient (16.30). He knows heavenly things (3.11f.): he comes from above, and has seen the Father and spoken with him. He knows things which take place afar off (1.42, 47f.; 11.4, 11ff.), men's past (4.17f.), their inward heart (2.24f.). Of course, he also knows his own future (6.64, 70; 13.21ff.). All this corresponds with the traditional conception. The Johannine reduction is visible only in the fact that Jesus does not disclose the content of the mysteries of the beyond. He does not outline any pictures of the heavenly world, and does not communicate any formulas from the beyond; he describes no ways of ascent and does not initiate anyone into mysteries of knowledge and ritual procedure.[1] He offers his knowledge by offering himself. He bears witness of God and thus of himself as the emissary of his Father. The content of his teaching is simply that he is the revelation and that his testimony is true. Jesus' discourses deliberately move in a circle, and therefore they are a σκληρὸς λόγος (6.60). The truth of his testimony is shown by the fact that God bears witness to him. But God's witness is made through him. In him, Father and Son may be seen together. Can a meaning be obtained from this paradox which goes beyond the paradox as such? It shows that the revelation must avoid worldly criteria if it is to be revelation. In positive terms, this negative position means that what Jesus says about himself is eo ipso a disclosure of the world, an appropriate and understandable word. How deliberate this dialectic is is shown by statements which formally contradict each other: cf. 5.30–34 with 10.25; further, 14.10; 15.22, 24. On the one hand, Jesus declares: if I bear witness to myself, then my witness is not true (5.31); on the other hand: then is my witness true (8.14). This contradiction expresses the notion of revela-

[1] Bultmann, Theology of the New Testament II, pp. 61ff.

tion: God can only bear witness to himself. His word proves itself to be the word of God in the self-evident quality and sufficiency of the revelation.

Jesus' wonderful knowledge is thus not particularized as mythological doctrine, but in the fact that he sees all and uncovers the hearts of men. In this way, he opens up faith as an offer to them to become his friends. In so doing, he gives life and opens up the future; by making possible discipleship along the course that he traverses, he frees the way to the heavenly dwellings, to which he goes before. This discipleship is not understood in gnostic terms, as though we were taken up with him in his ascension. Rather, after his death, Jesus returns to his own in the world. He himself remains the way.

III The Wonderful Capability of the θεῖος ἀνήρ: the Signs

The miracle stories of the gospel of John are cruder than those of the synoptic gospels. This is certainly a result of the source from which they come. But why does John take them over, and in what sense does he revise them? The Johannine use of the word σημεῖον gives some information about this.[1]

The literary-critical evidence: Bultmann may well be right in his assumption that the evangelist uses a source with miracle stories in which the miraculous element was more fully developed than that in the synoptic tradition. It is possible that the word σημεῖον already appeared in this source, but it is by no means certain. Rather, against Bultmann, analysis makes it probable that it has in all cases been inserted by the evangelist at a later stage. Bultmann argues that the signs were numbered in the source (2.11; 4.54), but that this enumeration does not fit the present account, as John mentions further miracles in between. It must, therefore, have been there before him. On the other hand, it has to be pointed out that no further miracles are narrated between 2.11 and 4.46 and that the numeration is not continued. It must therefore be regarded as redactional. This is absolutely true of the end of the book (20.30f.). The other σημεῖον passages also clearly come from the evangelist. 'Unless you see signs and wonders, you will not believe' (4.48) is a redactional insertion into the source which abruptly disturbs the context.

The miracles are a demonstration of the 'glory' of Jesus, not only for the source, but also for the evangelist (2.11). 2.23: many believe, because they see his signs. 3.2: Nicodemus knows of Jesus' miracles and acknowledges them (cf. 6.2, 14; 7.31; 9.16; 12.18). At the end of

[1] Bultmann, *Das Evangelium des Johannes*; K. H. Rengstorf, σημεῖον, *TWNT* VII, 241ff.

the book, all Jesus' activity is described in a summary as the doing of signs. This is one side. The other is that faith on the basis of the signs is shown to be questionable. 6.2: the crowd follows him because they saw his miracles. 6.14f.: the people conclude that he is the prophet – a twilight knowledge! He is, but not as they think. They want to make him king – and Jesus escapes them. The play is continued in 6.26: 'You seek me, not because you saw signs, but because you ate your fill of the loaves'. Thus they have experienced the miracle, but have not understood it as a sign. They do not want to understand the true sense of the miracle which lies beyond what is visible, i.e. in the word: 'I am the bread of life'. They want what is transitory, the momentary satisfaction of βιός, and hope for further acts of the same kind. They think only of the momentary, transitory need, which draws new need after it. They have not received what Jesus offered: the bread that satisfies for ever.

The miracle is a demonstration of power, but the narrative keeps being interrupted: 'Unless you see signs and wonders, you will not believe' (4.48). Anyone who requires a sign as a proof is repudiated (2.18; 6.30).[1] A man can see a miracle and yet refuse faith (12.37). How is this to be explained?

John preserves the starting point, the community's belief in miracles. Even his further development is primarily carried out on the basis of the understanding of miracle that generally prevails in the community: only faith understands the miracle. But all this is now incorporated into the specifically Johannine interpretation of faith. The miracle is only understood if it is realized that Jesus does not offer *something*, but *himself* – himself as the bread, as life. The miracle is only understood if the 'I am' which is presented in every miracle is also understood. Then no more miracles will be needed as proof. The miracle is ambiguous in the same way that the revelation that is identical with the revealer is ambiguous. Before the end of the book, in which its whole content is summed up as a report on the signs of Jesus, we read, 'Blessed are those who do not see and yet believe' (20.29). John 1.14 gives a further indication. It is no coincidence that here the language is in the first person: we saw (not, one saw) his glory. It is the we of the confessing community. Of the world, it can only be said that they did not accept Jesus who offered himself close enough to be touched.

---

[1] As in the synoptic gospels, the wonder is contingent: it cannot be acquired, but only received as a gift.

THE SENDING OF THE SON

What significance do the miracles have for John after the departure of Jesus? For Paul, what remains is the proclamation of the cross. He has no historical material from the life of Jesus and can therefore work out the character of the revelation as word without reference to it. But can a historical narrative be developed theologically in the same way? Can miracles be narrated in such a way that a presentation of them is not only possible but necessary, because the miracle is only understood when it is seen to be directed towards us and to determine us? In that case, do we not find ourselves involved in an unreal picture of the world or in pure symbolism: ταῦτα δὲ ἐγένετο μὲν οὐδέποτε, ἔστι δὲ ἀεί (Sallust, περὶ θεῶν καὶ κόσμου, section 4)? Following John, we could say, the answer to this question is not to be obtained from history, or from miracle, but only from the word, from the revelation in the word. The question disappears if the preaching is not the communication of knowable doctrine but the present uncovering of man, the present disclosure of faith as the possibility of living. It can only be this if it does not bypass the stumbling block, not the stumbling block in the miracle, but the stumbling block that God's word is present only as a human word. Where that is understood as salvation, 'the problem of miracle' is no longer a theological theme.

The Johannine reduction, the concentration on the point at which the revelation enters the world without becoming part of it, appears even more clearly in another demonstration of the wonderful power of Jesus, in the passion.

IV The Passion

E. Haenchen, 'Historie und Geschichte in den johanneischen Passionsberichten', in: F. Viering (ed.), *Zur Bedeutung des Todes Jesu* (1967), pp. 55–78.

The position of the passion narrative as a specific significance in the construction of the gospel:

1. Revelation before the world;
2. Revelation before Jesus' own (interpretation of the Coming One in the farewell discourses);
3. Passion – again before the public. Now they are offered nothing but helplessness. Faith understands that it is precisely this that is the unveiling of the glory: the cross is the exaltation.

The passion of Jesus is the reaction of the world to his claim. In the way in which the world reacts, it shows that in reality it is not the active, but the passive part. It has no choice in the way in which it is to act. It is given two alternatives. Either it can believe, in which case it is what it really is, world, creation, or it can remain as it is, and thus in face of the revelation make itself 'world' in the negative sense. And it can do this only if it puts the revelation out of the way. But its action is in vain. After it has killed the revealer, it learns that he does not remain dead. Precisely in this way, the revelation finds an abode in the world: the judgment of the world lives on in the community. The helplessness of the world is depicted in narrative form: Jesus' opponents try time and again to get him in their grasp. Each attempt fails. Jesus cannot be taken before his hour comes (7.30, 44; 8.20, 59; 10.39). Jesus meets his hour freely. His opponents only reach him when he has said his ἐγείρεσθε, ἄγωμεν ἐντεῦθεν (14.31). We have the impression that an other-worldly being is going through the world, appearing, disappearing. But now John stresses the reality of Jesus' humanity by making clear the reality of his death.

But is that enough to show that the revelation is a historical (and not a mythical) event? Is Jesus' death really more than a mere transition? The test will be the trace which this heavenly being leaves behind in the world: will it be enough to show that the revelation remains in the world without becoming world?

In investigating this question, we come extremely close to Paul's theology: the point of contact between the revelation and the world is the cross. For John, this is not the extreme point of humiliation which precedes the exaltation, but the nadir of the exaltation itself. John in fact has a play on 'lift up' in a double sense (3.14; 8.28; 12.34).

Thüsing: 'exaltation' in John primarily means the crucifixion. This is the only content which can certainly be ascertained from John's frequent use of 'exaltation'. But the word 'exaltation' contains more than the cross. After Jesus' departure, in the time of his rule with the Father, this is also the determinative reality of the work of salvation. 'Exaltation' brings out the character of Jesus' death on the cross as revelation: the cross is the permanent structural principle of revelation. Cf. Blank, p. 84: the 'more' is already there. The exaltation is the appointment of Jesus to honour. The new element is that the cross is taken up into the process of exaltation. The one who departs is already glorified (12.23, 28), yet the glorification takes places in the historical course of the passion (13.31f.; 17.1). It is completed at the moment of death: τετέλεσται (19.30).[1]

If the crucifixion is already the exaltation, then why does John distinguish crucifixion, resurrection and ascension as events? Why does he not make Jesus go

---

[1] Bultmann stresses the paradox: the hour of *glorification* is the hour of the *passion*. Blank (p. 269) wants to change the accents: the *cross* is already the *exaltation*. But in terms of Johannine theology that is no alternative.

to heaven at the moment when he dies on the cross? Because this conception would lead straight to docetism. Then only the spirit would have ascended into heaven, and the body would be left behind. This would do away with the ὁ λόγος σάρξ ἐγένετο. The realism of the Easter accounts is no inconsistency for John. It is necessary, in order to depict the unity of incarnation and exaltation, coming and going. John begins from the traditional conception of the resurrection, but then brings it into the suspense that is typical of his work: he concludes his book without a farewell scene or a narrative account of the ascension. Jesus' last word runs: 'Blessed are those who do not see, yet still believe' (20.29). Then John adds his own conclusion: 20.30f. Jesus' remark to Thomas does not negate history, but presupposes it, and is meant to show the way in which it can remain present: by concentration on the self-presentation of the revealer in his 'It is I'. That can be seen from the narrative itself: John often begins from the ideas of the tradition. But then he identifies Good Friday, Easter and Ascension. Furthermore, by making the risen Jesus – and not the ascended Jesus – bestow the spirit, he also equates Easter and Pentecost. Finally, he makes Easter and the parousia identical by incorporating the future in the present. Here, of course, the relationship differs from that between Easter and the passion. The historical events (in John's sense) of the passion and resurrection are interpreted, but they do not disappear by being interpreted. This is not true of the future 'events'. They completely coalesce with their significance for the present. And this poses the problem of Johannine eschatology.

45 · JESUS' ACCOUNT OF HIMSELF: ἐγώ εἰμι

E. Schweizer, *Ego Eimi*, FRLANT NF 38 (1965²); R. Bultmann, *Das Evangelium des Johannes*, pp. 167f. (note on John 6.35); H. Becker, *Die Reden des Johannesevangeliums und der Stil der gnostichen Offenbarungsrede*, FRLANT 68 (1956); H. Zimmermann, 'Das absolute ἐγώ εἰμι als die nt. Offenbarungsformel', *BZ* NF (1960), pp. 54–69, 266–76.

John puts the proclamation of faith in Jesus, which is related to the whole saving work (including cross and resurrection) on the lips of the historical Jesus. This raises a hermeneutical problem; the possibility of interpreting these discourses. It is usually said that John makes the earthly Jesus act already as the exalted Jesus. In fact, he means to make clear Jesus' glory by means of the incarnate Jesus (1.14). How is this possible in a description? Things are simpler in the case of the wonders, as they contain a miraculous element. But in the discourses? The glorified, present Jesus certainly speaks in them, but they are still constructed as historical past discourses. Why?

Why are they not made direct revelation discourses in the spirit today? Because John must show that the truth is not reached simply by the repetition of discourses. The truth is the speaker himself. He must therefore be as it were incorporated into his discourses, so that in hearing the discourse the reader can be led to Jesus himself. This happens through the present proclamation of the church. This is essential for the process of understanding. John makes this clear by his introduction of the Paraclete (see below): after Jesus' death and resurrection, it is no longer possible to learn anything about him without experiencing him as the one who speaks today. By means of the dialectical concept of revelation, John finds a mode of presentation that transcends the alternatives of either a historical, past picture or a mythical, present picture (or a mythical revelation discourse). The condition on which he escapes these alternatives is that he must keep any concrete content to his conceptions out of the discourses – apart from the one statement 'It is I', and the interpretation of it. Does this reduction of faith to a statement which consists only of subject and copula still allow one to speak of a comprehensible content?

But a counter-question can also be posed. How is real particularization to be achieved? Through the most vivid description possible of Christ as a heavenly being? Through a picture of history? Through a vision of the future in glowing colours? Would those not in reality be abstractions, pictures, instead of the thing itself?

John achieves particularization precisely by his renunciation of imagery. Instead of using imagery, he makes it clear that revelation happens here and now, in such a way that man comes to know himself through conversation with the revealer and thus becomes transparent to himself. The content of the revelation is not the description of physical or metaphysical entities, nor the description of the process of illumination in the religious believer. The revelation is illuminating address. Understanding is always open to the future, is always on the move. I do not know Christ if I know a definition of his nature, but only if I understand what he is for me now, because he is the word to the world. Jesus' 'It is I' is the concrete interpretation of God's constant communication with the world. The refusal of illustrative 'descriptiveness' and all 'comprehensible' content beyond Jesus' presentation of himself (this apparent negative) displays an eminently positive significance: the content of faith reveals itself in the process of my unveiling of myself, which becomes understandable to me as salvation; the revealer may be experienced as bread, as light, as life. Faith leads to the particularization of freedom to live in the world in peace, which realizes itself as worldly insecurity and thus as the possibility of love.

Of course, John makes Jesus say 'It is I' in more than a formal sense. He has to make clear the saving significance of this expression. He has to show not only that the giver presents himself as gift in this saying, but also how it is done. For this he uses the following pattern:[1]

6.35: ἐγώ εἰμι ὁ ἄρτος τῆς ζωῆς. ὁ ἐρχόμενος πρὸς ἐμὲ οὐ μὴ πεινάσῃ, καὶ ὁ πιστεύων εἰς ἐμὲ οὐ μὴ διψήσει πώποτε.

8.12: ἐγώ εἰμι τὸ φῶς τοῦ κόσμου. ὁ ἀκολουθῶν μοι οὐ μὴ περιπατήσῃ ἐν τῇ σκοτίᾳ, ἀλλ' ἕξει τὸ φῶς τῆς ζωῆς.

In addition, there are the pictures of the door (10.9), the shepherd (10.11, 14), the vine (15.1, 5). In other passages, the meaning is not expressed symbolically, but directly: the resurrection and the life (11.25); the way, the truth and the life (14.6).

In the statement 'I am the light', Bultmann takes the 'I' as the predicate: 'The light, it is I'. Jesus distinguishes himself from a false offer of salvation. The starting point is the absolute, fixed significance of light as salvation. Now Jesus declares, 'It is I'. In fact, the statement contains a differentiation, but this is not in the foreground. The primary significance lies more in the positive interpretation of the nature of Jesus. 'I' is thus the subject.

The starting point for an understanding of the 'I am' sentences is the traditional confession of the community: Jesus is the Son of God. This is interpreted by John in his symbolic language, in such a way that the interpretation of Jesus is put in his own mouth.

Light is already to be found as a symbol of salvation (life) and revelation in the Old Testament: 'The Lord make his face to shine'; 'Thy word is a lamp to my feet and a light along my ways'; 'In thy light we see light'. The servant of Yahweh is made a light for the nations.[2] But this does not go as far as the absolute significance of light in John: 'the' light. Although the 'I am' formula stands out strikingly in Deutero-Isaiah, who describes the servant of Yahweh as the light,[3] John's terminology cannot be derived directly from there. In the Old Testament, light is always a metaphor, even when the servant of Yahweh is rhetorically spoken of in this way. In John, however, the language is not metaphorical, but literal. 'The light' designates the nature of Jesus directly. He is not like a light; he is 'the' light. He is the vine, the bread, etc. Bultmann has rightly recognized this. What appears to us

---

[1] For the distribution of the formula see E. Schweizer, R. Bultmann and H. Becker.

[2] The passages quoted are: Num. 6.25; Ps. 119.105; Ps. 36.10; Isa. 49.6.

[3] Isa. 45.22 etc.

as light is not the *true* light, i.e. the power of life. If we look for bread, we are not really looking for bread, but for life. This Jesus offers, by offering himself. At the same time, there is also a differentiation here; but that is not the starting point for the formula.

The statement 'I am the light' delivers a judgment on the world and brings it about at the same time – as a disclosure: the world comes 'to light' for what it is: world.

46 · WORLD AND MAN (THE DISCLOSURE)

The world is dark, but it is not dark in itself (say, because it is matter). John outlines no mythical picture of the world, no myth of the fall, etc. True, the world is fallen, but its fall takes place in actual confrontation with the revelation. The word *cosmos* primarily designates the world of men (1.10f.), but not, of course, simply the sum-total of individual men. As a result of its attitude, the cosmos has become a trans-subjective power, a sphere which the individual cannot escape, which he constantly helps to constitute. In itself the world is creation, it is good, it is illuminated; that is, it presents itself as creation and is understandable as such. It has been created by the Logos, who 'was' the light of men. It is evil if, or in so far as, it does not act in accordance with its nature as creation. In that way, it becomes 'this' world.[1] But even after its fall, God has not given it up. It can only be world in the negative sense because the light shines in it. Its attitude is constant repudiation of its origin (3.19).

Now a strange duality is to be observed: if the shining of the light describes the historical appearance of Jesus, then sin is on the one hand the rejection of Jesus, unbelief. Then the difficulty arises: has there only been sin since Jesus appeared? John cannot, of course, say that. He cannot explain that the world was in order before Jesus came; in that case, the incarnation would be senseless. Nor can he assert that there was no relationship between God and the world before Jesus' historical appearance. That this indeed existed, and that

---

[1] Cf. Paul, 'this aeon'. Even Paul does not speak of the 'aeon to come', and John does not at all, as he does not objectify the world in an apocalyptic way.

there is no world 'in itself', is expressed by the pre-existence of the Logos, by its position as mediator of creation. On the other hand, it follows from this that the world had already succumbed to sin before Jesus – but this sin was rejection of the Logos. John can therefore say the two things: both that the world already sinned before the appearance of Jesus and that the sin came about through encounter with him. This is possible because he avoids cosmological objectification. Were he to extend the conception, he would have to describe a twofold coming of the Logos into the world. In the prologue he in fact comes very near to such a conception. But what John really wants to say is this: the revelation has taken place, and in confrontation with it men experience what sin is. Then they know at the same time that the world has always been confronted by revelation and has wanted to avoid this confrontation. That means, that the cosmological conception of the pre-existent being of the Logos becomes comprehensible to the individual as a disclosure of his own past, his solidarity with the world, his sin. Revelation discloses to the world what its nature is by telling the world what it was from the beginning. The well-known Johannine antitheses, light and darkness, above and below, truth and lie, freedom and slavery, are all meant historically and soteriologically; they serve to define the relationship to God, to the world and to oneself which has now been disclosed. 'Light' is the manifestation of God in Christ, the offer of life. Where there is no light, i.e. where the light is not accepted, where faith is refused, there is darkness, and man finds himself involved in falsehood about himself. Truth is not a formal concept, establishing the correctness of a statement; in qualified terms it means the divine truth, which is identical with the word.[1] Similarly, falsehood is not a matter of telling a lie or an attitude of untruthfulness, but a general condition: anyone who remains in unbelief finds himself involved in falsehood about himself. He shows this by evading the disclosure (3.19–21).

Despite the antithetical conceptuality, one can only speak with caution of a Johannine dualism. Just as no cosmological dualism is developed, so, too, no anthropological dualism is to be found.[2] Light and darkness are neither cosmic powers nor ingredients of fallen man, but possibilities of existence. One can speak of a dualism of decision,[3]

[1] J. de la Potterie, 'L'arrière-fond du thème johannique de vérité', TU 73 (Studia Evangelica I) (1959), pp. 277–94.
[2] There is no doctrine of the soul, and no depreciation of the body.
[3] Cf. the unmythological dualism of decision in Qumran.

as long as one notes that 'possibility' does not denote a subjective choice that I make in free resolve: rather, revelation shows me whence I am. I am whence I am. Of course, John does not mean this biologically, as he shows by means of the Jews: they stem from Abraham, but they are children, not of Abraham, but of the devil, because they do not believe. John defines two objective, fundamental possibilities for man: to be from below or from above.[1] The former is the impossibility, and it is this that has been chosen by men and by the world. We find a confrontation between: ἐκ τοῦ θεοῦ (7.17; 8.42) = ἄνωθεν (3.3, 7; cf. 8.23) = ἐκ τῆς ἀληθείας (18.37) and ἐκ τοῦ διαβόλου (8.44) = ἐκ τῶν κάτω (8.23) = ἐκ τούτου τοῦ κόσμου (8.23) = ἐκ τῆς γῆς (3.31).

In these concepts – 'to be', 'to come' etc. 'from' – the Johannine understanding of predestination becomes clear: man cannot create salvation for himself. It comes to him, he perceives it in the word, and does so in such a way that at the same time he experiences the objective priority of salvation. The idea of election is understood in historical terms. Man cannot be other than what he is, a being of the world; i.e. he has succumbed to sin. Therefore he is not free to decide on his own salvation. The world has already decided for itself. But this situation does not remain a fatal doom; as a result of the revelation it becomes a situation of decision. As a result, too, the crisis is brought about in which it emerges what the world was. Faith becomes possible by being disclosed by the revelation. In the face of the world which unveils man, it becomes free to transcend itself and, in the language of Johannine predestination, to acquire a new past. The idea of predestination does not exclude God's free act of election, but forms its horizon (John 15.16). The past hitherto is not ignored, but transcended. In this way it is shown that election is a wonder and that it embraces all of being. Paul speaks in this sense of the new creation, whereas John talks about rebirth (3.3). The miraculous character of the renewal is expressed in 3.8.

Only the man who is of the truth can understand the word. And the possibility of being of the truth is offered precisely by this word. In the hearing of it, a man becomes either elect (i.e. he understands) or lost. Judgment cannot be separated from salvation. The same holds for John as for Paul: the message does not offer a doctrine about salvation and damnation; it offers salvation – to faith. Salvation is

[1] The two are contrasted in 3.6: τὸ γεγεννημένον ἐκ τῆς σαρκὸς σάρξ ἐστιν, καὶ τὸ γεγεννημένον ἐκ τοῦ πνεύματος πνεῦμά ἐστιν.

the only aim of the sending of the Son (3.17; 12.47).[1] The judgment is not the aim of revelation, but an actual result of it. It is identical with the decision of unbelief itself.

47 · THE COMMUNITY IN THE WORLD

E. Schweizer, 'Der Kirchenbegriff im Evangelium und den Briefen des Johannes', TU 73 (*Studia Evangelica* I) (1959), pp. 363–81 (=*Neotestamentica* (1963), pp. 254–71).

This theme forms the content of the farewell discourses. In this way the existence of the community is closely bound up with Jesus' departure from the world. His departure brings about a fundamental separation of the community and the world: the community incurs the hate of the world, and does so of necessity. Its hate is not arbitrary, nor could it be explained in historical or psychological terms. It arises on the one hand from the nature of revelation and on the other from the nature of the cosmos, from the encounter of light and darkness, in which the latter seeks to assert itself. The stumbling block which the revelation brings with it is given with the thing itself.

Therefore there is no possibility of the church escaping hatred by some kind of tactic, say by demonstrating by its conduct how law-abiding and innocuous it is, or by giving out its teaching as a positive contribution to the ordering of the world.

This separation from the world, this purely esoteric definition of the common life of the believers, gives the Johannine community the appearance of a sect, which cultivates its religious life by retreating from the world.

E. Schweizer underlines this feature: there is no longer the multiplicity of the gifts of the spirit, but the one gift of the spirit. Anyone who (in the Son) has seen the Father, no longer really needs the brother. On the other hand, the commandment to love the brethren is sharpened up, though the call is *only* to love the brethren; John does not formulate any general commandment of love. This community does not pursue any mission; the place of mission is taken by testimony through love of

---

[1] The opposite is said in 5.22: the Father judges no man, but he has given all judgment to the Son.

the brethren. Schweizer speaks of a danger of de-historicization. But this does not describe the Johannine idea of the church completely.

The doctrine which is cultivated in the community does not become a secret doctrine, as it does in a sect. It leads to the public confession of faith. Jesus' departure from the world and his return to the community as the Exalted One means the lowering of the boundaries which were set by the incarnation. If the church lives as an enclosed brotherhood, then its existence is still the constant confrontation of the world with revelation, and along with it, the offer of faith.

48 · ESCHATOLOGY (RESURRECTION, JUDGMENT, THE PARACLETE)

J. Behm, παράκλητος, *TWNT* V 798–812; J. Blank, *Krisis*, pp. 316ff. (literature).

The eschatology of John is often described as 'present eschatology': the whole of the saving work is accomplished; there is no need for it to be supplemented by new facts, e.g. the parousia. The apocalyptic expectation of the parousia is excluded; thus there is also no future judgment and no future resurrection (3.18f.; 5.21–25).

There is a debate as to whether there is not at least a remnant of apocalyptic expectation left (cf. 5.28 and similar passages). Bultmann ascribes these future statements to what he calls 'ecclesiastical redaction'.[1] Schweizer, on the other hand, notes that even if one accepts Bultmann's analysis, a remnant of future statements remains which wait for consummation in the future (6.27; 12.25; 14.2f.; 17.24; cf. 11.24). Blank goes still further in his criticism: Bultmann neglects christology and makes it a function of eschatology. In John, however, the reverse is true. Blank uses 5.19ff. as an example: the eschatological statement in 5.21ff. is made possible by the christological presupposition of 5.19f. The passage καὶ μείζονα τούτων δείξει marks the transition from christology to eschatology. This is the development of the christological foundation. Then the line leads straight to vv. 28f.: we have salvation, but we have it in faith, and are thus oriented to a future consummation. The reference to the concept of faith is apt (see below). But because of their position in the context, vv. 28f. give the impression of being an interpolation.

With this making present of salvation, John is on the verge of

---

[1] For criticism, cf. L. van Hartingsveld, *Die Eschatologie des Johannesevangeliums* (1962). He regards the apocalyptic passages as authentic.

gnosticism. But his correctives mark the difference. The presence of salvation holds for faith. The element of futurity is not excluded, but actualized. John does not need apocalyptic statements to present true futurity. The future is in fact the orientation of faith. Of course, John knows the expectation of the parousia (and indeed of the resurrection and the judgment). He does not exclude it, but integrates it into his understanding of salvation as present. The work of salvation is complete. But salvation, once realized, must now remain present in the world; it must continually happen anew, from above. In Johannine terms, the dead one must return to the world and be in it in such a way that the same salvation is offered as was offered by Jesus – that is, himself. In that case, there can be no empty intermediate stage between Jesus' death and the parousia. I am going and I am coming to you (14.28): or, rather, the intermediate period is concentrated in a single point (16.16). This statement refers primarily to Jesus' coming at Easter, but in addition it contains the prospect of the final return and presence of Jesus for faith, which replaces the apocalyptic parousia.

Right alongside the promise of the return of Jesus stands the prophecy that he is going and will send another to represent him, the Paraclete, the spirit ('of truth'). He will bring further revelation and will lead men into all truth. Here a second hypostasis, the spirit, seems to take its place alongside the Logos. What is the significance of this remarkable duplication? Is Jesus' teaching not enough? What will make up the additional teaching? Are the believers promised inner illumination, mystic or visionary disclosures?

Windisch:[1] the spirit brings christological and eschatological doctrine: 15.26; 16.7b–11, 13. It can be put that way as long as one defines the Johannine character of this christology and eschatology precisely.

So, like Jesus, the Paraclete makes no factual statements about the beyond and the future. He still does not bring metaphysical teaching. But if he brings no new content, then what does he bring? The answer emerges from the definition of his relationship to the Logos: the Logos is a real hypostasis – the only one. In the case of the spirit, the hypostatization is a metaphor, even if a mythological figure may stand in the background. If the Paraclete is regarded as a real hypostasis, then the remarks about Jesus and the spirit become enigmatic. The

---

[1] H. Windisch, 'Die fünf johanneischen Parakletsprüche', *Festgabe für A. Jülicher* (1927), pp. 110–37.

Paraclete has no independent existence alongside the Logos. It is related to him, indeed it *is* the relationship to him. Its 'teaching' does not consist in positive statements, but in the fact that it constantly discloses the truth of the revelation. It *is* the disclosing of the truth. Only one thing goes beyond the content of Jesus' teaching, and that is that his death and resurrection are now incorporated into the teaching.

Retrospect and prospect correspond: just as John does not subordinate the revelation to a past conceived of in terms of salvation history, but to the pre-existence of the Logos and the origin of the world, so, too, he does not develop any apocalyptic picture of the future. In that case, what is the believer to expect from the future? Nothing that he does not already have. He already has life. What he can expect is that he no longer has to live in being exposed in the world. The farewell of Jesus means that he has gone in advance to the heavenly abode in order to prepare a place there for his own. This seems to be a radical individualization of the hope of the future world.[1] Indeed, I can hope for *myself*; that is disclosed to me. But the hope is the hope of those who form the eschatological brotherhood in the world. At his departure, Jesus left behind his word, through which he established peace. In so doing he created the eschatological freedom that particularizes itself as love. The one who departed has returned and makes possible the life of this community today, makes possible faith, and finally makes it possible to endure the world and in so doing already to have life in anticipation.

[1] The word ἐλπίς does not appear in the gospel of John.

INDEX OF NAMES

INDEX OF SUBJECTS

SELECT INDEX OF BIBLICAL REFERENCES

NON-BIBLICAL CHRISTIAN LITERATURE